June 18-20, 2018
Buffalo-Niagara Falls, NY, USA

**Association for
Computing Machinery**

Advancing Computing as a Science & Profession

SIGMIS-CPR'18

Proceedings of the 2018 ACM SIGMIS Conference on
Computers and People Research

Sponsored by:

ACM SIGMIS

Supported by:

Prospect Press & Brock University

**Association for
Computing Machinery**

Advancing Computing as a Science & Profession

The Association for Computing Machinery
2 Penn Plaza, Suite 701
New York, New York 10121-0701

ISBN: 978-1-4503-5768-5 (Digital)

ISBN: 978-1-4503-6160-6 (Print)

Additional copies may be ordered prepaid from:

ACM Order Department
PO Box 30777
New York, NY 10087-0777, USA

Phone: 1-800-342-6626 (USA and Canada)
+1-212-626-0500 (Global)
Fax: +1-212-944-1318
E-mail: acmhelp@acm.org
Hours of Operation: 8:30 am – 4:30 pm ET

ACM SIGMIS CPR 2018 Chairs' Welcome

It is our great pleasure to welcome you to the Annual Computers and People Research Conference – ACM SIGMIS-CPR 2018. For more than 50 years, ACM SIGMIS CPR has engaged the academic and practitioner communities in understanding the issues related to the interaction of people with computers, what we now broadly refer to as information technology (IT).

The theme of this year's conference is 'Transforming Healthcare through IT'. From transformation of healthcare delivery through the application of new tools to support information sharing and decision making, to transformation of the clinician-patient relationship through vastly increased information for patients through social media and other sources, to applications of data analytics to identify new treatments and new approaches to population health – virtually no area of healthcare is left unchanged by IT. This interdisciplinary topic spans multiple levels of analysis (individual, team, organization, and societal), and draws on a variety of perspectives (healthcare, information systems, operations management, organizational behavior, computer science, economics, sociology, psychology, etc.). Our theme-related papers are similarly diverse in their foci and perspectives, but they share a desire to understand how applications of IT support the transformation of our health and our healthcare organizations.

Our other papers address the traditional SIGMIS theme of computers and people. They showcase topics of current theoretical and practical relevance – such as implications of emerging technologies such as social media and gamification for the IT workforce, effects of IT on the workforce such as technostress, workforce development, and IT workforce practices such as agile and crowdsourcing.

Of special note this year are two keynote addresses, one by Daniel Porreca, the executive director of HEALTHeLINK the clinical information exchange and HEALTHeNET the administrative data exchange for Western New York (WNY), on the topic "Connecting at the Intersection of Technology and Healthcare," and the other by Viswanath Venkatesh, Distinguished Professor and Billingsley Chair in Information Systems at the Walton College of Business, University of Arkansas and one of the most influential and highly-cited scholar in the IS discipline, on the topic "Doing Research That Matters: Reflecting on the Past and Charting a Future for ICT4D." Also of special note this year is an industry-academia panel that will address issues related to the conference theme and that is comprised of two senior industry executives who have shaped and continue to shape the transformation in the healthcare industry, and two professors who are engaged in understanding the digital transformation occurring around us in general, and that occurring in the healthcare arena, and its implications on work in healthcare services and on our individual lives. Last but not the least, the doctoral consortium at the conference provides an opportunity to doctoral students, who are the budding scholars of our discipline, to refine their scholarly ideas through their interactions with faculty mentors, many of whom are and were journal editors, and with fellow students, in addition to growing their professional networks.

The various volunteer committees at any scholarly conference play a critical role in making it happen, and this conference is no exception. However, it is the authors, the reviewers, and many other volunteers and supporters who are really critical to the success of any conference. This conference in Buffalo – Niagara Falls, USA would really not have been possible without the many authors and doctoral students who submitted their high-quality work, without the many reviewers who provided their timely and constructive reviews to submitted papers and doctoral proposals, and the faculty mentors who
willingly agreed to give their time to interact with invited doctoral students in the doctoral consortium, and we would like to thank them all for their consideration and dedicated efforts. We are sincerely thankful to the keynote speakers – Mr. Daniel Porreca and Dr. Viswanath Venkatesh – for readily accepting our request for giving a keynote address on the theme of the conference despite their very busy schedules. We would like to thank all the panelists on the industry-academia panel – Ms. Leslie

Feidt (Vice President of IT Strategic Initiatives, Great Lakes IT Managed Services Organization), Dr. Ann Fruhling (Professor of the Peter Kiewit Institute at the University of Nebraska – Omaha and founding Director for the School of Interdisciplinary Informatics), Dr. T. Ravichandran (Associate Dean for Research and the Irene and Robert Bozzone'55 Distinguished Professor of Management & Technology in the Lally School of Management, Rensselaer Polytechnic Institute), and Mr. Lawrence Zielinkski (Executive-in-Residence for Health Care Administration at the University at Buffalo School of Management) – for willingly agreeing to give their time to participate in the panel to discuss issues of direct relevance to the theme of the conference. We are also very thankful to Leigh-Ellen Potter (Griffith University, Australia) who is generously giving her time to mentor students in the doctoral consortium. Further, we are indebted to Stacie Petter (Baylor University, USA) and Tom Stafford for lending their full support to the conference by way of fast-track publishing of high quality articles from the conference in The Data Base for Advances in Information Systems. We are also very thankful to David Carroll, Andrea Grover, and all the other staff at the Doubletree by Hilton at Niagara Falls, NY hotel for all their services and support for successfully hosting this conference at their hotel, and for making the stay of our conference attendees at their hotel a smooth and enjoyable experience. No conference can be successfully organized without the support of student volunteers, and we wish to recognize Ruochen Liao and Xunyi Wang, doctoral students in the Management Science and Systems Department in the School of Management at the State University of New York at Buffalo, for providing their excellent support prior to and during the conference. We would be remiss if we did not acknowledge the strong and unstinting support of Fred Niederman (Saint Louis University, USA), the Chair of ACM SIGMIS, both through his words and through his actions (e.g., by generously increasing the doctoral consortium student travel budget for the conference) for this Buffalo – Niagara Falls edition of the conference. We would also like to acknowledge the support of the other SIGMIS officers, including Leigh-Ellen Potter (Griffith University, Australia), Jeria Quesenbery (Carnegie Mellon University, USA), and Monica Adya (Marquette University, USA), who provided their help throughout the planning and organizing of this conference. Last but not the least, our sincere thanks also go to our supporters at ACM and Sheridan Communications, particularly to Diana Brantuas, Donna Cappo, Cindy Edwards, Irene Frawley, April Mosqus, John Otero, and Lisa Tolles, for their support with budgeting, doctoral student travel, conference proceedings, membership, registration, and the many other things that are necessary to make a conference successful. Thank you everyone!

We hope that you will find the conference program interesting and thought-provoking, and that the keynotes, industry-academia panel, and industry visit will provide you with valuable opportunities to learn first-hand from those who are directly engaged in shaping our digital world.

Rajiv Kishore
CPR'18 Conference Chair
University of Nevada, Las Vegas, USA

Daniel Beimborn
CPR'18 Conference Chair
Frankfurt School of Finance &
Management, Germany

Rajendra K. Bandi
CPR'18 Conference Chair
Indian Institute of Management
Bangalore, India

Benoit Aubert
CPR'18 Program Chair
Dalhousie University, Canada

Deborah Compeau
CPR'18 Program Chair
Washington State University, USA

Monideepa Tarafdar
CPR'18 Program Chair
Lancaster University, UK

Atreyi Kankanhalli
CPR'18 Doctoral Consortium Chair
National University of Singapore,
Singapore

Pankaj Setia
CPR'18 Doctoral Consortium Chair
University of Arkansas, USA

Tim Weitzel
CPR'18 Doctoral Consortium Chair
University of Bamberg, Germany

Tejaswini Herath
CPR'18 Local Arrangements Chair
Brock University, Canada

Indira Guzman
CPR'18 Communications Chair
Trident University International, USA

Table of Contents

Paper Session 2.1: Social Media and Gamification
Session Chair: Luvai F. Motiwalla *(University of Massachusetts Lowell)*

Paper Session 2.2: Technology and the Workforce
Session Chair: Ann L. Fruhling *(University of Nebraska Omaha)*

Paper Session 3.1: Patient Perspectives in Healthcare
Session Chair: Andreas Eckhardt *(German Graduate School of Management & Law)*

Paper Session 3.2: IT and Innovation
Session Chair: Leigh E. Porter *(Griffith University)*

Paper Session 4.1: Analytics to Improve Health and Well-being
Session Chair: Sara Moussawi *(Carnegie Mellon University)*

Paper Session 4.2: Emerging Trends in Workforce Development - 1
Session Chair: Stacie Petter *(Baylor University)*

Paper Session 5.1: Emerging Trends in Workforce Development - 2
Session Chair: Yi Wang *(Rochester Institute of Technology)*

Paper Session 5.2: New Pathways
Session Chair: Damien Joseph *(National University of Singapore)*

Poster Session
Session Chair: Mike Gallivan *(Kennesaw State University)*

Doctoral Consortium

Session Chairs: Atreyi Kankanhalli *(National University of Singapore)*, Pankaj Setia *(University of Arkansas)*, Tim Weitzel *(University of Bamberg)*

Author Index

ACM SIGMIS CPR 2018 Conference Organization

Conference Chairs: Rajiv Kishore (*University of Nevada, Las Vegas, USA*)
Daniel Beimborn (*Frankfurt School of Finance & Management, Germany*)
Rajendra K. Bandi (*Indian Institute of Management Bangalore, India*)

Program Chairs: Benoit Aubert (*Dalhousie University, Canada*)
Deborah Compeau (*Washington State University, USA*)
Monideepa Tarafdar (*Lancaster University, UK*)

Doctoral Consortium Chairs: Atreyi Kankanhalli (*National University of Singapore, Singapore*)
Pankaj Setia (*University of Arkansas, USA*)
Tim Weitzel (*University of Bamberg, Germany*)

Local Arrangement Chair: Tejaswini Herath (*Brock University, USA*)

Communications Chair: Indira Guzman (*Trident University, USA*)

Reviewers:

Khushboo Agarwal	Wei Gao
Mohammad Al-Ramahi	Kinnis Gosha
Chintan Amrit	Ashish Gupta
Deb Armstrong	Gaurav Gupta
Shankhadeep Banerjee	Sumeet Gupta
Simon Bourdeau	Ye Han
Christopher Califf	Teju Herath
Ann-Frances Cameron	Tim Jacks
Shalini Chandra	Jennifer Jewer
Yi-Te Chiu	Damien Joseph
John Cotton	Sven Laumer
Jocelyn Cranefield	Kyung Lee
Michael Curry	Diane Lending
Rodreck David	Ruochen Liao
Jesse Dinneen	Liu Liu
Indika Dissanayake	Markus Luczak-Roesch
Linying Dong	Christian Maier
Cathal Doyle	Kristijan Mirkovski
Andreas Drechsler	Luvai Motiwalla
Andreas Eckhardt	Sara Moussawi
Shadi Erfani	Bogdan Negoita
Ann Fruhling	Abhipsa Pal

Sponsor:

Supporters:

Keynote:
Doing Research That Matters:
Reflecting on the Past and Charting a Future for ICT4D

Viswanath Venkatesh

Distinguished Professor & Billingsley Chair in Information Systems
University of Arkansas
vvenkatesh@vvenkatesh.us
vvenkatesh.com

ABSTRACT

ICT4D has emerged as an important research area within the IS discipline, with special issues in leading journals. Research on societal problems and a focus on the grand challenges facing the planet is crucial to do research that matters and changes the lives of the poorest people on the planet. In this presentation, against the backdrop of the presenter's work in rural India, suggested future research directions that call for a paradigm shift will be proposed spanning from human-computer interaction to IS theories.

ACM Reference format:
Viswanath Venkatesh. Doing Research That Matters: Reflecting on the Past and Charting a Future for ICT4D. In the Proceedings of *SIGMIS-CPR'18: 2018 Computers and People Research Conference, Buffalo-Niagara Falls, NY, USA*, ACM, NY, NY, USA. 1 page. https://doi.org/10.1145/3209626.3226590

BIOGRAPHY

Viswanath Venkatesh, who completed his PhD at the University of Minnesota in 1997, is a Distinguished Professor and Billingsley Chair in Information Systems at the Walton College of Business, University of Arkansas. He is widely regarded as one of the most influential scholars in business and economics, both in terms of premier journal publications and citations. His research focuses on understanding the diffusion of technologies in organizations and society. For over a decade, he has worked with several companies and government agencies, and has rigorously studied real-world phenomena. His favorite project focuses on rural India and improving the quality of life of the poorest of the poor—which he has presented in various forums including at the United Nations. The sponsorship of his research has been about US$10M. His work has appeared in leading journals in human-computer interaction, information systems, organizational behavior, psychology, marketing, medical informatics, and operations management. Over various periods, including the most

Permission to make digital or hard copies of part or all of this work for personal or classroom use is granted without fee provided that copies are not made or distributed for profit or commercial advantage and that copies bear this notice and the full citation on the first page. Copyrights for third-party components of this work must be honored. For all other uses, contact the Owner/Author.
SIGMIS-CPR '18, June 18-20, 2018, Buffalo-Niagara Falls, NY, USA
© 2018 Copyright is held by the owner/author(s).
ACM ISBN 978-1-4503-5768-5/18/06.
https://doi.org/10.1145/3209626.3226590

recent 5-, 10-, and 15-year periods (e.g., 2013-'17, 2008-'17, 2003-'17), he has been the most productive in terms of publications in the premier journals in information systems (i.e., *ISR* and *MISQ*). His works have been cited about 76,000 times and 20,000 times per Google Scholar and Web of Science, respectively. He has been recognized to be among the most influential scholars in business and economics (e.g., Thomson Reuters' highlycited.com, Emerald Citations, SSRN). He has taught a wide variety of undergraduate, MBA, exec MBA, PhD, and executive courses. Student evaluations have rated him to be among the best instructors at the various institutions, and he has received teaching awards at the school and university levels. He has performed extensive administration and service including a long stint at Arkansas as the director of the information systems PhD program. In 2009, he launched an IS research rankings web site, affiliated with the *Association for Information Systems* (AIS), that has received many accolades from the academic community including *AIS' Technology Legacy Award*. He has served in editorial roles in various journals including *Management Science, MISQ, ISR, Journal of AIS, POM, OBHDP, and DSJ*. He is a Fellow of the *AIS* and the *Information Systems Society, INFORMS*.

Keynote: Connecting at the Intersection of Technology and Healthcare

Daniel E. Porreca
Executive Director, HEALTHeLINK
dporreca@wnyhealthelink.com

ABSTRACT

Healthcare in the United States continues to evolve in its use of information technology. Health Information Exchange (HIE) organizations have been in existence across the country for nearly two decades and we are now beginning to see the benefits of the unique qualities they bring and the value to both the quality of patient care and the cost of care. This keynote address will focus on the evolution of the HIEs to their present state, the benefits and value they create for the various involved stakeholders in the healthcare arena, and further developments we expect to see in this arena as HIEs continue to evolve.

Author Keywords

Healthcare; Health information exchange organizations, Health IT

ACM Reference format:
Daniel E. Porreca. Keynote: Connecting at the Intersection of Technology and Healthcare. In the Proceedings of *SIGMIS-CPR'18: 2018 Computers and People Research Conference, Buffalo-Niagara Falls, NY, USA, ACM, NY, NY, USA.* 1 page. https://doi.org/10.1145/3209626.3226591

BIOGRAPHY

Daniel E. Porreca is executive director of HEALTHeLINK the clinical information exchange and HEALTHeNET the administrative data exchange for Western New York (WNY).

HEALTHeLINK is a collaborative effort among the WNY region's leading health care providers and health plans to share clinical information in efficient and meaningful ways to improve the delivery of care, enhance clinical outcomes and help control healthcare costs.

Porreca has been leading HEALTHeLINK since 2007. Under his leadership, HEALTHeLINK has become one of the leading clinical exchange networks in the United States.

Porreca serves as chair of the board of directors for the Strategic Health Information Exchange Collaborative (SHIEC) and on the governing board of the Buffalo Clinical and Translational Sciences Institute (CTSI). Porreca also serves on the New York State Commissioner of Health's Transparency, Evaluation, and HIT Workgroup, serves as an advisor to the board of Stella Technologies and previously served on the board for the New York eHealth Collaborative (NYeC).

With more than 25 years of experience in the health care and technology industry, Porreca has a wealth of knowledge and a strategic understanding of healthcare technology and its application in the clinical setting. Prior to joining HEALTHeLINK, he served as president and chief sales officer for a healthcare software company which he co-founded that provided software and other technology and support services.

Panel – Looking Back at 18 Years of Best Papers at SIGMIS CPR: The Authors Speak

Mike Gallivan
Information Systems Department
Coles College of Business
Kennesaw State University
Kennesaw, GA, USA
mgalliv1@kennesaw.edu

Deborah Armstrong
Information Systems Department
College of Business
Florida State University
Tallahassee, FL, USA
djarmstrong@business.fsu.edu

Andreas Eckhardt
Department of Management
German Graduate School
of Management & Law
Heilbronn, Germany
andreas.eckhardt@ggs.de

Damien Joseph
IT & Operations Management
Nanyang Technological University
Singapore
adjoseph@ntu.edu.sg

Jeria Quesenberry
Information Systems Program
Carnegie Mellon University
Pittsburgh, PA, USA
jeriaq@andrew.cmu.edu

Eileen Trauth
College of Information
Sciences & Technology
Pennsylvania State University
University Park, PA, USA
etrauth@psu.edu

ABSTRACT

This panel will highlight papers that have received the Best Paper Award at the SIGMIS CPR conference going back to 2000 (with those since 2004 named the "Magid Igbaria Best Paper Award"). We will start the panel with a high-level overview of papers that received the Best Paper Award – a summary of the topics, research methods, types of organizations or populations studied, and publication outcomes after receiving the Best Paper Award. The main portion of the panel will feature authors describing how they regard conference papers as part of their research portfolio. A key goal of the panel is to elicit authors' perspectives regarding whether conference papers are end goals themselves, an intermediate outcome that has value to their career only if later published in a journal, or a stepping stone to multiple later options.

KEYWORDS

ACM proceedings; Magid Igbaria Best Paper Award

ACM Reference Format:
M. Gallivan, D. Armstrong, A. Eckhardt, D. Joseph, J. Quesenberry, and E. Trauth. 2018. Panel – Looking Back at 18 Years of Best Papers at SIGMIS CPR: The Authors Speak. In Proceedings of ACM *SIGMIS-CPR, June 18–20, 2018, Buffalo-Niagara Falls, NY, USA* ACM, NY, NY, USA, 3 pages. https://doi.org/10.1145/3209626.3210255

[1] ACM maintains a website indicating the recipients of the Best Paper Award as far back as 2004, when the "Magid Igbaria Best Paper Award" was created to honor our colleague who contributed to the conference for many years (see sigmis.org/events/awards/). Other recipients of Best Paper Awards were located back to 2000 based on the author's familiarity with colleagues who won the award, as confirmed by Google searches for details of the Best Papers listed on authors' websites for 2000 to 2003.

1 INTRODUCTION

The panel will allow the audience to hear from six former recipients of the Best Paper Award, representing a total of 9 Best Papers, regarding their perspectives on the questions listed above, as well as their experiences with conference papers as achievements that may lead to a range of outcomes – such as a journal papers, grant funding, and the opportunity to meet future editors, reviewers, or even coauthors.

The panelists reflect diversity in several areas: country of origin and current employment, research methods, epistemological orientation and finally, publication outcomes[1]. The latter include former SIGMIS Best Papers that were subsequently published in journals, those receiving major grant funding, papers never submitted to journals, and those submitted, rejected, and later abandoned as research efforts.

Considering the past 18 years of Best Papers (2000-2017), the raw statistics reveal a mixed picture of outcomes, in terms of subsequent journal paper publication of these Best Paper. A total of 9 such Best Papers have produced one or more journal papers to date, including one forthcoming in *Information Systems Journal* [2]. Thus, 50% of conference Best Papers have journal counterparts. A more positive picture emerges if we recognize that some of the Best Papers yielded multiple journal papers each (the 2000 Best Paper yielded three journal papers [5, 6, 7]; the 2007 Best Paper yielded two [10, 11]). In addition to journal papers, one Best Paper led to a chapter in an edited book (the 2009 Best Paper) [12], while many others yielded other conference papers in the same year or later years later after receiving the award (e.g., AMCIS, HICSS, etc.).

The main part of the panel will consist of six authors of best papers, describing their perspective about the value of conference papers, how they are recognized and rewarded at their institutions, and how they value the opportunities that conference papers yield.

2 PANELISTS ABSTRACTS

Deb Armstrong (Florida State University, USA), author on both 2006 and 2014 Best Papers (with Cindy Riemenschneider, Baylor University, USA) on the topic of women in the IT profession [16, 17], will describe her experiences leading to publication of both papers in journals [1, 2]. Deb subscribes to the "publish or perish" worldview, where she experiences the tension between publishing in conference proceedings vs. journals (and specifically, certain journals). She will discuss her view of the value of conference papers, in terms of developing ideas, careers, and doctoral students.

Andreas Eckhardt (German Graduate School of Management & Law, Germany), coauthor of the 2011 Best Paper [15], will explain the reward system for journal and conference papers in German business schools and other departments. He will also explain his beliefs about the value of submitting and presenting papers at small conferences (e.g., SIGMIS CPR) and pre-ICIS workshops (e.g., SIG ADIT) as opportunities to present new work to the potential audience of reviewers and editors. In contrast to the value of such intimate venues, he will also question whether large conferences are able to play a similar role due to their size.

Damien Joseph (Nanyang Technological University, Singapore), recipient of Best Paper Awards for the past three years [14, 18, 19] all on IT Human Resource topics, will discuss his view of the value of conference papers, in terms of his overall approach to research. He regards a conference paper as a step towards a journal paper, a test-bed for ideas, and an opportunity to gauge acceptance with the community with which he seeks to have a conversation. Damien's approach to writing and to deriving value from a conference paper is largely driven by both internal convictions and by external pressure. Damien believes that the endpoint must be the communication of research to the community. The context within which he operates is influenced by journal rankings. So, he belongs to the camp of "publish (in an A+ journal) or perish." Receiving a Best Paper Award from SIGMIS is viewed favorably – a signal of quality by peers who should be very familiar with the research sub-field; however, such recognition is also not perceived as the end point for a given study by his institution. By these terms, Damien's values fit well with those of his institution.

Jeria Quesenberry (Carnegie Mellon University, USA), coauthor of the 2008 Best Paper Award [23], will consider the relationship between her conference paper and a follow-on action research project conducted in rural Pennsylvania. The foundational work in the Best Paper was replicated as an important part of an industry-university partnership. Jeria will also share her views of the recognition accorded to research in social good and community outreach, as seen from the perspective of an IS department within a college of social sciences.

Eileen Trauth (Pennsylvania State University, USA), coauthor of the 2008 Best Paper Award [23], will consider the relationship between conference papers and larger research streams by focusing on the ways in which her 2008 Best Paper later informed research, grant writing, further conference papers, and a journal paper. The project on which the Best Paper was based yielded two more conference papers [20, 21], received NSF funding on regional economic development and was later published in *Economic Development Quarterly* [22].

Mike Gallivan (Kennesaw State University, USA), recipient of the 2003 best paper award [7] will describe his experience in publishing a new paper with the same dataset as his 2003 Best Paper, but with a different theoretical lens in Database for Advances in IS [8]. He will also describe further splitting the original Best Paper, which was on the subject of gender, stress and job turnover among IT workers, into two separate papers submitted to different IS journals.

Other perspectives on the value of conference papers were suggested by some Best Paper authors who are unable to attend the conference. One former author argued that receiving a Best Paper Award attracts attention from editors, who may solicit the paper for their journal. Other options include the possibility of journals creating a special issue to focus on all nominated papers from a conference, or otherwise "fast tracking" papers through the review process. We anticipate that, in a 90-minute block of time, we will have time for 30 minutes of question and answers from the audience.

REFERENCES

[1]   Armstrong, D. J., & Riemenschneider, C. K. (2014). The barriers facing women in the information technology profession: An exploratory investigation of Ahuja's model. *Proceedings of the 52nd ACM Conference on Computers and People Research*, 85-96. ACM Press.

[2]   Armstrong, D. J., Riemenschneider, C. K., & Giddens, L. (2018). The Advancement and persistence of women in the information technology profession: An investigation of Ahuja's model," *Information Systems Journal*, forthcoming.

[3]   Benamati, J., & Lederer, A. (2000). The emerging IT group and rapid IT change. *Proceedings of the 2000 ACM SIGCPR conference on Computer Personnel Research*, pp. 23-32.

[4]   Benamati, J. S., & Lederer, A. (2000). Rapid change: Nine information technology management challenges. *INFOR: Information Systems and Operational Research*, 38, 336-358.

[5]   Benamati, J., & Lederer, A. (2001). Rapid information technology change, coping mechanisms, and the emerging technologies Group. *Journal of Management Information Systems*, 17, 183-202.

[6]   Benamati, J., & Lederer, A. L. (2001). Coping with rapid changes in IT. *Communications of the ACM*, 44, 83-88.

[7]   Gallivan, M. (2003). Examining gender differences in IT professionals' perceptions of job stress in response to technological change. *Proceedings of the 2003 SIGMIS Conference on Computer Personnel Research*, 10-23. ACM Press.

[8]   Gallivan, M. (2004). Examining IT professionals' adaptation to technological change: The influence of gender and personal attributes. *Database for Advances in Information Systems*, 35(3), 28-49.

[9]   Klaus, T., Wingreen, S., & Blanton, J. E. (2007). Examining user resistance and management strategies in enterprise system implementations. *Proceedings of the 2007 ACM SIGMIS CPR Conference on Computer Personnel Research*, pp. 55-62. ACM Press.

[10] Klaus, T., Blanton, J. E., & Wingreen, S. C. (2015). User resistance behaviors and management strategies in IT-enabled change. *Journal of Organizational and End User Computing*, 27(1), 57-76.

[11] Klaus, T., Wingreen, S. C., & Blanton, J. (2010). Resistant groups in enterprise system implementations: A Q-methodology examination. *Journal of Information Technology*, 25(1), 91-106.

[12] Mgaya, K., Uzoka, F.-M., Kitinidi, E., & Shemi, A. (2009). Examining career orientations of IS personnel in an emerging economy context. *Proceedings of SIGMIS 47th Conference on Computer Personnel Research*, 41-56. ACM Press.

[13] Mgaya, K. V., Uzoka, F. M. E., Kitindi, E. G., Akinnuwesi, A. B., & Shemi, A. (2012). An empirical study of career orientations and turnover intentions of information systems personnel in Botswana. A. Usoro, G. Majewski, P. Ifinedo & I. Irikpo (eds.) *Leveraging Developing Economies with the Use of Information Technology: Trends and Tools*, 120-153.

[14] Koh, C. & Joseph, D. (2016). Experienced meaningfulness and calling: effects on IT professionals' retention intention, *Proceedings of the 2016 ACM SIGMIS Conference on Computers and People Research*, pp. 97-103. ACM Press.

[15] Laumer, S., Maier, C., Eckhardt, A., & Weitzel, T. (2011). The trend is our friend: German IT personnel's perception of job-related factors before, during and after the economic downturn. *Proceedings of the 49th SIGMIS Annual Conference on Computer Personnel Research*, pp. 65-70. ACM Press.

[16] Reid, M. F., Allen, M. W., Riemenschneider, C., & Armstrong, D. J. (2006). Affective commitment in the public sector: The case of IT employees. *Proceedings of 2006 ACM SIGMIS CPR conference on Computer Personnel Research: Forty-Four Years of Computer Personnel Research*, pp. 321-332. ACM Press.

[17] Reid, M. F., Riemenschneider, C., Allen, M. W., & Armstrong, D. J. (2008). Information technology employees in state government: A study of affective organizational commitment, job involvement, and job satisfaction. *American Review of Public Administration*, 38, 41-61.

[18] Setor, T. and Joseph, D. (2017). Executive pay before and after technology IPOs: Who receives more? *Proceedings of the 2017 ACM SIGMIS Conference on Computers and People Research, 155-160. ACM Press.*

[19] Setor, T., Joseph, D. and Srivastava, S. (2015). Professional Obsolescence in IT: Relation-ships between the Threat of Professional Obsolescence, Coping and Psychological Strain. *Proceedings of the 2015 ACM SIGMIS Conference on Computers and People Research*, 117-122. ACM Press

[20] Trauth, E. M. & Juntiwasarakij, S. (2010). Knowledge transfer challenges for universities and SMEs in the USA. *Proceedings of Americas Conference on Information Systems*, paper 127.

[21] Trauth, E. M. (2012). Barriers to knowledge acquisition, transfer and management in regional knowledge economy development. *Proceedings of Hawaii International Conference on System Science*, pp. 3612-3621.

[22] Trauth, E. M., DiRaimo Jr, M., Hoover, M. R., & Hallacher, P. (2015). Leveraging a research university for new economy capacity building in a rural industrial region. *Economic Development Quarterly*, 29, 229-244.

[23] Trauth, E. M., Quesenberry, J.., Huang, H., & McKnight, S. (2008). Linking economic development and workforce diversity through action research. *Proceedings of the 2008 ACM SIGMIS CPR Conference on Computer Personnel Research*, pp. 58-65. ACM Press

Industry-Academia Panel:
Transforming Healthcare with IT

Rajiv Kishore
University of Nevada, Las Vegas
rkishore@unlv.edu
(Moderator)

Leslie Feidt
Vice President of IT Strategic Initiatives, Great Lakes IT Managed Services Organization
lfeidt@KaleidaHealth.org

Ann Fruhling
University of Nebraska, Omaha
afruhling@unomaha.edu

T. Ravichandran
Rensselaer Polytechnic Institute
ravit@rpi.edu

Lawrence J. Zielinski
State University of New York at Buffalo
ljzielin@buffalo.edu

ABSTRACT

The purpose of the Industry-Academia Panel session is to provide attendees with an opportunity to hear the views of a distinguished group of panelists on the theme of the conference, particularly as they relate to the future opportunities and challenges that arise the implementation and use of information technologies by various stakeholders in the various facets of the healthcare landscape.

KEYWORDS

Digital transformation; healthcare IT; healthcare transformation.

ACM Reference format:
Rajiv Kishore, Leslie Feidt, Ann Fruhling, T. Ravichandran and Lawrence J. Zielinski. Industry-Academia Panel: Transforming Healthcare with IT. In the Proceedings of *SIGMIS-CPR'18: 2018 Computers and People Research Conference, Buffalo-Niagara Falls, NY, USA*, ACM, NY, NY, USA. 3 pages.
https://doi.org/10.1145/3209626.3226589

1 PANEL OVERVIEW

In this conference theme-focused panel, the panelists will discuss the current and future issues and trends in the healthcare arena and the role that IT is playing and can play in transforming healthcare and making it more accessible and affordable with higher quality of service, experiences, and outcomes. In particular, the panel will discuss how IT is transforming healthcare services, including their clinical, administrative, process-related, epidemiological or public health aspects as well as how IT apps impact individual health behaviors and health outcomes. The panelists may not be able to cover all the topics listed below during their panel discussion. Also, the list below is just an indicative list and the panelists are not restricted to this list of topics. The panel moderator and the panelists may bring up any topic that is not listed below and that they feel is important and should be addressed during the course of the panel discussion.

Individual

- Use of information systems, m-health, telemedicine, telehealth, etc. to transform individual health-related behaviors and health outcomes
- Wearable devices and their impacts on various healthy behaviors and habits such as lifestyle, diets, and exercise habits
- Individuals' role in healthcare delivery (e.g., co-creation of healthcare knowledge, healthcare-focused online social networks)
- User-generated content and its impact on healthcare practices and providers
- Online virtual communities and their impact on patient empowerment and patient safety
- Ways in which healthcare services and personal lives intersect to impact health outcomes
- Privacy and security of individual healthcare data

Organizational

- Digital transformation of healthcare delivery processes and operations
- IT's role in enhancing patient safety
- The role of health information exchanges and collaborative platforms in improving patient care and reducing costs
- Use of data analytics and artificial intelligence for healthcare decision support
- Telehealth and telemedicine applications and their impacts on health delivery and outcomes
- Technology-enabled care coordination and care pathways
- New payment methods and new ways of care delivery (e.g., Accountable Care Organizations and Patient-Centered Medical Home)
- Impacts of IT on payer and provider practices
- IT enabling emerging organizational configurations and structures of healthcare delivery (e.g., private, public, private-public partnership, ACOs)

Societal

- Personalized medicine

- Smart health and artificial intelligence developments and applications
- Impacts of big data on healthcare delivery, costs, and outcomes
- Privacy and ethical concerns with big data use in healthcare
- Population level impacts of IT on public health (e.g., analysis of large-scale epidemiological data)

2 PROFILE OF PANELISTS

Leslie Feidt serves as the Vice President of IT Strategic Initiatives for the newly formed Great Lakes IT Managed Services Organization (MSO). Previously, she served as the Chief Information Officer (CIO) at Erie County Medical Center Corporation (ECMC). Her nine plus years as CIO at ECMC in which she assumed full oversight of the information technologies, telecommunication and clinical informatics along with her 20+ past years of experience as a registered respiratory therapist and healthcare IT leader allows her to nicely transition to her new strategic role. With Great Lakes Health IT MSO she will be responsible for GLH Population Health strategy along with bringing the 10+ hospital systems solution together. She received an A.A.S in Respiratory Therapy from Eric Community College along with a BS in Management from the University of New York at Buffalo. She also attended Canisius College in Buffalo New York. Leslie, a native Western New Yorker, resides in Lancaster NY with her husband Bob and is most proud of her twin teenage daughters Samantha and Grace.

Dr. Ann Fruhling, PhD, MBA is an Information Technology Professor and the founding Director of the School of Interdisciplinary Informatics and the Public Health Informatics Research lab, University of Nebraska Omaha, College of Information Science and Technology. Her field of research is analyzing and solving information systems development problems that span the spectrum from efficient requirements elicitation processes and best practices in user interface design and systems development methods to post-implementation evaluation of user acceptance. Her specialty niche is public/clinical health informatics. Dr. Fruhling has been a principal investigator or co-principal investigator on over 40 research projects with total funding in excess of $8.2 million. She has been awarded funding from several national agencies such as NIH, NASA, DOD, DOT, CDC, U.S. Department of Justice, U.S. Department of Housing and Urban Development. Dr. Fruhling's journal publications have appeared in Journal Management Information Systems, Communications of the Association for Information Systems, Journal of Computer Information Systems, International Journal of Electronic Health Care, International Journal of Cooperative Information Systems, Journal of Electronic Commerce Research and the Journal of Information Technology Theory and Application.

Dr. Rajiv Kishore will start a new job in July 2018 as Professor and Chair of the Department of Management, Entrepreneurship, and Technology in the Lee Business School at the University of Nevada, Las Vegas. Dr. Kishore's research interests are in IT governance, healthcare IT, knowledge management, and IT innovation. His research has been funded by premier federal funding agencies including the National Science Foundation and the Agency for Healthcare Research and Quality. Dr. Kishore's research papers have been accepted and/or published in premier journals including Strategic Management Journal, MIS Quarterly, Journal of Management Information Systems, Journal of the American Medical Informatics Association, Information & Management, Decision Support Systems, Journal of Strategic Information Systems, and IEEE Transactions on Engineering Management. He has also presented numerous research papers and participated in panels at international and national conferences. He currently serves as an Associate Editor for Information & Management, a premier journal in the IS field. He is also currently serving as the conference co-chair for the Computers and People Research (CPR) 2018 Conference sponsored by ACM SIGMIS. He earlier served as the conference co-chair for CPR 2017 and as program co-chair for CPR 2014. He has also served as track-chair and associate editor at the premier International Conference on Information Systems (ICIS), and as track chair and mini-track chair at various international, national, and regional conferences including AMCIS, AOM, and PACIS annual conferences. He also continues to speak with industry and professional groups on topics of his research interests.

Dr. T. Ravichandran is the Associate Dean for Research and the Irene and Robert Bozzone'55 Distinguished Professor of Management & Technology in the Lally School of Management, Rensselaer Polytechnic Institute. His long term research interests focuses on digital strategies of firms and the mechanisms through which digitization is transforming firms, markets, supply networks and industries. He has published in leading scholarly journals in information systems (Information Systems Research, Journal of Management Information Systems, MIS Quarterly; Decision Sciences; European Journal of Information Systems), strategic management (Organization Science), technology management (IEEE Transaction on Engineering Management) as well as in leading practitioner journals (Communications of the ACM). His research has won several awards including the 1) Best Information Systems Publication in 2010 (Association of Information System); 2) Best Published Paper Award, 2010 (Information Systems Research); 3) Best Paper Award, Software Technology Track (HICSS, 2010); 4) Best Paper Award Honorable Mention (IEEE Transactions on Engineering Management, 2007); 4) Best Academic Paper Award (Second Supply Chain Management Symposium, McMaster University, 2004); 6) Best Paper Award (OCIS Division, Academy of Management, 2001). He currently serves as a Senior Editor of MIS Quarterly and as a Department Editor for IEEE Transactions on Engineering Management. He recently completed a four year term as an Associate Editor of MIS Quarterly and a three year term as an Associate Editor of Information Systems Research. Dr. Ravichandran led the effort to design, launch and scale two new graduate programs, MS in Business Analytics and MS in Supply Chain Management. He founded and directs RPI's Center for Supply Networks and Analytics. Prior to joining Rensselaer, Dr. Ravichandran had extensive business experience having served as a Consultant to the Reliance Group, as the Assistant Director of

National Productivity Council, India and as a Production Manager in Flakt AB (now Asea Brown Boweri). He has also been a successful entrepreneur; he started, built and ran an IT services firm.

Lawrence J. Zielinski, MBA, has led successful, market-leading organizations in both health care and banking over the last 35 years. He served as the President of Buffalo General Hospital, the flagship center of the Kaleida Health System. Prior to that, he was the President of the Visiting Nursing Association of Western New York, developing that organization into the leading home health provider in the regional marketplace and one of the most prominent agencies in the country. He now serves as the Executive-in-Residence for Health Care Administration at the University at Buffalo School of Management, and also runs his own health care consulting practice. His health care expertise covers the entire delivery system, including acute, ancillary, and post-acute care in both adult and pediatric settings. He also has extensive experience working with physicians on collaborative strategies to build their practices, both in private and academic settings. Prior to his career in health care, Larry was a successful banking executive at Goldome, an $11 billion regional institution serving New York and Florida. His banking and finance background are a unique complement in today's challenging world of health care economics.

Larry is also a former Trustee of the University at Buffalo Foundation and a member of the Finance and Gift Stewardship Committees, the Past President of the University at Buffalo Alumni Association, Past President of the University at Buffalo School of Management Alumni Association, Original member of the New York State Action Coalition Steering Committee on the Future of Nursing, Former Board Member for Upstate New York Transplant Services, and Chairman of the Finance Committee for Annunciation Church, his parish in Elma, NY. His academic credentials include Program for Management Development (Harvard Business School), MBA with a concentration in Finance and Marketing (University at Buffalo), and BA in Sociology (University at Buffalo).

Panel – The IS Student and Professional: Current, Past, and Future

Munir Mandviwalla
Temple University
mandviwa@temple.edu

Fred Niederman
Saint Louis University
Fred.niederman@slu.edu

Craig Van Slyke
Louisiana Tech University
crvanslyke@gmail.com

Monica Adya
Marquette University
Monica.adya@marquette.edu

Keywords

IT workforce, information systems, jobs, careers

ACM Reference Format:
M. Mandviwalla, F. Niederman, C. Van Slyke, and M. Adya. 2018. Panel – The IS Student and Professional: Current, Past, and Future. In Proceedings of ACM *SIGMIS-CPR, June 18–20, 2018, Buffalo-Niagara Falls, NY, USA*, 2 pages.
https://doi.org/10.1145/3209626.3210255

INTRODUCTION AND MOTIVATION

In this panel, we will focus on the demographics, preparedness, jobs, and salaries of IS students today as well as contrast with the past and in the future. First, we will quickly review relevant results from the Information Systems Job Index, a longitudinal national project, which in 2017 assessed more than 2100 information systems (IS), management information systems (MIS), and computer information systems (CIS) recent graduates from 58 universities across the nation.

OVERVIEW OF PRESENTATIONS

The panelists will focus on the following specific questions:

- Demographics: What are the current demographics of IS students? What can we do to address gaps in race? Have we made sufficient progress on gender or is there more to do?

- Preparedness: What do IS students know? How prepared are they for specific jobs (e.g., cyber-security)? Has the underlying tension between technical vs. business knowledge shifted?

- Jobs: What kinds of jobs are IS students getting? Why is salary growth slow? What role does preparedness play in salaries?

STRUCTURE OF THE PANEL

Munir Mandviwalla will moderate the panel and focus on summarizing the data and its direct implications. Fred Niederman, Craig Van Slyke, and Monica Adya will apply their extensive experience to comment on the results focusing on the three major categories above, along with potential action items for the field. All four panelists will identify research gaps with the intent to create a future research agenda with audience participation. Each of the four panelists will speak for about 10 minutes, and we hope to have about 40-45 minutes for audience engagement. The panelists will drive audience participation by posing interesting questions based on the above categories and results.

PANELISTS

Munir Mandviwalla is Associate Professor of Management Information Systems at the Fox School of Business, Temple University. He is also the Executive Director of the Institute for Business and Information Technology. He has published articles on collaborative systems, design science, social media, virtual teams, software training, peer review, globalization, and universal access and use in journals such as *MIS Quarterly, Information Systems Research, ACM Transactions on Computer Human Interaction, Journal of MIS, Journal of the Association for Information Systems, Information Systems Journal, MIS Quarterly Executive, Decision Support Systems, Communications of the ACM,* and *Public Administration Review.* He has received grants from the National Science Foundation (NSF), SIM Advanced Practices Council, Lockheed Martin, IBM, Microsoft, CIGNA, Lilly Endowment, and others. Mandviwalla has taught executive education seminars on systems thinking for NBCUniversal and QVC. Mandviwalla founded the Fox School's MIS department in 2000 and led the department until 2017. He has contributed to the field by leading the creation of AIS student chapters, the first national analysis of jobs in information systems, and the AIS Leadership Excellence Award. The Institute for Business and Information Technology (IBIT), which he leads, focuses on industry engagement through the Fox IT awards, The IBIT Report, Analytics Challenge, and the Cyber Analyst Challenge.

Dr. Fred Niederman serves as Shaughnessy Endowed Professor at Saint Louis University. His PhD is from the University of Minnesota in 1990. He has published peer reviewed studies in numerous top IS journals including *MIS*

Quarterly, Journal of AIS, Journal of Strategic Information Systems, and Journal of MIS. He serves as senior editor for the *Journal of AIS*, and on the editorial boards for *DATABASE, Communications of AIS, AIS Transactions on Replication Research, Human Resource Management, and Journal of International Management.* He serves as a Department Editor for ICT on the editorial board of *Project Management Journal.* He has edited or co-edited numerous special issues on a wide variety of topics include current ones on agile approaches to project management for *Project Management Journal* and digital workforce for *MIS Quarterly Executive.* His areas of research interest include: philosophy of science applied to IS, IS research methods – particularly qualitative ones, IS project management, effects on IS of mergers and acquisitions, global IS, IS personnel, and group collaboration and teams. He served as co-program chair for the 2010 ICIS conference in St. Louis, Missouri, has served as the first official "facilitator" for the AIS College of Senior Scholars and is proud to be counted as a member of the "circle of compadres" for the KMPG PhD Project.

Craig Van Slyke is the Mike McCallister Eminent Scholar Chair in Information Systems at Louisiana Tech University. Prior to joining Tech, he was professor and dean of the W.A. Franke College of Business at Northern Arizona University. He has also held faculty positions at Saint Louis University, University of Central Florida, and Ohio University. He holds a Ph.D. in Information Systems from the University of South Florida. Dr. Van Slyke has published over 30 articles in respected academic journals including *Decision Sciences, Communications of the ACM, European Journal of Information Systems and Journal of the Association for Information Systems.* His fourth co-authored textbook, *Information Systems in Business: An Experiential Approach,* is in its third edition. Craig's first trade book, *On Leadership and Life: Essays on Leading and Living Well* was published in June 2017. The book combines psychology and philosophy with his experiences to provide insights in to leadership and living well.

Monica Adya is Professor and Chair of Management at Marquette University. She received her PhD in Management Information Systems from The Weatherhead School of Management, Case Western Reserve University. Monica's research spans two areas: (a) IS workforce wherein she examines career choice and experiences among women and (b) knowledge-based systems with applications to business forecasting in which she has examined the use of DSS in forecasting complex and simple time series. She is currently working on studying benefits of mentoring and e-mentoring among IS professionals. Her work has been published in *Communications of the AIS, Decision Support Systems, Decision Sciences Journal of Innovative Education, Human Resource Management, Information Technology & People, International Journal of Forecasting, Information Systems Research,* and *Journal of Global Information Management* among others. Monica has been co-investigator on several research grants including those from *3M Foundation* and *Naval Surface Warfare Center.*

REFERENCES

[1] Mandviwalla, M., Harold, C., and Boggi, M. "Information Systems Job Index." The IBIT Report. Institute for Business and Information Technology, Temple University and The Association for Information Systems, ISSN 1938-1271 (January 2018). Available at: isjobindex.com.

Patient Preferences for Authentication and Security: A Comparison Study of Younger and Older Patients

Ann Fruhling[1], Devika Ramachandran[1], Tamara Bernard[2], Ryan Schuetzler[1], John Windle[2]

[1]University of Nebraska Omaha, Omaha, Nebraska, 68182, USA,

afruhling@unomaha.edu, dramachandran@unomaha.edu, rschuetzler@unomaha.edu

[2]University of Nebraska Medical Center, Omaha, Nebraska, 98198-2265, USA, tbernard@unmc.edu, jrwindle@unmc.edu

ABSTRACT

We examine authentication and security preferences of younger versus older patients in the healthcare domain. Previous research has investigated users' perception of the acceptability of various forms of authentication in non-healthcare domains, but not patients' preferences. First, we developed an interactive prototype to test three authentication methods: passwords, pattern, and voice. Our results indicate that younger patients prefer passwords by a significant margin. Older patients indicated more mixed preferences. In addition, we evaluated the level of security patients desired for protection of health information compared to financial information. We found no difference based on age: both groups felt financial security is more important than health data security. The findings of this research can be used to improve and enhance usability of future PHRs and overall PHR usage by patients. While this study is specific to cardiology patients we believe the results are generalizable to all patients with chronic conditions.

ACM Reference format:

Ann Fruhling[1], Devika Ramachandran[1], Tamara Bernard[2], Ryan Schuetzler[1], and John Windle[2] 2018. Patient Preferences for Authentication and Security: A Comparison Study of Younger and Older Patients. In Proceedings of ACM SIGMIS-CPR'18, Buffalo-Niagara Falls, NY, USA, June 2018, 7 pages. https://doi.org/10.1145/3209626.3209702

CCS Concepts

• **Security and privacy~Authentication** • **Human-centered computing~Empirical studies in interaction design**

KEYWORDS

PHRs; usability; authentication; privacy; security; prototype; patients; cardiology

SIGMIS-CPR '18, June 18–20, 2018, Buffalo-Niagara Falls, NY, USA
© 2018 Copyright is held by the owner/author(s).
ACM ISBN 978-1-4503-5768-5/18/06.
https://doi.org/10.1145/3209626.3209702

INTRODUCTION

Patient authentication to access personal health records (PHRs) is mandated by the Health Insurance Portability and Accountability Act of 1996 (HIPAA) due to the sensitive nature of health information [18]. Health information includes identifiable information about the patient's health conditions, contact information (name, address, telephone number), and other personal information (insurance policy number, credit card number, banking information, etc.) that may be linked to their finances. In computing, authentication is the process of verifying the identity of the person attempting to access a resource [26]. In the case of PHRs, it is used to verify a patient's identity before allowing access to his or her health information.

Although a username (unique identifier) and password combination is the most common authentication method used to access PHRs [3], the difficulty of remembering a username and password was a frequent complaint by patients in a recent study of the wants and needs of patients using PHRs [5]. Alternative authentication methods such biometric scans (e.g., fingerprint, face, voice, or retina), token-based authentication, recognition-based graphical password techniques [23], and login through email notification [16] could remedy this problem. When implementing new technology—including novel authentication techniques—it is important to evaluate how users, in this case patients, perceive the new technology and the likelihood of acceptance.

BACKGROUND

HITECH

The 2009 Health Information Technology for Economic and Clinical Health (HITECH) Act placed new requirements on health care organizations in terms of Meaningful Use criteria which drive reimbursements from the US government for patient-centered care [17]. Meaningful use Stage 1 focuses on data capture and sharing. Stage 2 focuses on advanced clinical processes such as health information exchange and increased patient-controlled data. Increasing PHR usage is required to achieve Stage 2 [19].

Health organizations are motivated to continue to offer more features in their patient portals [25] due to governmental pressure to meet the Meaningful Use Stage 2 requirement,. They recognize that patients have an increased interest and desire to securely message with their care providers as well as to actively manage and monitor their diseases. The ability for patients to view their health information electronically meets the Meaningful Use Stage 2 requirement.

Older Adults

Older adults are poised to be the fastest growing patient group of PHR users. Due to smart phones and social media such as Facebook older adults appear to be interested in investing time in learning needed computer skills. Further, older adults often have a higher need to access online health information than younger adults. Older adult populations, when compared to younger adult populations, have a higher proportion of having some type of disability. According to the Administration on Aging (2002) 44.5% of older adults ages 65-69 have a disability, and this increases to 73.6% for those 80 years and older [1]. Chronic disabilities (e.g. arthritis, hearing impairments, cataracts, hypertension, heart disease, and diabetes) are the leading types of disabilities. Older adults are also more likely to be in regular contact with a healthcare professional than younger adults, with 86% of adults aged 65-74 reporting contact with a healthcare professional in the last six months, compared with 59% for adults age 18-44 [8].

Many older adults are realizing the Internet provides immediate access to a wealth of health information and resources that might not otherwise be available. On the other hand, accessing these health resources and understanding how to find the information can be more of a challenge for older adults due to aging, lower education, and unfamiliarity with technology.

Older adults tend to face more barriers than younger adults in terms of eyesight, memory, and computer self-efficacy. Key website usability factors identified for older adults were vision, cognition, and motor skills. Becker (2004) assessed 125 websites evaluating usability barriers that impact older adult users. In their study they identified several barriers including: pull-down menus and small font size impacting readability, screen length increasing cognitive load, and missing help features such as contact us, privacy statement, and site maps [6].

Toscos et al. (2016) found a "novelty effect" in the level of continual patient usage of PHRs [33]. Patients' interest in PHR usage started out high because it was something new and then their interest and usage declined. Toscos et al. (2016) also noted PHR training and age as factors of usage. In their study, the authors reported older adults were more likely to be super users and utilized the PHR more often. However, older adults self-reported their computer and Internet abilities being lower than younger adults. In another study, Chrischilles et al. (2014) found older adults were especially interested in tracking their medication and health information [12].

Patient Health Records

For most healthcare organizations, increasing patient engagement and patient activation is a universal healthcare goal. One of the first steps to patient activation is accessing the PHR. PHRs provide an important communication avenue between healthcare providers and patients [34]. Patients who use PHRs report several positive effects such as knowing more about their health care, more communication with their providers, and taking more steps to improve their health such as actively monitoring their health and care by emailing or messaging their providers [29, 34]. In a systematic review on

which conditions (e.g. asthma, diabetes, fertility, glaucoma, HIV, hyperlipidemia, and hypertension) were potentially sensitive to the PHR as an intervention Price et al. (2015) reported a need for more studies on how PHRs are designed, what features they have and how they are adopted [28]. Engaging more patients to use PHRs are likely to have important public health benefits [24].

Authentication

Authentication is a concept complementary to identification. When authenticating with a computer system, users (patients) must first identify who they are claiming to be. Typically, identification is done with a username. After identification, users must then take steps to prove their identity. These steps are known as authentication.

Authentication takes three primary forms: something a user *knows*, something a user *has*, or something a user *is* [36]. Each form has advantages and limitations.

The first form, *something the user knows*, typically refers to the most common form of authentication: the password. It might also refer to other secret-based authentication methods such as the PIN used in ATMs, or the pattern frequently used on Android phones [20]. There are also knowledge-based authentication methods such as cognitive questions, most commonly seen as security questions [21]. While very widespread, these forms of authentication are not without their problems. Users, for example, frequently reuse passwords or PINs [22], share passwords with others, or choose poor passwords that provide little security [7, 9]. Passwords have an advantage in user acceptance, however. Through widespread exposure over decades, passwords have become the *de facto* standard for authentication [36].

The *something the user has* factor includes such authentication factors as smart cards and authentication tokens that authenticate based on possession [36]. This form of authentication might frequently be seen for authorizing building access, but is less common as the sole factor of authentication for a computer system. However, it has become more common for sites to use the possession factor to supplement knowledge-based authentication like a password. For example, many popular websites (e.g., Gmail, GitHub, and Facebook) allow users to use two-factor authentication combining passwords and a message or unique code sent to a smartphone. In this case, the user *has* a phone and *knows* a password, providing two forms of authentication to log into the site.

The final factor included in most descriptions of authentication types is *something the user is*. This factor typically refers to biometric authentication, including through methods such as fingerprint, iris, retina, face, and voice recognition. Biometrics are often proposed as an answer to the weaknesses of secret-based authentication. Some of the biggest challenges to the adoption of biometric authentication is user acceptance [22]. Users may fear the privacy implications of having their biometric information gathered and stored [11], or they might not feel they are acceptable and useful in a given application [22]. In addition, biometrics face technical issues—

such as accuracy and scalability—not present in other traditional means of authentication.

While previous research has investigated users' perception of the acceptability of various forms of authentication in a variety of domains [11], we are the first to look exclusively at *patients'* authentication preferences in a healthcare domain. We are also the first to examine age as a moderating factor influencing authentication preferences. It is important to understand user preferences in security, as well as the perceived security associated with various authentication methods. When users believe a site is well designed for security, they have a greater sense of trust in the security of their data [32].

Our study examines patients' authentication method preferences and the preferred security level protection for health versus demographic/financial information. We compare three authentication methods: password, pattern, and voice. We also examine the influence of demographic factors such as age, gender, current PHR usage on individual security risk tolerance. Patients rated each authentication method's usability, which is defined according to ISO 9241-11, as "The effectiveness, efficiency and satisfaction with which specified users achieve specified goals in particular environments [21]."

METHOD

Although there are many potential authentication methods, not all of them satisfy security policies required in the healthcare environment. To determine acceptable authentication methods, the research team met with a Chief Security Officer at a large university medical center. In addition to the standard username/password combination, voice recognition, pattern recognition, and fingerprint were identified as acceptable authentication alternatives. For our study, we compared three methods of authentication: password, pattern recognition, and voice recognition. These authentication methods were selected because they are commonly available on smart phones and tablet computers.

Participants - Patients

Our study focused on cardiovascular patients who access their PHRs on a routine basis to manage their health care because of their chronic (ongoing) illness. We chose to study patients with cardiovascular disease because of the large impact that cardiovascular disease has on healthcare in the US and around the world. According to the American Heart Association's 2017 Heart Disease and Stroke Statistics Update, cardiovascular disease accounts for over 800,000 deaths in the US, which is equivalent to about 1 in every 3 deaths. Heart disease remains to be the number one cause of death in the US. It was estimated that about 92.1 million American adults are living with a form of cardiovascular disease or the after-effects of a prior stroke. Combined direct and indirect cost of cardiovascular disease and stroke amounts to about $316 billion [4].

Recruitment and Study Methodology

A convenience sample of diverse patients were recruited at the time of their regularly scheduled clinic appointment. At the

onset of the session, the patient was asked to 1) create a username and password, 2) save a pattern with a minimum of nine dots, and 3) audio record a passphrase. Next, the patient was presented the following scenario:

> *"You have completed your follow-up visit with your cardiologist at University Medicine. The next day you would like to take a look at your updated current medications and also view your lab test results that your physician had ordered during the visit. In order to access this information, you will need to access your patient health record (PHR)."*

Subsequently, the patient was asked to use each authentication method to access the PHR prototype. The order of the authentication methods was randomly assigned to prevent bias. The PHR prototype also included other functionalities, but the patients were only required to gain access to the PHR.

A usability survey was presented to the patient after each authentication method was tested. The usability survey was derived from the System Usability Scale [10] and Weir's scale [35]. At the completion of the authentication exercise, the patients completed a survey that measured the authentication preferences, PHR usage, gender, age and the patient's desired security protection of health information and financial information. All study protocols were reviewed and approved by the university's IRB.

User Profile Setup Guidelines

We researched several sources on the best practices for pattern recognition and password creation [5, 30, 31]. The following rules were given to the patients to setup their login profile.

For Pattern Recognition the unlock pattern has 9 dots on the screen organized in a 3×3 matrix. To login using pattern recognition, a pattern has to be drawn on the screen, connecting certain points in a certain order. The rules for setting up pattern recognition are:

- At minimum, 4 dots must be used.
- At maximum, 9 dots can be used.
- Each dot can be used only once.
- The order in which the dots are connected matters (thus making it a directed graph).
- Dots are connected with a straight line meaning that all points on the path of the line get connected.

For alphanumeric passwords, the unlock screen requires entering an alphanumeric password (numbers, letters, and symbols). The rules for setting up an alphanumeric password are:

- Must be at least 8 characters in length.
- Use a combination of at least one uppercase character (A through Z) and at least one lowercase character (a through z).
- Use at least one digit (0 through 9).
- Use at least one non-alphabetic character (~!@#$%^*&;?.+_).

For voice recognition, the prototype simulated recording the patient's voice. The patient was asked to say this statement: "This is my voice password".

PHR Wireframe Prototype

An interactive PHR wireframe prototype with a user interface for each authentication method was developed for a tablet computer. Figures 1, 2 and 3 are the wireframes created for the patients to setup their user profile. Each patient was given a tablet computer to use during the study.

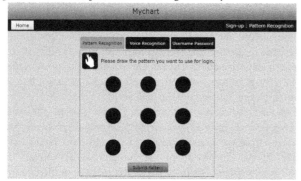

Figure 1. Setup Pattern Recognition Wireframe.

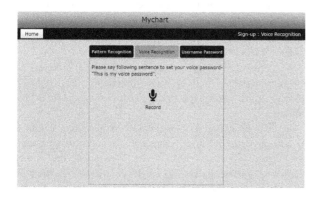

Figure 2. Setup Voice Recognition Wireframe.

Figure 3. Setup Password Login.

Survey Development

The System Usability Scale (SUS) [10] is a commonly used light-weight, reliable tool for measuring user interface usability. SUS was selected for this study because it is easy to administer, scalable, and clearly distinguishes between high and low usability in user interfaces. After reviewing the ten SUS questions it was determined three of the questions relating to system integration did not directly apply; these questions were not included.

The survey questions that assessed the patient's preference on the level of security desired for protection of patient health information and personal financial information aligned with the definitions for security levels established by NIST 800-122 (National Institute of Standards and Technology) [27]. The levels of security are:

- **None**: No login security protection required for the data.
- **Low**: Low security level is used for the protection of low risk data.
- **Low risk data**: The loss of confidentiality, integrity, or availability of the data would have no adverse impact on your mission, safety, finances, or reputation.
- **Moderate**: Moderate security level is used for the protection of moderate risk data.
- **Moderate risk data**: The loss of confidentiality, integrity, or availability of the data could have a mildly adverse impact on your mission, safety, finances, or reputation.
- **High**: High security level is used for the protection of high risk data.
- **High risk data**: The loss of confidentiality, integrity, or availability of the data could have a significant adverse impact on your mission, safety, finances, or reputation.

RESULTS

Patient Statistics

Thirty-six patients participated in our study. Two were removed for failing to complete the survey correctly. This left 15 females and 19 males in the study. Twenty-three (68%) were under 65 and eleven (32%) were 65 and over. Sixteen (50%) indicated that they were currently using their PHR, while sixteen (50%) reported not being current users (two people failed to answer this question). Of those who reported using the PHR, 13 (81%) indicated they used their PHR at least once a month, with only 3 (19%) reporting less frequent use. Usability items for password (α=.93), pattern (α=.92), and voice recognition (α=.94) were found reliable.

Preference Ranking

In our study 22 (64.7%) of the patients ranked password as their first choice, five (14.7%) preferred voice and seven (20.5%) preferred pattern. Pattern recognition ranked second for most patients (59%), with voice recognition last (59%).

A repeated measures linear model showed a statistically significant difference ($\chi2(2) = 9.88$, $p = .007$) in rated usability between password (M = 1.92, SD = 0.57), pattern (M = 2.20, SD = 0.74), and voice (M = 2.26, SD = 0.78) authentication methods (in this case, a lower score indicates higher usability). A planned orthogonal contrast between password and other methods revealed that password has significantly higher usability than pattern and voice (b = .11, t(65) = 2.93, p s= .005). There was no significant difference in usability between pattern and voice authentication (b = -.09, t(65) = -1.29, p = .20). Seventeen patients (50%) indicated their preferences were in the following order: (1) password, (2) pattern, (3) voice.

Age

A linear mixed effects model with ranking as a repeated measure showed that there was a marginally significant interaction effect between the ranking of authentication types and age ($\chi2(3)$ = 7.56, p = .056) and no significant interaction between authentication preference and current PHR usage ($\chi2(3)$ = 3.54, p = .32). A post hoc analysis of mean rank indicates that younger patients prefer passwords by a significant margin. Older patients indicated more mixed preferences, with password authentication showing the best mean rank, but by a much smaller margin than for younger patients (see Table 1).

Table 1. Mean rank of authentication type by age group

Authentication Type	Age	
	<65	>=65
Password	1.30	1.91
Pattern	2.13	2.09
Voice	2.57	2.00

Post hoc analysis of the mean ranking of authentication preference for PHR users versus non-users indicated a difference not in the order of the preferences, but in the strength of those preferences. Current PHR users indicated a strong preference for password authentication, with pattern and voice showing lower ratings. For non-users, the preferences are not as strong, but the mean ranks fall in the same order of password first, followed by pattern, then voice (see Table 2).

Table 2. Mean rank of authentication type by PHR usage

Authentication Type	Currently using PHR?	
	Yes	No
Password	1.31	1.69
Pattern	2.19	2.00
Voice	2.50	2.31

Security

In general, patients wanted their data to be secure. For financial data, 32 of 34 patients indicated they wanted the highest level of security (M = 3.91, SD = 0.38). For health information, 20 of 34 wanted the highest level (M = 3.44, SD = 0.79). The results of an ordinal logistic regression [2] show a statistically significant difference between security preferences for financial and health data (b = 2.38, t = 2.95, p = .003), with people showing stronger preferences for security of their financial data.

DISCUSSION

The basic question we seek to answer with this research is this: what authentication method do patients prefer for accessing their PHR? The approach we took was to perform within-subjects comparisons allowing patients to rank their preferences for authentication with the system. The data for younger patients (under 65) tells a clear story: password is by far the most preferred option, followed by pattern, and finally voice. Despite the problems of having to remember a username and password, it is still the most preferred authentication method and reported the highest perceived usability. This finding may be due to the younger patients' familiarity with this method and its alignment with the authentication method commonly used for accessing other internet applications (e.g. online banking, online shopping, etc.). A few of the patients commented that they save the password for logging into the PHR on the login page which lets them login without having to remember or type it in every time they visit the site. Since some of the patients have found a way to use the password login method without needing to remember the password, they are quite comfortable with the password method, and are reluctant to use or try any other login option.

There are significant differences in authentication preference by age group. For our analysis, we compared age broadly: those aged under 65 years with those aged 65 years and older. From this data, we see that those aged under 65 overwhelmingly prefer password authentication (mean rank = 1.29) over pattern and voice, while for those in the 65-and-older demographic, preferences are far more mixed. In the 65+ group we see a slight preference for password authentication (mean rank = 1.91), but not a strong preference, since the lowest ranked option, pattern, is only slightly behind (mean rank = 2.09). On the face, it makes sense that younger patients would prefer password authentication, the method with which they are most familiar. Younger people are likely used to remembering passwords for a variety of systems (or, more likely, reusing passwords between systems). Adding another system and another password to remember, while potentially burdensome, fits with these patients' expectations of what authentication looks like. Older patients may have poor eyesight, difficulty using a keyboard, have a hard time remember their password or do not have as much experience with password authentication, and thus would prefer a system using a method that has higher physical usability and rely less on cognitive memory.

Second, we see differences in ranking between PHR users and non-users. As shown in Table 2, the order of preferences between password, pattern, and voice (in that order) remains the same between the two groups, but for users of the PHR the preference is slightly stronger for passwords. Interestingly, there was no correlation between age and PHR use, with the same percentage of people in each age group reporting that they were currently using the PHR (50%). Like the finding with age, we see again that it is likely that experience with a PHR, or experience with computer applications in general, seems to push the users' preference toward password authentication, the more familiar option. This finding makes sense when considering that a big issue with passwords is people's ability to remember them. More infrequent use, or non-use, correlates with a desire to use an authentication method that does not require remembering a nonsensical string of letters and numbers.

Some of the patients who were not frequent keyboard users and were not used to typing on the keyboard were happy to learn about the pattern login and voice login method. They commented that typing letters/digits, especially on a mobile device is difficult. Some mentioned they preferred pattern recognition and voice login over passwords especially on a smartphone or tablet. A few of the patients commented that they thought the voice login would affect their privacy if they tried to login using voice in public areas and therefore preferred the other login methods.

One of the patients who preferred the password login method commented that he thought the password was the most secure login method as it was more complex compared to pattern recognition or voice recognition method. He thought it was easier to hack a pattern login compared to the text password. However, when he was asked if he could remember and keep track of the passwords for logging in, he said that he usually writes down all his passwords in a book and stores them in front of his computer and therefore there is no need to remember the passwords. The patient did not consider writing down passwords could possibly compromise security.

Together, these results suggest that younger patients and more frequent users prefer to use the most commonly used authentication method: passwords. Less frequent PHR users and older patients have different and more varied preferences for authentication. It was outside the scope of this research to consider the relative security of the various authentication options. Users frequently use short passwords, easy to guess passwords, and passwords that are reused between several different sites. Each of these issues reduces the security of password authentication. Future research should investigate how people feel about the various authentication options if they are forced to choose unique passwords or patterns for each site, a recommended security practice.

In general, patients indicated strong security preferences for both their financial and health data. Our data show that patients care more about the security of their financial data than they do about their health data. This is likely due to the perceived level of risk associated with unauthorized access. While there are privacy implications to unauthorized medical record access, there are much more obvious and immediate consequences if someone gains illicit access to a financial institution account. This would be expected to vary depending on the context of the healthcare. Our study was conducted with cardiology patients, for whom there is likely little stigma. Patients receiving care for other conditions such as sexually

transmitted diseases may have a different view on the privacy of their healthcare information.

CONCLUSIONS

In our study we found a statistically significant interaction effect between the ranking of authentication types and age. Further, a post hoc analysis of mean rank indicates that younger patients prefer passwords by a significant margin. Older patients indicated more mixed preferences.

Patients indicated a desire for security of their health information, though not as strong as their requirements for financial data. This could have significant implications on PHR designs and simplification of HIPAA laws, i.e. two-factor authentication for financial data but simpler authentication for health data.

While this study included a diverse group of patients and achieved significant results, the sample size was small and was intended as a proof of concept. It was also conducted with only patients in a cardiology clinic. More research to confirm and expand this research is necessary. Future studies should consider formal usability evaluations to compare patient authentication and security preferences.

This study has several contributions. First, it suggests that while passwords are the most popular, other authentication methods could be made available to patients to meet their needs and desires. Second, addressing the authentication usability barrier to PHR use by further understanding older patients' authentication preferences may help tip the scale to increased PHR adoption and regular usage. Third, to our knowledge this one of the first studies that evaluates *patients'* PHR authentication preference. We know that studying the usability from a user (e.g. patient) centered design approach is key to adoption and regular usage of PHRs by patients.

ACKNOWLEDGEMENTS

This project was supported by grant number HS022110-01A10 from the Agency for Healthcare Research and Quality. The content is solely the responsibility of the authors and does not necessarily represent the official views of the Agency for Healthcare Research and Quality. The authors would like to express their gratitude to the patients in the study. The authors would like to thank Aditya Chouhan a MIS graduate student for technical assistance in creating the prototype.

REFERENCES

[1] Administration on Aging. A profile of older Americans. 2002.
[2] Agresti A. 2002. Categorical Data Analysis. Hoboken, NJ: Wiley.
[3] Allaert FA, Le Teuff G, Quantin C, Barber B. 2004. The legal acknowledgement of the electronic signature: a key for a secure direct access of patients to their computerised medical record. International Journal of Medical Informatics;73(3):239-42.
[4] American Heart Association Statistics Committee and Stroke Statistics Subcommittee. Heart disease and stroke statistics 2017 at-a-glance.
[5] Android unlock pattern security analysis. 2012. [updated May 21]. Available from: https://sinustrom.info/2012/05/21/android-unlock-pattern-security-analysis/   .   Archived   at: http://www.webcitation.org/6uerL1mOR.
[6] Becker S. 2004. A study of web usability for older adults seeking online health resources. ACM Transactions on Computer-Human Interaction (TOCHI). Dec 1,;11(4):387-406.

[7] Berry N. 2012. PIN Analysis. Available from: http://www.datagenetics.com/blog/september32012/

[8] Blackwell DL, Villarroael MA. 2015. Summary Health Statistics: National Health Interview Survey, 2015.

[9] Bonneau J. 2012. The Science of Guessing: Analyzing an Anonymized Corpus of 70 Million Passwords. 2012 IEEE Symposium on Security and Privacy, San Francisco, California.

[10] Brooke J. SUS-A quick and dirty usability scale. In: Jordan PW, Thomas B, Weerdmeester BA, McClelland IL, editors. Usability Evaluation in Industry. London: Taylor & Francis, Ltd; 1996. pp. 189-94.

[11] Chandra A, Calderon T. 2005. Challenges and Constraints to the Diffusion of Biometrics in Information Systems. Communications of the ACM. Dec;48(12):101-6.

[12] Chrischilles EA, Hourcade JP, Doucette W, Eichmann D, Gryzlak B, Lorentzen R, et al. Personal health records: a randomized trial of effects on elder medication safety. Journal of the American Medical Informatics Association. 2014 Jul;21(4):679-86.

[13] Clarke MA, Sitorius M, Windle T, Fruhling AL, Bernard TL, Windle JR. 2016A qualitative study of user-desired personal health record functionality: impact of age on desired PHR functionality. Abstract presented at the 40th American Medical Informatics Association (AMIA) Annual Symposium, Nov, 2016, Chicago, IL.

[14] Furnell SM, Dowland PS, Illingworth HM, Reynolds PL. 2000. Authentication and Supervision: A Survey of User Attitudes. Computers & Security. 2000;19(6):529-39.

[15] Furnell SM, Papadopoulos I, Dowland P. 2004. A long-term trial of alternative user authentication technologies. Information Management & Computer Security. 2004;12(2):178-90.

[16] Garfinkel SL. Email-based identification and authentication: an alternative to PKI? IEEE Security and Privacy. 2003;1(6):20-26. DOI: 10.1109/MSECP.2003.1253564.

[17] Health Information Technology for Economic and Clinical Health Act. 2009. HHS.gov

[18] Health Insurance Portability and Accountability Act of 1996, (Aug 21, 1996). HHS.gov

[19] How to attain meaningful use. [Internet].; 2013. Available from: https://www.healthit.gov/providers-professionals/how-attain-meaningful-use   .   Archived   at: http://www.webcitation.org/6tST2tjYh.

[20] Irakleous I, Furnell SM, Dowland PS, Papadaki M. An experimental comparison of secret-based user authentication technologies. Information Management & Computer Security. 2002;10(3):100-108.

[21] International Organization Standardization (ISO). Ergonomic Requirements for Office Work with Visual Display Terminals (VDTs) - Part 11: Guidance on Usability. 1998 Jun 15,:22.

[22] Jones LA, Ant 'on AI, Earp JB. Towards Understanding User Perceptions of Authentication Technologies. Proceedings of the 2007 ACM Workshop on Privacy in Electronic Society; Alexandria, Virginia, USA. New York, NY, USA: ACM; 2007.

[23] Kahate A. Cryptography and network security. Tata McGraw-Hill Education; 2013.

[24] Krist AH, Woolf SH, Rothemich SF, Johnson RE, Peele JE, Cunningham TD, et al. Interactive preventive health record to enhance delivery of recommended care: a randomized trial. Annals of Family Medicine. 2012 Jul;10(4):312-319.

[25] Kruse CS, Bolton K, Freriks G. The effect of patient portals on quality outcomes and its implications to meaningful use: a systematic review. Journal of medical Internet research. 2015;17(2):e44.

[26] Lowe G. A hierarchy of authentication specifications. Computer Security Foundations Workshop Proceedings. IEEE Xplore. 1997. DOI 10.1109.CSFW.1997.596782.

[27] McCallister E, Grance T, Scarfone KA. Guide to protecting the confidentiality of personally identifiable information (PII). 2010. NIST. SP 800-122.

[28] Price M, Bellwood P, Kitson N, Davies I, Weber J, Lau F. Conditions potentially sensitive to a personal health record (PHR) intervention, a systematic review. BMC Medical Informatics and Decision Making. 2015;15(1):32.

[29] Ricciardi L, Mostashari F, Murphy J, Daniel JG, Siminerio EP. A national action plan to support consumer engagement via e-health. Health Affairs (Project Hope). 2013 Feb;32(2):376-384.

[30] Selecting good passwords. 2017. [Internet]. [updated N.d.;]. Available   from: https://csguide.cs.princeton.edu/accounts/passwords. Archived at: http://www.webcitation.org/6uerRKFmV. Princeton University.

[31] Selecting secure passwords. 2017. [Internet]. [updated N.d.;]. Available   from: https://msdn.microsoft.com/en-us/library/cc875839.aspx   .   Archived   at: http://www.webcitation.org/6uerbOzWn. Microsoft.

[32] Shah MH, Peikari HR, Yasin NM. The determinants of individuals' perceived e-security: Evidence from Malaysia. Int J Inf Manage. 2014;34(1):48.

[33] Toscos T, Daley C, Heral L, Doshi R, Chen Y, Eckert GJ, et al. 2016. Impact of electronic personal health record use on engagement and intermediate health outcomes among cardiac patients: a quasi-experimental study. Journal of the American Medical InformaticsAssociation. Jan;23(1):119-28.

[34] Undem T. 2010. Consumers and health information technology: a national survey. Lake Research Partners. Oakland, CA:.

[35] Weir CS, Douglas G, Richardson T, Jack M. Usable security: User preferences for authentication methods in eBanking and the effects of experience. Interact Comput. 2010;22(3):153-164.

[36] Zviran M, Erlich Z. 2006. Identification and Authentication: Technology and Implementation Issues. Communications of the Association for Information Systems. 2006;17(4):90-105.

Can IT Improve Cardiac Treatment Quality? A Quantitative Study of Interaction between Technology and External Factors

Shounak Pal
Information Technology and Systems
Indian Institute of Management,
Lucknow India
fpm15015@iiml.ac.in

Arunabha Mukhopadhyay
Information Technology and Systems
Indian Institute of Management,
Lucknow India
arunabha@iiml.ac.in

Girja Kant Shukla
Indian Institute of Technology,
Kanpur India
gkshukla78@gmail.com

ABSTRACT

The scope of healthcare information systems (HIS) is immense. It can not only help in providing easy access to data and taking decisions, but also ensure following standard procedures and improve quality. Prior literature have discussed on technology impact while controlling for the organizational and economic factors. However, there is a dearth of research on the effect of their interaction with technology. Moreover, overall technology impact misses the depth of application-level impact. Our work discusses the application-level impact and also empirically shows the effect of its interaction with other external factors. Our finding for 2010 show that use of HIS in nursing activities was significant in improving care quality. Disease-specific applications also have a positive effect under the influence of organizational factors. In 2013, per-capita income has significant effect on the impact of technology. Moreover our results show a considerable increase in the significance of technology and the interplay between technology and external factors in 2013 from that in 2010. Thus, our work motivates researchers to explore factors influencing the effect of technology. It directs managers to prioritize their investment on applications based on their impact on healthcare quality.

KEYWORDS

Mortality rate, healthcare information systems, Moderator, Socio-Economic Factors, Organization variables

1 INTRODUCTION

Information technology (IT) was introduced in healthcare for the purpose of improving delivery efficiency and quality. The use of information systems (IS) in healthcare has come a long way from just storing medical records to a decision-making tool that helps in treatment plan [1]. Consequently, the market for healthcare IT (HIT) is expected to grow at a compounded growth rate (CAGR) of 11.80% for the USA and Europe [2]. Aligning health IS to existing healthcare processes has been a major concern for healthcare organizations since its inception [3]. The presence of different players like physicians, nurses, administrators and regulators have made HIT adoption a complex phenomenon [4]. Although using standard procedures and order entry might lead to faster health information retrieval [5], improper HIT adoption may result in fatal consequences [6].

Extant literature on HIT has helped us to understand its impact on hospital quality, mortality rate and cost reduction [7, 8]. Subsequently, research works on misalignment, over-optimistic prediction and counter-productive impact of IT on healthcare quality, also known as IT productivity paradox, is an essential barrier to HIT adoption [9]. However, most of the papers are qualitative in nature and does not appreciate the importance of application-level impact. Although hospital characteristics and other social factors are controlled [8, 10] in most research discussing on IT impact, we found very few researches which discuss on their direct impact or their interaction with HIT. This is due to the scarcity of available information and low impact factor of these parameters when considered as an impacting variable.

In our paper, we model an exploratory framework to understand the impact of HIT on healthcare quality. Healthcare quality, as defined by Devaraj and Kohli in 2003, can be expressed in terms of mortality rates. We used cardiac disease mortality rate (CDMR) of each hospitals for the limited purpose of our study. We compare the results on same sets of hospitals for the years of 2010 and 2013.We also dig for involvement of *hospital characteristics* like bed size or physician number, and *socio-economic factors* like state-wise literacy and per capita income (PCI) in affecting HIT impact on CDMR. Our work will have significant effect on investment policies of future managers and will motivate use of interaction effects between technology and socio-economic characteristics.

2 LITERATURE REVIEW

Healthcare facilities of a nation influence the quality of lives of its people. A single mistake may have serious and fatal consequences [6]. IT was introduced in healthcare for efficient care delivery, cost-efficiency and improved competitive advantage [11, 12]. Since then there have been a growing interest in the use of IS research in healthcare. The existing literature can be broadly

ACM Reference Format:
Shounak Pal, Arunabha Mukhopadhyay, and Girja Kant Shukla 2018. Can IT Improve Cardiac Treatment Quality? A Quantitative Study of Interaction between Technology and External Factors. In Proceedings of ACM *SIGMIS-CPR, June 18–20, 2018, Buffalo-Niagara Falls, NY, USA* ACM, NY, NY, USA, 8 pages. https://doi.org/10.1145/3209626.3209704

classified into HIT adoption and impact [13]. Prior works have dealt with factors influencing adoption and diffusion of HIT and electronic medical records (EMR) [14]. Successful HIT adoption is not only influenced by the coordination among people-process-technology but also by the external environment [15, 16].

Impact of IT has been measured through affecting organization efficiency, quality and faster healthcare delivery [9, 17]. The presence of factors resulting in gap between the actual and the expected performance of IT have been pointed out by several researches [9]. Most of these research papers focused on routine process automation while discussing about workflow integration and process transition during IT implementation [3] as solution. Thus we observed that there is a general tendency for automation of repetitive processes.

Several works have been observed that include predictive models for medical conditions like heart attack [18] or use of IS in prolonged care and monitoring of diabetes patients [19]. Most of these research were empirical in nature and used regression analysis of primary or secondary data. HIT impact on payoff and outcome measure [7, 8]. A successful HIT implementation and its desired impact require a deeper understanding of the technology function for improved process integration. The work by [4] discussed several research opportunities related to influence of social media, personalized medicine for specific medical interventions and use of evidence-based medicine in medical decision making.

Our work is inspired by the lack of quantitative studies that explain the nature of IT impact on cardiac disease treatment. Our work is an extension to technology-organization-environment framework (TOE). Furthermore, the work by [7] showed how improvement in mortality rate is linked with HIT usage and is influenced by hospital characteristics like hospital age and number of employees. Researchers also used process care quality [8] and patient readmission rate [20] to demonstrate the effect of HIT on hospital performance. All these works take hospital type and hospital characteristics as control variables. Our work differs from all these works as we try to find the impact of individual applications and other socio-economic and hospital demographics quantitatively. We also try to establish the importance of their interactions on hospital mortality rates for cardiac patients.

3 THEORY FOUNDATION

Resource-based view (RBV) in IS [21] states that sustained competitive advantage can be attained by optimal usage of resources. Concepts like "IS capabilities lead to sustained competitiveness" [22] and "mutual adaption between technology and user environment" [23] are core to effective IS implementation and usage.

IT productivity has been a major concern since 1990s which resulted in the discussion of IT productivity paradox [24]. This paper contributes towards providing insight on factors that can further explain productivity. Our work is also in line with the integrative model of IT business value where the authors [25] believe that IT and organizational performance are divergent. Although technology is important as a value creation component,

the extent and dimension depends largely on internal organizational factors and external environment [25].

4 MODEL AND HYPOTHESES

We used linear equation to determine the effect of technology and other factors in improving cardiac disease care quality in terms of negative mortality rates. We used *expert physician opinion* to categorize the IT applications into routine and disease-specific categories. The routine and disease applications are further categorized based on their functionality using application categories from one of the databases. Figure 1 illustrates the framework based on which the resultant equation is formulated as below,

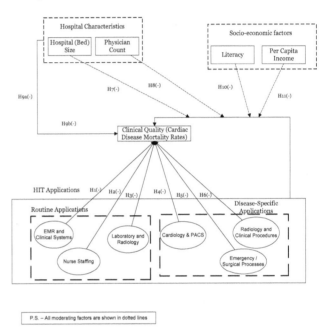

Figure 1: Proposed model to demonstrate factors affecting Cardiac Disease Mortality Rates

$Cardiac\ Disease\ Mortality\ Rates\ (CDMR) = \beta_0 +$
$\beta_1 NofBeds + \beta_2 Physician\_Total +$
$\sum_i \beta_{i1}(EMR\ and\ Clinical\ Systems) +$
$\sum_j \beta_{j1}(Nurse\ Staffing) +$
$\sum_k \beta_{k1}(Laboratory\ and\ Radiology) +$
$\sum_l \beta_{l1}(Cardiology\ and\ PACS) +$
$\sum_m \beta_{m1}(Emergency\ and\ Surgical\ Processes) +$
$\sum_n \beta_{n1}(Radiology\ and\ Clinical\ Procedures) +$
$\sum_o \beta_{o1}(HIT\ applications)(NofBeds) +$
$\sum_p \beta_{p1}(HIT\ applications)(Physician\_Total) +$
$\sum_q \beta_{q1}(HIT\ applications)(PCI) +$
$\sum_r \beta_{r1}(HIT\ applications)(Literacy)$ (1)

Where the terms $\{\beta_{i1} \dots \beta_{r1}\}$ represent the coefficients of different applications within the mentioned categories and $\{EMR\ and\ Clinical\ Systems,\ Nurse\ Staffing,$

Laboratory and Radiology, Cardiology and PACS,
Emergency and Surgical Processes, Radiology and
Clinical Procedures} ⊆ {HIT applications}

4.1 Routine Applications

Routine CIT applications are part of the daily clinical workflow like nurse scheduling, primary care, patient monitoring, diagnosis and medication, patient care, access to medicine, diagnostic tests among others. Our data consists of 24 applications which are part of standard clinical workflow. They are categorized in the following three categories.

4.1.1 EMR and Clinical Systems

Prior researches have shown that while IT was used for billing and other administrative purposes, there is a considerable reluctance to use EMR for keeping patient medical records or ordering prescriptions [26]. While multiple researches have claimed the lack of connection between EMR usage and treatment quality [27], several papers have explained qualitatively as well as quantitatively that clinical decision-making quality can be improved using HIT [26]. In a research, EMRs are specifically found significant for cardiac disease treatment [28]. Thus, EMR systems like clinical decision support systems (CDSS) and computerized physician order entry (CPOE) might affect care quality in a positive way by reducing mortality rates.

Hypothesis 1 (H1): EMR and clinical systems have a negative effect on cardiac disease mortality rates.

4.1.2 Nurse Staffing

Effective nurse staffing and scheduling is an essential part of a hospital's operation and cost management. Moreover, high patient-to-nurse ratio leads to high mortality rates [29]. Better cost management will help hospitals to keep more staffs which will improve care quality. Use of IS is often associated with cost-efficiency [11, 12]. Hence nurse staffing systems are supposed to improve care quality.

Hypothesis 2 (H2): Nurse staffing systems have a negative effect on cardiac disease mortality rates.

4.1.3 Laboratory and Radiology

The laboratory systems mostly include clinical and pathological testing processes that are handled by technicians. One natural change due to the use of IS in laboratory and radiology information system is the faster report generation. Few researches highlight both positive (effective keeping of records and automation of image generation) and negative (infrastructure issue, integration with other software and high cost) side of laboratory IS [30]. Hence, we hypothesize that IS in laboratory and radiology improves the quality of care.

Hypothesis 3 (H3): Laboratory and Radiology systems have a negative effect on cardiac disease mortality rates.

4.2 Disease-specific Applications

HIT applications that have usage specific to a disease is termed as disease-specific HIT applications. Hence, they are not a part of the day-to-day activities of the healthcare organization. Here we investigated 16 applications which are specifically used for cardiac disease treatment. **Table 1** summarizes the list of applications.

4.2.1 Cardiology and PACS

Cardiology and PACS help in patient safety by keeping repository of patient cardiac information and helping in monitoring, nuclear cardiology and other related treatments [23].

Thus use of Cardiology IS and PACS should lead to improved care quality.

Hypothesis 4 (H4): Cardiology and PACS have a negative effect on cardiac disease mortality rates.

4.2.2 Emergency or Surgical Procedures

The presence of more surgical IS is negatively related with risk during surgical procedure [31]. Thus information systems like OR scheduling, and peri, post, pre-operative equipment are supposed to make cardiac surgeries less risky which also decreases the mortality rate.

Hypothesis 5 (H5): Emergency and surgical systems have a negative effect on cardiac disease mortality rates.

4.2.3 Radiology and Clinical Procedures

There are disease-specific applications too that are handled by technicians for like anesthetics or radiology angiography. They are used for proper diagnosis and other surgical and clinical purposes. Radiology automation helps in better imaging and efficiency and effectiveness, specifically for cardiac patients. Anesthetic information management system (AIMS) helps in better care quality by storing information about anesthesia dosage of patients and any record of side-effects for better decision making.

Hypothesis 6 (H6): Specialized Radiology and clinical systems have a negative effect on cardiac disease mortality rates.

Table 1: To demonstrate categorization of applications

	Processes	Applications
Routine Applications	EMR and Clinical Systems	CDSS
		Clinical Data Repository
		CPOE
		EMR
		Physician Documentation
		Physician Portal
		Patient Portal
		Intensive Care
		Respiratory Care Information System
	Nurse Staffing	Nurse Acuity
		Nurse Call System
		Nursing Documentation
		Nurse Staffing_Scheduling
		Order Entry
		Staff Scheduling
		Medication Reconciliation Software
		Patient Acuity
		EMAR
		RFID
	Laboratory and Radiology	Anatomical Pathology
		Pharmacy Management System
		Radiology Information System

		RadiologyDR
Disease-specific Applications		Transfusion Management System
	Cardiology & PACS	Cardiology - Cath Lab
		Cardiology - CT
		Cardiology - Echocardiology
		Cardiology – Intravascular Ultrasound
		Cardiology - Nuclear Cardiology
		Cardiology 3D
		Cardiology Information System
	Emergency or Surgical Processes	EDIS
		OR Peri-Operative
		OR Post-Operative
		OR Pre-Operative
		OR Scheduling
	Disease-specific Radiology and Clinical Procedures	Radiology - US
		Radiology 3D
		Radiology - Angiography
		AIMS

4.3 Hospital Characteristics

Hospital characteristics is often used as a factor that determines the performance level of the hospital. It also affects the vision and policies related to implementation and adoption of information systems.

4.3.1 Hospital (Bed) Size

The size of the hospital greatly determines the vision and the investment policy of the hospital as well as the effect of changes [10, 32] caused by technological intervention. Introduction of technology is expected to improve efficiency of the hospital. Technology usage reaches significance mainly in larger hospitals where it is difficult to work manually. Thus hospital size enhances the significance of technology in most of the cases.

Hypothesis 7(H7): Number of beds, as a moderator to information systems, has negative effect on mortality rates.

4.3.2 Physician Count

A positive correlation is observed between patient satisfaction and physician number [33]. Patient satisfaction is an indication of quality of care in most cases [34]. More physicians reduce work pressure and improves physician productivity.

Hypothesis 8(H8): Physician Count, as a moderator to information systems, has negative effect on mortality rates.

Although we observed negative correlation of number of beds with respect to heart attack and heart failure mortality rates [35], smaller hospitals have higher patient satisfaction compared to larger hospital [37]. However in [37] it is also mentioned that larger hospitals have higher quality than smaller hospitals. So we also check for the individual effect of both these hospital characteristics on cardiac disease mortality rates for comparison, if any, between the two years, 2010 and 2013.

Hypothesis 9a (H9a): Number of beds have negative effect on mortality rates.

Hypothesis 9b (H9b): Physician Count has negative effect on mortality rates.

4.4 Socio-Economic Factors

4.4.1 *Literacy*

Information systems show the best result when coupled with user's knowledge on using it. Thus positive technology adoption has been often associated with literacy [36]. The literacy and involvement of an official who has influence and knowledge in both medical and administrative field is essential requirement [37]. Although we were unable to get such individual-level information, a state-level literacy rate can help determining the technology acceptance level of individuals within that particular state or community. Literate individuals are much receptive towards disruptive technology and hence can do better justice towards its implementation and effect.

Hypothesis 10(H10): Literacy, as a moderator to information systems, has negative effect on mortality rates.

4.4.2 *Per-Capita Income*

Technology installation and developing proper infrastructure requires investment. Healthcare expenditure is directly related to income of the state or per capita income [38]. Thus, only states and organizations in a state where PCI is high, can sustain technology implementation.

Hypothesis 11(H11): Per capita income, as a moderator to information systems, has negative effect on mortality rates.

5 DATA

We used two different secondary data sources on U.S. hospitals – Dorenfest Institute for Health Information (HIMSS), Hospital Compare Website maintained by the Centers for Medicare & Medicaid Services (CMS). We matched the provider number of hospitals in CMS database with the Medicare number of Dorenfest database for combining the hospital details. America's Health Rankings (AHR) published by United Health Foundation provides access to state by state data ranking based on public health statistics. We used state-specific data of the socio-economic factors like literacy and PCI. The data collected consisted 952 hospitals over a period of 2008-2013 for a study that included three-year average of the availability of different applications for the years 2010 and 2013 for a longitudinal view of technology effect. The resultant data is reduced to 615 hospitals and 501 hospitals for 2010 and 2013 respectively due to few missing data.

6 METHODOLOGY

In this paper, we check for the factors which affect cardiac disease mortality rate in a hospital. For this purpose, we consider the different IT applications used by a hospital, hospital characteristics, socio-economic factors and the interactions between IT applications and hospital characteristics and socio-economic factors [39].

Step 1:	Merging of Data from Dorenfest, CMS and AHR for the years 2008 to 2013.
Step 2:	Data Transformation: i) Used physician's expertise to segregate routine and disease-specific applications. Then we used Dorenfest

database categories to segregate applications based on functionality.

ii) Created separate columns for each of the applications: 0 for absent and 1 for present.

iii) Merged IT application's availability from 2008-2010 and from 2011-2013 to create a three year average availability for each application for the years 2010 and 2013.

iv) Transforming State to obtain Literacy rate and Per Capita Income.

Step 3: *Moderator Formation:*
i) Multiplying application's availability with hospital characteristics (number of beds and physician number) and socio-economic factors (literacy rate and per capita income) to obtain the interaction variables.

Step 4: *Run backward linear regression with CDMR as dependent variable and individual applications and their interaction with hospital characteristics and socio-economic factors as independent variables..*

Step 5: *We compare three models: Model 1 includes no interaction, in Model 2 we add interaction of each application with hospital characteristics; and Model 3 includes interaction of technology with any one socio-economic factor, in addition to interactions present in Model 2.*

7 Result

We compared three models to determine the influence of hospital characteristics and socio-economic variables on each of the applications. We checked between step-wise, forward and backward regression to obtain the best model fit in terms of adjusted R-square. The best model fit was obtained from backward linear regression.. As socio-economic factors could only be captured state-wise and not on an individual or patient-level, we consciously tried to include only those factors which are very significant in the model. Thus, explained in the previous section, we included literacy rate of the state for 2010 and per capita income for 2013. Finally we obtained the model fit adjusted R-square values which helped us to stop at Model 3, as shown in **Table 2**.

Table 2: Goodness of fit of models tested for 2010 and 2013

Models	2010	2013
Model 1	0.042	0.081
Model 2	0.06	0.126
Model 3	0.13	0.181

In the upcoming **Table 3** and **Table 4**, we illustrate the results of Model 3 for 2010 and 2013 respectively. The backward regression stopped at model 110, since only a few variables came up to be significant for both the years. All the variables reported in the resultant table are significant with p-value < 0.10. We have also highlighted variables which are negatively affecting mortality rate and hence are in line with our hypotheses.

Table 4: Model 3 coefficients to explain Cardiac disease mortality rates for 2010

	Standardized Coefficient Beta Value			
	Individual Effects	Interaction effects		
Applications		Bed Size	Physician Count	Literacy
EMR and Clinical Systems				
Clinical Data Repository	1.031			-1.051
CPOE	0.080			
EMR	0.142		-0.232	
Nurse Staffing				
EMAR	1.120			-1.165
Medication Reconciliation Software	-1.621			1.659
Nurse Call System	-1.032			1.044
Nursing Documentation	-1.241			1.227
Order Entry		0.470	-0.304	
Laboratory and Radiology				
Radiology Information System		-0.564	0.806	
Cardiology & PACS				
Cardiology - Echocardiology	2.418	-0.274		-2.243
Cardiology - Nuclear Cardiology	-1.484			1.407
Cardiology - Cath Lab	0.113			
Emergency or Surgical Processes				
OR Pre-Operative		-0.184		
OR Scheduling	0.104		-0.225	
Disease-specific Radiology and Clinical Procedures				
Radiology – US		-0.875	0.891	
Adjusted R-square	0.130473545			
Durbin-Watson	2.054			

Table 5: Model 3 coefficients to explain Cardiac disease mortality rates for 2013

	Individual Effects	Bed Size	Physician Count	Per Capita Income
Applications				
EMR and Clinical Systems				
Intensive Care	0.131			
Physician Documentation	-1.201			1.169
Physician Portal			-0.220	
Respiratory Care Information System			0.228	
Nurse Staffing				
EMAR		-0.237		
Medication Reconciliation Software	-0.158	0.611	-0.426	
Nurse Acuity		0.116		
Nurse Staffing and Scheduling	0.796			-0.833
Order Entry		-0.570	0.427	
Staff Scheduling	0.871			-0.890
Laboratory and Radiology				
Anatomical Pathology		-0.549	0.435	
Pharmacy Management System	1.276			-1.253
Radiology Information System		0.376		-0.188
Transfusion Management System	0.975			-1.025
Cardiology & PACS				
Cardiology - Cath Lab				0.237
Cardiology - Echocardiology	-0.887			0.815
Cardiology - Intravascular Ultrasound	0.948	-0.341		-0.799
Cardiology - Nuclear Cardiology		0.162		
Cardiology 3D	1.275	-0.196		-1.084
Emergency or Surgical Processes				
EDIS		-0.489	0.614	
OR Post-Operative	-1.074			1.070
OR Scheduling	1.308		-0.418	-1.282
Disease-specific Radiology and Clinical Procedures				
Radiology - Angiography	0.111		-0.736	
Radiology – US		0.973		-0.133
Adjusted R-square	0.181137568			
Durbin-Watson	1.75			

8 Discussion

As shown in **Table 3**, for 2010, the model fit did not improve much from Model 1 to Model 2 while there is a huge jump from Model 2 to Model 3. This shows that literacy rate can foster growth in technology adoption and usage, also observed in several researches like [36] and [40]. Literacy might not have direct effect on mortality rates. This is because technology adoption is time-consuming [41] and difficult to align with existing processes [9]. In 2010 model, physician number in a hospital gives negative mortality rates, both as a separate measure as well as a moderator. In **Table 4**,

physician number impacts care quality positively and also impacts order entry and EMR positively and OR scheduling.

We also observe that information systems used for nurse staffing are quite significant in improving care quality by reducing mortality rates. We also observe that EMR and clinical systems show positive coefficient towards mortality unlike hypothesized. This may be due to the fact that physicians were wary of using it due to poor adoption strategy [9] and lack of training and awareness [24]. Our results also show that cardiology information system also showed limited negative influence on mortality rate. However, disease specific applications showed improved care quality for larger hospitals. Based on scatter-plot explanation of hospital size and technology interaction, we can say that smaller hospitals are better off than larger hospitals in absence of technology. Moreover, for larger hospitals, effect of technology diminishes while mid-sized hospitals show the most impact of technology.

In 2013 model, we observe a significant increase in applications' model participation. This gives an idea of the maturity attained by HIT in 2013 compared to 2010. Moreover, we also observed significant effect of PCI as a moderator for HIT applications towards improving clinical quality. Hospital characteristics, too, show certain significance as a moderator. EMR applications have started showing some effect towards improving quality. Significance of physician portal and physician documentation gives an idea about the gradual penetration of HIS among practitioners. We also find significant improvement in participation of laboratory and radiology, especially for states with higher PCI.

Table 6: Summarized result of the hypotheses

Hypothesis	2010	2013
H1	?	?
H2	✓	?
H3	X	X
H4	?	?
H5	X	?
H6	X	X
H7	✓	✓
H8	✓	✓
H9a	X	X
H9b	✓	X
H10	✓	NA
H11	NA	?

✓ → hypothesis proved
X → hypothesis not proved
? → hypothesis result opposite or partially proved

In 2010 and 2013 models, we observe a gradual improvement in the interplay between technology and other factors like hospital characteristics and socio-economic factors. The goodness of fit of our model for 2010 and 2013 shows only 13% and 18.1% respectively. One of the primary reason is that mortality rates of critical diseases is highly dependent on patient condition during admission. There are several other factors too, like security concerns, policies within a state or country [42], physician's unwillingness to adopt technology and steps followed for proper technology diffusion [43], which affect the optimal usage of HIT. This motivates us to look into the technology-organization-environment (TOE) perspective in future [44]. We have also tested for autocorrelation using Durbin-Watson. We faced several challenges due to the variability in the method of capturing the different predictors of the regression model. While mortality rates were captured as a three-year average for each years, socio-economic factors were mentioned for the overall state. Although, it is worth noting that we have observed some genuine effect of the state-wise socio-economic factors on the overall model. However, patient condition during admission, their economic condition and

literacy, and hospital's policy should help get closer to the factors on which technology's contribution on quality depends.

9 CONCLUSIONS

Our paper is an exploratory framework that consists of HIT applications used for routine as well as disease-specific process automation. We also used hospital characteristics and socio-economic factors as moderators to check the contribution of technology due to interaction as well as on its own. Our result shows a dominance of hospital characteristics both in 2010 and 2013. It also shows an improvement in technology's significance in predicting mortality rate reduction (or improvement of hospital clinical quality). The increased maturity of technology as information systems is understood by its interaction with PCI and hospital characteristics in 2013 model. Thus our paper motivates researchers to use the concept of interactions and interplay between technology and other social and organizational factors. Our work also motivates managers to prioritize investment in installing applications to ensure better return on investment in terms of quality.

10 REFERENCES

[1] Reinhold Haux, 2006. Health information systems–past, present, future. International journal of medical informatics, 75, 3 (March–April 2006), 268-281.
[2] Digital Journal 2016. Global IT-Enabled Healthcare Market: Developing Economies Stealing the Spotlight. (January 2016). http://www.digitaljournal.com/pr/2827294
[3] Richard Lenz, and Klaus A. Kuhn, 2004. Towards a continuous evolution and adaptation of information systems in healthcare. International journal of medical informatics, 73, 1 (February 2004), 75-89.
[4] Robert G. Fichman, Rajiv Kohli, and Ranjani Krishnan, eds., 2011. Editorial overview—the role of information systems in healthcare: current research and future trends. Information Systems Research, 22, 3 (Septmeber 2011), 419-428.
[5] Janet M Morahan-Martin, 2004. How internet users find, evaluate, and use online health information: a cross-cultural review. CyberPsychology & Behavior, 7, 5 (November 2004), 497-510.
[6] David C. Classen, Stanley L. Pestotnik, R. Scott Evans, James F. Lloyd, and John P. Burke. 1997. Adverse drug events in hospitalized patients: excess length of stay, extra costs, and attributable mortality. Jama, 277, 4 (January 1997), 301-306.
[7] Sarv Devaraj, and Rajiv Kohli, 2003. Performance impacts of information technology: Is actual usage the missing link?. Management science, 49, 3 (March 2003), 273-289.
[8] Indranil R. Bardhan, and Mark F. Thouin, 2013. Health information technology and its impact on the quality and cost of healthcare delivery. Decision Support Systems, 55, 2 (May 2013), 438-449.
[9] Basit Chaudhry, Jerome Wang, Wu Shinyi, Margaret Maglione, Walter Mojica, Elizabeth Roth, Sally C. Morton, and Paul G. Shekelle, 2006. Systematic review: impact of health information technology on quality, efficiency, and costs of medical care. Annals of internal medicine, 144, 10 (May 2006), 742-752.
[10] Budsakorn Watcharasriroj, and John CS Tang, 2004. The effects of size and information technology on hospital efficiency. The Journal of High Technology Management Research, 15, 1 (February 2004), 1-16.
[11] J. Yannis Bakos, and Michael E. Treacy. 1986. Information technology and corporate strategy: a research perspective. MIS quarterly, (June 1986), 107-119.

[12] Kyu K. Kim, and Jeffrey E. Michelman. 1990. An examination of factors for the strategic use of information systems in the healthcare industry. MIS quarterly, (June 1990), 201-215.

[13] Ritu Agarwal, Gao Guodong, Catherine DesRoches, and Ashish K. Jha. 2010. Research commentary—The digital transformation of healthcare: Current status and the road ahead. Information Systems Research, 21, 4 (December 2010), 796-809.

[14] Corey M. Angst, Ritu Agarwal, Vallabh Sambamurthy, and Ken Kelley. 2010. Social contagion and information technology diffusion: the adoption of electronic medical records in US hospitals. Management Science, 56, 8 (August 2010), 1219-1241.

[15] Ken Trimmer, Leigh W. Cellucci, Carla Wiggins, and William Woodhouse. 2009. Electronic medical records: TAM, UTAUT, and culture. International Journal of Healthcare Information Systems and Informatics (IJHISI), 4, 3 (July 2009), 55-68.

[16] Fons Wijnhoven, Ton Spil, Robert Stegwee, and Rachel Tjang A. Fa. 2006. Post-merger IT integration strategies: An IT alignment perspective. The Journal of Strategic Information Systems, 15, 1 (March 2006), 5-28.

[17] Felicia M. Bowens, Patricia A. Frye, and Warren A. Jones. 2010. Health information technology: integration of clinical workflow into meaningful use of electronic health records. Perspectives in Health Information Management/AHIMA, American Health Information Management Association, 7(Fall).

[18] Srinivas, K., B. Kavihta Rani, and A. Govrdhan. 2010. Applications of data mining techniques in healthcare and prediction of heart attacks. International Journal on Computer Science and Engineering (IJCSE), 2, 2 (February 2010), 250-255.

[19] Marc Berg, 1999. Patient care information systems and health care work: a sociotechnical approach. International journal of medical informatics, 55, 2 (August 1999), 87-101.

[20] Indranil Bardhan, Jeong-ha Oh, Zhiqiang Zheng, and Kirk Kirksey. 2014. Predictive analytics for readmission of patients with congestive heart failure. Information Systems Research, 26, 1 (November 2014), 19-39.

[21] Jay Barney, 1991. Firm resources and sustained competitive advantage. Journal of management, 17, 1(March 1991), 99-120.

[22] Dorothy Leonard-Barton. 1992. Core capabilities and core rigidities: A paradox in managing new product development. Strategic Management Journal, 13, 1 (June 1992), 111-125.

[23] Dorothy Leonard-Barton. 1988. Implementation as mutual adaptation of technology and organization. Research Policy, 17, 5 (October 1988), 251-267.

[24] Erik Brynjolfsson. 1993. The productivity paradox of information technology. Communications of the ACM, 36, 12 (December 1993), 66-77.

[25] Nigel Melville, Kenneth Kraemer, and Vijay Gurbaxani. 2004. Information technology and organizational performance: An integrative model of IT business value. MIS quarterly, 28, 2 (June 2004), 283-322.

[26] Abby S. Kazley, and Yasar A. Ozcan. 2008. Do hospitals with electronic medical records (EMRs) provide higher quality care? An examination of three clinical conditions. Medical Care Research and Review, 65, 4 (August 2008), 496-513.

[27] Jeffrey A. Linder, Jun Ma, David W. Bates, Blackford Middleton, and Randall S. Stafford. 2007. Electronic health record use and the quality of ambulatory care in the United States. Archives of internal medicine, 167, 13 (July 2007), 1400-1405.

[28] Amy Hennington, and Brian D. Janz. 2007. Information systems and healthcare XVI: physician adoption of electronic medical records: applying the UTAUT model in a healthcare context. Communications of the Association for Information Systems, 19, 1 (March 2007), 5.

[29] Linda H. Aiken, Sean P. Clarke, Douglas M. Sloane, Julie Sochalski, and Jeffrey H. Silber. 2002. Hospital nurse staffing and patient mortality, nurse burnout, and job dissatisfaction. Jama, 288, 16 (October 2002), 1987-1993.

[30] David U. Himmelstein, Adam Wright, and Steffie Woolhandler. 2010. Hospital computing and the costs and quality of care: a national study. The American journal of medicine, 123, 1 (January 2010), 40-46.

[31] Jennifer Daley, Maureen G. Forbes, Gary J. Young, Martin P. Charns, James O. Gibbs, Kwan Hur, William Henderson, and Shukri F. Khuri. 1997. Validating risk-adjusted surgical outcomes: site visit assessment of process and structure. Journal of the American College of Surgeons, 185, 4 (October 1997), 341-351.

[32] Stephen Lee Walston, Lawton Robert Burns, and John R. Kimberly. 2000. Does reengineering really work? An examination of the context and outcomes of hospital reengineering initiatives. Health Services Research, 34, 6 (February 2000), 1363.

[33] Mehmet Sahin Gok, and Bulent Sezen. 2013. Analyzing the ambiguous relationship between efficiency, quality and patient satisfaction in healthcare services: the case of public hospitals in Turkey. Health policy, 111, 3 (August 2013), 290-300.

[34] Paul D. Cleary, and Barbara J. McNeil. 1988. Patient satisfaction as an indicator of quality care. Inquiry. (April 1988) 25-36.

[35] Shounak Pal, Baidyanath Biswas, and Arunabha Mukhopadhyay. 2016. Can HIT Work Alone? A Security and Socio-Economic Perspective of Healthcare Quality. In the Proceedings of 22nd AMCIS Conference, San Diego, California. ISBN: 978-0-9966831-2-8

[36] Surabhi Mittal, and Praduman Kumar. 2000. Literacy, technology adoption, factor demand and productivity: An economic analysis. Indian Journal of Agricultural Economics, 55, 3 (July 2000), 490.

[37] John R. Kimberly, and Michael J. Evanisko. 1981. Organizational innovation: The influence of individual, organizational, and contextual factors on hospital adoption of technological and administrative innovations. Academy of management journal, 24, 4 (December 1981), 689-713.

[38] Badi H. Baltagi, and Francesco Moscone, 2010. Health care expenditure and income in the OECD reconsidered: Evidence from panel data. Economic Modelling, 27, 4 (July 2010), 804-811.

[39] James Jaccard, and Robert Turrisi. 2003. Interaction effects in multiple regression. No. 72. Sage University Paper.

[40] Chung-pin Lee, Kaiju Chang, and Frances Stokes Berry. 2011. Testing the development and diffusion of e-government and e-democracy: A global perspective. Public Administration Review, 71, 3 (May 2011), 444-454.

[41] Zhen-Yu Wu, Yueh-Chun Lee, Feipei Lai, Hung-Chang Lee, and Yufang Chung. 2012. A secure authentication scheme for telecare medicine information systems. Journal of medical systems, 36, 3 (June 2016), 1529-1535.

[42] Ajit Appari, M. Eric Johnson, and Denise L. Anthony. 2009. HIPAA compliance: an institutional theory perspective. AMCIS 2009 proceedings, (January 2009). 252.

[43] Mary Cain, and Robert Mittman. 2002. Diffusion of innovation in health care. http://www.ehealthstrategies.com/files/diffusionofinnovation.pdf

[44] Jeff Baker, 2012. The technology–organization–environment framework. In Information systems theory 231-245. Springer New York.

A Meta-Review of IS Health IT Research and Development of a New Framework

Mike Gallivan
Information Systems Department Coles
College of Business
Kennesaw State University
Kennesaw, Georgia, USA
001 (470) 578-7763
mgalliv1@kennesaw.edu

ABSTRACT

In the past decade, research on healthcare IT (HIT) has become an established domain in the IS field [33]. Given the large number of HIT papers published in IS journals, as well as the many special issues dedicated to HIT, and the role of IS special interest groups (e.g., AIS SIG Health) and specialized HIT conferences, it is time to take stock of the contributions of the IS community with regard to HIT. This paper provides a meta-review of HIT research – a review of nine prior IS HIT review papers from journals and conferences. Based on insights from our analysis, we create a new framework to classify IS HIT research (the PRECIOUS model). We argue that our framework leverages and extends the well-known PICO framework used in medical research to render it useful for IS scholars who seek to locate or classify the contributions of IS scholars to HIT research. In creating our PRECIOUS model, we also seek to remedy several problems that have previously been noted regarding the limitations of the conventional PICO model.

Keywords

Co-citation analysis; Healthcare information technology; Research methods; Meta-analysis; Meta-review; Literature review

ACM Reference format:
Mike Gallivan. 2018. A Meta-Review of IS Health IT Research and Development of a New Framework. In *SIGMIS-CPR'18: SIGMIS-CPR'18, June 18-20, 2018, Buffalo-Niagara Falls, NY, USA*, 7 pages.
https:// doi.org/10.1145/3209626.3209714

1. INTRODUCTION

Health IT has become an important topic within the IS field, especially given the importance of providing care to aging populations, and the need to increase access while reducing costs. In the past decade, the domain of health IT (HIT) research has become an established research stream within the IS discipline [33]. Given the number of published studies in IS, as well as the many journal special issues dedicated to HIT and the role of special interest groups (SIG Health), is time to take stock

of the contributions of the IS community regarding HIT research. Most HIT scholars are aware of a comprehensive review of this area by Chiasson & Davidson [5]); however, their review appeared nearly 15 years ago. With the rapid growth in the number of HIT scholars and studies in IS, plus new generations of HIT systems that have emerged in the past decade, it is important to take stock of where we are and where we have been, and to understand how IS scholars contributes to HIT research.

In this paper, we present a meta-review of HIT (a review of nine prior review papers in IS journals and conferences), and based on insights from these reviews, we develop a framework to represent a structure for classifying IS HIT research. We believe our framework (the PRECIOUS model), reflecting an extension to the well-known "PICO" framework (referring to Patient, Intervention, Control group, and Outcomes), which is commonly used to classify medical research and guide health-related literature reviews, can resolve several gaps that medical researchers have identified in the "PICO" model [6, 11, 28].

2. CONCEPTUAL DEVELOPMENT

Within medical and medical informatics research, the "PICO" acronym is often used as an organizing framework to support several goals. These include classifying prior research, structuring a literature review, and formulate medical research questions. For instance, in the medical research and medial librarian community, the dimensions of "PICO" are used to guide the mechanics of an online search. Based on years of tradition in these communities, it is assumed that the four dimensions of the "PICO" model will help to identify relevant studies of interest. According to this guiding framework, "P" refers to the Patient type or Population with a given medical condition being studied; "I" is the medical Intervention, "C" refers to the presence of a Control group (or comparison); "O" refers to the Outcome of interest – such as mortality, average length of hospital stay, or cost. While 'PICO' is widely embraced by medical researchers and librarians, ironically, it has been virtually ignored in the IS community of scholars who study HIT. While this lack of uptake by IS scholars of the PICO framework is surprising – given its broad use in medical research and health informatics – use of PICO represents but one artifact by which IS discipline research vastly differs from HIT research published in medical journals and in medical informatics journals. We support this claim by noting that, our own focused search in several online databases covering IS journals revealed a recent paper in *Communications of the AIS* [29], based on a 2016 ICIS conference panel, and one conference paper by Shirley Gregor [9] from a design science conference.

Although 'PICO' was originally developed for formulation of clinical questions, medical researchers have criticized it for both providing insufficient guidance for conducting searches to support Evidence-based Medicine or for being too restrictive. According to Huang et al. [13], who conducted an analysis of 59 real-world clinical care searches on two medical databases, they identified several problems with the limitations of PICO:

We found ... only two questions in our corpus [of 59 queries] contain all four PICO elements and [that only] 37% of questions contain both Intervention and Outcome... We found that the PICO framework is primarily centered on [clinical] therapy questions, and [it] is less suitable for representing other types of clinical information needs [13, p. 359].

While Huang et al [13] noted that specifying the therapeutic Intervention (the 'I' in PICO) is overly-restrictive, there are other problems with PICO. Several medical researchers seeking to conduct systematic literature reviews [11, 16] report that other forms of search guidance are needed. In disciplines other than medical research (such as IS, health education, and psychology). In the IS field, the model it is problematic – since PICO's assumption of controlled experiments is unrealistic and thus, unable to capture the diversity of research methods in IS. Moreover, some dimensions of the model – such as the 'I' (intervention) and C' (control group) are criticized for not generalizing to qualitative research [15].

3. RESEARCH METHODS

Given our understanding of such limitations of PICO for classifying IS HIT research or for supporting searches, we chose to review papers in the IS HIT literature that themselves serve as reviews in order to identify the various frameworks, classification approaches, and dimensions of such models. We engaged in two rounds of searches to retrieve, analyze, and summarize insights of these HIT review papers published in IS journals and conferences. While we were already familiar with Chiasson and Davidson's [5] comprehensive study of HIT research, we sought both more and more recent reviews to guide us in developing a useful model.

In our first round, we searched for IS HIT review papers containing the word "Review" in the title. We searched many databases, including Google Scholar, ProQuest, Science Direct, and the AIS eLibrary. In this round, we located five review papers. Three were from 2015 IS conferences – either AMCIS [14, 18] or ICIS [1] – while two appeared in IS journals [2, 32]. We discuss these papers by explaining how the authors classified HIT papers – whether according to the PICO model, the type of user, type of system, research methods, or other approaches.

The five papers are summarized in the top half of Table 1. Each paper focuses on part of the health IT literature; this means that we were unable to find any comprehensive reviews of the IS HIT literature since Chiasson and Davidson [5] published their review in *Information and Organization*. Each of the reviews focused on a small part of the HIT literature – either a specific type of HIT, such as electronic health records [2], or clinical knowledge management systems [32], a specific adopter group, physicians [5], or a specific outcome: health literacy [14], or health quality [18].

Since we did not want to limit our review of HIT review papers to just those containing the word "review" in the title, we repeated our search process (using the same range of online databases as before); however, in this second phase, we sought to broadly include review papers based on those containing the word "review" or "meta-analysis" in the Abstract (but not necessarily the title). After excluding many papers that just mentioned the word "review" as a precursor to the authors' empirical study (as their primary research method), or papers that described their research method as reviewing health websites, we located four papers featuring reviews of the IS HIT literature – even if the word "review" did not appear in the title.

For each empirical study, we identified the number of informants or subjects, type of subjects (e.g., employees, under-graduate, graduate, or secondary school students), the number of men and women, and subjects' country of origin.

4. RESULTS

Table 1 summarizes this aspect of the review papers (i.e., what subset of papers each author included in their review). While all reviews were focused – either in terms of the specific HIT technology reviewed, the adopter group, or the outcome variable – we also classify whether the reviews were broad, focused, or ambiguous in terms of three attributes: (a) the time period of papers covered – whether all years or a subset; (b) the number of publications covered; and (c) whether the authors included IS journals in their searches of HIT papers. Table 1 shows whether each review paper was broad, focused, or ambiguous according to each of these dimensions.

While all reviews were published in IS outlets, some authors intentionally excluded IS journals in performing their searches – for example, by searching only medical databases, like *PubMed*, that exclude IS journals. Others simply lacked any IS papers in their results set, despite the fact that they searched online databases containing IS journals. We summarize each review paper, focusing on how the authors classified the HIT papers they retrieved, including any frameworks or conceptual models that these authors created or used for classification purposes.

The first paper, by Abouzahra et al. [5] focused on a specific adopter group (physicians), locating a total of 175 papers. The authors conducted a broad search on doctors' adoption and use of HIT as well as adoption of clinical guidelines across a broad range of databases and journals. As one part of their search protocol, they searched the AIS "Basket of Eight" journals for papers, finding 9 such papers in IS journals (less than 5% of papers they retrieved). One-third of the papers the authors retrieved and analyzed (58 out of 175 papers) concerned physician's adoption of clinical guidelines rather than HIT, leaving 117 remaining papers that focus on physicians' adoption and use of IT.

Abouzahra et al performed various analyses – including coding and summarizing the journal source (IS vs. health informatics journals) (their Table 2), the primary topic (adoption of HIT or clinical guidelines) (their Table 3), the underlying theories used to guide the hypotheses and analyses (their Table 4). They also separately analyzed the primary constructs employed in IS papers (their Table 5), and in health informatics papers (their Table 6). In comparing research published in IS journals with medical informatics journals, the authors first highlight the much greater importance of theory in IS papers; moreover, they list the leading theories in IS journal papers (e.g., TAM, Social Network Theories, Theory of Planned Behavior, Innovation Diffusion Theory, and Institutional Theory) (their Table 4). Notably, the authors underscored the strong role of theory in IS papers and conversely, the lack of theory in health informatics papers. Referring to their classification based on topic and publication source, Abouzahra et al explain such differences:

> As Tables 3 and 4 show, two distinct streams of research are evident. The first stream considers HIS as business information systems and applies business IS theories to study HIS, with TAM being the prevailing theory ... [A] second stream, research ... by medical researchers, is characterized by a clear lack of theory behind the study of physicians' behavior ... Surprisingly, the number of HIS studies in the second stream is larger than in the first [5, p. 4].

The second paper by Ben-Zion et al. [2] focused on electronic health records (EHR), analyzing the critical success factors that lead to implementation success. These authors reviewed over 500 papers from academic journals and various non-academic sources (newspapers, magazines, white papers, and dissertations). Their objective was to provide advice about how to implement EHR technology. These authors leveraged the *IT Interaction Model* from Silver, Markus & Beath [31] to classify factors leading to implementation success.

The third paper by Wills et al [32] also focused on a specific type of HIT, clinical knowledge management systems. They organize their review using two frameworks: first, four clinical processes of diagnosis, treatment, monitoring, and prognosis. Next, they also use the four knowledge management stages (creation, capture, transfer, and application). Among various analyses they offer, one identifies the various technologies that support these processes for different clinical stages. They identify many technologies for knowledge creation (Table 5), knowledge sharing (Table 6), and knowledge application (their Figure 3). The authors conclude that most research on clinical KMS is conducted by health informatics scholars, with much less from IS scholars. They observe that "IS researchers have played a limited role in past clinical KMS research ...[but] there is considerable potential for IS researchers to contribute their expertise" [32, p. 565].

The fourth paper by Hur et al [14] focused on a specific outcome: consumer health literacy. In their analysis of 45 paper about health literacy (none of which appeared in IS outlets, despite having included one database that indexes several IS journals as one part of their search), the authors created a framework to summarize their results (their Table 1). Hur et al. identify five steps that consumers take to reach health literacy, starting with Access to information, then Building Knowledge (with explicit and tacit knowledge identified separately), and finally, Knowledge Use (with behavior change and use of decision-making aids as separate steps).

The final paper focuses on studies of healthcare quality [8]. In this paper, Parthasarathy and Steinbach searched for papers containing keywords *quality* and *errors* across a broad range of media that "included search engines, academic journals, medical research portals, and academic research on publication portals" (*ibid*, p. 3). They did not state whether they searched for papers in IS journals or conferences.[1] Among various analyses that they performed were coding of the methods that researchers used to collect their data (e.g., surveys, case studies, archival data) [18, Table 1] and the types of HIT that physicians use [18, Table 2].

Overall, these reviews of HIT suggest that it is useful to distinguish and classify different types of HIT studies, such as the journal source in which papers appeared (i.e., IS vs. medical journals) [5, Table 2], different outcome measures that HIT use may influence – such as health literacy [14] vs. healthcare quality [18]. Finally, it is important to consider different types of HIT (even those employed by the same adopters), since different classes of HIT will have different effects.

Based on these comments and our classification of these reviews, we note that the "PICO" model does not consider the research methods used in the study, although we regard this as essential for IS research, since only a small fraction of IS research is based on controlled experiments, and many more IS studies use surveys or case studies, in contrast to medical research. Along these lines, Chiasson and Davison [5, p. 178] recognized the breadth of IS research on HIT and cautioned that we should not just assume that all IS HIT research "follow[s] normative research designs modeled on experimental clinical trials." Another aspect in which IS research differs from research in medicine or health informatics is the importance of theory (as observed in [5]), such that IS publications are evaluated primarily on the basis of contributions to theory, in contrast to medical research, where evidence of statistical findings matters most.

The lower half of Table 1 shows HIT papers with 'review' in the Abstract, but not the title. We discuss each one, again with a goal of identifying the types of conceptual frameworks that the authors created or borrowed. Chiasson and Davidson's [5] paper in *Information and Organization* is a comprehensive review of all health IT research published from 1985 to 2002. Unlike other papers that we discussed above, their selection of papers was not limited to a specific topic (e.g., health quality) or a specific type HIT (e.g., telemedicine, nursing systems, online data). Their review was broad but focused mostly on papers published in IS journals (a total of 17 IS journals), plus a few non-IS journals.[2]

For the 165 papers they located, Chiasson and Davidson conducted two primary analyses. First, they analyzed the papers in terms of Orlikowski & Iacono's [17] typology of different *views* of the IT artifact – categorizing HIT studies in terms of whether IT is seen as a tool, an ensemble, a computational system, or only nominally (i.e., not present). Second, they created a typology of papers depending on the relative importance of general IS theory vs. the importance of the health context and a specific technology. The latter typology shows a continuum from, at one end, papers that focus most on creating and testing generalizable IS theories (which they label "IS Only"), where the healthcare context is incidental to the paper, to studies at the other end, that focus on the specific healthcare technology or context, with no attempt to create or test generalizable theories.

- IS Only (the primary goal is generalizable theory without regard to any healthcare context)

- IS-Healthcare (the primary goal is generalizable theory, but analyzes specifics of the health context)

- Healthcare-IS (explains behavior in a health context, using general theory to frame it)

---

[1] The 29 papers they analyzed lacked IS journal papers.

[2] In addition to 17 IS journals, they added *Organization Science*, *Organization Studies*, and *Human Relations*.

- Healthcare Only (the primary goal is to describe a healthcare technology in its context; less concern for generalizable theory)

The 165 papers they analyzed were spread across the entire continuum, but the largest category was "Healthcare Only" – papers offering descriptive applications of a specific technology, algorithm or solution – without any attempt to generalize what the findings to other industry contexts or to general IS theory. It is also noteworthy that they conducted an analysis that showed, when they excluded *Communications of the ACM* (a practitioner magazine containing the most papers: 36 papers), from their analysis, then the majority of the remaining papers (i.e., 55% of the remaining 129 papers) featured either a medium-high or very high role for generalizable IS theory. Chiasson and Davidson's reanalysis of their own data after they excluded *Communications of the ACM* is supplemented by our re-analysis of their results, after we excluded a different practitioner magazine that ceased publication in 1996 (*Journal of Systems Management*), to reveal that 59 of the remaining 118 papers had a strong role for generalizable theory (after omitting *Journal of Systems Management* and *Communications of the ACM*).

Of course, in addition to deriving a typology to classify papers based on the relative importance of generalizable theory in the original study (as Chiasson and Davidson did), the other way to consider theory is to classify research according to different IS theories – whether the primary theory is TAM, Theory of Planned Behavior, Social Network Theories, etc. [5, Table 4].

We discuss three additional reviews, each focused on a specific area within HIT: reviews focusing on a specific outcome variable (healthcare quality) [20], a specific data source (Internet-based health data) [27], and a specific topic (patient-centered e-health) [34]. While each review develops a detailed framework relevant to their own topic within the larger HIT domain, they offer analyses that can be useful to a broad range of HIT scholars for future research. These frameworks include analyses of the effects of different forms of HIT on the same dependent variable (as [7] show in their Figure 1; see also [20, Table 1].

One study classified HIT papers based on the different outcomes considered (e.g., patient access to information vs. better decision-making (Table 2 in [7]). A second study classified the research methods used (Figure 3 in Rozenkranz et al [7]) while a third created a typology to identify various "players" within the health sector (Table 1 in [7]). We found the typology of health industry players useful since the range of players distinguish healthcare contexts from other industries that IS scholars study.[3]

Recognizing the various players highlights the Environment in which HIT is used – which necessarily includes the institutional setting, plus the country, geographic region, and culture in which the study is situated. Moreover, Environment also includes the regulations and institutional practices

that shape practitioners' and patients' behavior. As with other medical library scholars who noted the limitations of the PICO model [6, 28], we recognize the need to consider the Environment in which a given HIT is used ('E'), as well as the underlying theory or framework ('U'), and finally, the type of research methods ('R') employed.

Based on these insights, we propose an expanded version of the traditional 'PICO' model:

P – Represents the Patient, but, in IS HIT research, research subjects are not always patients

I – Intervention represents a clear construct, but not all HIT studies feature interventions. While interventions occur in controlled experiments, IS studies often consist of surveys, case studies, ethnographies, and design science research – which often lack interventions and control groups

C – Control group (or comparison), which is assumed by experimental studies, but often does not exist in IS research using survey research, case studies, or analysis of archival data

O – Outcomes are retained as a construct in our model

To this model, we propose the following new attributes to understand and classify IS research:

S – Subjects of study. In most HIT studies, the subjects are doctors or hospital workers who are distinct from patients. For example, subjects may be nurses using HIT to care for diabetics.

R – Research Methods (as we described above)

U – Underlying theoretical model (characteristic of IS research; less common in medicine).

E – Environmental context where the research occurs (country, region, type of institutions)

Based on these additional attributes, we introduce the acronym "PRECIOUS" to serve as an extension to the PICO model. One value of our framework is that it can serve as the basis to classify IS papers about HIT to facilitate searches and literature reviews. For example, a given researcher may be interested in identifying all prior HIT studies that employed a specific Underlying theory ("U"), studies focused on a specific subject type ("S") (e.g., nurses, hospital administrators), or they may seek to locate only papers that use a specific research method ("R") (e.g., interpretive case studies, controlled experiments, etc.).

Based on insights provided by the prior reviews, we believe the PRECIOUS framework can be useful to IS scholars to retrieve and classify previous studies, as well as for comparing their work to prior studies. It may be time-consuming to locate and classify HIT research in terms of the PRECIOUS model, especially if the goal is to locate *all* studies (or at least a range of HIT studies on various topics). It is not surprising that the prior review papers we analyzed in Table 1 focus on a single type of adopter, a specific outcome, or a specific HIT system type.

5. DISCUSSION

Our paper features a meta-review of nine prior HIT review papers, and on the basis of insights we derived from our analysis, we proposed to extend the traditional PICO model from medical research to better reflect elements of IS research that distinguish it from medical research, including the Research Methods (R), the Environmental context of study (E), the Underlying theoretical model (U), and type of Subjects (S). Based on

---

[3] The full list of "Players in the Health System" (Rozenkranz et al. 2013, Table 1) specifies: "Individual Level" (patients, hospitals, physicians, health professionals, pharmacists, researchers, statutory health insurance, private health insurance companies); "Organizational Level" (medical associations, hospital associations, patient associations, associations of health professionals, pharmacy associations), and "Others" (pharmaceutical industry, medical technology industry, state-run organizations, institutes).

these extensions, we propose the acronym, PRECIOUS, for use by IS scholars to help classify the diversity of IS research and to support searches of IS HIT papers, as medical librarians do with the PICO model.

In our future work, we plan to conduct a type of automated analysis of HIT research by using patterns of citations that appear in HIT research, in order to identify the overall macro patterns of topics and themes. Our goal is to see whether the patterns by which various sets of IS HIT studies group together will reflect either the original elements of the PICO model (e.g., patient disease, outcomes), or the new dimensions we introduce here (research method, underlying theoretical framework, environmental context). Our future work will use co-citation analysis. Co-citation analyses is typically considered a way to understand the intellectual structure of a discipline. Some co-citation analyses have sought to analyze the IS discipline as a whole, including Culnan's reviews of the IS field in its early days [7, 8], as well as reviews of fields like operations management [3], and strategic management [10, 24]. Co-citation analysis is becoming more frequently used in the IS field; however, it has been over 30 years since this approach has been applied to the IS discipline as a whole [7, 8]. It has also been used for analyzing topics such as software maintenance [25], operations management [19], or virtual teams [23]. Scholars have conducted co-citation analysis for all papers based on a single theory, such as TAM [12] and Strategic Alignment Model [26].

Recent studies applied co-citation analysis to HIT research published in IS journals [4], or in health informatics [21, 30].

Table 2 shows topics that emerged from co-citation analyses of a subset of authors (editorial board members) who published in five health informatics journals, as reported by Raghupathi and Nerur [21] or in eight such journals, as reported in a later paper by the same authors [22]. The results in Table 2 illustrate the types of topics and themes that emerge from co-citation analysis.

Our future work will demonstrate the themes and clusters of studies that result from co-citation analysis of HIT research as well as our interpretation of the results using PRECIOUS framework, described here. We anticipate that the underlying factors that determine groups related IS HIT studies will include attributes such as the underlying theoretical framework, research method used (e.g., surveys, case studies, etc.), as well as the healthcare context (e.g., hospitals, outpatient clinics), and the type of respondents in the study.

6. REFERENCES

[1] Abouzahra, M., Guenter, D. & Tan, J. Integrating IS and healthcare research to understand physician use of health information systems: A literature review. *Proceedings of ICIS*, 2015.

[2] Ben-Zion, R., Pliskin, N. & Fink, L. Critical success factors for adoption of electronic health record systems: Literature review and prescriptive analysis. *Information Systems Management*, 31, 2014, 296-312.

[3] Charvet, F.F., Cooper, M. C. & Gardner, J. The intellectual structure of supply chain management: A bibliometric approach. *Journal of Business Logistics*, 2, 2008, 47-73.

[4] Chen, L., Baird, A. & Straub, D. The evolving intellectual structure of the health informatics discipline: A multi-method investigation of a rapidly-growing scientific field. Social Science Research Network (SSRN) papers, 2014.

[5] Chiasson, M. W. & Davidson, E. Pushing the contextual envelope: developing and diffusing is theory for health IS research. *Information and Organization* 14, 2004, 155-188.

[6] Cooke, A., Smith, D. & Booth, A. Beyond PICO: The SPIDER tool for qualitative evidence synthesis. *Qualitative Health Research*, 22(10), 2012, 1435-1443.

[7] Culnan, M. J. The intellectual development of management information systems, 1972-1982: A co-citation analysis. *Management Science* 32(2), 1986, 156-172.

[8] Culnan, M. J. Mapping the intellectual structure of MIS, 1980-1985: A co-citation analysis. *MIS Quarterly*, 11, 1987, 341-353.

[9] Gregor, S. Building theory in the sciences of the artificial, Proceedings of *DESRIST '09*, 2009.

[10] Gregoire, D., Noel, M., Déry, R. & Béchard, J.P. Is there conceptual convergence in entrepreneurship research? A co-citation analysis, 1981-2004. *Frontiers of Entrepreneurship Research*, 30, 2006, 333-373.

[11] Hoogendam, A., De Vries R. & Overbeke, A.J. Comparing patient characteristics, type of intervention, control, and outcome queries with unguided searching. *Journal of Medical Library Association*, 100, 2012, 121-128.

Topics Found in 5 Health Informatics Journals Raghupathi & Nerur (2008) [21]		Topics Found in 8 Health Informatics Journals Raghupathi & Nerur (2010) [22]	
(Topics sorted from largest to smallest eigenvalues)			
1.	HIS Evaluation	1.	Communication and e-health
2.	Communication and e-health	2.	Medical imaging technology
3.	E-Heath	3.	A.I. / Decision Support
4.	Clinical DSS	4.	Ontology and medical terminology
5.	Adoptions, outcome, policy	5.	Remote monitoring, mobile computing
6.	Telemedicine and communication	6.	User acceptance, quality
7.	Mobile computing	7.	Bioinformatics
8.	Internet and web-based health care	8.	Clinical information systems
9.	Quality, integration	9.	User interface
10.	Public health informatics	10.	Natural language processing
11.	Use and impact of HIS	11.	Health informatics
12.	Medical safety	12.	e-Health
13.	Health policy, quality of care	13.	Computational genomics
		14.	Analysis and extraction in genomics

Table 2. Topics in Health Informatics Journals

[12] Hsiao, C.H. & Yang, C. The intellectual development of the technology acceptance model. *International Journal of Information Management*, 31(2), 2011, 128-136.

[13] Huang, X., Lin, J. & Demner-Fushman, D. PICO as a knowledge representation for clinical questions *American Medical Informatics Association 2006 Proceedings*, 2006, 359-363.

[14] Hur, I., Lee, R. & Schmidt, J. How healthcare technology shapes health literacy? A systematic review. *Proceedings of AMCIS Conference*, 2015, Puerto Rico.

[15] Methley, A. M., Campbell, S., Chew-Graham, C., McNally, R. & Cheraghi, S. PICO, PICOS and SPIDER: A comparison study of specificity and sensitivity in three search tools for qualitative systematic reviews. *BMC Health Services Research*, 14, 2014, 1-44.

[16] Murad, M. H., Montori, V. M., Ioannidis, J. P., Jaeschke, R., & Meade, M. O. How to read a systematic review and meta-analysis and apply the results to patient care: Users' guides to the medical literature. *Journal of American Medical Association* (JAMA), 312, 2014, 171-179.

[17] Orlikowski, W. & Iacono, C. Desperately seeking the 'IT' in IT research: a call to theorizing the IT artifact. *Information Systems Research*, 12, 2001, 121-134.

[18] Parthasarathy, R. & Steinbach, T. Health informatics for healthcare quality improvement: A literature review of issues, challenges, findings. *Proceedings of AMCIS*, 2015, Puerto Rico.

[19] Pilkington, A., & Meredith, J. The evolution of the intellectual structure of operations management 1980-2006: A citation/co-citation analysis. *Journal of Operations Management*, 27(3), 2009, 185-202.

[20] Pinaire, K. & Sarnikar, S. Identifying optimal IT portfolios to promote healthcare quality. *Proceedings of ICIS*, 2012, Orlando, FL.

[21] Raghupathi, W. & Nerur, S. Research themes and trends in health information systems *Methods of Information in Medicine*, 47, 2008, 435-442.

[22] Raghupathi, W. & Nerur, S. The intellectual structure of health and medical informatics. International *Journal of Healthcare Information Systems & Informatics*, 5, 2010, 20-34.

[23] Raghuram, S., Tuertscher, P. & Garud, R. Mapping the field of virtual work: A co-citation analysis. *Information Systems Research* 21(4), 2010, 983-999.

[24] Ramos-Rodríguez, A. & Ruíz Navarro, J. Changes in the intellectual structure of strategic management research: A bibliometric study. *Strategic Management Journal* 25, 2004, 981-1004.

[25] Ramanujan, S. & Nerur, S. An exploratory analysis of the state of software maintenance research: An author cocitation analysis. *Journal of Systems and IT*, 11, 2009, 117-130.

[26] Renaud, A., Walsh, I. & Kalika, M. Is SAM (Strategic Alignment Model) still alive? A bibliometric and interpretive mapping of strategic alignment research field. *Journal of Strategic Information Systems*, 25, 2016, 75-103.

[27] Rozenkranz, N.; Eckhardt, A., Kuhne, M. & Rosenkranz, C. Health information on the Internet. Business & Information Systems Engineering, 5(4), 2013, 259-273.

[28] Schardt, C., Adams, M., Owens, T., & Keitz, S. Utilization of the PICO framework to improve searching PubMed for clinical questions. *BMC Medical Informatics & Decision Making*, 7, 2007, 16-21.

[29] Schryen, G., Benlian, A., Rowe, F., Gregor, S., Larsen, K., Petter, S., Paré, G., Haag, S., & Yasasin, E. Literature reviews in IS research: What can be learnt from the past and other fields? *Communications of the Association for Information Systems*, 41(30), 2017.

[30] Schuemie, M. J., Talmon, J.L., Moorman, P.W. & Kors, J.A. Mapping the domain of medical informatics. *Methods of Information in Medicine*, 48, 2009, 76-95.

[31] Silver, M.S., Markus, M. L., & Beath, C. M. The information technology interaction model: A foundation for the MBA core course. *MIS Quarterly*, 19, 1995, 361-390.

[32] Wills, M.J., Sarnikar, S., El-Gayar, O., & Deokar, A.V. Clinical knowledge management systems: Literature review and research issues, *Communications of the AIS*, 26, 2010, 565-598.

[33] Wilson, E.V. & Tulu, B. The rise of a health-IT academic focus. *Communications of the ACM*, 53, 2010, 147-150.

[34] Wilson, E.V., Wang, W. & Sheetz, S. Underpinning a guide theory of patient-centered e-health. *Communications of the AIS*, 34(16), 2014, 337-350.

Authors	Year	Outlet	Topic Coverage	Time Range	Outlets Covered	Focus on IS Journals?	# of Papers Coded	Is Typology Used to Classify Papers?
IS HIT papers containing the word "Review" in the title								
Abouzahra, Guenter & Tan	2015	ICIS	Physician Use of IT	1970-2014	Not stated	Partly (9 papers in IS journals)	190	Yes, (see Table 3 - Table 6)
Ben-Zion, Pliskin & Fink	2014	ISM	EHR Adoption	2001-2013	Not stated	No (none) (searched relevant IS databases)	500 (incl. news-papers)	Yes, CSFs for IS Success (see Tables 1 – 5)
Wills, Sarnikar, El-Gayer & Deokar	2010	CAIS	Clinical Knowledge Systems	1991-2008	10 IS and non-IS	Partly (7 papers in IS journals) (see Table 4)	372	Yes, various IT artifacts (Table 6), Stages of Knowledge Management (Table 2)
Hur, Lee & Schmidt	2015	AMCIS	Health Literacy	Up to 2014	Not stated	No (none)* (searched relevant databases)	45	Yes, 5 topics (Table 1) Populations (Table 2)
Parthasarathy & Steinbach	2015	AMCIS	Quality Improvement	Up to 2014	Not stated	No (none)* (searched relevant databases)	29	Yes, 4 topics (Table 2) Data Collection Method (Table 1)
IS HIT papers containing the word "Review" in abstract								
Chiasson & Davidson	2004	I&O	All Health IT	1985-2002	17 total journals (14 IS, 3 non-IS)	Mostly (a few non-IS journals)	165	Yes: Views of the IT artifact 4 part framework of the importance of generalizable theory
Pinaire & Sarnikar	2012	ICIS	Health Quality	2000-2011	PubMed data	No (not in PubMed)	39	Yes, 4 types of HIT (Table 1) Concept Model (Table 2)
Rozenkranz, Eckhardt, Kühne & Rosenkranz	2013	B&ISE	Internet-based Health Data	1995-2010	Not stated	Not spec.	352	Health Players (Table 1) Types of IT (Table 3)
Wilson, Wang & Sheets	2014	CAIS	E-Health	2007-2011	PubMed data	No (not in PubMed)	17	Concept Model (Figure 1)

Table 1. Summary Table of HIT Review Papers

The Influence of Agile Practices on Performance in Software Engineering Teams: A Subgroup Perspective

Leonard Przybilla
Chair for Information Systems,
Technical University of Munich
Boltzmannstr. 3
85748 Garching, Germany
+49 (0)89 289-19529
leonard.przybilla@in.tum.de

Manuel Wiesche
Chair for Information Systems,
Technical University of Munich
Boltzmannstr. 3
85748 Garching, Germany
+49 (0)89 289-19539
wiesche@in.tum.de

Helmut Krcmar
Chair for Information Systems,
Technical University of Munich
Boltzmannstr. 3
85748 Garching, Germany
+49 (0)89 289-19532
krcmar@in.tum.de

ABSTRACT

This research explores the influence of the agile practices daily stand-ups and retrospectives on negative effects of subgroups, i.e. of having several smaller groups within a team, on group conflict, satisfaction, and performance. Based on extant literature in agile software development (ASD) and group research, a model of effects of ASD practices and the constructs elaboration, i.e. direct sharing, of information and team reflexivity, i.e. how much teams reflect on processes and outcomes, is developed and assessed using a survey of agile teams. Previous findings on negative effects of subgroups on conflict and satisfaction are corroborated in an agile setting. Retrospectives enhance team reflexivity and elaboration of information. As expected, elaboration of information significantly attenuates effects on conflict. Surprisingly, reflexivity is seen to further exacerbate the negative effects of perceived subgroups on conflict and satisfaction.

Keywords

agile software development; subgroups; daily stand-up; retrospective; team dynamics.

ACM Reference format:

Leonard Przybilla, Manuel Wiesche, and Helmut Krcmar 2018. The Influence of Agile Practices on Performance in Software Engineering Teams: A Subgroup Perspective. In Proceedings of ACM SIGMIS-CPR'18, BuffaloNiagara Falls, NY, USA, June 2018, 8 pages. https://doi.org/10.1145/3209626.3209703

1. INTRODUCTION[i]

The agile manifesto is arguably the very basis on which most agile software development (ASD) methods are built. It prominently calls for putting people first in development activities–as opposed to processes or documentation [3]. As an operationalization of this proposition, ASD has been described to promote diversity in work teams [29]. This is to say team members differ regarding for example gender, age, or functional background [28]. Diverse team members can contribute diverse viewpoints, which fosters creativity, problem-solving, and ultimately achieves "agile," efficient response to change [28, 32]. As an example, a team comprised of both women and men, young and old members, who are trained in different areas such as business and computer science, can draw on a rich repository of different viewpoints and experiences. Even members having suffered project failures can bring positive effects [34].

The preceding description suggests increased diversity as a sure bet to increase performance. There is, however, research describing negative consequences of diversity, which may hinder progress in ASD projects. For example, the above-mentioned diverse viewpoints can clash and thus increase team conflict [33]. In turn, conflict has been found to reduce performance of agile practices [13]. How do such negative effects come about? Members of diverse groups may bond with people they perceive as similar to them. Such behaviour can lead to the emergence of subgroups in a team that act in opposition to one another and thus lead to increased conflict [28]. Emergence of perceived subgroups is described to be dependent on contextual factors, e.g. how much a group is kept together by a shared goal [28].

With its foundation in the agile manifesto and the resulting propositions how development projects should be executed, ASD has been described several times to shape a unique working environment. ASD has been characterized by several terms: it has been said to be about change and feedback [52], to be a cooperative game [6], and to be a culture of its own [49]. Given the consistent description of far-reaching effects and benefits of ASD, it stands to reason that using ASD practices may constitute a contextual factor that moderates the negative effects of subgrouping.

We are, however, not aware of any research that has empirically tested the effects of using ASD practices on subgrouping effects, which is a critical void since effects may have far-reaching implications for team dynamics and thus project success. Drawing on subgroup theory and extant literature in ASD, we therefore pose the following research question:

What are the effects of the ASD practices daily stand-ups and retrospectives on the effects of perceived subgroups?

In order to answer this question, a model of the effects of subgroups on team outcomes and the moderating effect of daily stand-ups and retrospectives is analysed and validated using a survey among ASD teams.

2. THEORETICAL BACKGROUND

We provide a brief overview of extant works on teams in agile software development, subgrouping and its effects, as well as proposed moderators of subgrouping effects.

2.1 Teams in Agile Software Development

ASD has been described as very impactful in computer science during the past years [10] and found to significantly improve success of projects [42]. A common thread in ASD methods is harnessing heterogeneous project teams [29] and promoting people aspects, as prominently put forth in the agile manifesto [3]. For the purpose of this research, we see ASD practices, e.g. daily stand-up meetings [46], as constituents of ASD methods or frameworks, e.g. Scrum or eXtreme Programming.

While ASD has been described to be mostly based on practitioners' experiences and to be underresearched in academia [10], research has made strides to understand how exactly ASD works and its effect on final outcomes. In this quest, different levels of abstraction have been considered.

At the team level, the picture of a special type of work environment is corroborated on several dimensions. At a general level, ASD projects are characterized as complex adaptive systems, which means team dynamics cannot be explained by investigating team constituents since they are constantly changed by inputs and outputs–leading to a need for constant communication [1]. For insights into this complex adaptive system, social aspects have been studied extensively in ASD research [10] on a wide range of topics such as recruitment and training, social skills, or conflict [7, 13]. Naturally, characteristics of members are also of relevance [50]. Considering work principles in ASD teams to incorporate a culture of change and feedback [52], and to heavily emphasize direct interaction via face-to-face communication [3]. From a structural perspective, decentralized work, which is typical of ASD, has been found well-suited for coordinating expertise in design tasks, but less beneficial for completing technical tasks [26]. Adding the influence of context factors, a complex trade-off interaction with the effects of ASD has been described: Autonomy and diversity impact ASD work differently, which in turn has differential effects on project success [29].

Agile practices have been found to improve project success, e.g. through helping teams to achieve shared cognition [41]. As an example of an individual practice, pair programming has been described to have several positive effects, e.g. increased satisfaction in programmers [2]. These effects are, however, also found to be contingent on contextual factors, e.g. task complexity [15], and therefore do not come to fruition in every case. As with other methodologies and tools, use thus should be considered carefully [51].

To put it briefly, current evidence points to generally positive effects of ASD but investigations at more detailed levels expose these effects to be contingent on specific situational factors. It is thus hardly possible to anticipate the effects of ASD in a given situation.

2.2 Subgroups and their effects

Subgroups can be defined as entities comprised of members sharing a distinctive common relation based on their characteristics. These entities form part of a larger, overarching team [5]. Emergence and dynamics of subgroups can be predicted by so-called faultlines, which are based on e.g. demographic attributes [28]. Faultlines that go unnoticed have

been said to be "dormant" and can become "active," i.e. as perceivable subgroups [21]. Figure 1 provides an exemplary case, in which job title, sex, group size, and geography align to form highly distinct subgroups.

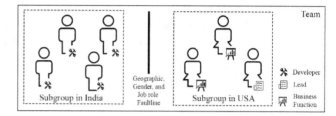

Figure 1 Exemplary illustration of subgroups based on several characteristics, adapted from [27]

According to meta-analytic review, both dormant and active faultlines have been found to negatively affect team outcomes with active faultlines showing stronger effects. Specifically, performance, satisfaction, and conflict have been studied [45]. If conflict arises, each subgroup may act as one cohesive entity in opposition to all other groups, which in turn reinforces subgrouping behavior [28]. The choice of development methodology has been found to influence the basis for subgroup formation with agile teams showing groups based on previous ties [35].

Albeit most research emphasizes the negative effects of faultlines and subgrouping, previous meta-analysis also cites instances in which faultlines are seen to be positive [45]. Since most research focuses on the negative implications of faultlines and subgroups, we constrain our investigation to negative effects.

2.3 Moderators of subgroup effects

The emergence and impact of subgroups are described to be contingent on situational factors [28]. Several known moderators have been proposed to fit conceptually with ASD practices [27]. *Elaboration of information* and *team reflexivity* will be described in the following as examples of such moderators.

Elaboration of information is described to be a key mechanism through which diversity can benefit team performance: "Elaboration is defined as the exchange of information and perspectives [... and] the process of feeding back the results of [...] individual-level processing into the group" [25]. Means of directly sharing knowledge are described to enable easy communication, which reduces task conflict and thus is proposed to deactivate faultlines [23]. Such direct communication facilitates constructive discussions, which can prevent misunderstandings and thus ensure smooth teamwork.

Team reflexivity has been found to moderate the negative effects of perceived subgroups on performance [47]. It encompasses discussions of processes, task-related issues and members' reflections on group goals and strategies [40]. The aspects of team reflexivity enable team members to render themselves a more detailed picture of their current context, to identify and mitigate information-sampling biases, and lastly to consider information beyond the perceived subgroups they may belong to [8, 47]. As another consequence, members may develop a shared understanding of the task at hand and its requirements [12], which enables members to reframe cognitive representations, and lastly helps transcending intergroup bias, and thus to mitigate conflicts [23].

3. RESEARCH MODEL

Subgroups are described to negatively affect team dynamics and outcomes. These effects are, however, dependent on context [28] and multiple moderators have been proposed in literature. Several of these seem conceptionally very close to core principles operationalized in ASD practices [27]. This leads us to propose that using for example daily stand-ups or retrospectives may attenuate the effects of subgroups. We chose these two practices since they are widely applied [48] and share common characteristics, see below. Figure 2 offers an overview of the research model. In the following, we will motivate each hypothesized interaction.

Effect of subgroups on conflict and satisfaction

Subgroups have been found to increase task and relationship conflict as well as reduce satisfaction, cohesion, and performance [21, 44]. At a more detailed level, negative categorization is summarized to lead to frustration, anxiety, and discomfort in teams [21], which in turn decrease satisfaction and increase conflicts. While these observations and propositions have been made in the domain of general group research, we expect them to hold in the context of ASD and thus posit:

H1a: Perceived subgroups negatively influence satisfaction in agile software development teams.

H1b: Perceived subgroups positively influence the prevalence of conflicts in agile software development teams.

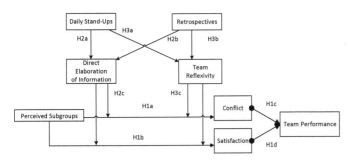

Figure 2 Overview of research model

Relation between conflict, satisfaction and performance

Moreover, the relation between conflict, satisfaction, and performance is to be validated. Previous research has described both task- and relationship-conflict to be detrimental to performance [9]. In addition, conflict has been linked to reduced cohesion, cooperation, and support [21]. While satisfaction has been found to positively correlate with performance, meta-analytic research discusses the possibility this result may be spurious [4]. Since this relation is not the focus of this research, we limit our model to the expectation of a positive relation. Combining extant research, we posit:

H1c: Satisfaction positively influences the performance of agile software development teams.

H1d: Conflict negatively influences the performance of agile software development teams.

Elaboration of information, i.e. especially face-to-face communication, has been described to be beneficial in

attenuating negative effects of subgroups and to reduce task conflict [23]. These positive effects have also been reported in the realm of software development: direct forms of communication are seen to foster knowledge on members' capabilities and a common understanding of tasks [16].

At a theoretical level, ASD supports elaboration of information by prescribing direct, face-to-face communication [3]. Moreover, ASD oftentimes is conducted in collaborative workspaces, which support communication [30]. In addition, ASD extends the requirement of frequent and informal communication to business people [20], which arguably can help in bridging professional divides.

At the operational level, practices such as daily standups provide a venue in which communication helps achieve work outcomes [24]. Arguably, this assertion extends to retrospectives, in which members are expected to communicate on past issues and experiences–thus integrating personal information with collective group memory.

Empirical results support the preceding argumentation since ASD practices have been found to improve team communication [36]. Given theoretical and empirical descriptions of how ASD fosters communication in teams and evidence of such communication being a moderator of subgroup effects, we posit:

H2a: Daily stand-ups positively influence the elaboration of information and knowledge in agile software development teams.

H2b: Retrospectives positively influence the elaboration of information and knowledge in agile software development teams.

H2c: ASD practices moderate the negative relationship between perceived subgroups and performance/satisfaction and the positive relationship between perceived subgroups and team conflict through the elaboration of information.

Team reflexivity–defined as discussing task-related issues, processes, and reflecting on group goals and strategies [40]–has been found to create a shared understanding in groups [12], which in turn is described to attenuate subgroup effects [23].

The construct of team reflexivity can be readily related to ASD: Reflexivity forms part of the core principles put forth in the agile manifesto [3] and ASD practices, e.g. stand-ups require team members to reflect on their behavior and performance [53]. Retrospectives for reflecting on how things have been done and what has happened during a project increment have been described as a critical success factor in agile work and been recommended to be done habitually [6].

Theory on shared mental models as outcomes of team reflexivity has been used to theoretically describe the effects of three agile practices [53]. Empirical evidence points to the creation of shared mental models through using ASD, which in turn improve performance [41]. Moreover, the presence of shared mental models has been related to effective work in ASD [22].

Extant evidence describes team reflexivity as a moderator of subgroup effects. ASD methods and practices put a strong focus on reflexivity and have been linked to contribute to and profit from shared mental models. Drawing on this extant research, we posit:

H3a: Daily stand-ups positively influence team reflexivity in agile software development teams.

H3b: Retrospectives positively influence team reflexivity in agile software development teams.

H3c: ASD practices moderate the negative relationship between perceived subgroups and performance/satisfaction and the positive relationship between perceived subgroups and conflict through team reflexivity.

4. METHOD

In order to test the theoretical model of the effects of ASD practices on the effects of subgroups in ASD, we have distributed an online survey to agile development teams. For the survey, we have identified tested scales from extant research and where necessary slightly adapted them to the context of this research. All items are measured on Likert scales, with items concerning ASD practices using 7-point scales, whereas all other items use 5-point scales. Table 1 provides an overview of the measures used.

Table 1 Measures used to assess constructs in online survey

Construct	Scale Source	Construct	Scale Source
Information elaboration	[18]	Perceived subgroups	[38]
Team reflexivity	[40, 43]	Performance	[17]
ASD practices	[46]	Conflict	[31]
		Satisfaction	[21]

For assessing *perceived subgroups* the 4-item scale developed by Rico et al. [38], which measures whether there are salient subgroups, task-based cohesiveness, and the existence of "us vs. them" feelings, has been employed. Three items each from the scale by Tripp et al. [46] have been used for the agile practices *daily stand-ups* and *retrospectives*. *Satisfaction* is assessed using a 3-item scale asking participants about their happiness, satisfaction, and intention to continue working in this team [21]. For conflict, the 4-item scale by Li & Hambrick [31] gauging both task and relationship conflict on two items each is used. *Performance* is assessed relatively by asking participants to gauge efficiency, quality, innovativeness, work excellence, and schedule and budget adherence, relative to the best team they have worked in [17]. For gauging *team reflexivity*, evaluation and learning dimensions of the scale by Shin [43] have been chosen, which encompass six items and are adapted from Schippers et al. [39]. *Elaboration of information* is operationalized using an instrument built on the original description that asks participants to assess the use of information in their team [18].

In addition to the constructs of main interest, single items for colocation, i.e. how spread out teammates are ranging from the same room to off-shore, and agile experience are included as control variables as well as demographic data on age and team size for characterizing the sample. Previous research on ASD effects has proposed to control for programming experience when assessing performance [2]. Given our interest in effects of ASD practices, this aspect is slightly adapted to reflect experience with ASD. Colocation is deemed relevant given previous research on the negative effects of geographical distance on teamwork in software development [11].

5. RESULTS AND DISCUSSION

We find the hypotheses regarding effects of subgroups mostly supported with subgroups reducing satisfaction and increasing conflict. Conflict and satisfaction show the anticipated effects on performance. The moderating effects of agile practices are found to be a double-edged sword: As expected, elaboration of information ameliorates the effects of subgroups on conflict and satisfaction, whereas reflexivity is found to further add to conflict and reduce satisfaction. While we can thus partly confirm findings on elaboration of information, results on team reflexivity are in opposition to extant research–implying a special relation in ASD.

Since the perception of subgroups can differ within teams, analysis is aimed at the individual level. The survey was distributed to members and project managers of a convenience sample of agile teams in several domains. Of the 102 survey participants we removed three for not filling in any items for satisfaction, which we deemed inappropriate for inclusion since it is a key latent construct. Table 2 gives an overview of demographic characteristics of the remaining participants regarding team size, age, and agile experience. Answers on these dimensions imply the sample to be quite homogeneous.

Table 2 Overview of demographic data

Age (in years)		Agile Experience (in years)		Team Size	
21 - 25	7.07%	None	3.03%	0 - 3	18.18%
26 - 30	30.30%	<1	18.18%	4 - 5	18.18%
31 - 35	28.28%	1 - 2	28.28%	6 - 8	38.38%
36 - 40	13.13%	3 - 4	28.28%	9 - 11	11.11%
41 - 45	3.03%	5 - 10	14.14%	12 - 14	5.05%
46 - 50	1.01%	>10	4.04%	15 - 17	2.02%
>50	5.05%	NA	4.04%	>17	2.02%
NA	12.12%			NA	5.05%

All constructs are interpreted to be reflective. To estimate validity, we have surveyed factor loadings and the reliability criteria of Cronbach's alpha, composite reliability, and average variance extracted. Items not attaining the threshold loading of .70 have been eliminated iteratively: two items on performance innovation and schedule, the fourth item on perceived subgroups, and three items of the reflexivity scale. For both retrospectives and daily stand-ups one item has been removed due to a high variance inflation factor. Despite eliminating several indicators, all but the agile practices constructs are operationalized using at least three indicators.

With the exception of elaboration of information and team reflexivity at .69, all latent constructs have Cronbach's alpha values in excess of .70. Following advice not to primarily consider Cronbach's alpha we surveyed composite reliability and average variance extracted [14], which have been found to be satisfactory for all constructs. Table 3 provides an overview of the reliability measures.

Considering crossloadings, the criterion that all items should load most on the expected underlying factor is satisfied. There are, however, some items with relatively high loadings on other factors, e.g. items for daily stand-ups and retrospectives have loadings of >.50 on the respective other factor. This is an expected finding and in line with our theoretical model, where we hypothesize both daily stand-ups and retrospectives to be linked to a common methodological core.

Table 3 Reliability of Constructs

Construct	R^2	Alpha	Comp. Reliability	AVE
Perceived Subgroups		.73	.84	.63
Daily Stand-ups		.81	.91	.84
Retrospectives		.80	.91	.83
Elaboration of Information	.13	.70	.83	.62
Reflexivity	.32	.70	.83	.62
Conflict	.34	.87	.91	.71
Satisfaction	.47	.88	.93	.81
Performance	.39	.76	.86	.68

PLS was chosen for analysis as it has been found to outperform traditional methods concerning violations of some assumptions [19], which given our sample size and the number of variables cannot be ruled out. Following the approach by Hair et al. [14], a maximum of 1000 iterations and Simple Bootstrapping without sign changes using the bias-corrected and accelerated method on 10,000 subsamples have been used to calculate the structural model. Figure 3 illustrates the results. Moderating effects are operationalized as interactions of perceived subgroups and the respective moderator, i.e. elaboration of information or team reflexivity. For latent constructs, R^2 values are shown, for paths the weight and in parentheses the p-value are given.

Considering the fuzziness of some constructs, the resulting R^2 values seem satisfactory. While only 13% of the variance in elaboration of information is explained by daily stand-ups and retrospectives, medium-levels of R^2 are attained for conflict, performance, and reflexivity. The R^2 of .47 for satisfaction is considered to be quite strong given it is not feasible to assume reflexivity and direct elaboration of information to be the only determinants of satisfaction.

Effects of perceived subgroups on team outcomes

Regarding the influence of perceived subgroups on team outcomes, hypotheses 1a and 1b are mostly supported. Perceived subgroups exert a highly significant negative effect on satisfaction, which mirrors previous findings. This result is promising since it implies effects found in general group settings translate to ASD teams. The relationship between perceived subgroups and conflict is positive–as expected, albeit not significant at the 5% level (p=.057). Both task and relationship

conflict are operationalized with two items each. Keeping only the items on relationship conflict results in a significant weight of .24 (p=.038), which implies the relation may be more pronounced. We therefore confirm hypothesis 1b and tentatively reject hypothesis 1a for a slight lack of significance.

In line with prior research, conflict and satisfaction both relate to performance: conflict is significantly negatively related, whereas satisfaction exhibits a highly significant positive relation. We can thus confirm hypotheses 1c and 1d. Taken together, the results of the current model support most of the propositions regarding the effects of subgroups on performance in ASD teams.

Considering its effect on satisfaction, conflict, and performance, the control variable agile experience is not significantly related to any of the outcomes with all p-values >.20. Colocation, however, exhibits a highly significant effect on performance with more distance leading to inferior performance (-.27, p=.003).

Relation between ASD practices and psychological constructs

In line with expectations, retrospectives are highly significantly related to the construct *team reflexivity* and to a lesser extent positively related to *elaboration of information*–confirming hypotheses 2b and 3b. Based on this finding, we expect ASD practices to not map directly to constructs proposed in psychology, no matter how closely related they may appear. Engaging in a retrospective seems to also contribute to elaboration of information. This is readily understandable given the definition of elaboration of information as group-based information exchange [25], which arguably is part of what happens in a retrospective.

Contrasting with retrospectives, the relationships of daily stand-ups are more surprising. While given their operational nature, daily stand-ups are expected to contribute to *elaboration of information*, this relationship is very weak and highly insignificant. Following theory stating daily stand-ups to be helpful in creating shared mental models [53], the relationship with *team reflexivity* is positive, albeit also considerably smaller than either of the effects of retrospectives. This may be due to the dataset, in which daily stand-ups were apparently widely used with median values for daily stand-ups at 6 and mean values > 5.7 on a 7-point Likert scale. In addition to use-driven explanations, it is conceivable that the focus of daily stand-ups on operational updates does not qualify them for elaboration of information. In addition, it may be the case that items on elaboration of information were attributed to a specific task without any involvement of daily stand-ups. While the expected effects of daily stand-ups on psychological constructs could not be corroborated, a general direction of effects can still be inferred. Investigating the effective mechanism through which daily stand-ups affect outcomes is thus an issue for future research.

We therefore tentatively reject hypotheses 2a and 3a for a lack of statistical power, noting that the direction of the effect is as expected. Agile practices are found to relate to several psychological constructs, which means results from general group research cannot be transferred directly.

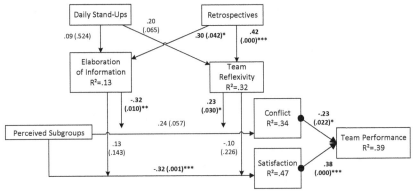

To maintain readability, the control variables Agile Experience and Colocation are not included .

Figure 3 Overview of Results

Table 4 Total effects of Daily Stand-Ups and Retrospectives

Path	Original Sample (O)	Sample Mean (M)	P Values
DSU -> Conflict	-.05	-.05	.334
DSU -> Performance	.03	.04	.366
DSU -> Satisfaction	.06	.06	.370
Retrosp. -> Conflict	-.14	-.15	.095
Retrosp. -> Performance	.09	.10	.072
Retrosp. -> Satisfaction	.16	.17	.054

Moderating effect of agile practices: conflict

Both *team reflexivity* and *elaboration of information*, as explained by using ASD practices, are expected to negatively moderate the relation between subgroups and conflict. *Elaboration of information* indeed highly significantly attenuates the relationship with conflict, which supports our proposition that the conflict-reducing effect of direct communication [23] is achieved by ASD practices. While the moderating effect of *team reflexivity* on conflict is only significant at the 5% level (p=.030), the sign of the effect is worth noting: Reflexivity seems to further add to conflict in presence of perceived subgroups, contradicting predictions based on extant research that reflexivity reduces negative effects of faultlines [47].

This result can, however, be related to extant research describing limits to the positive effects of *team reflexivity*. In the setting of software development, reflexivity has been found to benefit effectiveness but not efficiency [22], where many arguments for the positive effects of reflexivity seem conceptually closer to *elaboration of information*. Moreover, content of communication has been theorized to be decisive for the effect [40]. Following this line of thought, it may be the case that for task-focused work in ASD, the dimensions captured by *team reflexivity* pale in terms of informational value compared to e.g. *elaboration of information*. In addition, the effects of differences between members are found to be strengthened through increased interactions when teams have a large span of control [37]. We suspect the planned and intense communication in daily stand-ups and retrospectives to frequently show team members potential divides and dissent with their colleagues and thus leading to increased conflict.

Moderating effect of agile practices: satisfaction

Neither *elaboration of information* nor *team reflexivity* have been found to significantly moderate the relationship between perceived subgroups and satisfaction, leading us to reject parts of hypotheses 2c and 3c because of lack of statistical power. Analogously to the effects on conflict, *elaboration of information* is positively related as expected, whereas *team reflexivity* further exacerbates negative tendencies.

Following the conflict-enhancing effect of *team reflexivity*, this result may be explained by seeing *team reflexivity* performed in retrospectives and daily stand-ups as instances in which negative experiences may be triggered, come to mind, and thus reduce satisfaction. Positive effects of ASD practices on satisfaction by influencing *elaboration of information*, but missing the contingencies that explain when this result holds is in line with previous research. An overall positive effect of ASD practices on satisfaction has been found but some ASD practices have been

described to be excluded from this assertion [46]. By shedding light on a pathway and interaction of psychological constructs through which this effect may come about, the current research adds to this finding.

Lastly, the total effects of daily stand-ups and retrospectives are to be considered and are shown in table 4. The direction of all effects is as expected: Reducing levels of conflict and increasing performance and satisfaction. While none of the effects is significant at the 5% level, the effect sizes for retrospectives are consistently stronger than for daily stand-ups, which is in line with individual analysis.

6. CONTRIBUTION AND LIMITATIONS

The present study makes both academic and practical contributions. From an academic perspective, it provides insights into how a much researched group topic affects and is affected by ASD. It thus contributes to an increased insight into the contingencies of ASD. Especially, it adds further details to the existing knowledge on contingencies regarding diversity [29], effects of conflict in ASD [13], and the effects of practices on satisfaction [46]. For practitioners, knowledge on possible (side) effects of ASD practices helps in estimating their potential and effects to influence group dynamics.

The current research does, however, present only a first step in understanding the role of ASD practices in light of subgroups and has several limitations. First, the sample could be improved. Given the number of constructs and their complex interaction, the 99 members of ASD teams in the current study may not be sufficient for fully reliable results. In addition, as outlined previously, the sample is quite homogenous regarding demographics, which may limit generalizability. A second potential issue lies in the operationalization of constructs. While scales have been taken from validated sources, some–especially *elaboration of information* and *team reflexivity*–have not shown the anticipated statistical power. While they are close to the .70 threshold on Cronbach's alpha, results are contrasting the original ones: *Team reflexivity* has attained a value of .91 [43] and *elaboration of information* of .85 [18]. This stark deviation is peculiar. On the one hand, the result could be an artifact associated with our specific sample or, on the other hand, being part of an ASD team and its context may have affected validity of these items.

7. CONCLUSION

Working in an agile manner prominently emphasizes diversity in teams. A possible consequence of diversity is the emergence of subgroups, which can negatively affect team outcomes. We argue that daily stand-ups and retrospectives moderate these effects since they can be related to the proposed moderators elaboration of information and team reflexivity.

To test the proposed relationship, we have surveyed members of ASD teams. Results of the partial least squares model mostly confirm the expected relations between perceived subgroups and group processes. The practice of retrospectives exhibits a significant positive relation with elaboration of information and team reflexivity. Contrary to expectations, daily stand-ups have relatively weak relations to both dimensions.

Elaboration of information is found to significantly moderate the relation between perceived subgroups and conflict. Surprisingly, results imply a negative effect of reflexivity on the effects of subgroups: a significant increase in conflict and a further decrease in satisfaction are found. The results provide first insights into subgroup effects in ASD and add to previous works on contingencies of ASD work.

8. REFERENCES

[1]   Augustine, S., Payne, B., Sencindiver, F. and Woodcock, S. 2005. Agile Project Management: Steering from the Edges. *Communications of the ACM.* 48, 12 (2005), 85–89.

[2]   Balijepally, V., Mahapatra, R., Nerur, S. and Price, K.H. 2009. Are two heads better than one for software development? The productivity paradox of pair programming. *MIS Quarterly: Management Information Systems.* 33, 1 (2009), 91–118.

[3]   Beck, K. et al. 2001. Manifesto for Agile Software Development. *Business People.* (2001).

[4]   Bowling, N.A. 2007. Is the job satisfaction-job performance relationship spurious? A meta-analytic examination. *Journal of Vocational Behavior.* 71, 2 (2007), 167–185.

[5]   Carton, A.M. and Cummings, J.N. 2012. A theory of subgroups in work teams. *Academy of Management Review.* 37, 3 (2012), 441–470.

[6]   Cockburn, A. 2006. *Agile software development: the cooperative game.* Pearson Education.

[7]   Conboy, K., Coyle, S., Wang, X. and Pikkarainen, M. 2011. People over process: Key challenges in agile development. *IEEE Software.* 28, 4 (2011), 48–57.

[8]   De Dreu, C.K.W. 2007. Cooperative outcome interdependence, task reflexivity, and team effectiveness: a motivated information processing perspective. *The Journal of applied psychology.* 92, 3 (2007), 628–638.

[9]   De Dreu, C.K.W. and Weingart, L.R. 2003. Task versus relationship conflict, team performance, and team member satisfaction: A meta-analysis. *Journal of Applied Psychology.* 88, 4 (2003), 741–749.

[10]   Dyba, T. and Dingsoyr, T. 2009. What Do We Know about Agile Software Development? *IEEE Software.* 26, 5 (2009), 6–9.

[11]   Espinosa, J.A., Slaughter, S.A., Kraut, R.E. and Herbsleb, J.D. 2007. Team Knowledge and Coordination in Geographically Distributed Software Development. *Journal of Management Information Systems.* 24, 1 (2007), 135–169.

[12]   van Ginkel, W., Tindale, R.S. and van Knippenberg, D. 2009. Team reflexivity, development of shared task representations, and the use of distributed information in group decision making. *Group Dynamics: Theory, Research, and Practice.* 13, 4 (2009), 265–280.

[13]   Gren, L. 2017. The Links Between Agile Practices, Interpersonal Conflict, and Perceived Productivity. *Proceedings of the 21st International Conference on Evaluation and Assessment in Software Engineering - EASE'17.* June (2017), 292–297.

[14]   Hair Jr, J.F., Hult, G.T.M., Ringle, C. and Sarstedt, M. 2016. *A primer on partial least squares structural equation modeling (PLS-SEM).* Sage Publications.

[15]   Hannay, J.E., Dybå, T., Arisholm, E. and Sjøberg, D.I.K. 2009. The effectiveness of pair programming: A meta-analysis. *Information and Software Technology.* 51, 7 (2009), 1110–1122.

[16]   He, J., Butler, B.S. and King, W.R. 2007. Team Cognition: Development and Evolution in Software Project Teams. *Journal of Management Information Systems.* 24, 2 (2007), 261–292.

[17]   Hinds, P.J. and Mortensen, M. 2005. Understanding Conflict in Geographically Distributed Teams: The Moderating Effects of Shared Identity, Shared Context, and Spontaneous Communication. *Organization Science.* 16, 3 (2005), 290–307.

[18]   Homan, A.C., Hollenbeck, J.R. and Humphrey, S.E. 2008. Facing Differences With an Open Mind: Openness To Experience , Salience of Intragroup Differences , and Performance of Diverse Work Groups. *Academy of Management Journal.* 51, 6 (2008), 1204–1222.

[19]   Hulland, J., Ryan, M.J. and Rayner, R.K. 2010. Modeling Customer Satisfaction: A Comparative Performance Evaluation of Covariance Structure Analysis Versus Partial Least Squares BT - Handbook of Partial Least Squares: Concepts, Methods and Applications. V. Esposito Vinzi, W.W. Chin, J. Henseler, and H. Wang, eds. Springer Berlin Heidelberg. 307–325.

[20]   Hummel, M., Rosenkranz, C. and Holten, R. 2013. The role of communication in agile systems development: An analysis of the state of the art. *Business and Information Systems Engineering.* 5, 5 (2013), 343–355.

[21]   Jehn, K.A. and Bezrukova, K. 2010. The faultline activation process and the effects of activated faultlines on coalition formation, conflict, and group outcomes. *Organizational Behavior and Human Decision Processes.* 112, 1 (2010), 24–42.

[22]   Kakar, A.K. 2017. Do Reflexive Software Development Teams Perform Better? *Business & Information Systems Engineering.* (2017).

[23]   van der Kamp, M., Tjemkes, B. V and Jehn, K.A. 2015. Faultline Deactivation: Dealing with Activated Faultlines and Conflicts in Global Teams. *Leading Global Teams: Translating Multidisciplinary Science to Practice.* J.L. Wildman and R.L. Griffith, eds. Springer New York. 269–293.

[24]   Kim, Y. 2007. Analyzing scrum agile software development with development process, social factor, and project management lenses. *Association for Information Systems - 13th Americas Conference on Information Systems, AMCIS 2007: Reaching New Heights.* 3, (2007), 1937–1945.

[25]   van Knippenberg, D., De Dreu, C.K.W. and Homan, A.C. 2004. Work Group Diversity and Group Performance: An Integrative Model and Research Agenda. *Journal of Applied Psychology.* 89, 6 (Dec. 2004), 1008–1022.

[26]   Kudaravalli, S., Faraj, S. and Johnson, S.L. 2017. A Configurational Approach to Coordinating Expertise in Software Development Teams. *MIS Quarterly.* 41, 1 (Mar. 2017), 43–64.

[27]   Lassak, S., Przybilla, L., Wiesche, M. and Krcmar, H. 2017. Explaining How Agile Software Development Practices Moderate the Negative Effects of Faultlines in Teams. *ACIS 2017 - Australasian Conference on Information Systems* (Hobart, Australia, 2017).

[28]   Lau, D.C. and Murnighan, J.K. 1998. Demographic diversity and faultlines: The compositional dynamics of organizational groups. *Academy of Management Review.* 23, 2 (1998), 325–340.

[29]   Lee, G. and Xia, W. 2010. Toward Agile: an Integrated Analysis of Quantitative and Qualitative Field Data on Software Development Agility. *MIS Quarterly.* 34, 1 (2010), 87–114.

[30]   Levy, M. and Hazzan, O. 2009. Knowledge Management in Practice: The Case of Agile Software Development. *2009 Icse Workshop on Cooperative and Human Aspects of Software Engineering.* (2009), 60–65.

[31]   Li, J. and Hambrick, D.C. 2005. Factional groups: A new vantage on demographic faultlines, conflict, and disintegration in work teams. *Academy of Management Journal.* 48, 5 (2005), 794–813.

[32]   Nerur, S.. and Balijepally, V.. 2007. Theoretical reflections on agile development methodologies. *Communications of the ACM.* 50, 3 (2007), 79–83.

[33]   Pelled, L.H., Eisenhardt, K.M. and Xin, K.R. 1999. Exploring the black box: An analysis of work group diversity, conflict, and performance. *Administrative Science Quarterly.* 44, 1 (1999), 1–28.

[34]   Pflügler, C., Jäschke, T., Mälzer, T., Wiesche, M. and Krcmar, H. 2018. " Do I Want to Have Losers In My Team?" – A Quantitative Study of Learning from IT Project Failure. *Proceedings of the 51st Hawaii International Conference on System Sciences* (2018).

[35]   Pflügler, C., Wiesche, M. and Krcmar, H. 2018. Subgroups in Agile and Traditional IT Project Teams. *Proceedings of the 51st Hawaii International Conference on System Sciences* (2018).

[36]   Pikkarainen, M., Haikara, J., Salo, O., Abrahamsson, P. and Still, J. 2008. The impact of agile practices on communication in software development. *Empirical Software Engineering.* 13, 3 (2008), 303–337.

[37]   Rico, R., Molleman, E., Sanchez-Manzanares, M. and Van Der Vegt, G.S. 2007. The effects of diversity faultlines and team task autonomy on decision quality and social integration. *Journal of Management.* 33, 1 (2007), 111–132.

[38]   Rico, R., Sánchez-Manzanares, M., Antino, M. and Lau, D. 2012. Bridging Team Faultlines by Combining Task Role Assignment and Goal Structure Strategies. *Journal of Applied Psychology.* 97, 2 (2012), 407–420.

[39]   Schippers, M.C., Den Hartog, D.N. and Koopman, P.L. 2007. Reflexivity in teams: A measure and correlates. *Applied Psychology.* 56, 2 (2007), 189–211.

[40]   Schippers, M.C., Den Hartog, D.N., Koopman, P.L. and Wienk, J. a 2003. Reflexivity and diversity in teams: The moderating effects of outcome interdependence and group longevity. *Journal of Organizational Behavior.* 24, (2003), 779–802.

[41]   Schmidt, C.T., Heinzl, A., Kude, T. and Mithas, S. 2014. How Agile Practices Influence the Performance of Software Development Teams: The Role of Shared Mental Models and Backup. *ICIS 2014 Proceedings.* (2014), 1–18.

[42]   Serrador, P. and Pinto, J.K. 2015. Does Agile work? - A quantitative analysis of agile project success. *International Journal of Project Management.* 33, 5 (2015), 1040–1051.

[43]   Shin, Y. 2014. Positive Group Affect and Team Creativity: Mediation of Team Reflexivity and Promotion Focus. *Small Group Research.* 45, 3 (2014), 337–364.

[44]   Thatcher, S.M.B. and Patel, P.C. 2011. Demographic faultlines: A meta-analysis of the literature. *Journal of Applied Psychology.* 96, 6 (2011), 1119–1139.

[45]   Thatcher, S.M.B. and Patel, P.C. 2012. Group Faultlines. *Journal of Management.* 38, 4 (2012), 969–1009.

[46]   Tripp, J.F.., Riemenschneider, C.K.. and Thatcher, J.B.. 2016. Job satisfaction in agile development teams: Agile development as work redesign. *Journal of the Association of Information Systems.* 17, 4 (2016), 267–307.

[47]   Veltrop, D.B., Hermes, N., Postma, T.J.B.M. and de Haan, J. 2015. A tale of two factions: Why and when factional demographic faultlines hurt board performance. *Corporate Governance (Oxford).* 23, 2 (2015), 145–160.

[48]   Versionone 2017. *11th Annual State of Agile Report.*

[49]   Whitworth, E. 2008. Experience report: The social nature of agile teams. *Proceedings - Agile 2008 Conference.* (2008), 429–435.

[50]   Wiesche, M. and Krcmar, H. 2014. The relationship of personality models and development tasks in software engineering. *Proceedings of the 52nd ACM conference on Computers and people research - SIGSIM-CPR '14.* May (2014), 149–161.

[51]   Wiesche, M., Schermann, M. and Krcmar, H. 2013. When IT Risk Management Produces More Harm than Good: The Phenomenon of 'Mock Bureaucracy'. *System Sciences (HICSS), 2013 46th Hawaii International Conference on* (2013), 4502–4511.

[52]   Williams, L. and Cockburn, A. 2003. Agile Software Development: It's about Feedback and Change. *Computer.* (2003).

[53]   Yu, X. and Petter, S. 2014. Understanding agile software development practices using shared mental models theory. *Information and Software Technology.* 56, 8 (2014), 911–921.

[i] Acknowledgement: This research and development project was funded by the German Federal Ministry of Education and Research (BMBF) within the Program Innovations for Tomorrows Production, Services, and Work (02K14A080) and managed by the Project Management Agency Karlsruhe (PTKA). The authors are responsible for the contents of this publication. We would like to thank the two anonymous reviewers for their detailed and very helpful comments.

Determinants of Open Source Software Project Performance: A Stage-wise Analysis of GitHub Projects

Senthilkumar Thangavelu
Amrita School of Business
Amrita Vishwa Vidyapeetham
Bangalore, India
senmalkisasb@gmail.com

Amalendu Jyotishi
Amrita School of Business
Amrita Vishwa Vidyapeetham
Bangalore, India
amalendu.jyotishi@gmail.com

1. INTRODUCTION

The phenomenon of open-source software (OSS) has gained importance among the information technology (IT) firms in the recent years due to its advantages over proprietary or closed source software (CSS). The advantages include low cost of development, availability of reusable architectural and functional components, free and unrestricted access to the source codes, and high level of innovation [2]. Firms have started recognizing the importance and value of OSS over CSS. Successful OSS projects such as Linux, Apache, Gnome, R, STATA, Perl, Python, and MySQL have created a significant impact [3] on the paradigm of software development. In recent times, firms and government institutions are giving much importance to OSS adoption [7] and it is an integral part of their strategy. The choice between growth and control plays a very important role in developing OSS adoption strategy. This choice can shift from one to another over the lifecycle of the business, [1] keeping the value it brings to the firm. Firms explore how to appropriate returns from innovations happening outside their boundaries [4] by getting involved in OSS development and balancing intellectual property rights (IPR). The innovation strategies of the firms are also changing from a closed structure within the firm to outside their boundaries [6]. The [10] R&D expenses and IPR impact the performance of IT firms. In CSS the level of advancement of that particular project is limited, but in OSS the projects are available to everyone and hosting services like GitHub, OpenSource, and SourceForge [8] enable them to modify the projects better. The delivery of the software services over the internet, the cloud computing, the reduced hardware cost, the

ACM Reference format:
Senthilkumar Thangavelu, and Amalendu Jyotishi. 2018. Determinants of Open Source Software Project Performance: A Stage-wise Analysis of GitHub Projects. In Proceedings of ACM SIGMIS-CPR, June 18–20, 2018, Buffalo-Niagara Falls, NY, USA, 4 pages. https://doi.org/10.1145/3209626.3209723

improved speed of the digital services, play major roles in making OSS a popular choice. They are able to bring a new outlook and innovation to the existing mechanism which seems to be superior to the CSS. GitHub is one of the most popular OSS hosting services firms that hosts and supports a large number of OSS projects. The contributors of OSS projects develop programs with a freedom to introduce new features and advancement in the functionalities and create a social identification and reputation. The key objective of this study is to address the research question:

What are the characteristics of firm, team and project that influence the performance of an OSS project at various development stages?

2. THEORETICAL FOUNDATIONS

The authors invoke the Self-Determination Theory (SDT) [9], the theory of collaboration through open superposition [5] and the Affective Events Theory (AET) [11] to understand the development of OSS project. The SDT explains the behavior of human beings, self-motivation, self-regulation, and well-being. When the three innate psychological needs of human beings namely competence, autonomy, and relatedness are satisfied, it enhances the self-motivation and well-being. This applies in the OSS project development phenomenon, where the contributors expect the autonomy in their actions, involved in activities related to their knowledge, and a competitive environment to develop their expertise. The complex functionalities of OSS projects are developed by dividing them into smaller units which are developed by individuals or teams. This theory helps to explain the OSS development by the communities. According to the AET, the emotions and moods of contributors are important aspects of work experience which influence the participation and performance in OSS projects [11].

3. THE CONCEPTUAL MODEL

Figure 3.1 provides the conceptual model of this research study showing different stages of performance indicators being influenced by not only a number of independent variables discussed above but also by the previous stage performance.

Figure 3.1: The Conceptual Model

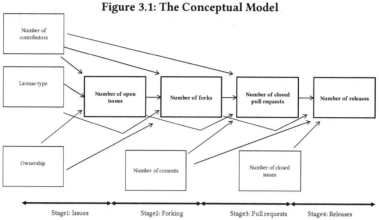

4. RESULTS AND DISCUSSION

This study uses the OLS regression for the estimation. In this study, we theorize and empirically examine the influence of various factors on the success of OSS project at different levels using staged approach.

In Stage1, the regression coefficient of the number of contributors, the license type, and the ownership shows that they positively and significantly influence the number of open issues. Thus H1a, H1b, H1c are supported.

In Stage2, the open issues count and the number of contributors positively and significantly influence the number of forks. The license type and the ownership do not show any significant influence and hence do not support H2c and H2d. This shows an interesting finding that license type and ownership show significant influence in Stage1 but not in Stage2.

In Stage3, the square of open issues count and the number of commits show positive influence on the number of pull requests and support H3b and H3c. The square of the number of forks shows positive influence and hence supports H3a. The number of contributors are not showing any significant influence and hence not supporting H3d.

In Stage4, the number of closed pull requests and the square of the number of closed issues shows positive and significant influence on the number of releases and support H4a, H4b. These results show that the output of one stage has a positive and significant influence as input to the next stage. We will present the full results and findings at the SIGMIS CPR 2018 conference.

5. CONTRIBUTIONS AND IMPLICATION

This paper has presented a conceptual model of the factors of projects, users, contributors, and property rights that influence the OSS project performance. This study is unique in this perspective and contributes to the academic research by shedding light on the internal dynamics and development of OSS projects, hence structural aspects of OSS project performance. The findings of this study significantly contribute to the software development methodology and the study on internal dynamics of the development lifecycle. The findings also contribute to change in the way the IT firms develop OSS

projects and contribute to the OSS communities. The study also helps to design suitable governance mechanisms in order to get the maximum benefits from the OSS projects and OSS communities.

REFERENCES

[1]   Appleyard, M.M. and Chesbrough, H.W. 2017. The Dynamics of Open Strategy: From Adoption to Reversion. *Long Range Planning*. 50, 3 (2017), 310–321.

[2]   Bonaccorsi, A. and Rossi, C. 2003. Why open source software can succeed. *Research Policy*. 32, 7 (2003), 1243–1258.

[3]   Crowston, K. et al. 2003. Defining Open Source Software project success. *International Conference on Information Systems (ICIS)* (2003).

[4]   Dahlander, L. 2005. Appropriation and appropriability in open source software. *International Journal of Innovation Management*. 9, 3 (2005), 259–285.

[5]   Howison, J. and Crowston, K. 2014. COLLABORATION THROUGH OPEN SUPERPOSITION: A THEORY OF THE OPEN SOURCE WAY. *MIS Quarterly*. 38, 1 (2014), 29–50.

[6]   Kumar, K.G.S. and Jyotishi, A. 2014. Differences in approach to and output of innovation. *Proceedings of the 52nd ACM conference on Computers and people research - SIGSIM-CPR '14*. (2014), 59–68.

[7]   van Loon, A. and Toshkov, D. 2015. Adopting open source software in public administration: The importance of boundary spanners and political commitment. *Government Information Quarterly*. 32, 2 (2015), 207–215.

[8]   Medappa, P.K. and Srivastava, S.C. 2017. License Choice and the Changing Structures of Work in Organization Owned Open Source Projects. *ACM SIGMIS-CPR 2017* (2017), 118–123.

[9]   Ryan, R.M. and Deci, E.L. 2000. Self-Determination Theory and the Facilitation of Intrinsic Motivation, Social Development, and Well-Being. *American Psychologist*. 55, 1 (2000), 68–78.

[10]   Thangavelu, S. and Jyotishi, A. 2017. Influence of R & D and IPR Regulations on the Performance of IT Firms in India: An Empirical Analysis using Tobin ' s Q Approach. *ACM SIGMIS-CPR 2017* (2017), 161–168.

[11]   Weiss, H.M. and Cropanzano, R. 1996. *Affective Events Theory: A theoretical discussion of the structure, causes and consequences of affective experiences at work*.

If You Can't Say Something Nice: Factors Contributing to Team Member Silence in Distributed Software Project Teams*

Stacie Petter
Baylor University
Waco, TX 76798 USA
stacie_petter@baylor.edu

ABSTRACT

Managing software projects is complex. Increasingly, organizations are using different methods and forms of teams to ensure software projects are developed on time, on budget, and meet functionality requirements. One factor that can affect the success of a software development team is the willingness of team members to be fully engaged and to share concerns throughout the effort. Employee silence is the unwillingness of an individual to express concerns. This exploratory research study examines three factors that influence a team member's choice to remain silent when participating in a distributed software project: the individual's level of experience, the role of the offending team member, and the individual's personal responsibility to report. Using a scenario-based experiment, this study finds that some of the factors that are assumed in other contexts of employee silence may not be related in the context of distributed teams in which there is a need to voice concerns among peers.

CCS CONCEPTS

• **Social and professional topics** → **Project and people management**   • Social and professional topics → Systems development

KEYWORDS

team member silence; employee silence; mum effect; whistleblowing; IS project teams; team dynamics

ACM Reference format:

S. Petter, 2018. If You Can't Say Something Nice: Factors Contributing to Team Member Silence in Distributed Software Project Teams. In Proceedings of ACM SIGMIS-CPR '18, June 18–20, 2018, Buffalo-Niagara Falls, NY, USA. 8, 7 pages. https://doi.org/10.1145/3209626.3209718

1 INTRODUCTION

Managing software development projects is challenging; the statistics regarding failed and challenge projects are widely cited

among research and practice. Typically, the success of IS projects is determined based on the management of time, schedule, and functionality needs; yet, these constraints are constantly changing throughout the project as requirements shift, schedules are shortened, or budgetary constraints emerge. As these changes in constraints occur, the team must respond effectively. Yet, individuals within the team may choose to remain silent about the nature or impact of changes occurring in the project, which creates a situation in which the project's true status is unknown [1-3]. When the software project's status is unknown, this can lead to a runaway project that is over budget, over schedule, and/or fails to meet user requirements [4].

When individuals choose not to express concerns or share important information that can impact the status of the project, this is referred to as employee silence or the mum effect [5, 6]. Employee silence in information systems (IS) projects is a dangerous phenomenon that can negatively impact project outcomes, team members, and the organization [7]. Silence in IS projects occurs in a variety of ways, including withholding information, reframing information in a more positive light, or delaying the reporting of information [8].

Existing literature has investigated reasons why individuals choose to remain silent (i.e., mum effect) or to speak up (i.e., whistleblowing) in software project teams. Some studies have considered employee silence in vendor/client relationships [e.g., 8, 9], but most have focused on internal reporting of information to project managers or other leaders in the organization [e.g., 10, 11]. Research on employee silence in the IS project literature also tends to focus on when individuals fail to voice concerns to someone in a position of authority, such as a project sponsor or senior management [e.g., 1, 3]. Other limited research has examined if individuals selectively bias information (positively or negatively) when reporting the status of projects [1, 8]. Finally, the majority of studies that examine employee silence, mum effect, whistleblowing, or status reporting tend to assume that interactions are face-to-face [e.g., 11, 12].

While prior research has provided interesting insights on employee silence in IS projects, the increasing adoption of agile software development methods and use of distributed teams are changing the nature of project teams. Agile software development assumes that client needs are changing and emphasizes rapid responses to new requirements or shifting timelines [13]. As such, this approach emphasizes high levels of interaction among team members and clients. Consequently, status reporting is not purely hierarchical, but also occurs laterally within the team through daily team meetings [14]. Increasing use of distributed teams, in which team members interact virtually, change the nature of IS projects since communication is mediated via technology [15]. Although many IS projects are evolving in one or more of these ways, current research on employee silence has not considered how the changing nature of project teams impacts team members' decisions to remain silent.

What is unknown in our current research is what factors affect silence among peers in a distributed project team. Further, when team members focus on their self-interest rather than the needs of the team, how does this impact the team member's decision to remain silent? Therefore, the objective of this research is to examine the factors that encourage a project team member to remain silent when another team member engages in self-interested behavior that could negatively impact the team. To investigate employee silence, this study reports the results from a scenario-based experiment based on responses from 231 information systems professional to examine a research model that identifies potential predictors of team member silence.

The rest of the paper is organized as follows. To provide a theoretical foundation, the current understanding of employee silence is explained. Next is the research model along with a description of the research study and results. The paper concludes by explaining how the findings extend our current understanding of employee silence.

2 THEORETICAL BACKGROUND

In the organizational behavior literature, employee silence is defined as "the withholding of any form of genuine expression about the individual's behavior, cognitive, and/or affective evaluations of his or her organizational circumstance to persons who are perceived to be capable of effecting change or redress" [16, p. 334]. Most studies in organizational behavior and in information systems that examine employee silence focus on the failure to share negative information to someone in a position of power [17-19]. Employee silence has been investigated at the organizational level [17, 20, 21] and, more recently, at the workgroup level [e.g., 22, 23, 24]. While studies often focus on how the phenomenon impacts the organization, employee silence could also refer to withholding information from other parties, such as subordinates, those external to the organization, or peers [18]. Studies have found many reasons why individuals choose to remain silent, including being fearful of the consequences of voicing concerns [20], centrality within one's workgroup [24], and an individual's perceptions of others' receptiveness to information [25].

A related area of literature to employee silence is the "mum effect", which refers to an individual's reluctance to convey negative information [6]. This stream of research assumes individuals often choose to withhold negative information because of a desire to protect themselves from risk or disengagement due to a lack of personal responsibility [11]. In the IS field, the mum effect has been investigated as one factor influencing IT project escalation. Here, studies have focused on why individuals fail to report bad news to managers (i.e., project manager or supervisor) or senior managers within the organization. IS researchers have examined characteristics of the individual, the information, and the organization as determinants of individuals' decisions to remain "mum." Prior research finds that fault responsibility [5], risk propensity [11], concern for one's self and the organization [26], and national culture identity [27] are characteristics of the individual that are influential in this regard. The urgency of information [5], one's ability to hide negative information [10, 27], and the ability to shift blame to a third party [26] have been identified as characteristics of information that influence the mum effect.

Another related area of literature related to employee silence is whistleblowing. Whistleblowing occurs when an individual reports wrongdoing, which includes "illegal, immoral or illegitimate practices" [28]. In the IS domain, much of the research on whistleblowing, *per se*, is not focused on illegal practices, but rather reporting missed deadlines, defects, or failing projects to managers or senior managers. The reason these individuals choose to speak up is due to perceived responsibility they have toward a project, their role, or the organization. Individuals that see themselves as similar to others in the organization [5] and see a benefit that outweighs the cost of reporting negative information about a project [29] are more likely to share information. In a study of IS auditors, Keil and Robey [4] found that auditors are more willing to report failing projects to management when there are larger audit staffs, management is receptive to auditor reports, and formal reporting mechanisms exist. Conversely, organizations that have poor policies for reporting and/or have management that appear unwilling to respond to negative information are less likely to have employees blow the whistle on troubled projects [5, 29].

Yet, there are several aspects of employee silence (and its related research streams) that are unexplored. In terms of content, while employee silence is defined as any information that is withheld, delayed, or reframed; yet, typically research focuses on negative content or bad news rather than other forms of information that could impact the team. Further, IS has focused on silence in the context of sharing information to someone else that is in a position of authority or power, such as a manager, auditor, or client. However, there is no examination of factors that affect silence among peers within the IS discipline. Finally, the IS field has focused on self-protection as the reason for remaining silent; however, there are other reasons for remaining silent, such as a desire to be cooperative (i.e., protect the interests of the organization or team) or disengagement (i.e., lack of interest).

The limitations of the current study of employee silence in IS projects fails to consider how software development projects have evolved. As many IS project teams move toward more collective goals through the use of agile methodologies, there is an assumption that the team will work together to reach their collective goal. Yet, teams are comprised of individual team members with their own interests and aspirations. It is unknown if the contributing factors that promote employee silence are also applicable in a team context. Furthermore, as teams become increasingly distributed in which team members are communicating through online digital collaboration tools, a team member's ability to voice their concerns become more limited. While a person may be verbally silent about their concern, sometimes non-verbal cues can signal discontent [30]. These non-verbal cues are not present in an online context, making the effort to voice opinions to the team more deliberate [31]. Our existing theory regarding employee silence, mum effect, and whistle-blowing have not considered these contexts that are becoming increasingly common in IS projects.

3　RESEARCH MODEL

Research examining employee silence has found that team members with less experience (in terms of organizational tenure and in the domain) are more likely to remain silent than those with more experience because they are more concerned about negative consequences that may arise if they voice their opinion [20, 21]. Less experienced team members may choose not to reveal their vulnerabilities to project a sense of knowledge, skill, or ability to others in the team; however, this may be in conflict with the team member's desire to help the team reach their goals. Furthermore, team members with less experience within the team may perceive that they have less responsibility to report information to fellow team members. Those that are novices might perceive that they do not have an obligation to report information, particularly if other more experienced team members are present within the group.

H1: The higher the level of experience of an individual, the less likely the individual will engage in team member silence behaviors about an offending team member's actions.

H2: The level of experience of an individual within a team will be positively related to his/her personal responsibility to report.

One's position within the team can alter the team dynamics [32]. Within a team, some members of the team may be viewed as more important due to their knowledge or role within the team. Although a more prominent team member does not have legitimate power within the team, this team member may be perceived to have referential power within the group [33]. If this prominent team member acts in a self-interested manner that may harm the team, there may be more pressure for others in the team to remain silent about the actions [20], even though a more prominent person may have the ability to instill more damaging effects upon the team. Other team members may fear offending the prominent member or may perceive that they are alone in their struggle with the problem. If there is a perception that others in the group may not hold the same opinion, a reinforcing spiral of silence develops among the group creating additional pressures to remain silent even as the problem escalates [17]. Furthermore, for teams engaging in a distributed context, team members are communicating via digital collaboration tools and non-verbal cues are not present. Therefore, it is unknown if others may be

experiencing the same problems, further reinforcing team member silence.

H3: When the offending team member has a more prominent role within the team, an individual will be more likely to engage in team member silence behaviors.

H4: When the offending team member has a more prominent role within the team, an individual will perceive a higher sense of personal responsibility to report.

Prior research has identified a relationship between one's personal responsibility to report information and one's willingness to express concerns or remain silent [11, 34, 35]. The relationship between personal responsibility and the need to voice concerns has been studied in the context of whistleblowing, in which there was an ethical dilemma or concern. Even in a non-ethical context, this study expects that this relationship a strong responsibility to report and team member voice (and vice versa) will still be applicable.

H5: A team member with a stronger sense of a personal responsibility to report will be less likely to engage in team member silence behaviors.

Figure 1 identifies the research model posited in this study that identifies factors that contribute to silence among team members in a distributed software project teams.

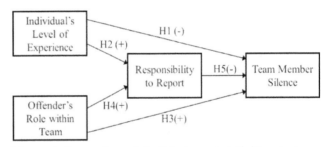

Figure 1: Research model of factors contributing to team member silence.

4　RESEARCH STUDY

4.1　Experimental Task

To examine the research model, a scenario-based experiment consistent with research in information systems examining the mum effect was used [e.g., 11]. Subjects read a scenario that explained that they were a member of a global distributed software development team. In the scenario, a fellow team member was encouraging the team to finish the project quickly for the team member's personal gain. The scenario told the participants about potential problems associated with complying with the offending team member's request. Then, participants then answered a series of questions about the actions that they may take to address this issue (i.e., team member silence), their personal obligation to report information (i.e., responsibility to report), and questions related to their perceived level of experience within the team (i.e., individual experience) and the role of the offending team member (i.e., offender's role).

The experiment used a 2 x 2 factorial design to manipulate the level of experience of the individual and the role of the offending team member. Participants were randomly assigned to the four conditions. The level of the individual's experience had a high and low condition in which the participants were instructed in the scenario that they were either a novice in the organization, team, and role (i.e., low experience) or the individual had extensive experience in the organization, team, and role (i.e., high experience). To manipulate the role of the offending team member, participants were told that the offending team member had extensive experience and knowledge that made him difficult to replace on the project (i.e., highly prominent role); another scenario noted that this team member would be relatively easy to replace within the team (i.e., less prominent role).

As a manipulation check, each subject evaluated the difficulty of replacing the offending team member within the project and the level of experience of the subject within the scenario. The items used to measure perceived experience and the offender's role were created by the authors based on techniques used in other studies [11]. The measures for responsibility to report and team member silence were adapted from items used in prior research [11, 30]. To measure team member silence, items that represent two specific forms of silence behaviors were used: waiting for someone else to handle a problem or hoping the problem will go away [30]. The measures and scenario were pilot tested to ensure that the manipulations were significantly strong and the items were robust prior to conducting the research study.

4.2 Research Participants

Often the subjects of scenario-based experiments include students [e.g., 11]. Yet for this study, subjects were obtained via a market research firm to access participants that have experience in the information technology profession. Participants were screened to ensure that they had at least one year of work experience in the information technology field. Further, screening questions and manipulation checks administered during the survey ensured that subjects read the scenario and questions.

Subjects were assigned to one of the four treatment conditions within the experiment. Of the 250 subjects that participated in the experiment, 231 subjects successfully completed the experiment and questionnaire by passing the screening questions and manipulation checks. The average age of participants was 37.6 years (standard deviation = 11.0) with 15.6 years of work experience (standard deviation 10.5). 26.8% of the sample was female, consistent with the percentage of women in the IT workforce. Each of these demographic variables were also examined as potential control variables within the research model.

4.3 Measurement Model Assessment

Each of the participants answered questions related to their perceived experience within the team as well as the offender's role within the team. This allowed for a manipulation check to ensure that the respondents had carefully read the scenario. Table 1 demonstrates that the means for the manipulated variables are consistent with the treatment.

Table 1: Effects of experimental manipulations

| | | Offender Role within Team (ROLE) | |
		Less Prominent	More Prominent
Individual Experience with Team (EXP)	Novice	N = 51 Mean (Std Dev) EXP = 2.46 (1.50) ROLE = 2.81 (1.11)	N = 56 Mean (Std Dev) EXP = 2.18 (1.32) ROLE = 4.96 (1.14)
	Experienced	N = 58 Mean (Std Dev) EXP = 5.60 (1.56) ROLE = 2.70 (1.04)	N = 66 Mean (Std Dev) EXP = 5.67 (1.62) ROLE = 5.31 (1.25)

To further examine the experimental manipulations, a 2x2 multiple analysis of variance test (MANOVA) was performed. Each participant was identified as being in the low or high experience condition and a low or high role condition. The independent variable was the manipulation and the subjective scores that participants provided related to the participant's experience level with the team or the offender's role within the team were the dependent variables. As expected, there was a significant main effect for each of the manipulations on their own dependent variable with no interaction effects (see Table 2).

Table 2: Results of MANOVA

| | Dependent Variable: EXP | | Dependent Variable: ROLE | |
	Sum of Squares	F-Value (sig)	Sum of Squares	F-Value (sig)
Main Effect: EXP	522.189	261.305 (0.000)	0.777	0.591 (0.443)
Main Effect: ROLE	0.913	0.457 (0.500)	324.240	246.701 (0.000)
Interaction Effect: EXP*ROLE	0.596	0.298 (0.585)	3.091	2.352 (0.127)

To examine the measurement model, construct validity was established by examining the item-to-construct loadings, the average variance extracted (AVE), and the relationship between the AVE and the squared correlations of the latent constructs. One item from each of the constructs created to measure the individual's level of experience and the offender's role had low item-to-construct values. Therefore, these two constructs had two items each remaining after the poor performing items were dropped. Table 3 identifies the correlations among the constructs with the AVEs are provided on the diagonal.

Table 3: Correlation matrix with AVEs on diagonals.

	1.	2.	3.	4.
1. Individual Experience	**0.896**			
2. Offender's Role	-0.028	**0.774**		
3. Responsibility to Report	-0.042	0.160	**0.654**	
4. Team Member Silence	0.194	-0.555	-0.255	**0.764**

4.4 Results

The research model was analyzed using SmartPLS 3.0 [36]. Figure 2 presents the results of the structural model analysis.

Figure 2: Results of research study.

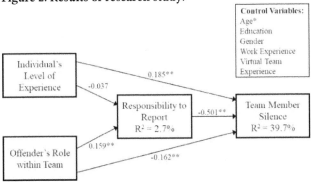

Hypothesis 1 was not supported in that as team members have more experience, individuals were found to be more likely to engage in team member silence behaviors. This relationship is significant and in the opposite direction compared to the hypothesized relationship. Hypothesis 2 was not supported in that there was no relationship between one's level of experience and one's sense of responsibility to act upon the information from the offending team member.

Hypothesis 3 was not supported. This study proposed that if an offending team member had a more prominent role within the team, an individual would be more likely to engage in team member silence behaviors; however, the opposite relationship was found to be true. Hypothesis 4 was supported in that as an offending team member's role is more prominent, there is a stronger responsibility to report.

Hypothesis 5 was supported in that there was a strong, significant inverse relationship in the relationship between one's sense of personal responsibility to report and one's likelihood to engage in team member silence behaviors.

Among the control variables, only Age was significantly related to team member silence behaviors. Those that are older were more likely to engage in team member silence behaviors.

5 DISCUSSION AND CONCLUSIONS

As explained earlier, employee silence occurs as individuals withhold one's opinions or concerns to others that can effect change [16, p. 334]. In this research study, I examined factors that contribute towards employee silence behaviors when there are messages communicated within a team that may negatively impact the team. In this scenario, it is the team members themselves that have the opportunity to effect change through action. Those that choose to hope that things will resolve on its own or that others will address a problem are engaging in silence behaviors. Many organizations are relying on agile software development methods to improve their ability to results more quickly and to adapt to changing needs in a dynamic environment. This places a greater need for intra-project team interaction. Agile practices, such as the daily stand-up used in Scrum or some other practice in XP or other methods, require team members to communicate their accomplishments and challenges. Furthermore, many organizations are leveraging distributed teams for software development, which exacerbates the issues associated with team member silence as distributed teams must rely on technology to communicate which can introduce problems with communication and trust [37].

This study examines the boundaries of research on employee silence to see how well the existing theories and principles apply in the context of silence among team members as well as when team members are in a distributed context. Given that several hypotheses, identified based on existing theory, were not supported in this context, there is a need for additional research to examine the phenomena of employee silence among team members as well as employee silence in a distributed context.

The dynamics within a software development team bring about a host of challenges as individuals with varying backgrounds, skill sets, and roles must come together to achieve a common set of goals [38]. The adoption of agile methods in project teams in which there is a need for high levels of team member collaboration and cooperation has also increased the need for team members to hold fellow team members accountable as the team seeks to accomplish its goals. This changing nature of dynamics within project teams that focus more on lateral, as opposed to hierarchical relationships, could affect the team dynamic and may alter our current understanding of employee silence. A team member that places his/her own needs above the needs of the team may prevent the team from accomplishing their goals. If the team is negatively affected by a self-interested team member, the fellow team members may need to alert the team member about the problem to ensure the team is able to accomplish their goals. However, team members may not feel comfortable discussing the issue with the self-interested team member. It was expected that as one had more experience with the team, that s/he would be less likely to engage in team member silence behaviors, but our results suggest did not support this finding. More research is needed to understand the reason for this unexpected result. There might have been issues with the scenario or it might be that there are different factors that affect silence among team members as opposed to silence to someone in authority.

This study also posited that if a team member was prominent in the team, individuals would be more likely to engage in team member silence behaviors out of fear of disrupting someone that was deemed to be an important team member. This is based on prior literature that has examined the role of status effects in influence employee silence. In this peer-oriented context, the opposite was true. It might be that team members expect that those in more prominent positions should be more focused on the goals of the team and are willing to hold those members accountable for their actions. Additional research should examine if our result was an anomaly of this particular study or if the status effects are interpreted differently among peers.

Further, the increasing use of non-traditional teams for projects have increased in frequency as more firms utilize digital technologies for collaboration as team members span geographical and organizational boundaries [39]. This, factor, too could be a reason for the surprising results obtained in this study. It might be that individuals that are engaging with one another in distributed format may make very different decisions or have different factors that affect the choice of engaging in employee silence.   Additional research should explore the role of communications, cohesion, and the degree of distributedness within the team as factors that positively or negatively affect a team member's choice to remain silent.

In contrast to employee silence is the concept of employee voice. Employee voice occurs when there is an intentional choice by an individual to express their concerns to someone in the organization that can enact change [30]. In the IS literature, employee voice has been examined in the context of whistleblowing which is when an employee voices concerns regarding an unethical decision or process within the project [11, 35]. Yet, employee voice has received less attention in the information systems literature in situations in which a concern or need should be expressed that is not necessarily ethical in nature. Future research could examine the factors that contribute to voice in both team and distributed settings.

This research introduces the need to study team member silence within the domain of information systems. To date, the research on employee silence in software projects focuses on hierarchical relationships; however, there is a need to consider reasons why individuals choose to remain silent or enact voice among peers, particularly as the focus on agile software development methods promote strong team interaction. Next, this study identifies that some of the factors that affect silence in hierarchical relationships may not be applicable when considering silence among team members, particularly as team members are distributed. The results from this study could inspire other studies to study the phenomena in other settings using other research methods, such as academic or organizational, to identify the boundaries of research on employee silence in the context of distributed teams. As we learn more about when team members remain silent as opposed to voicing concerns, we can be more proactive in managing team dynamics in distributed software development project teams.

REFERENCES

[1] Iacovou, C. L., Thompson, R. L. and Smith, H. J. Selective Status Reporting in Information Systems Projects: A Dyadic-Level Investigation. *MIS Quarterly*, 33, 4 (2009), 785-A785.

[2] Snow, A. P. and Keil, M. The Challenge of Accurate Software Project Status Reporting: A Two-Stage Model Incorporating Status Errors and Reporting. *IEEE Transactions on Engineering Management*, 49, 4 (2002), 491-504.

[3] Snow, A. P., Keil, M. and Wallace, L. The Effects of Optimistic and Pessimistic Biasing on Software Project Status Reporting. *Information & Management*, 44, 2 (2007), 130-141.

[4] Keil, M. and Robey, D. Blowing the Whistle on Troubled Software Projects. *Communications of the ACM*, 44, 4 (April 2001), 87-93.

[5] Park, C., Im, G. and Keil, M. Overcoming the Mum Effect in IT Project Reporting: Impacts of Fault Responsibility and Time Urgency. *Journal of the Association for Information Systems*, 9, 7 (2008), 409-431.

[6] Rosen, S. and Tesser, A. On Reluctance to Communicate Undesirable Information: The MUM Effect. *Sociometry*, 33, 3 (1970), 253-263.

[7] Thompson, R. L., Smith, H. J. and Iacovou, C. L. The Linkage between Reporting Quality and Performance in IS Projects. *Information & Management*, 44, 2 (2007), 196-205.

[8] Jain, R. P., Simon, J. C. and Poston, R. S. Mitigating Vendor Silence in Offshore Outsourcing: An Empirical Investigation. *Journal of Management Information Systems*, 27, 4 (2011), 261-297.

[9] Ramingwong, S. and Sajeev, A. Offshore Outsourcing: The Risk of Keeping Mu. *Communications of the ACM*, 50, 8 (2007), 101-103.

[10] Keil, M., Smith, H. J., Pawlowski, S. and Jin, L. "Why Didn't Somebody Tell Me?" Climate, Information Assymetry, and Bad News about Troubled Projects. *The DATA BASE for Advances in Information Systems*, 35, 2 (2004), 65-84.

[11] Smith, H. J., Keil, M. and Depledge, G. Keeping Mum as the Project Goes Under: Toward an Explanatory Model. *Journal of Management Information Systems*, 18, 2 (2001), 189-227.

[12] Smith, H. J. and Keil, M. The Reluctance to Report Bad News on Troubled Software Projects: A Theoretic Model. *Information Systems Journal*, 13 (2003), 69-95.

[13] Ramesh, B., Cao, L. and Baskerville, R. Agile Requirements Engineering Practices and Challenges: An Empirical Study. *Information Systems Journal*, 20, 5 (2010), 449-480.

[14] Schwaber, K. and Sutherland, J. V. *Software in 30 Days: How Agile Managers Beat the Odds, Delight Their Customers, and Leave Competitors in the Dust*. Wiley, Hoboken, NJ, 2012.

[15] Persson, J. S., Mathiassen, L. and Aaen, I. Agile Distributed Software Development: Enacting Control through Media and Context. *Information Systems Journal*, 22, 6 (2012), 411-433.

[16] Pinder, C. C. and Harlos, K. P. *Employee Silence: Quiescence and Acquiescence as Response to Perceived Injustice*. JAI Press, City, 2001.

[17] Bowen, F. and Blackmon, K. Spirals of Silence: The Dynamic Effects of Diversity on Organizational Voice. *Journal of Management Studies*, 40, 6 (September 2003), 1393-1417.

[18] Brinsfield, C. T., Edwards, M. S. and Greenberg, J. *Voice and Silence in Organizations: Historical Review and Current Conceptualizations*. Emerald Group Publishing Limited, City, 2009.

[19] Detert, J. R., Burris, E. R. and Harrison, D. A. Debunking Four Myths about Employee Silence. *Harvard Business Review*, 88, 6 (June 2010), 26.

[20] Milliken, F. J., Morrison, E. W. and Hewlin, P. F. An Exploratory Study of Employee Silence: Issues that Employees Don't Communicate Upward and Why. *Journal of Management Studies*, 40, 6 (September 2003), 1453-1476.

[21] Morrison, E. W. and Milliken, F. J. Organizational Silence: A Barrier to Change and Development in a Pluralistic World. *Academy of Management Review*, 25, 4 (2000), 706-725.

[22] Tangirala, S. and Ramanujam, R. Employee Silence on Critical Work Issues: The Cross Level Effects of Procedural Justice Climate. *Personnel Psychology*, 61 (2008), 37-68.

[23] Tangirala, S. and Ramanujam, R. Exploring Nonlinearity in Employee Voice: The Effects of Personal Control and Organizational Identification. *Academy of Management Journal*, 51, 6 (2008), 1189-1203.

[24] Venkataramani, V. and Tangirala, S. When and Why Do Central Employees Speak Up? An Examination of Mediating and Moderating Variables. *Journal of Applied Psychology*, 95, 3 (2010), 582-591.

[25] Vakola, M. and Bouradas, D. Antecedents and Consequences of Organisational Silence: An Empirical Investigation. *Employee Relations*, 27, 5 (2005), 441-458.

[26] Keil, M., Im, G. and Mahring, M. Reporting Bad News on Software Projects: The Effects of Culturally Constituted Views of Face-Saving. *Information Systems Journal*, 17, 1 (2007), 59-87.

[27] Tan, B. C. Y., Smith, H. J., Keil, M. and Montealegre, R. Reporting Bad News about Software Projects: Impact of Organizational Climate and

Information Asymmetry in an Individualistic and a Collectivistic Culture. *IEEE Transactions on Engineering Management*, 50, 1 (2003), 64-77.

[28] Near, J. P. and Miceli, M. P. Organizational Dissidence: The Case of Whistle-Blowing. *Journal of Business Ethics*, 4, 1 (1985), 1-16.

[29] Keil, M., Tiwana, A., Sainsbury, R. and Sneha, S. Toward a Theory of Whistleblowing Intentions: A Benefit-to-Cost Differiential Perspective. *Decision Sciences*, 41, 4 (2010), 787-812.

[30] van Dyne, L., Ang, S. and Botero, I. C. Conceptualizing Employee Silence and Employee Voice as Multidimensional Constructs. *Journal of Management Studies*, 40, 6 (2003), 1360-1392.

[31] Davis, A., Murphy, J., Owens, D., Khazanchi, D. and Zigurs, I. Avatars, People, and Virtual Worlds: Foundations for Research in Metaverses. *Journal of the Association for Information Systems*, 10, 2 (2009), 90-117.

[32] Petter, S. and Petter, R. To Tell or Not to Tell: Examining Team Silence and Voice in Online Ad Hoc Teams. In *Proceedings of the International Conference on Information Systems* (Shanghai, China, 2011). Association for Information Systems, [insert City of Publication],[insert 2011 of Publication].

[33] French, J. P. R. and Raven, B. *The Bases of Social Power*. Harper and Row, City, 1960.

[34] Dozier, J. B. and Miceli, M. P. Potential Predictors of Whistle-Blowing: A Prosocial Behavior Perspective. *Academy of Management Review*, 10, 4 (1985), 823-838.

[35] Petter, S., Randolph, A., DeJong, J. and Robinson, A. T. The Trouble with Troubled Projects: Keeping Mum during Times of Crisis. *AIS Transactions on Replication Research*, 2, 1 (2016).

[36] Ringle, C. M., Wende, S. and Becker, J.-M. *SmartPLS 3*. SmartPLS GmbH, http://www.smartpls.com., City, 2015.

[37] Greenberg, P. S., Greenberg, R. H. and Lederer, A. Y. Creating and Sustaining Trust in Virtual Teams. *Business Horizons*, 50, 4 (2007), 325-333.

[38] Katzenbach, J. R. and Smith, D. K. The Discipline of Teams. *Harvard Business Review* (March-April 1993), 111-119.

[39] Zigurs, I. Leadership in Virtual Teams: Oxymoron or Opportunity. *Organizational Dynamics*, 31, 4 (2003), 339-351.

Avoidance of Social Media Advertising: A Latent Profile Analysis

Completed Paper

Jens Mattke
University of Bamberg
An der Weberei 5,
96047 Bamberg
Germany
jens.mattke@uni-bamberg.de

Lea Müller
University of Bamberg
An der Weberei 5,
96047 Bamberg
Germany
lea.mueller@uni-bamberg.de

Christian Maier
University of Bamberg
An der Weberei 5,
96047 Bamberg
Germany
christian.maier@uni-bamberg.de

Heinrich Graser
University of Bamberg
An der Weberei 5,
96047 Bamberg
Germany
heinrich-axel-theodor.graser@stud.uni-bamberg.de

Abstract

Some individuals actively avoid social media advertising, for instance by scrolling over ads or ignoring ads. Therefore, this research aims to identify distinct profiles of individuals avoiding social media advertising. We build upon the advertising avoidance model and take a person-centered approach, using latent profile analysis to identify different profiles of individuals, who avoid social media advertising. We identified three distinct profiles of individuals, differing in their perception and their level of avoidance: *unconcerned users, playful avoiding users and goal-oriented users.* We contribute by characterizing individuals avoiding SMA, so that companies can use these profiles to derive different strategies how to deal with different profiles.

Keywords

Online advertising; advertising avoidance; LPA (latent profile analysis); social media advertising, avoidance

ACM Reference Format:
Jens Mattke, Lea Müller, Christian Maier, and Heinrich Graser. 2018. Avoidance of Social Media Advertising: A Latent Profile Analysis. In Proceedings of ACM *SIGMIS-CPR, June 18–20, 2018, Buffalo-Niagara Falls, NY, USA* ACM, NY, NY, USA, 8 pages. https://doi.org/10.1145/3209626.3209705

Introduction

Imagine John, a casual IT user. Whenever he acts in his personal or professional life, he is surrounded with IT and IT-enabled services: e.g., he works with the computer using business software, he uses a smartphone to book a table in his favorite restaurant at night and he routinely checks his social media accounts on his mobile device to keep up with friends and news. He thereby leaves traces of his behavior and preferences behind, which can be used by organizations to contact John and convince him of buying their products [18]. Therefore, they show him personalized online ads, which – in the best case – match John's specific characteristics and interests. The most promising surrounding for organizations to display to John an optimally matching online ad, is on social media sites, via social media advertising [14]. Using social media advertising, they can utilize the information, John has stated in his social media account, such as favorite books, hobbies or brands he likes, to find out about his characteristics and interests and consequently, to show him a social media ad he might actually like while he is browsing his social media newsfeed [14].

Given that situation, John has two possible ways to react to the displayed social media ad: Either he wants to see more information and so he clicks on the social media ad or he does not want to see the social media ad and actively avoids it by scrolling over [11]. As organizations around the world spend about 40 billion USD on social media advertising to hopefully reach potential customers like John [8, 11, 40], it depicts a huge issue to them, if John decides to actively avoid the social media ads they display to him [29, 33]. Therefore, organizations need to know, who actually avoids the displayed social media ads, which implies to enlighten why those individuals actively avoid the social media ads and which of their perceptions result in the active avoidance of social media ads. Using that information, organizations optimally could derive specific profiles of individuals, who are actively avoiding social media advertising, to identify a potential starting point to convince those profiles not to avoid.

We know from the advertising avoidance model (AAM) that social media advertising avoidance can be explained with individuals' perception of advertising impeding from current activities, individuals' perception of ad clutter and individuals' prior negative experiences with social media advertising [6]. Additionally, individuals' motivation for browsing social media — their browsing mode — might also influence individuals' avoidance [1, 36]. The AAM explains individual's active avoidance on a generalized level. Existing research in IS [17, 20, 23] and psychology [9] indicates again that individuals differ in their profiles, meaning that their perceptions and behavior differ. Therefore, we need to derive specific profiles, thus configurations of characteristics in relative strengths, based on the perceptions identified in the AAM to provide organizations the possibility to address those characteristics and reduce social media advertising avoidance. Bringing this aim into the focus of research, we want to answer the following research question: Which distinct profiles of individuals exist within the context of social media?

To answer this research question, we base on the AAM and collect data via an online survey. We take a person-centered approach and use a latent profile analysis (LPA) to reveal profiles of individuals within the context of social media advertising avoidance. We furthermore conduct an analysis of variance (ANOVA) to test for different levels of active avoidance. Using LPA, we identified three distinct profiles of users: *unconcerned users, playful avoiding users and goal-oriented users*. We thereby contribute to theory by indicating that active avoidance of social media advertising only occurs for individuals in a playful browsing mode. We contribute to practice by providing firms three distinct user profiles that can be used to adapt the different social media advertising strategies and thus, to reduce social media advertising avoidance.

The manuscript is organized as follows. Next, we will outline the AAM and existing research in the field of avoidance, followed by the methodology and the findings. Then, we will discuss the findings and provide theoretical and practical contributions. The manuscript will result in a conclusion.

Research Background

Based on early research on advertising avoidance [38], we define avoidance of social media advertising as *all actions of individuals that reduce their exposure to social media advertising*. This includes individuals' behavior, for example scrolling down ads or actively ignoring ads. We will next outline the Advertising Avoidance Model (AAM) with its extensions [6], which explains individuals' avoidance of online advertising and will be used here to explain avoidance of social media advertising, which depicts a subcategory of online advertising. The AAM [6] identifies three main concepts influencing individuals' advertising avoidance: goal impediment, perceived ad clutter and prior negative experience. Furthermore, the extended AAM [36] states that individuals' avoidance is influenced by the browsing mode of the individuals. Individuals browsing mode is determined by individuals' motives to use social media, therefore individuals can be in a goal oriented browsing mode or in a playful browsing mode.

Concepts of Advertising Avoidance Model. The first main concept **goal impediment** steams from the information theory [37], which describes advertising as a form of perturbation that averts individuals from performing the desired activity, which

yields avoidance. According to the AAM [6], goal impediment positively influences avoidance and can be described as individuals' perception that *social media advertising hinders individuals' search for information and disrupts or distracts individuals from their current activities*. The second main concept **perceived ad clutter** also steams from information theory [37] referring to the excessive amount of ads an individual is exposed to, which results in avoidance [7]. Perceived ad clutter positively influences avoidance and can be defined as *the perception that social media is an exclusive and irritating advertising medium* [6, 36]. The third main concept **prior negative experience** draws on the experience theory [15], stating that prior negative experiences influence individuals' behavior. According to the AAM [6, 36], individuals' empirical knowledge about social media advertising influences individuals' information processing of social media advertising as well as individuals' behavior, thus the avoidance of social media advertising. Therefore, this concept positively influences avoidance and can be defined as individuals' perception that *the reaction to a social media ad does not yield any benefits* [6, 36].

Furthermore, the extended AAM [36] bases on reversal theory [1], which states that individuals can either be in a goal oriented browsing mode or in a playful browsing mode. According to the extended AAM individuals' browsing mode influences individuals' avoidance. For instance, individuals within a **goal-oriented browsing mode** are surfing in social media to pursue a specific purpose, such as to find specific information. It was found that individuals, being in a goal-oriented browsing mode, experience a higher goal impediment and develop negative attitudes towards brands featured in the ads [5]. Based on prior research [1, 4, 36], a goal-oriented browsing mode can be defined as *individuals surfing in social media and being motivated by the achievement of future goals*. On the other side, an example for a **playful browsing mode** in social media would be a situation, where individuals browse social media to kill time and not to pursue a specific goal. Prior research found that individuals being in a playful browsing mode experience a higher influence of negative experiences [36]. Therefore, playful browsing mode can be defined as *individuals surfing in social media and being motivated by seeking excitement to avoid boredom* [1, 36].

Summary and Research Gaps. In sum, the extended AAM identifies three main concepts and two browsing modes. We know how the different concepts and browsing modes influence individuals' avoidance of online advertising and transfer this to social media advertising, as a subcategory of online advertising. The context of social media advertising is specifically interesting for this field, as it represents the most person-centered type of online advertising. Social media advertising delivers advertising based on a person's preferences and interests and thereby depicts a highly personalized user-IS relationship. Existing research in IS indicates that individuals differ in their profile and behavior when using IS [2, 29]. Yet, despite the knowledge that social media, especially social media advertising, is an example of a very person-centered system, the different profiles of individuals confronted with social media advertising have been not addressed in the context of advertisings avoidance, so far. For instance, it remains unclear, whether all individuals behave the same in response to social media advertising. More precisely, there is a gap of knowledge whether different profiles of individuals exist and how they differ in their level of avoidance of social media advertising. Furthermore, despite the research on individuals' browsing mode [4], there is a need to further examine the link of individuals' browsing mode and individuals' avoidance of online advertising. For instance, recent research indicates that playful browsing mode is associated with a positive response to advertising such as clicking on ads [4]. Yet, no research has considered whether a playful or a goal-oriented browsing mode is associated with the avoidance of social media advertising. To illumine this, this study aims at identifying different profiles of individuals and explaining how the browsing mode is linked to individuals' avoidance of social media advertising.

Methodology

This section provides a detailed description of our research methodology. As we want to know about different profiles of Internet users and their online advertising avoidance, we need to apply a person-centered approach, here LPA, which is explained in detail within this section. To specify our research attempt, we further outline the data collection procedure.

Data collection

As the goal of this study is to test for different profiles of individuals and to test whether these different profiles differ in the avoidance of social media advertising, we conducted an online survey using Amazon Mechanical Turk (mTurk). The data collection approach based on mTurk has become established within IS [41] and marketing research [4, 16] and is seen as equivalent to traditional data collection [19]. Furthermore, mTurk has become an established way of data collection when testing for different profiles of individuals [3], as using mTurk provides access to a large participant structure.

For participating in the survey, participants needed to have a level of at least 80 percent successfully completed tasks in mTurk. We followed recommendations from previous literature and used reverse coded questions, screening questions and attention tests to filter the answers [19, 41], we furthermore tracked the overall time the participants needed for completing identifies and compares profiles within a given population. A person-centered approach identifies individuals with similar characteristics and groups them into profiles based on the the survey. Those who passed the filtering received $ 0.15 for participation. We overall removed 50 participants, as they failed some of the predefined filters. For instance, 29 participants failed reverse coded items, 15 participants failed attention tests, six participants completed the survey within an unrealistic period of time and were removed. The demographics are displayed in Table 2. For the survey, we focused on Facebook, as the respective social media site, because Facebook has widely been used to study negative effects of social media on individuals [21, 22].

Participants were asked to remember the last time when they spend time in Facebook and answer questions about their browsing mode and their perceptions about Facebook advertising accordantly.

Table 1: Constructs

Constructs	M	SD	1	2	3	4	5
1. Goal-oriented browsing mode	3.34	1.55					
2. Playful browsing mode	5.05	1.36	-0.59				
3. Goal impediment	4.78	1.34	-0.28	0.14			
4. Perceived ad clutter	4.28	1.14	-0.15	0.07	0.74		
5. Negative experience	4.34	0.90	0.19	-0.07	-0.14	-0.04	
6. Avoidance	4.67	1.35	-0.18	0.11	0.59	0.57	-0.02
M= Mean; SD = standard deviation							

Table 2: Demographic Data (n=118)

Age (in years)	
<21	2.00%
21-30	51.00%
31-40	32.00%
41-50	9.00%
>50	6.00%
(mean = 33.40; standard deviation = 10.60)	
Gender	
Male	46.61%
Female	53.39%
Highest education level	
Less than High School	0.85%
High School / GED	4.24%
Some College	14.41%
2-year College Degree	4.24%
4-year College Degree	46.61%
Master's Degree	23.73%
Doctoral Degree	2.54%
Professional Degree (JD, MD)	3.39%

We adapted the original items (goal impediment, perceived ad clutter, negative experience) of the AAM [6] to the context of Facebook. To measure goal-oriented and playful browsing mode we used measures from previous research [4]. The constructs were measured on a 7-point Likert scale. To assess the validity and reliability of the construct measures, we tested for Cronbach's alpha which exceeded the threshold of 0.70 [31]. We furthermore examined the correlations (see Table 1).

Person-Centered Approach

A person-centered approach, such as the latent profile analysis (LPA) [30], aims at identifying distinct profiles [26] and examines how different constructs are combined within these groups of individuals. This takes into account that constructs can combine differently for different types of individuals [25]. Therefore, a person-centered approach focuses on individuals, configuration of the characteristics [26]. Consequently, a person-centered approach allows researchers to identify profiles in a given sample and analyze those profiles individually.

We used LPA as a person-centered approach based on advantages over other clustering methods. First, when using LPA there is no need for artificial dichotomization of continuous input variables, as LPA is a mixture modeling technique and uses continuous indicators as input [30]. Second, LPA is an inductive approach, meaning that the number of profiles is not known a priori. Consequently, there is no need to specify the number of profiles in advance of the analysis, such as in common clustering methods (e.g., K-means) [27]. LPA rather uses a iterative process of testing multiple number of profiles and thereby leads to an optimal number of profiles. Third, in contrast to other traditional cluster methods, LPA uses the maximum-likelihood method to estimate the models' parameters. That in turn creates a consistent criterion for allocating individuals to a specific profile. Last and most important, LPA is based on formal criteria such as Bayesian Information Criterion (BIC) [23], Akaike Information Criterion (AIC), Bootstrap likelihood ratio test (BLRT) [32] to determine the optimal number of profiles.

Data Analysis: Latent Profile Analysis (LPA)

As we want to identify which different profiles of individuals exist and how they differ in their avoidance of social media advertising we take a person-centered approach. In this case, we used latent profile analysis (LPA) that generates different profiles of individuals that differ in their patterns. Each profile has a distinct, prototypical pattern of individuals. LPA examines, whether the three constructs (goal impediment, perceived ad clutter, negative experience), the two browsing modes (goal-oriented browsing mode, playful browsing mode in our model) and the level of avoidance can be attributed to different profiles of individuals.

To identify the optimal number of different profiles of individuals, we iteratively conducted LPA with different numbers of profiles. Following recommendations from LPA literature [9, 32], we started with one profile and increased the number of profiles until the increase in the number of profiles did no longer improve the model. The optimal number of profiles was assessed, based on log likelihood (LL), Akaike Information

Criterion (AIC), Bayesian Information Criterion (BIC [32]), sample-size-adjusted BIC (SSA-BIC [43]), entropy and Bootstrap likelihood ratio test (BLRT [32]). We furthermore base on parsimony and interpretability of the emergent profiles from LPA [24]. The ideal profile solution contains smaller LL, AIC, BIC and SSA-BIC values compared to other solutions, whereas a higher entropy in comparison to other solutions indicates a good fit of the solution. Additionally, the entropy must be larger the 0.70 for classification accuracy [12]. The BLRT examines whether a solution with k profiles depicts a significant improvement in fit over a solution with $k-1$ profiles. Thereby, a significant p value indicates a significant improvement by using a higher number of profiles [13].

For the LPA, we used a package supplied on GitHub[1] for R (www.r-project.org). Furthermore, the analysis of variance (ANOVA) was conducted to understand how the identified profiles differ in their level of avoidance.

Results

The interpretability of the profiles suggested three profiles as the optimum number of distinct types of profiles. The analysis revealed that the BLRT is only significant for up to profile three, therefore only the solutions with a significant BLRT are re levant [32]. Consequently, we examined the solution for one profile (see Table 4 row two), the solution for two profiles (see Table 4 row three) and the solution for three profiles (see Table 4 row four). The results show that comparing the three solutions, LL, AIC, BIC and SSA-BIC are the lowest for a solution with three profiles in comparison to other solutions. The BTRT depicts a significant improvement for using three profiles instead of a solution with two profiles (see Table 4). Furthermore, there is a sufficient high number of cases in each profile, ranging from 12 to 59. The mean posterior probability, which indicates whether an individual belongs to the assigned profile, is high with an average value of 0.95. Overall, this attests the stability and validity of the solution.

(I) profile	(J) profile	Mean difference (I-J)	SD Error	Sig.	95% Confidence interval	
					Lower bound	Upper bound
Unconcerned user (mean 3.87)	Playful avoiding user	-1.45	0.98	0.000	-1.94	-0.96
	Goal-oriented user	1.49	0.32	0.000	0.69	2.28
Playful avoiding user (mean 5.32)	Unconcerned user	1.45	0.20	0.000	0.96	1.94
	Goal-oriented user	2.94	0.33	0.000	2.13	3.75
Goal-oriented user (mean 2.38)	Unconcerned user	-1.49	0.32	0.000	-2.28	-0.69
	Playful avoiding user	-2.94	0.33	0.000	-3.75	-2.13
Note: SD = standard deviation; Sig,= significance (p < 0.001)						

Table 3: Results ANOVA

n-profile	LL	AIC	BIC	SSA-BIC	Entropy	BLRT	BLRT p
1	1166.60	2357.19	2390.43	2352.50	1.00	111.15	p<0.001
2	1110.80	2259.64	2312.28	2252.22	0.95	60.45	p<0.001
3	**1080.60**	**2213.10**	**2285.14**	**2202.95**	**0.95**	**55.40**	**p<0.001**
4	*1052.90*	*2171.73*	*2263.16*	*2158.84*	*0.95*	*-10.63*	*p>0.90 (ns)*
...							

Note: Only the solution with one profile, two profiles and three profiles are relevant as those solutions show a significant BLRT. Starting with the solution of four profiles, the BLRT is not significant anymore.

Table 4: Model Fit Statistics

To represent the solution with three profiles, we used a mean plot for each of the three profiles (see Figure 1). The results of the ANOVA tests showed significant differences between all three profiles for the avoidance of social media adverting. Using post hoc analyses (Scheffe's Test), we confirmed significant differences between the three profiles in regard to the avoidance of social media advertising (see Table 3). This attests the differences and the meaningfulness of the profiles [39]. We named the three different profiles based on the differences that emerge from the comparison of the profiles and based on relative levels of constructs, such as very high level of particular constructs. The three different profiles will be discussed hereafter.

Profile 1 (n=59), hereafter labeled 'unconcerned user', shows a relative low level for perceived ad clutter and goal impediment. On the other side, the *unconcerned user* depicts also a low level of negative experience with social media advertising. Additionally, this profile can be classified into a rather goal oriented-browsing mode. Finally, this profile shows a low level of avoidance.

Profile 2 (n=47), hereafter called 'playful avoiding user', can be described with a low level of negative experience with social media advertising. Yet the *playful avoiding user* comes along with a high level of perceived ad clutter and a high level of goal impediment. Furthermore, this profile depicts individuals that are in a playful browsing mode, which is indicated by the positive level for playful browsing mode and the negative level of goal-oriented browsing mode. Most important, the *playful avoiding user* shows the highest level of avoidance of social media advertising compared to all three profiles.

Profile 3 (n=12), hereafter called 'goal-oriented user', depicts the lowest perception of goal impediment and perceived ad clutter. At the same time, this profile has relative high negative experience with social media advertising. The 'goal-oriented user' clearly depicts a highly goal-oriented profile, yet with the lowest level of avoidance. According to the conducted ANOVA tests, all three profiles show significant differences in their avoidance of social media advertising, meaning that the *playful avoiding user* has a significant higher level of avoidance than the other two profiles. The *unconcerned user* has a significant lower level of avoidance than the *playful avoiding user*, yet a significant higher level of avoidance than *goal-oriented user*.

Discussion

Remember John, who is surrounded by IT in his personal or professional life, leaving traces of data about his behavior and preferences behind. Organizations try to use these data, which John creates by using IT such as social media, to reach John and sell their products [18] using social media advertising. Therefore, they spend rising amounts of money in social media advertising to reach individuals in a person-centered way. Individuals do not always react positively to social media ad exposure: a major group of them actively avoids social media advertising [8, 11, 40].

To downsize this group of individuals, organizations need to enlighten and address the personal characteristics of those individuals. To address this, we adopted the AAM in its extended form and applied it in the context of social media advertising. Further we applied a person-centered approach, based on LPA, to identify different profiles and their differences in the level of avoidance of social media advertising.

Theoretical contributions. Our theoretical contributions are threefold. First, our LPA findings extend the existing knowledge on advertising avoidance by providing a tripartite typology of individuals. We identified three distinct profiles of individuals, where each profile significantly differs regarding the avoidance of social media advertising. Furthermore, this manuscript also contributes by demonstrating how LPA can be used to generate profiles among individuals in the context of social media advertising. We thereby show that LPA can make a significant contribution to the ongoing debate about individuals heterogeneity [2, 9, 23]. Furthermore, with this manuscript, we follow recent calls for research to use a person-centered approach [9, 25, 26, 28].

Second, as the AAM does not consider any profiles, we extend this knowledge by providing evidence that the model needs to consider three distinct profiles of individuals. The *unconcerned user* profile and the *goal-oriented user* depict profiles browsing in a goal-oriented browsing mode. Both profiles show a low level of goal impediment and perceived ad clutter and a high level of negative experience. Additionally, both profiles show a low level of avoidance. The finding that individuals within a goal-oriented browsing mode show lower levels of goal impediment is in contrast with prior findings [36]. The *playful avoiding user* depicts a profile in a playful browsing mode with a high level of perceived ad clutter, goal impediment and avoidance. The three different profiles improve the accuracy of the so fare universal AAM, as the identified profiles differ in their characteristics and consequently need to be treated and explained separately. With our findings, we show that the AAM depicts a special case and is not valid for every profile. Therefore, different models for different profiles are needed to fully explain individuals' avoidance of social media advertising. For instance, individuals in a goal-oriented browsing mode behave differently to individuals in a playful browsing mode.

Third, we furthermore provide evidence that individuals in a goal-oriented browsing mode show a low level of active

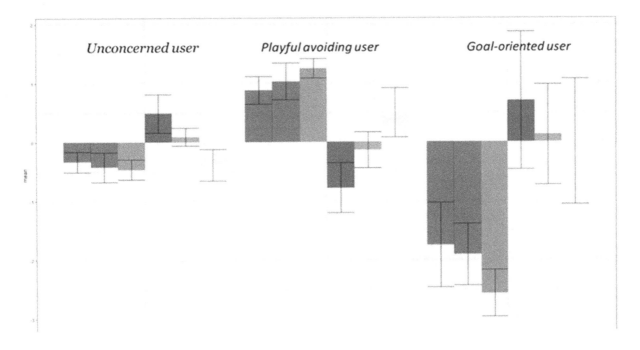

■ Perceived ad clutter;   ■ Avoidance of social media advertising;   ■ Goal impediment;
■ Goal-oriented browsing mode;   ■ Negative experience   Playful browsing mode

Figure 1: Profiles using Standardized Mean

avoidance. In contrast, the *playful avoiding user* profile shows the significant highest level of active avoidance. With this, we provide further evidence, that individuals in a playful browsing mode are more likely to avoid social media adverting. This finding is in contrast to present knowledge indicating that playful browsing mode is associated with positive reactions, such as clicking [4]. An explanation for this could be that individuals in a goal-oriented browsing mode do not notice advertising. On the other hand, individuals in a playful browsing mode may be more likely to process the advertising. That means that individuals in a goal-oriented browsing mode do not even realize ads, e.g. because they learned to dismiss them, due to prior negative experiences and therefore, they do not engage in active avoidance of advertising. These results are in line with research finding that individuals in a goal-oriented browsing mode are blind for distraction, such as advertising [35]. This furthermore explains the relative high level of goal impediment for the *playful avoiding user*. As individuals who are in a goal-oriented browsing mode do not process advertising, individuals in a playful browsing mode, process ads and feel impeded while browsing.

Practical contributions. The contribution to practice is the segmentation of individuals into three different profiles. Having three distinct profiles, organizations can target individuals based on these profiles. The profile of the *playful avoiding user* and the profile of the *goal-oriented user* are of special interest for organizations, as the *unconcerned user* does not show any high level in the constructs.

Looking at the *playful avoiding user*, we see that this profile is not characterized by negative experience with social media

advertising. The purpose of surfing in social media is to get entertained, yet those individuals perceive social media advertising as excessive and disturbing. The issue is that even though individuals in this profile seek for entertainment, they do not perceive social media advertising as entertaining. What organizations can learn from these findings is that they need to encounter those individuals with a '*entertaining advertising strategy*'. This means these individuals are open for entertainment, therefore organizations need to target those individuals with more entertaining, funnier and more emotional advertising. Social media advertising that is based on facts or pure information is inappropriate for this profile. These recommendations are enforced by similar findings indicating that advertising needs to be adapted to the current emotional mode of the individual [34].

Looking at the profile of the *goal-oriented user,* we see an individual who is highly goal-oriented and is characterized by negative experience with social media advertising. An explanation for the low level of avoidance even though this profile is goal-oriented and depicts a negative experience with social media advertising, is banner blindness. Banner blindness, in the context of social media advertising, means that individuals do not realize social media advertising at all and it is assumed that the experience with ads and the goal-oriented browsing mode influences the banner blindness positively [10, 42]. This reflects our findings as the *goal-oriented user* depicts a high level of negative experience and a highly goal-oriented browsing mode. This means for organizations, that they can encounter individuals within this profile with a '*do not target strategy*', as even if they expose social media advertising to *goal-oriented user,* they will most likely not realize a reaction to the ad, due to banner blindness [42].

Conclusion

As a large group of individuals actively avoids social media advertising, we test for different profiles of individuals and the different levels of the avoidance of social media advertising within these profiles. We identify three distinct profiles of individuals and found that individuals being in a playful browsing mode show a higher degree of avoidance of social media advertising.

References

[1] Apter, M.J. *The experience of motivation: The theory of psychological reversals*: Academic Pr, 1982.

[2] Bapna, R; Goes, P; Gupta, A; and Jin, Y. User heterogeneity and its impact on electronic auction market design: An empirical exploration. *MIS Quarterly* (2004), 21–43.

[3] Bennett, A.A; Gabriel, A.S; Calderwood, C; Dahling, J.J; and Trougakos, J.P. Better together? Examining profiles of employee recovery experiences. *The Journal of applied psychology, 101,* 12 (2016), 1635–1654.

[4] Bleier, A. and Eisenbeiss, M. Personalized Online Advertising Effectiveness: The Interplay of What, When, and Where. *Marketing Science, 34,* 5 (2015), 669–688.

[5] Campbell, C; Mattison Thompson, F; Grimm, P.E; and Robson, K. Understanding Why Consumers Don't Skip Pre-Roll Video Ads. *Journal of Advertising, 46,* 3 (2017), 411–423.

[6] Cho, C.-H. and Cheon, H.J. Why do people avoid advertising on the internet? *Journal of Advertising, 33,* 4 (2004), 89–97.

[7] Elliott, M.T. and Speck, P.S. Consumer Perceptions of Advertising Clutter and Its Impact Across Various Media. *Journal of Advertising Research, 38,* 1 (1998), 29–41.

[8] Fortune. Social Media Ad Spending Is Expected to Pass Newspapers by 2020. (11 October 2017) (available at http://fortune.com/2016/12/05/social-media-ad-spending-newspapers-zenith-2020/).

[9] Gabriel, A.S; Daniels, M.A; Diefendorff, J.M; and Greguras, G.J. Emotional labor actors: a latent profile analysis of emotional labor strategies. *The Journal of applied psychology, 100,* 3 (2015), 863–879.

[10] Hervet, G; Guérard, K; Tremblay, S; and Chtourou, M.S. Is banner blindness genuine? Eye tracking internet text advertising. *Applied cognitive psychology, 25,* 5 (2011), 708–716.

[11] Infolinks. The Banner Blindness Infographic. (3 February 2017) (available at http://www.infolinks.com/blog/infographic/the-banner-blindness-infographic/).

[12] Jung, T. and Wickrama, K.A.S. An introduction to latent class growth analysis and growth mixture modeling. *Social and personality psychology compass, 2,* 1 (2008), 302–317.

[13] Kabins, A.H; Xu, X; Bergman, M.E; Berry, C.M; and Willson, V.L. A profile of profiles: A meta-analysis of the nomological net of commitment profiles. *The Journal of applied psychology, 101,* 6 (2016), 881–904.

[14] Knoll, J. Advertising in social media: A review of empirical evidence. *International Journal of Advertising, 35,* 2 (2016), 266–300.

[15] Kolb, D. Experiential education: Experience as the source of learning and development. *Englewood Cliffs, NJ* (1984).

[16] Kouchaki, M. and Jami, A. Everything We Do, You Do: The Licensing Effect of Prosocial Marketing Messages on Consumer Behavior. *Management Science,* 2016 (2016).

[17] Laumer, S; Maier, C; Eckhardt, A; and Weitzel, T. User personality and resistance to mandatory information systems in organizations: A theoretical model and empirical test of dispositional resistance to change. *J Inf Technol, 31,* 1 (2016), 67–82.

[18] Li, G; Yang, H; Sun, L; and Sohal, A.S. The impact of IT implementation on supply chain integration and performance. *International Journal of Production Economics, 120,* 1 (2009), 125–138.

[19] Lowry, P.B; D'Arcy, J; Hammer, B; and Moody, G.D. "Cargo Cult" science in traditional organization and information systems survey research: A case for using nontraditional methods of data collection, including Mechanical Turk and online panels. *The Journal of Strategic Information Systems, 25,* 3 (2016), 232–240.

[20] Maier, C. Personality within information systems research: A literature analysis. *ECIS 2012 Proceedings, Barcelona, Spain* (2012).

[21] Maier, C; Laumer, S; Eckhardt, A; and Weitzel, T. Giving too much social support: Social overload on social networking sites. *Eur J Inf Syst, 24,* 5 (2015), 447–464.

[22] Maier, C; Laumer, S; Weinert, C; and Weitzel, T. The effects of technostress and switching stress on discontinued use of social networking services: A study of Facebook use. *Info Systems J, 25,* 3 (2015), 275–308.

[23] Melas, C.D; Zampetakis, L.A; Dimopoulou, A; and Moustakis, V.S. An empirical investigation of Technology Readiness among medical staff based in Greek hospitals. *Eur J Inf Syst, 23,* 6 (2014), 672–690.

[24] Merz, E.L. and Roesch, S.C. A latent profile analysis of the Five Factor Model of personality: Modeling trait interactions. *Personality and individual differences, 51,* 8 (2011), 915–919.

[25] Meyer, J.P. and Morin, A.J.S. A person-centered approach to commitment research: Theory, research, and methodology. *Journal of Organizational Behavior, 37,* 4 (2016), 584–612.

[26] Meyer, J.P; Stanley, L.J; and Vandenberg, R.J. A person-centered approach to the study of commitment. *Human Resource Management Review, 23,* 2 (2013), 190–202.

[27] Meyers, L.S; Gamst, G; and Guarino, A.J. *Applied multivariate research: Design and interpretation*: SAGE Publications, 2016.

[28] Morin, A.J.S; Meyer, J.P; Creusier, J; and Biétry, F. Multiple-group analysis of similarity in latent profile solutions. *Organizational Research Methods, 19,* 2 (2016), 231–254.

[29] Müller, L; Mattke, J; Maier, C; and Weitzel, T. The Curse of Mobile Marketing: A Mixed Methods Study on Individuals' Switch to Mobile Ad Blockers. *ICIS 2017 Proceedings* (2017).

[30] Muthén, L.K. and Muthén, B.O. Mplus User's Guide (7th ed.). *Los Angeles, CA: Muthén &* (1998-2015).

[31] Nunnally, J. *Psychometric methods*. New York: McGraw-Hill, 1978.

[32] Nylund, K.L; Asparouhov, T; and Muthén, B.O. Deciding on the number of classes in latent class analysis and growth mixture modeling: A Monte Carlo simulation study. *Structural equation modeling, 14,* 4 (2007), 535–569.

[33] PageFair. 2016 Mobile Adblocking Report. (9 January 2017) (available at https://pagefair.com/blog/2016/mobile-adblocking-report/).

[34] Puccinelli, N.M; Wilcox, K; and Grewal, D. Consumers' Response to Commercials: When the Energy Level in the Commercial Conflicts with the Media Context. *Journal of Marketing, 79,* 2 (2015), 1–18.

[35] Resnick, M. and Albert, W. The impact of advertising location and user task on the emergence of banner ad blindness: An eye-tracking study. *International Journal of Human-Computer Interaction, 30,* 3 (2014), 206–219.

[36] Seyedghorban, Z; Tahernejad, H; and Matanda, M.J. Reinquiry into advertising avoidance on the internet: A conceptual replication and extension. *Journal of Advertising, 45,* 1 (2016), 120–129.

[37] Shannon, C.E. and Weaver, W. *The mathematical theory of communication*: University of Illinois press, 1998.

[38] Speck, P.S. and Elliott, M.T. Predictors of advertising avoidance in print and broadcast media. *Journal of Advertising, 26,* 3 (1997), 61–76.

[39] Stanley, L; Kellermanns, F.W; and Zellweger, T.M. Latent Profile Analysis. *Family Business Review, 30,* 1 (2017), 84–102.

[40] Statista. Global social network ad revenues 2017 | Statistic. (7 November 2017) (available at https://www.statista.com/statistics/271406/advertising-revenue-of-social-networks-worldwide/).

[41] Steelman, Z.R; Hammer, B.I; and Limayem, M. Data Collection in the Digital Age: Innovative Alternatives to Student Samples. *MIS Quarterly, 38,* 2 (2014).

[42] Sun, Y; Lim, K.H; and Peng, J.Z. Solving the Distinctiveness – Blindness Debate: A Unified Model for Understanding Banner Processing. *Journal of the Association for Information Systems, 14,* 2 (2013), 49–71.

[43] Tofighi, D. and Enders, C.K. Identifying the correct number of classes in growth mixture models. *Advances in latent variable mixture models,* Information Age Publishing, Inc (2008), 317–341.

Effects of Leaderboards in Games on Consumer Engagement*

Extended Abstract

Laura C. Amo
State University of New York at Buffalo
lccasey@buffalo.edu

Ruochen Liao
State University of New York at Buffalo
rliao2@buffalo.edu

H. Raghav Rao
University of Texas at San Antonio
hr.rao@utsa.edu

Gretchen Walker
The Tech Museum of Innovation
gwalker@thetech.org

ACM Reference format:
L. C. Amo, R. Liao, H. R. Rao, and G. Walker. 2018. Effects of Leaderboards in Games on Consumer Engagement. In *SIGMIS-CPR '18, June 18–20, 2018, Buffalo-Niagara Falls, NY, USA,* 2 pages.
https://doi.org/10.1145/3209626.3209708

1 INTRODUCTION

Gamification is the process of adding games or game-like elements to a non-game task in order to encourage participation and engagement [8]. Gamification, as a means of engaging consumers [6, 10, 16], has become more and more popular and implemented in a range of user-oriented applications. However studies have shown that it may not always have the type of impact as initially projected [12, 13]. Gamification yields different, sometimes contradictory, results with regard to the engagement outcomes. Researchers have argued that gamification is not always properly implemented and may not have consistent positive effects [14], as the reward mechanisms and intensified competition could create a controlling gaming environment that could dampen the intrinsic motivation of the participants [13]. Therefore, it is important for businesses and organizations to be able to gauge the impact of gamified interventions and evaluate return on investment.

In this study, we first review prior research on consumer engagement, and posit that the different findings related to engagement outcomes may be due to the multi-facet nature of consumer behavior. Specifically, we divide engagement outcomes on four indicators and examine the effect of gamification on each of them: time-on-task, the number of attempts, the number of re-attempts, and the number of unique attempts. We compare differences between a control group and a treatment group in an informal learning environment across a 10-month period wherein a leaderboard was introduced in the treatment kiosk in the fifth month, allowing us to evaluate the change in outcomes while controlling for existing differences.

The National Science Foundation (NSF), DGE-1523174, supported data collection associated with this study; all disclaimers apply.

2 LITERATURE REVIEW

Consumer engagement originated from the relationship marketing literature in the 1990s [1, 2, 16]. However, consumer engagement lacks a clear definition, and related psychological and behavioral outcomes tend to be context-specific [11]. For example, there is evidence that certain game elements may actually be negatively related to motivation [12, 15] or at least not associated with long-term behavioral change [4]. Prior literature that attempts the explain the contradictory findings in the effect of gamification generally agree that while gaming elements appeal to the intrinsic motivation of individuals by making the game more interesting and engaging, material rewards and the competition for reputation and ranking would actually hurt intrinsic motivation by making the individuals feeling coerced and controlled [15].

We propose that while external factors such as ranking and reputation could potentially exert social- and peer-pressure on the participants, the participants may adopt different coping strategies in the presence of such pressure [3, 5]. We integrate literatures on pride [21] and social comparison [5], and posit that while certain individuals may perceive the game environment to be controlling and harming their autonomy, other individuals may be driven to achieve higher symbolic places under the pressure.

3 RESEARCH MODEL AND HYPOTHESES

In certain studies, leaderboards are positively associated with time-based outcomes. Pride is a powerful motivator of time spent on a task [8] particularly when such pride is authentic and tied to a specific experience [19]. Leaderboards publicly display achievement and establish ranking, and may represent the opportunity for a consumer to take public ownership of an achievement. As such, we posit that there will be a significant increase in the average time spent at the kiosk among consumers as they would try harder to come out top of the competition. Following the same line of logic, leaderboards will likely encourage consumers to make more attempt when they run into obstacles. Literature has shown that even if a task is difficult, the prospect of experiencing pride at the end by achieving success is a powerful motivator [9, 21]. Therefore, we hypothesize that there will be a significantly greater number of attempts by consumers once the leaderboard is added.

On the other hand, the leaderboard is just as likely to be negatively associated with re-attempts and unique attempts. Specifically, unlike points and levels, leaderboard does not provide task-related feedbacks and error cues. Participants could experience greater frustration when they perform below expectation but not knowing how to improve. Similarly, from a social comparison perspective [5], consumers may feel that attempting the game is not worth the effort as there are far better performers (i.e. top leaderboard scorers). As a result, we posit that the leaderboard will be negatively associated with re-attempts.

Lastly, we posit that the presence of a leaderboard will be associated with fewer unique attempts; in other words, fewer consumers will even attempt the game once the leaderboard is introduced. It may be that consumers feel that attaining a score comparable to that of high scorers is not very possible or economical. Social comparison in the form of a leaderboard may lead to a destructive form of competition and negatively affect motivation [7, 13]. If consumers are not competitive or are intimidated by competitive activities, the leaderboard may actually deter them.

4   DATA SOURCES AND METHODOLOGY

We conducted the study at the Tech Museum of Innovation in San Jose, California. School-age students visit this museum and informal learning occurs by interacting with the mini-games at kiosks to achieve goals. Our data included multiple observations for visitors over the course of about ten months: November 1, 2015 through August 28, 2016. A leaderboard is introduced to one of the game kiosks, Net-builder, in the middle of the study period, this intervention allows us to evaluate if changes made to one kiosk were associated with changes in engagement outcomes.

5   RESULTS

On average, consumer spend much longer time on Net-builder compared to other kiosks before the intervention. After the leaderboard was introduced to the Net-Builder kiosk, consumers spend an extra 60 seconds or about 35% more time per interaction at the Net-Builder kiosk. Contrary to our hypothesis, the addition of the leaderboard to the Net-Builder kiosk did not significantly affect the average number of overall attempts. This indicates that consumers are trying harder at each attempt, but not increasing the number of attempts. Average number of attempts made by consumers on Net-builder kiosk and other game kiosks were not significantly affected by the addition of the leaderboard. But the number of re-attempt decreased at the Net-builder kiosk compared to other kiosks, as we hypothesized, and unique attempts at the Net-builder kiosk also decreased after the leaderboard is in place.

6   DISCUSSION

Consistent with existing findings on leaderboard effectiveness, our results suggest that leaderboards have both positive and negative effects on consumer engagement. Our findings confirm that leaderboards are not necessarily an overall effective mechanism for increasing engagement. While leaderboards may motivate certain consumers to pursue opportunities to demonstrate pride over achievement [20, 22], these game

elements may also introduce an element of competition, eliciting fear and aversion in other consumers [12]. The overall goals and culture of the organization need to be taken into account when leaderboards are implemented as a game element.

REFERENCES

[1]   Christopher, M., Payne, A., and Ballantyne, D. 1991. *Relationship marketing: bringing quality customer service and marketing together.* Butterworth-Heinemann: Oxford, England.

[2]   Crumlish, C., and Malone, E. (2009). *Designing social interfaces: Principles, patterns, and practices for improving the user experience.* O'Reilly Media, Inc.,: Sebastopol, CA.

[3]   Deterding, S. 2011. *Situated motivational affordances of game elements: A conceptual model.* In Proceedings of Gamification: Using game design elements in non-gaming contexts. ACM Computer-Human Interaction [CHI], Vancouver, British Columbia.

[4]   Farzan, R., DiMicco, J. M., Millen, D. R., Dugan, C., Geyer, W., and Brownholtz, E. A. 2008. Results from deploying a participation incentive mechanism within the enterprise. In *Proceedings of the SIGCHI conference on Human Factors in Computing Systems.*

[5]   Festinger, L. (1954). A theory of social comparison processes. *Human Relations*, 7, 2 (1954), 117-140. DOI: https://doi.org/10.1177/001872675400700202

[6]   Hamari, J., Koivisto, J., and Sarsa, H. 2014. Does gamification work?--a literature review of empirical studies on gamification. In *Proceedings of the 2014 47th Hawaii International Conference on System Sciences.* IEEE Computer Society, Hawaii.

[7]   Hanus, M. D., and Fox, J. 2015. Assessing the effects of gamification in the classroom: A longitudinal study on intrinsic motivation, social comparison, satisfaction, effort, and academic performance. *Computers & Education, 80*, 152-161.

[8]   Landers, R. N., and Landers, A. K. 2014. An empirical test of the theory of gamified learning: The effect of leaderboards on time-on-task and academic performance. *Simulation & Gaming, 45*(6), 769-785.

[9]   Landers, R. N., Bauer, K. N., & Callan, R. C. 2017. Gamification of task performance with leaderboards: A goal setting experiment. *Computers In Human Behavior, 71*, 508-515.

[10] Liu, D., Santhaham, R., and Webster, J. 2017. Toward meaningful engagement: A framework for design and research of gamified information systems. *MIS Quarterly, 41*(4), 1011-1034.

[11] Malone, T. W. 1981. Toward a theory of intrinsically motivating instruction. *Cognitive Science, 5*(4), 333-369.

[12] Mekler, E. D., Brühlmann, F., Opwis, K., and Tuch, A. N. 2013. *Do points, levels and leaderboards harm intrinsic motivation?: An empirical analysis of common gamification elements.* Paper presented at the Proceedings of the First International Conference on Gameful Design, Research, and Applications.

[13] Orosz, G., Farkas, D., and Roland-Lévy, C. (2013). Are competition and extrinsic motivation reliable predictors of academic cheating? *Frontiers in Psychology, 4.*

[14] Richter, G., Raban, D.R., and Rafaeli, S. Studying gamification: the effect of rewards and incentives on motivation. *Gamification in education and business*: Springer, 2015, pp. 21-46.

[15] Ryan, R., and Deci, E. 2000. Intrinsic and Extrinsic Motivations: Classic Definitions and New Directions. *Contemporary educational psychology, 1*(25), 54-67. doi:10.1006/ceps.1999.1020 %\ 2017-01-22 15:39:00

[16] Schiff, J. L. (2017). How gamification improves customer engagement and retention. Retrieved from https://www.cio.com/article/3184368/small-business/how-gamification-improves-customer-engagement-and-retention.html

[17] Stieglitz, S., and Dang-Xuan, L. 2013. Emotions and information diffusion in social media—sentiment of microblogs and sharing behavior. *Journal of Management Information Systems, 29*(4), 217-248.

[18] Suh, A., Wagner, C., and Liu, L. 2016. Enhancing User Engagement through Gamification. *Journal of Computer Information Systems*, 1-10.

[19] Tangney, J. P. 1999. The self-conscious emotions: Shame, guilt, embarrassment and pride.

[20] Werbach, K., and Hunter, D. 2012. *For the win: How game thinking can revolutionize your business*: Wharton Digital Press.

[21] Williams, L. A., and DeSteno, D. 2008. Pride and perseverance: the motivational role of pride. *Journal of Personality and Social Psychology, 94*(6), 1007.

[22] Yee, N. 2006. Motivations for play in online games. *CyberPsychology & Behavior, 9* (6), 772-775.

The Classification of Aggressive Dialogue in Social Media Platforms

Jaida Langham
Spelman College
Department of Computer and Information Sciences
Atlanta, GA, USA
jlangham@scmail.spelman.edu

Kinnis Gosha
Morehouse College
Department of Computer Science
Atlanta, GA, USA
kinnis.gosha@morehouse.edu

ABSTRACT

The significance of aggression for the understanding of human behavior cannot be over amplified. It associates the individual, behavior, habits, environment, and health (mental). Understanding specificity when it comes to types of aggression and aggressive behavior can help with implementing appropriate countermeasures to those who demonstrate aggressive behavior within their speech and behavior on social media platforms. Through a research synthesis utilizing different search engines to find work on hate speech detection, hate, anger, aggressive behavior in social media, and the consequences associated with these terms, it can be concluded that previous work on hate speech detection have developed methods that ignore the variety in speech, possible other categories of hate speech, the correlation of speech to human behavior, and demonstrate minimal to no empathy toward the users from which this data was extracted from. Categorizations of hate speech currently only include hate and offensive language. Another category that should be added is anger. Future studies should specify their searches to including aggressive behavior since it is the connection when analyzing human behavior and hate speech.

CCS CONCEPTS

• **Social and professional topics** → **Hate speech**; • **Information systems** → *Social networks*;

KEYWORDS

Aggressive behavior, anger, hate, offensive language, social media, violence, hate speech

ACM Reference Format:
Jaida Langham and Kinnis Gosha. 2018. The Classification of Aggressive Dialogue in Social Media Platforms. In *SIGMIS-CPR '18: 2018 Computers and People Research Conference, June 18–20, 2018, Buffalo-Niagara Falls, NY, USA.* ACM, New York, NY, USA, 4 pages. https://doi.org/10.1145/3209626.3209720

1 INTRODUCTION

There have been several unfortunate cases of social media serving as a tool leading to suicides, murders and violence - especially with

teenagers and young adults [5, 8, 9, 14–18, 22, 25, 28, 29, 31], largely in part because of hate speech. Hate speech is considered an epidemic and as a primary tool in inciting violence onto others through various platforms [23]. In 2017, one of the largest social media firms, Twitter, adjusted their privacy policy rules pertaining to abusive behavior. This includes any tweet that promotes violence, self-harm, suicide, harassment, abuse, hate, and so on. [32] The problem is that current detection implementations that are used to support policies implemented to govern user language and interactions, ignore the multifaceted attributes of speech and negative aggressive behavior which leads to inaccurate categorizations and generalizations. A demonstration of hate speech is a confirmation of the presence of negative aggressive behavior within a user. Negative aggressive behavior includes offensive language, hate, and anger [21]. Currently, there is no consolidated way to detect anger within social media. A majority of the previous work that has focused on hate speech has attempted to detect hate speech in a binary method, meaning the tweet/post/comment is flagged for hate or not. A 2017 study on hate speech detection brought to light another category, offensive language, with a method that was used to categorize a tweet/post/comment into the categories of hate, offensive language, or neither. [11] Although this method considers hate speech as larger than a binary system, this method still ignores the variety in speech, possible other categories of hate speech, and demonstrates minimal to no empathy toward the users from which this data was extracted from. In 2013, there was a study conducted on the Chinese "Twitter"-like social media platform that concluded that anger is the most influential social media emotion. [13] Multiple studies have shown how anger in social media becomes contagious from one from user to another. [2, 12, 13, 19, 30, 35] Anger is inevitably heavily involved in the hate crimes, bullying, suicides, deaths, fights, and murders in social media. In this study, we argue that Anger should be considered in hate speech detection methods because it will effectively assist in proper categorization. The goal of this paper is to review the literature and develop a more accurate and inclusive classification of anger-related social media posts to be used for hate speech detection. Acknowledgment of the impact of negative aggressive behavior and the role of anger in hate speech is necessary for reducing aggressive behavior within social media and deciding the appropriate countermeasures for those who demonstrate it.

2 BACKGROUND

When discussing the flaws within a detection method used to categorize humans, the human behavior must be considered. The overarching category that includes hate speech, behavioral problems, anger, offensive language, and so on is the category of aggressive human behavior. A better understanding of aggression is necessary for learning how to prevent negative aggression in the future. Aggression can be applied to animal behavior as well as human behavior. When applied to human behavior, it is used to describe personality and attitudes, as well as to characterize behavior in both children and adults. Certain levels of aggression are considered unhealthy. [3, 21] Examples of difference in levels and context of aggression include the "aggressive" businessman, which is used in a daily context to designate forceful but legitimate actions or the "aggressive" and uncooperative man which is used in a context that denotes negative, antagonistic, and maybe even hostile actions of that man. It is important to consider the complex and multifaceted nature of aggression strictly because of differences in catalysts, psychological development, mental processes and so on. [21] The aggressive behavior that is commonly referred to in this paper can be defined as hostile, negative, inappropriate aggression, meaning its purpose is to induce injury or pain.

As stated before, negative aggressive behavior includes demonstrations of hate. Previous studies on hate and hate speech generalize hate to this one large idea of anything that has a negative context - hate vs. neither-, innately ignoring the diversity of emotions and human behavior. Anger and hatred are interrelated, but different in definition and behavior. Anger is an initial reaction to something and is also a more temporary emotion. Hatred is a more sustained, possibly permanent, reaction to something. [7] For example, you can be angry at someone for cutting you off in traffic, but maybe a few hours later, you won't be necessarily angry at that person anymore; but you can say that you hate being cut off in traffic in general. Anger and hatred exist on the same scale but are different in intensity and energy.

The general term used to describe aggressive behavior on social media is "hate speech." To define hate speech, the definition of hate in a social context must also be considered. The word "hate" can be understood as "extreme negative feelings and beliefs held about a group of individuals or a specific representative of that group because of their race, ethnicity, religion, gender or sexual orientation".[26] The term "hate speech" can be understood as covering all forms of expression that "spread, incite, promote or justify racial hatred, xenophobia, anti-Semitism or other forms of hatred based on intolerance, including intolerance expressed by aggressive nationalism and ethnocentrism, discrimination and hostility against minorities, migrants and people of immigrant origin".[24] Referring to these definitions, hate is a broad category that covers a large spectrum of potential tweet context but not all. A user can create a negative tweet that does not demonstrate hatred based on another's identity. People often use terms that are highly offensive to certain groups but in a qualitatively different manner. [11] A definition of offensive language can be generalized to mean language used in an amicable manner that does not intend for offense. For example,

African Americans using the term n*gga in daily online language [34], other profane terms such as b*tch, h*e, c*nt, *sshole, are used in quoting song lyrics and during affable conversations between peers. Profane language is common on social media and is seen as a normality [33], such that the category of offensive language is considered during hate speech detection. Anger is not an example of hate nor offensive language but is interrelated. For example, Team A just beat Team B in a sports game, fans of Team B goes to the main blog for fans of Team B and makes the comment "Team A is full of a bunch of b*tches," the word b*tch suggests offensive language but it is not, because the context was meant to be intentionally offensive; hate would not be a proper category either because this post did not promote hatred based on Team A's identity; anger would be the proper category because Team B posted this as an emotional response to losing the game and Team A's post. Fights, murders, suicides, are consequences of emotional responses like anger. For example, you fight someone because they offended you. You murder someone because they offended you deeply, inciting a large angry response.

Social media and other internet outlets have given freedom of expression a much larger platform [4]. Within this new platform, hate, anger, offensive language, and other examples of aggressive behavior can be shared freely. A common example of aggressive behavior within social media is trolling. Trolling means to "make a deliberately offensive or provocative online post with the aim of upsetting someone or eliciting an angry response from them" [1]. These angry responses turn into online arguments and debates which in some cases is contagious and can spread from user to user, especially on platforms like Twitter. Twitter gives users the options to like and to retweet tweets, both of which generally demonstrate unison or assent with each other in agreement with context. If a user tweets something hateful, offensive or even angry, there is an opportunity for other users to agree or speak out against with a reply or quote; these responses could potentially include profane language said in a manner to incite offense, whether the response includes a targeting based on the identity of the other user would determine if it is hate or anger. Sadly, not all free speech has positive implications [23]. Freedom of speech has created a hostile environment for many people [23]. Because of this growing issue [4], detection methods are relied on so executive decisions can be made and policies implemented to make the internet environment safer for the users. Social media platforms, like Twitter, have a reputation to randomly suspend accounts due to detection of spam, post-stealing, and improper or abusive language. [6, 20, 27, 32] Heavy reliance on detection methods leaves the platform vulnerable to error, because if the detection method is flawed or inaccurate, then users accounts will be shut down unjustly.

3 RESEARCH APPROACH

The goal of this paper is to review the literature and develop a more accurate and inclusive classification of anger-related social media post to be used for hate speech detection. Many people confuse a literature review with a research synthesis. According to Cooper [10], literature reviews can have one or more goals: to integrate (compare and contrast) what others have done and said, to criticize previous scholarly works, to build bridges between related topic areas, and/or to identify the central issues in a field. [10] The research approach for this paper follows along with the literature review goals outlined by Cooper [10]. The specific approach followed involved researching a topic, finding an area within that topic that could be expanded, formulating a hypothesis, researching keyword terms in specific search engines including Google, Google Scholar, ACM digital library, and integrating past research with the research findings and drawing overall conclusions related to the hypothesis.

4   RESULTS FROM REVIEW

Online blogs and news posts have discussed the power of anger and its influence in social media for the past five years [12, 13, 19, 30, 35], but there is hardly any published work relating anger and social media. Currently, studies do not consider anger as a plausible category to examine when detecting hate speech and analyzing social interactions, even with the vast amount of consequences that anger has presented in society. Table 1 can quantitatively show our findings after reviewing the literature.

In addition, there has been a scarce amount of published work relating aggressive behavior with computer-related social interactions. Hate speech relates to human behavior because it is an example of aggressive behavior. Ignoring the concept of aggressive behavior is an injustice to the studies of hate speech because it disregards the human aspect of the study. Overall, previous studies and papers are strictly focused on detecting hate language but have failed to acknowledge the variety of behaviors and emotions of the users and specify the category of human behavior that the study is focused on.

5   CONCLUSION

Future studies in hate speech detection should adopt our hypothesis of including anger in their detection methods and including an analysis of aggressive behavior in social media. When evaluating human and computer interaction, human behavior must be considered. Considering aggressive behavior as the overarching category puts a study into a better perspective when evaluating human behavior; aggressive behavior isn't a subcategory of hate, hate is a subcategory of aggressive behavior. Analyzing aggressive behavior in social media caters to the homogeneity of the users rather than strictly analyzing hate speech because it also considers offensive language, hate, anger, and other potential categories as well. Hate is interrelated with anger and offensive language. Hate

is a demonstration of negative emotions and actions toward someone because of their identity. Anger and offensive language are also demonstrations of negativity, but anger is intentional while offensive language could be considered non-intentional due to the qualitative manner it is used. These studies should also consider referencing the definitions located in table 2 which gives a definition, detection method, and an example statement to aid them within these analytical studies and algorithm building. The addition of anger in speech analysis and aggressive behavior as a concept allows the studies to be more specific in their analyses of certain user data. Being able to specifically analyze the intent of users posts and categorize the specific type of aggression opens the door to providing appropriate countermeasures to the users and provides properly organized and categorized data that can be used for future studies.

REFERENCES

[1] 2018. Trolling. https://www.merriam-webster.com
[2] Roy F Baumeister, Ellen Bratslavsky, Catrin Finkenauer, and Kathleen D Vohs. 2001. Bad is stronger than good. *Review of general psychology* 5, 4 (2001), 323.
[3] Leonard Berkowitz. 1993. *Aggression: Its causes, consequences, and control.* Mcgraw-Hill Book Company.
[4] Michal Bilewicz. 2018. A lecture: Hate speech Epidemics. Are We Far from March '68? http://www.polin.pl/en/event/a-lecture-hate-speech-epidemics-are-we-far-from-march-68
[5] Brittany Bostic. 2014. Does Social Media Perpetuate Youth Violence? http://yvpc.sph.umich.edu/social-media-perpetuate-youth-violence/
[6] Russell Brandom and Casey Newton. 2017. Twitter is locking accounts that swear at famous people. https://www.theverge.com/2017/2/24/14719828/twitter-account-lock-ban-swearing-abuse-moderation
[7] Joseph Burgo. 2013. The Difference Between Anger and Hatred. http://www.afterpsychotherapy.com/anger-vs-hatred/
[8] CBS/AP. 2016. Cyberbullying pushed Texas teen to commit suicide, family says. https://www.cbsnews.com/news/cyberbullying-pushed-texas-teen-commit-suicide-family/
[9] Elizabeth Chuck. 2017. Is Social Media Contributing to Rising Teen Suicide Rate. https://www.nbcnews.com/news/us-news/social-media-contributing-rising-teen-suicide-rate-n812426
[10] Harris Cooper. 2009. *Research Synthesis and Meta-Analysis: A Step-by-Step Approach.* SAGE.
[11] Thomas Davidson, Dana Warmsley, Michael Macy, and Ingmar Weber. 2017. Automated hate speech detection and the problem of offensive language. *arXiv preprint arXiv:1703.04009* (2017).
[12] Nick English. 2013. Anger is the Internet's most powerful emotion. https://www.usatoday.com/story/news/nation/2013/09/24/anger-internet-most-powerful-emotion/2863869/
[13] Rui Fan, Jichang Zhao, Yan Chen, and Ke Xu. 2014. Anger is more influential than joy: Sentiment correlation in Weibo. *PloS one* 9, 10 (2014), e110184.
[14] Natsuko Fukue. 2017. 'Social media suicide' in spotlight after Japan 'Twitter killer'. https://phys.org/news/2017-11-social-media-suicide-spotlight-japan.html
[15] Meredith E. Gansner. 2017. "The Internet Made Me Do It"-Social Media and Potential for Violence in Adolescents.". http://www.psychiatrictimes.com/blogs/internet-made-me-do-it-social-media-potential-violence-adolescents
[16] Jennifer Holladay. 2010. The stakes have never been higher for studentsâĂŤor schools. *teaching tolerance* (2010).
[17] Julia Jacobo. 2017. Family of cyber-bullied NJ girl who killed herself to sue school district for negligence. https://abcnews.go.com/US/family-cyber-bullied-nj-girl-killed-sue-school/story?id=48969586
[18] Tamara Jones. 2008. A Deadly Web of Deceit: A Teen's Online 'Friend' Proved False, And Cyber-Vigilantes Are Avenging Her. http://www.washingtonpost.com/wp-dyn/content/article/2008/01/09/AR2008010903367_pf.html
[19] Karen Pezza Leith and Roy F Baumeister. 1996. Why do bad moods increase self-defeating behavior? Emotion, risk tasking, and self-regulation. *Journal of personality and social psychology* 71, 6 (1996), 1250.
[20] Andrew Liptak. 2018. Twitter has suspended a number of accounts responsible for 'tweetdecking'. https://www.theverge.com/2018/3/11/17107192/twitter-tweetdecking-spam-suspended-accounts-mass-retweeting
[21] Jianghong Liu. 2004. Concept analysis: aggression. *Issues in mental health nursing* 25, 7 (2004), 693–714.
[22] David D Luxton, Jennifer D June, and Jonathan M Fairall. 2012. Social media and suicide: a public health perspective. *American journal of public health* 102, S2

Table 1: Quantitative results from review

	Journal/ Conference Papers	News Articles/ Editorials	Reports
Offensive Language	3	4	1
Hate	8	15	4
Anger	0	9	5

Table 2: Definition and detection method reference

Category	Definition	Detection Method	Example
Aggressive Speech	Any speech or language that demonstrates violence &/or induces (with or without intention) pain, harm, embarrassment, or injury.	Any examples of offensive language, hate or anger.	"Next person to bother me, is getting punched in the face" (Woman to another woman)
Offensive Language	Speech or language that could unintentionally offend, harm, or embarrass.	Specific terms that are deemed as offensive or hateful, but context and user profile is considered.	"You look so good b*tch" (AA to another AA) "Whatsup my n*gga" "I can't stand n*ggers"
Hate	Speech or language with the purpose to offend, harm, or embarrass a targeted group based on their identity.	Specific terms that are deemed as offensive or hateful that include offensive terms or offensive context related to the identity of a person or group.	"I'm f*cking sick of these Mexicans taking over all the available jobs, build the wall" "Black people annoy me always begging for handouts and affirmative action. Get out of my country!" "I'm f*cking pissed about that test"
Anger	Speech or language with the purpose of offending, harming, or embarrassing.	Specific terms that are deemed as offensive or hateful.	"Everyone can go jump off of a bridge"

(2012), S195–S200.

[23] Toni M Massaro. 1990. Equality and freedom of expression: The hate speech dilemma. *Wm. & Mary L. Rev.* 32 (1990), 211.

[24] Council of Europe. [n. d.]. Freedom of expression and information. https://www.coe.int/en/web/freedom-expression/freedom-of-expression-and-information-explanatory-memo

[25] Desmond Upton Patton, Jun Sung Hong, Megan Ranney, Sadiq Patel, Caitlin Kelley, Rob Eschmann, and Tyreasa Washington. 2014. Social media as a vector for youth violence: A review of the literature. *Computers in Human Behavior* 35 (2014), 548–553.

[26] Barbara Perry. 2002. *In the name of hate: Understanding hate crimes.* Routledge.

[27] Harry Pettit. 2017. Twitter's Time Out: Site's New Tool BLOCKS Users for 12 Hours for Abusive Behaviour. http://www.dailymail.co.uk/sciencetech/article-4230460/Twitter-blocking-users-12-hours.html

[28] Associated Press. 2017. Rise in teen suicide connected to social media popularity: study. https://nypost.com/2017/11/14/rise-in-teen-suicide-connected-to-social-media-popularity-study/

[29] Samantha Schmidt. 2017. After months of bullying, her parents say, a 12-year-old New Jersey girl killed herself. They blame the school.

https://www.washingtonpost.com/news/morning-mix/wp/2017/08/02/after-months-of-bullying-a-12-year-old-new-jersey-girl-killed-herself-her-parents-blame-the-school/ ?noredirect=on&utm_term=.4f2154c5911f

[30] Susanna Schrobsdorff. 2017. The Rage Flu: Why All This Anger Is Contagious and Making us Sick. http://time.com/4838673/anger-and-partisanship-as-a-virus/

[31] TeenSafe. 2016. Suicide Now the Second Leading Cause of Death For Teens; Is Social Media to Blame? https://www.teensafe.com/blog/suicide-now-second-leading-cause-death-teens-social-media-blame/

[32] Twitter. [n. d.]. The Twitter Rules. https://help.twitter.com/en/rules-and-policies/twitter-rules.

[33] Wenbo Wang, Lu Chen, Krishnaprasad Thirunarayan, and Amit P Sheth. 2014. Cursing in english on twitter. In *Proceedings of the 17th ACM conference on Computer supported cooperative work & social computing.* ACM, 415–425.

[34] William Warner and Julia Hirschberg. 2012. Detecting hate speech on the world wide web. In *Proceedings of the Second Workshop on Language in Social Media.* Association for Computational Linguistics, 19–26.

[35] Zoe Williams. 2017. We are all angry on social media âĂŞ at least try to listen to the rage of others. https://www.theguardian.com/commentisfree/2017/oct/09/angry-social-media-facebook-twitter-silicon-valley

The Effects of Anxiety and Preparation on Performance in Technical Interviews for HBCU Computer Science Majors

Phillip Hall, Jr.
Clemson University
School of Computing
Clemson, SC, USA
pwhall@g.clemson.edu

Kinnis Gosha
Morehouse College
Department of Computer Science
Atlanta, GA, USA
kinnis.gosha@morehouse.edu

ABSTRACT

Interview anxiety affects us all and research suggests that it can have a negative impact on interview performance. For that reason, a better understanding of how interview anxiety is affecting underrepresented minorities in computing should be a goal of academic institutions and companies who plan to hire these students. Technical computing interviews often require more than just knowing how to code, and students are not always aware of this. The current study investigates interview anxiety, interview performance among African-American students at Historically Black Institutions and the tools they use to prepare for interviews. Findings suggest that interview performance decreases as interview anxiety increases, supporting past research. Also, results suggest that experience going through interviews have a positive impact on interview anxiety. The major contributions of this work include: further understanding of the research literature for interview anxiety in relation to African American students in computing; incite in how this group of students prepare for interviews.

CCS CONCEPTS

• **Social and professional topics** → **Employment issues**; *Computing industry*; *Race and ethnicity*;

KEYWORDS

interview anxiety, technical interview, careers, HBCUs

ACM Reference Format:
Phillip Hall, Jr. and Kinnis Gosha. 2018. The Effects of Anxiety and Preparation on Performance in Technical Interviews for HBCU Computer Science Majors. In *SIGMIS-CPR '18: 2018 Computers and People Research Conference, June 18–20, 2018, Buffalo-Niagara Falls, NY, USA.* ACM, New York, NY, USA, 6 pages. https://doi.org/10.1145/3209626.3209707

1 INTRODUCTION

Preparing for a technical interview as a computer science student or graduate can be a stressful time. By the year 2020, software engineering jobs are expected to increase by 30% [28]. Recent diversity numbers released by bag tech companies like Google, Apple and

Facebook show a tremendous lack of African-American representation [2, 5, 18]. Not surprisingly, Google and Apple are two of the top three choices of where computer scientist graduates want to work according to a study by Global research and advisory firm Universum where 81,102 students from 359 US universities were surveyed [11].Less than 2% of technical roles are filled by African Americans at these top companies. Several top tech companies like Google, Facebook and Apple have developed relationships with HBCUs [13, 17, 19]in order to identify and interview candidates for entry level, software engineering positions however there has been no significant change in the number of African American technical workforce at those companies. The technical interview is seen as the major barrier for most students who wish to gain entry level software engineering positions at the top tech companies [22], thus how computer science students at HBCUs prepare for and perform on these interviews must be investigated in order to know why the diversity numbers at these top tech firms have not shown any significant growth in order to investigate this, two research questions will be addressed.

RQ1: How are CS students from Historically Black Institutions preparing for interviews?

The lack of African Americans in technical roles at top tech companies may come from one or combination of three things: lack of students that apply for entry level tech positions, lower performance on these interview by those who do apply or interest in applying altogether. In this paper, we will only investigate the option that students don't perform as well as their majority peers. The rationale for choosing this option is based on feedback provided to multiple CS faculty members at diversity events hosted by The United Negro College Fund and sponsored by these top tech companies: Ebay, Google, Amazon, Twitter, Facebook, NetApp, Uber [3]. Performance on the technical interview can be a product of the concepts that the students know and their problem solving ability, however other factors may contribute to the outcome of interview as well. One of those is anxiety.

RQ2: Does interview anxiety impact performance in technical interviews?

Technical interviews require more than being able to code, interviewees are rated on their problem solving, people, team working and critical thinking skills [15, 22]. All of these skills require cognitive functions that are influenced by stress and anxiety, specifically interview anxiety. Interview anxiety refers to nerves or jitters that individuals experience prior to and during the job interview. As a result, many candidates dread job interviews and experience negative thoughts about their performance in the days leading up to it [20]. Previous research by [30] suggests that anxious individuals are less likely to be hired in both simulated and real interview situations. As CS graduates leave their institutions behind they are expected to know how to deal with interview anxiety, what to expect on an interview, and to feel as if their institution prepared them adequately for interviewing.

The intent of the present investigation is to provide descriptive results to better understand the experience of interview anxiety among students at Historically Black Institutions in Computer Science majors by investigating the relationship between interview anxiety, interview performance and interviewing experience. To investigate this a few predictions have been made. Consistent with past research, first we hypothesized that interview anxiety and interview performance will be negatively correlated. Second, we predict that interviewing experience and interview anxiety will be negatively correlated. Thus, as interview experience increases, interviews anxiety levels on new interviews will decrease.

The following paper will present research on interview anxiety and its effects on performance, college students and how they prepare for technical interview and the representation of minorities in big tech. After that the study method and results will be discussed followed by a conclusion and future work section.

2 RELATED WORK
2.1 Interview Anxiety

Studies of anxiety and its negative effects on human performance are numerous and psychologists have theorized that moderate levels of anxiety are ideal [30]. Surprisingly, there are few studies of anxiety in employment interviewing contexts, where performance is a critical determinant in hiring decisions and anxiety levels are likely to be high. One study [14] says that most job applicants experience interview anxiety. Another study [26] found that interview anxiety negatively impacted interview self-efficacy, suggesting that one consequence of interview anxiety is reduced confidence that one can do well in an interview. Furthermore [14] found that individuals who are anxious in public-speaking situations and job interviews experience more verbal difficulties, and [8] discovered that anxiety has an effect on body language, communication, eye contact, voice levels, and projected confidence. The previously mentioned points are all hiring determinants [21]. Although interview specific anxiety may be related to long-term tendencies to be anxious (e.g., neuroticism), there is reason to believe that interview anxiety is a separate and specific state. For instance, having limited job prospects could increase interview anxiety, even for interviewees who would not normally be anxious during an interview, while having several offers in hand could decrease anxiety. Other cognitive research suggests that the ability to retrieve information from long-term memory tends to be impaired under conditions of stress [27]. For colleges, having a holistic understanding of interview anxiety can help with preparing students for interviews [8].

2.2 Preparing for Interviews
2.2.1 Interview Training in the Curriculum.
At Stanford University in California, CS students can register for a class entitled *Problem-Solving for the CS Technical Interview*. The course prepares students to interview for software engineering and related internships and full-time positions in industry [27]. The course requires students to synthesize information they have learned across different courses in the CS major. Emphasis is placed on the oral and combination written-oral modes of communication common in coding interviews, but which are an unfamiliar setting for problem solving for many students. According to [8], anxiety reduction therapy can be successfully embedded in classroom experiences. Stanford's efforts should cause a decrease in interview anxiety for students who complete the course. Laboratory work associated with an anxiety producing stimulus will reduce that performance anxiety dramatically without requiring additional"therapy time[8]." Other research conducted by [16, 23] suggest that best practices in interview training include variations of instructions and models of target skills, followed by practicing those skills and receiving feedback. This means that students do best in interviews when they are given a variety of"target skills" to practice and given feedback on their practice. According to the [1] 67% (N=699) of employers say that recent graduates need to improve their interview performance, suggesting that there is a need to improve interview training at academic institutions

Since high levels of anxiety are associated with inferior performance in many settings, it seems reasonable that instructors include employment interviewing and interview anxiety reduction mechanisms in the curriculum. Unless a student has experienced a technical interview, knows someone who has, or done their own research, they have no idea what to expect.

2.2.2 Online Interview Training.
With the popularity and demand for code rapidly growing, more ways for individuals to learn how to code, practice code and prepare for coding interviews are being introduced. There are several websites that offer code interview training. Leetcode.com, InterviewCake.com, InterviewBit.com offer practice on historically asked coding interview questions and claim to help interviewees land offers at companies like Google, Facebook and more. InterviewCake.com guarantees its paid users a job or their money back. InterviewCake.com offers free access to some of the site content but users have to pay a one-time fee of $599 to get full access to all courses on the site. Pramp.com is a site that believes its users should not prepare for interviews alone and gives them the opportunity to practice with real people. Using video conferencing, users can train with peers and professionals online to improve programming interview skills. Other websites like Coursera.com and Udacity.com offer courses that users take to learn how to code or to improve their coding skills, although these websites are not targeted toward interview training they do offer code practice outside of a classroom setting.

2.2.3 Textbook Training.
At the time of this writing, *Cracking the Coding Interview: 189 Programming Questions and Solutions 6th Edition* was the bestselling

book in the Data Structure and Algorithms section on Amazon.com, the largest book retailer in the world [9]. Another title by Adnan, Tsung-Hsien and Amit is *Elements of Programming Interviews: The Insiders' Guide* [6].

2.3 Resources at Historically Black Institutions

Historically Black Institutions have always lagged behind funding for predominantly White land-grant universities for over 100 years, and it is only getting worse [4]. This impacts the amount of quality professors, as well as the quality of learning resources institutions can provide for their students. This should concern CS departments at Historically Black Institutions, students are expected to not only be prepared to perform on the job but also to ace the interview.

Preparation is very important for a technical CS interview. [10] suggests that Black and Hispanic students are unaware of how to prepare for an interview for a major tech company. The article states that Black and Hispanic students are not aware of what the technical interview consists of therefore do not know how to prepare. It is also important to point out that very few CS professors at a Historically Black Institutions have experienced a technical interview at a major tech company. Ten professors (including the authors of this manuscript) representing 10 different Historically Black Institutions went through a software engineering interview at Google while participating in a six-week long faculty workshop. Researchers held interviews with three professors who were part of that group; they gave feedback on their experiences. For most of the professors it was their first time experiencing an industry style technical computing interview. One professor of over 10 years stated that during the interview they felt as if they were taking a final exam in college all over again, "I was extremely nervous" stated one professor. Another professor of 15 years also mentioned being very nervous. If professors have not experienced these types of interviews or are not aware of what they consist of; how can they be expected prepare their students for these interviews?

2.4 Underrepresented Minority Presence in Tech Industry

Currently the tech industry is experiencing an issue with diversity and lags when it comes to hiring minorities [29]. Many companies are currently going great lengths to fix this issue, but numbers continue to stay stagnant even when minorities are getting CS degrees [29]. Google recently pledged $265 million, while Apple and Microsoft pledged over $50 million towards increasing diversity numbers [5, 17]. In the summer of 2017, Google launched two major programs, "Howard West" and "HBCU Faculty in Residence". Howard West was a program that brought 25-30 juniors and faculty from Howard's CS program to Google's headquarters in Silicon Valley for 12 weeks to take courses co-taught by Google software engineers [19]. HBCU Faculty in Residence was a six week program (attended by by both authors of the paper) where 30 HBCU CS faculty worked at Google as interns, with the job of learning about the culture of Google as well as developing curriculum in collaboration with Google engineers based on what they learned. Another Google program, Google in Residence, is a program where a Google software engineer moves to the city where an HBCU is located and teaches a freshman level CS course [17]. In 2015, Apple made a $40 million dollar multi-year commitment, the largest and most comprehensive corporate investment ever given exclusively for students and faculty of four-year HBCUs [24].

Given the diversity numbers, one has to assume one of the following: interview performance must not be adequate, students are not applying for these jobs, or students are applying but not landing interviews. [7] says that minority college students often report higher rates of anxiety than their white peers, suggesting that white CS students experience less interview anxiety, which may result in better performance in interviews than their underrepresented peers. When discussing interview anxiety amongst this population, imposter syndrome must be addressed. Research has suggested that underrepresented minorities do exhibit higher levels of imposter syndrome than their white counterparts [12]. Those who suffer from impostor syndrome cannot grasp or believe in their successes, even if they are high achieving, leading them to feel like frauds. In some cases impostor syndrome can degrade mental health [12]. From all of this we can assume that interview anxiety among recent college graduates and students could affect diversity numbers in the computing industry.

3 EXPERIMENTAL DESIGN

A quantitative research study was conducted in order to answer the following two research questions,"How are CS students from Historically Black Institutions preparing for interviews?" and "Does interview anxiety impact performance in technical interviews?". Undergraduate computer science majors were recruited from a Historically Black Institution in southeastern United States to participate in the study. Students who were upperclassmen (junior and seniors) were preferred to participate in the study since they would have more experience participating in technical interviews. Additionally, students were not required to have had participated in a technical interview in order to participate in the study since they would be able to answer some questions about what they know in order to study for a technical interview. A convenience sample was chosen to give the largest number of responses with the small number of students available. The survey was administered to the participants electronically. The students who participated where all enrolled in a 400 level required CS course. Students were asked to complete a survey in exchange for a movie style box of candy.

3.1 Procedure

The survey asked questions about experiences with technical interviews. Participants were asked to answer questions for each technical interview they experienced. The following questions were used in analysis: How many technical computing interviews have you been on?, How many hours per week do you spend preparing for interviews? How familiar are you with the following interview prepping resources? The first question recorded the amount of interviews each participant had been on, this question was later used in the data analysis to split the participants into two groups. The second question was asked in intervals: None, 1-5 hours a week, 6-10 hours a week, 11-15 hours a week, more than 16 hours. This allowed researchers to gather data participant practice habits. The third was a likert scale question with five options: Extremely Familiar, Very Familiar, Moderately Familiar, Slightly Familiar, Not Familiar At All, that recorded participant familiarity with the following interview practice tools: Cracking the Coding Interview: 189 Programming Questions and Solutions Book, InterviewBit.com, InterviewCake.com, CourseEra.com, Udacity.com, Pramp.com and Mock Interviews. For each interview, students completed a State Trait Anxiety Inventory (STAI-Y) Scale. The STAI-Y is the most widely used self-reported measure of anxiety, developed in 1977 by Charles Spielberger.

3.2   Measures

Students were asked to complete a STAI-Y scale for every interview. An interview anxiety score was generated from the scale values. Students rated their performance for each interview. The students were also asked to report how many technical interviews they had experienced. Additionally, student were also asked about the number of hours they practice/prepare for technical interviews and what tools they used to prepare for those interviews.

4   RESULTS

Nine (9) juniors and 15 seniors were asked how familiar they were with the seven interview training tools listed previously, see Table 1.

There were five juniors and seven seniors, the average age was 21, with the oldest being 23, the youngest being 20. The amount of interviews per participant varied with 2(N=3) being the lowest and 6(N=1) being the most. Participants were put into two groups based off interview experience:

Group 1: <= 3 interviews (N=7)
Group 2: > 3 interviews (N=5)

Two independent sample t-tests were conducted to test for significance between groups for the first and last interview, used as two separate conditions. Interview anxiety means were calculated using interview anxiety levels from each condition. There was no

Table 1: Familiarity with Coding Interview Resources
1-Extremely familiar, 2-Very familiar, 3-Moderately familiar, 4-Slightly familiar, 5-Not familiar at all

How familiar are you with the following interview training resources?	1	2	3	4	5
InterviewBit.com	4%	0%	17%	17%	63%
Cracking the Coding Interview: 189 Programming Questions and Solutions Book	25%	33%	13%	21%	8%
InterviewCake.com	0%	4%	21%	8%	58%
CourseEra.com	8%	4%	21%	8%	25%
Udacity.com	21%	21%	25%	8%	25%
Pramp.com	0%	4%	12%	8%	75%
Mock Interviews	46%	8%	25%	8%	13%

significant difference between group anxiety levels in their first and last interviews.

4.1   Interview Anxiety effects on Interview Performance

For both groups, the relationship between interview anxiety and interview performance during their first and last interviews gave negative correlations (r = -.38, r = -.42). As anxiety went up performance went down, this supports past research on interview anxiety effects on performance.

4.2   Interview Experience effect on Interview Anxiety

A within group paired sample t-test revealed that students in Group 1 interview anxiety level in the last interview was significantly higher compared to the first interview (p=.04), while Group 2 showed no significance (p=.4).

Due to this finding, a one-way ANOVA was conducted for Group 1 to compare the effect of interview experience on interview anxiety for their first interview and their final interview. There was a significant effect of interview experience on interview anxiety at the p < .05 level for the two conditions [F(1,12) = 4.8, p = .048].

All participants anxiety levels went up on their second and/or third interview. But after four interviews participant interview anxiety level remained normal or decreased. This could suggest that because students in Group 2 had four or more interviews, their anxiety level on their last interview was not significantly higher than it was for participants in Group 1 on their last interview.

4.3   Interview Preparedness

Since every participant experienced a minimum of 2 interviews researchers decided to use the data reported for interviews 1 & 2 for the following analysis.

When preparing for interviews; students reported that they use mock interviews 58% of the time, online tools leetcode.com or hackeron.com 16% of the time, and 12% of the time students used the Cracking the Coding Interview book. Table 3 shows the complete analysis. Based on this data we can assume that students prefer mock interviews, over other interview training tools, and based on past research mock interviews have a positive impact on interview anxiety.

When asked how many hours were spent per week preparing for interviews, 50% spend between 1 and 5 hours, while 25% stated they do not practice at all, See Table 2 for full breakdown.

Table 2: Time Preparing for Interviews

How many hours do you spend a week preparing for interviews?		
1-5 hours	6-10 hours	None
50%	25%	25%

Table 3: Methods for Preparing for Interviews

What tools did you use to prepare for the interview?	
Mock Interviews	58.3%
Online Tools	16.7%
Cracking The Code Interview Book	12.5%
Did Not Prepare	12.5%

5 CONCLUSIONS

5.1 Discussion

The current study provided empirical support for our first hypothesis that an individual's interview performance will be negatively impacted as their anxiety increases, supporting previous research but offering new insight for this particular demographic. The current study also provides support for our second hypothesis, there was a significant effect on interview anxiety due to interview experience. Students who had more experience going on interviews were less likely to experience higher anxiety. This finding suggests that by going through more interviews students can improve their interview anxiety which should improve their performance. As mentioned earlier, underrepresented minority students are less likely to be aware of how to prepare for technical interviews, and many may not even go through an interview due imposter syndrome. But accordingly, to the concurrent data, experiencing as many interviews as possible could be the trick to performing well. This makes sense, but students who suffer from imposter syndrome may also feel like they don't have many chances to fail an interview at a prestigious company. Therefore, going through an interview and not getting the job, translates to many as never getting a job with that company. When the reality is that many of the employees at these prestigious companies failed the interview process more than once before getting the job [25]. Interview anxiety deserves the attention of universities and companies, in order to understand and be aware during interviews with individuals from certain demographics.

All participants stated they either reviewed old classwork, used an online tool, used the cracking the code book, used mock interviews, or nothing at all to prepare for the interviews they listed. Mock interviews were the most utilized interview preparation intervention across all participants. Past research suggests that mock interviews could be the best way to combat interview anxiety, but a downside to mock interviews is that they require time coordinating for at least two individuals. Time that is not always available or easy to come by for a college student, and in academic environments where resources are already limited, providing access to unlimited mock interviews is not realistic. Students should have unlimited access to interview training tools that incorporate, as best as possible, all the sensations experienced in a mock interview.

As time progresses, we believe more training tools will become available. Ideally, these tools will incorporate some mechanism to allow their users to simulate the technical interview process in order to mitigate the negative impacts of interview anxiety. If CS faculty wants to adequately prepare their students for an entry level software engineering position at a major tech company, curriculum should include activities or coursework to help students prepare for technical interviews.

InterviewCake.com guarantees a job or your money back, but in this group of students, majority of them never heard of the website.

5.2 Limitations & Future Work

Limitations in the study include a small sample size of participants and the lack of students from multiple HBCUs participating in the study. Also, gender was not asked nor was the career goals of each participant asked in the survey instrument. Future research should incorporate students from multiple HBCUs as well as students from non-HBCU institutions to serve as a control group. Also, the relation between how students prepare for interviews and interview performance should be investigated. Will certain tools, if available, cause students to perform better or worse? Also, research should be done creating and testing new tools that would give students an "authentic" interview experience, similar to mock interviews, but that do not require as much time sacrifice. Data on the amount of job offers, or interviews, participants had at the time of going through an interview was not included in this paper. Future work on this data could present some correlations between interview anxiety, or performance, and the amount of offers, or interviews, on an individual's schedule.

6 ACKNOWLEDGEMENTS

Funding for this research was made possible by the National Science Foundation, Division Of Human Resource Development (Award #1547793).

REFERENCES

[1] 2012. *The Role of Higher Education in Career Development: Employer Preparations*. The Chronicle of Higher Education. http://www.chronicle.com/items/biz/pdf/Employers%20Survey.pdf

[2] 2017. Facebook Diversity Update: Building a more diverse, inclusive workforce. (2017). https://fbnewsroomus.files.wordpress.com/2017/08/fb_diversity_2017_final.pdf

[3] 2017. HBCU ICE | 2017 UNCF HBCU Innovation Summit. (2017). http://www.hbcuinnovation.org/

[4] 2017. *A Looming Crisis for HBCUs? An Analysis of Funding Sources for Land Grant Universities*. National Education Association. http://www.nea.org/assets/docs/NEA%20CGPS%20Research%20HBCU%20Brief%202.pdf

[5] Apple. 2018. Inclusion & Diversity. (2018). https://www.apple.com/diversity/

[6] Adnan Aziz, Amit Prakash, and Tsung-Hsien Lee. 2012. *Elements of programming interviews.*

[7] Jeremy Bauer-Wolf. 2017. Feeling Like Imposters. (2017). https://www.insidehighered.com/news/2017/04/06/study-shows-impostor-syndromes-effect-minority-students-mental-health.

[8] Ralph R. Behnke and Chris R. Sawyer. 1999. Milestones of anticipatory public speaking anxiety. *Communication Education* 48, 2 (1999), 165–172. https://doi.org/10.1080/03634529909379164

[9] Jeff Bercovici. 2014. Amazon Vs. Book Publishers, By the Number. (2014). https://www.forbes.com/sites/jeffbercovici/2014/02/10/amazon-vs-book-publishers-by-the-numbers/#6d2e62934ef9.

[10] Quoctrung Bui and Claire Cain Miller. 2016. Why Tech Degrees Are Not Putting More Blacks and Hispanics Into Tech Jobs. (2016). https://www.nytimes.com/2016/02/26/upshot/dont-blame-recruiting-pipeline-for-lack-of-diversity-in-tech.html

[11] A Cain. 2017. 15 places where computer science majors dream of working. (2017). http://www.businessinsider.com/dream-companies-and-organizations-for-computer-science-students-2017-5.

[12] Kevin Cokley, Leann Smith, Donte Bernard, Ashley Hurst, Stacey Jackson, Steven Stone, Olufunke Awosogba, Chastity Saucer, Marlon Bailey, and Davia Roberts.

2017. Impostor feelings as a moderator and mediator of the relationship between perceived discrimination and mental health among racial/ethnic minority college students. *Journal of Counseling Psychology* 64, 2 (2017), 141–154. https://doi.org/10.1037/cou0000198

[13] Emily DeRuy. 2015. Apple Pledges $40 Million to HBCUs in Scholarships and Support. (2015). https://www.theatlantic.com/politics/archive/2015/09/apple-pledges-40-million-to-hbcus-in-scholarships-and-support/432726/

[14] Amanda R. Feiler and Deborah M. Powell. 2013. Interview anxiety across the sexes: Support for the sex-linked anxiety coping theory. *Personality and Individual Differences* 54, 1 (2013), 12–17. https://doi.org/10.1016/j.paid.2012.07.030

[15] George Forman. 2003. An extensive empirical study of feature selection metrics for text classification. *Journal of machine learning research* 3, Mar (2003), 1289–1305.

[16] John P. Galassi and Merna Dee Galassi. 1978. Preparing Individuals for job Interviews: Suggestions From More Than 60 Years of Research. *The Personnel and Guidance Journal* 57, 4 (1978), 188–192. https://doi.org/10.1002/j.2164-4918.1978.tb05142.x

[17] Google. 2017. Hiring diverse Googlers: We're expanding the ways we look for Googlers and creating additional pathways to Google. (2017). https://www.google.com/diversity/hiring.html

[18] Google. 2018. Our Workplace - Google Diversity. (2018). https://diversity.google/commitments/

[19] Jessica Guynn. 2017. Google opens Howard University West to train black coders. (2017). https://www.usatoday.com/story/tech/news/2017/03/23/howard-university-google/99518020/

[20] Richard G. Heimberg, Kevin E. Keller, and Theresa A. Peca-Baker. 1986. Cognitive assessment of social-evaluative anxiety in the job interview: Job Interview Self-Statement Schedule. *Journal of Counseling Psychology* 33, 2 (1986), 190–195. https://doi.org/10.1037//0022-0167.33.2.190

[21] Allen I. Huffcutt, Chad H. Van Iddekinge, and Philip L. Roth. 2011. Understanding applicant behavior in employment interviews: A theoretical model of interviewee performance. *Human Resource Management Review* (2011). https://doi.org/10.1016/j.hrmr.2011.05.003

[22] Gayle Laakmann McDowell. 2015. *Cracking the coding interview: 189 Programming Questions and Solutions* (6 ed.). CareerCup.

[23] Van M. Latham. 1987. Interviewee Training: A Review of Some Empirical Literature. *Journal of Career Development* 14, 2 (1987), 96–107. https://doi.org/10.1177/089484538701400204

[24] Samara Lynn. 2015. Apple Rewards 30 HBCU Students Scholarships in $40 Million Dollar Diversity Effort. (2015). http://www.blackenterprise.com/technology/apple-awards-30-hbcu-students-scholarships-in-40-million-diversity-effort/

[25] Shannon Shaper. 2017. How many interviews does it take to hire a Googler? (2017). https://rework.withgoogle.com/blog/google-rule-of-four/

[26] Stuart A. Tross and Todd J. Maurer. 2008. The effect of coaching interviewees on subsequent interview performance in structured experience-based interviews. *Journal of Occupational and Organizational Psychology* 81, 4 (2008), 589–605. https://doi.org/10.1348/096317907x248653

[27] Standford University. 2017. CS9: Problem-Solving for the CS Technical Interview. (2017). http://web.stanford.edu/class/cs9/

[28] U.S. Bureau of Labor Statistics. 2015. Computer and Information Technology Occupations. (2015). https://www.bls.gov/ooh/computer-and-information-technology/home.htm

[29] Elizabeth Weise and Jessica Guynn. 2014. Tech jobs: Minorities have degrees, but don't get hired. (2014). https://www.usatoday.com/story/tech/2014/10/12/silicon-valley-diversity-tech-hiring-computer-science-graduates-african-american-hispanic/14684211/

[30] Melissa J. Young, Ralph R. Behnke, and Yvonne M. Mann. 2004. Anxiety patterns in employment interviews. *Communication Reports* 17, 1 (2004), 49–57. https://doi.org/10.1080/08934210409389373

Technostress creators and burnout:
A Job Demands-Resources Perspective

Monalisa Mahapatra
Indian Institute of Management Kozhikode
IIMK Campus P. O., 673570
monalisam09fpm@iimk.ac.in

Surya Prakash Pati
Indian Institute of Management Kozhikode
IIMK Campus P. O., 673570
spp@iimk.ac.in

ABSTRACT

Although [1] prior research has examined the influence of technostress creators on various job outcomes, insights into the influence of individual technostress creators and their impacts on job outcomes are rather limited. In this research, by providing a technological component to the existing Job Demand-Resource framework, we investigate the relationship between individual technostress creators and burnout in an Indian context. We also examine the interaction among technostress creators to identify the mediating impact of techno-invasion and techno-insecurity. Analyzing a total of 163 responses, collected through an online survey we found encouraging pieces of evidence for our hypotheses. Specifically, our findings revealed that among the five technostress creators, only techno-invasion and techno-insecurity are positively related to burnout in an employee. The contributions of the study to theory and practice are also discussed.

KEYWORDS

IT and systems use; Technostress; Job Demands-Resources Model; Burnout

ACM Reference format:
Monalisa Mahapatra, Ryan, and Surya Prakash Pati. 2018. Technostress creators and burnout: A Job Demands-Resources Perspective. In Proceedings of ACM SIGMIS-CPR'18, June 18-20, 2018, Buffalo-Niagara Falls, NY, USA, 7 pages. http://dx.doi.org/10.1145/ 3209626.3209711

1 INTRODUCTION

The expeditious growth of Information and Communication Technologies [ICTs] over the past few decades has dramatically influenced organizations and individuals. Adoption of ICTs catalyzes business processes by redefining old organizational structures and creating new employment [36]. Even traditional non-IT sectors like agriculture and construction are now embracing ICTs to become competitive [2, 37, 30]. Organizations are implementing ICTs to increase their productivity, effectiveness and, efficiency [7, 27]. For employees across the globe, pervasive ICTs have made it feasible to connect anytime to support and improve business processes and organizational decision making [18, 10].

Although the ubiquity of ICTs provide a great deal of benefits, they have the potential to cause harmful and unintended consequences as well. In this study, we focus on one such adverse effects of ICTs known as Technostress [TS], which relates to the stress experienced by the employees due to their use of ICTs [36]. Recent studies in Information Systems [IS] have examined the antecedents and consequences of TS, which has been shown to negatively influence various job outcomes such as productivity, job satisfaction, end-user performance, job engagement etc. [45, 44, 43]. Prior research has also established that TS can be the outcome of information fatigue and perceived work overload that lead to demotivated and dissatisfied employees [36, 3].

Despite the well-documented research on the concept TS in an organization, there exist certain gaps that need further attention. First, except a few studies, the extant literature has described TS creators as a second-order construct in an aggregated form without considering the individual impact of its five major dimensions—techno-overload, techno-invasion, techno-complexity, techno-insecurity and techno-uncertainty on different dependent variables [9, 21]. It will be practically and theoretically interesting to understand how and to what extent each of these five dimensions individually influences various job outcomes under different context. While major empirical studies on TS were conducted and tested amongst European and American employees, in this article we aim to capture TS in Indian workplace [3,45]. With the widespread application of ICTs, India is becoming one of the largest and fastest growing economy across the globe supported by a rapidly developing technology infrastructure. As per NASSCOM report, India's Information Technology (IT) industry is projected to grow by 8% in FY2017 to USD 154 billion (NASSCOM, 2017). Not only the IT sector, ICTs adoption and diffusion can be seen almost all the sectors in India including healthcare, service industries, education systems, construction industry etc. Despite the potential benefits of ICTs use, various reports and articles showed that employees feel stressed out and face work-life imbalance. Hence managers need to understand the particular techno-stressors that have negative impacts on Indian employees. Secondly, the Job Demand-Resource (JD-R) framework, one of the widely used stress model listed down plenty of job demands that have negative impacts on employees [40]. However, the model is absent of a technological context and we argue that with the Omni-present nature of technology in organizational settings, it is important to include a technological component to the JD-R model.

Hence to address the above-mentioned gaps, using the JD-R Model, we proposed that each individual dimension of TS creator act as a demand that influence burnout. Burnout is a negative job outcome that comes in response to prolonged chronic stressors on the job [26].

Incorporating all the above points, the research question we aim to address in this study is:

RQ: How does each TS creators as a job demand individually influence burnout among employees?

The present study makes three key contributions. Firstly, by using the lens of JD-R model we provide a theoretical contribution to TS research. Secondly, by doing this, we added five new demands such as techno-overload, techno-invasion, techno-complexity, techno-insecurity and techno-uncertainty to the already existing demands of JD-R model [40]. Thirdly, this study can be used by IS managers and practitioners to understand how five different technological characteristics induce burnout amongst employees differently.

2 LITERATAURE REVIEW AND THEORY

2.1 Technostress

Clinical psychologist Craig Brod [1984] defined TS as "a modern disease of adaptation caused by an inability to cope with new computer technologies in a healthy manner." In 2007, Tarafdar et al. first extended the original concept of TS, developed and empirically validate the TS scale, thereby initiating active IS research in this field [45].

TS is defined as the stress experienced by the end users of ICTs [36]. It is also defined as the phenomenon of 'stress caused by an inability to cope with the demands of organizational computer usage' [44]. Based on the role theory and sociotechnical theory the second order construct TS creators were conceptually developed and empirically validated [45]. Drawing reference from the transaction based model of stress, TS creators represent the factors that create TS among an individual. The five different dimensions to TS creators are Techno-overload, Techno-invasion, Techno-complexity, Techno-insecurity and Techno-uncertainty. First, techno-overload deals with overloaded information in a limited time that forces employees to work faster and longer. Techno-invasion deals with the Omni-present effect of technology which essentially blurred the line between work-home balances and creates unnecessary disturbances. The third dimension, techno-complexity is about the complexities

associated with technologies. Due to this, employees may not be able to develop new skills frequently and their use of existing skills to new technologies may result in creating issues and errors. Techno-insecurity creates a fear of job loss in employees as they perceive new technologies may lead to automation or people with better skills and abilities will replace them in a long run. Finally, techno-uncertainty deals with the frequent and innovative technical changes that make workers uncertain about their work and job roles.

Thanks to all-pervasiveness nature of TS, research on it has invited significant attention from practitioners and scholars, examining both its antecedents and consequences. For example, studies showed TS creators negatively influenced employee productivity, job satisfaction and organizational commitment [45, 36]. However organizational mechanisms like literacy facilitation, technical support provision, involvement facilitations and perceived organizational support act as TS inhibitors that potentially reduce these negative impacts [36, 49]. Various factors like work culture, technology characteristics, and personality traits also play an important role in TS research. Study showed that employees from more centralized companies often perceive more TS and it is highest in companies that are highly innovative and centralize [47]. In another study, using Person-environment fit model as a theoretical lens, [3] proposed that specific technology characteristics like usability, intrusiveness, and dynamism are related to various workplace stressors by controlling negative affectivity and technology usage. Studies also showed that TS decreases with the increase in computer efficacy, education, and age while personality traits moderate the relationship between TS creators and job outcomes [42, 43].

Despite the widespread study of the phenomena, TS creators are always treated as the second order construct. Though there are two papers that emphasized on studying the individual dimensions, they do not provide any empirical results of such analysis [9, 21]. Other than these, to the best of our knowledge, none of the existing studies have examined the individual influence of TS creators on job burnout using the conceptual framework of JD-R model which is recognized as one of the leading job stress models [40]. To capture this gap, we used JD-R model to argue the positive impacts of individual TS creators on burnout among employees dealing with ICTs in their regular workplace setting

2.2 Burnout

Maslach characterized burnout as a syndrome of emotional exhaustion, depersonalization, and reduced personal accomplishment that can occur among people who do "people work" of some kind [55]. This definition highlights the relevance of burnout among professionals who primarily deals with human services, rather than information or things. Against this limitation, Demerouti et al. proposed a more generalized model of burnout i.e. the JD-R model [13]. This model assumes that irrespective of the type of work setting, high job demands and limited job resources can give rise to a negative consequence known as burnout. Conceptually burnout manifests as three different dimensions, i.e. overwhelming exhaustion, feelings of cynicism and detachment from the job, and a sense of ineffectiveness and lack of accomplishment [56].

Job burnout is one of the frequently used job outcomes in organizational studies. It has been associated with several negative work outcomes like high absenteeism, job dissatisfaction, low organizational commitment, higher turnover intention etc. (refer Maslach & Leiter, 2016 for a detailed review). Also, it has been widely examined amongst different professionals like teachers, police, health care professionals, athletes, social workers etc. (Kop et al., 1999; Ozyurt et al., 2006; Gustafsson et al., 2007; Kim & Stoner, 2008). In TS literature, Srivastava et al. (2015) studied the impact of TS creators on job burnout along with the moderating impact of big five personality traits. In our study, we also examine job burnout as the dependent variable as per JD-R model. However we consider the individual impact of each TS creators on burnout instead of considering the second order construct TS creators.

2.3. Job Demands-Resources model

The job demand-resource model [JD-R] is one of the leading job stress models that includes a broad range of job demands and job resources [4, 13]. The model was first developed to explain the antecedents of burnout and further revised multiple times. JD-R model assumes that employee health and well-being result from a balance between positive [resources] and negative [demands] job characteristics. Here job demands were defined as "those physical, social, or organizational aspects of the job that require sustained physical or mental effort and are therefore associated with certain physiological and psychological costs" [13]. While such job demands are not inherently negative in nature, the high effort associated with meeting those demands may lead to exhaustion. Similarly, job resources were defined as "those physical, social, or organizational aspects of the job that may do any of the following: [a] be functional in achieving work goals, [b] reduce job demands and the associated physiological and psychological costs, [c] stimulate personal growth and development" [13, p. 501]. Job resources are therefore important not only to accomplish work objectives but also personally for the individual [39]. Thus The JD-R framework assumes two processes, the energetic process of being worn out by high job demands that exhaust the individual, and the motivational process whereby the lack of resources siphon off resolve which foster mental withdrawal or disengagement [39]. The modified version of the initial JD-R model further added work engagement along with burnout, thus providing a holistic picture with both positive and negative psychological state [39]. The model is one of the leading job stress models due to its heuristic nature and flexibility to adhere to a wider variety of work settings [40].

In IS domain, a study among teleworkers demonstrates that time pressure, role ambiguity, and role conflict lead to exhaustion while autonomy, feedback, and social support increase engagement at work [38]. Another research highlights that interruptions and work-life conflicts are the demands and accessibility and efficient communication are resources associated with social media usage at work [53]. Similarly, Ghislieri et al. (2017) investigated the relationship between off-work hours technology assisted job demand and work-family conflict [17].

However, these studies mostly implemented the theoretical lens of JD-R to determine the job demands and resources that are related to particular IT artifacts or specific IS professionals. Also, the factors were always the physical, social, or organizational aspects of the job as defined originally [13, p. 501]. As technology inclusion is widely prevalence in various functionalities and business processes of an organization, ICTs have become a crucial part of daily work. It is becoming impossible to perform tasks and jobs without technology incorporation [51]. On one hand, the adoption and diffusion of ICTs have greatly improved the production efficiency, quality and effectiveness [7, 27]. On the other hand, from the perspective of employees, using ICTs requires high physical, social, and cognitive skills [3]. With the implementation of ever-evolving ICTs for competitive advantage jobs are becoming complex with increased interdependency which demands a lot of efforts from the employees. In such scenario, we argue that JD-R model is absent of a technological context which is highly essential in today's work environment. Hence, individual TS creators can act as job demands to essentially provide the required technological component to the existing JD-R model. The detailed elaboration of this argument will be given in the hypotheses development section.

3 RESEARCH MODEL & HYPOTHESES

3.1 Technostress Creators and Burnout

According to the JD-R framework every occupation may have its own specific factors that can give rise to job stress and these factors can be categorized to two broad groups, i.e. job demands and job resources [13]. A few examples of job demands in occupational context include role conflict, time pressure, problems planning, and reorganization while job resources can be safety climate, team harmony, performance feedback, and innovative climate [see 40 for the detailed list]. High job demands force employees to put additional effort to achieve work goals which comes with some psychological and physical costs such as fatigue and irritability [13]. Employees may recover from this by taking a break, switching tasks, or performing less demanding activities [40]. However, when such recovery is insufficient, the individual is in a continued state of activation that gradually exhausts her/him physically and/or mentally leading to burnout [40]. Referring to the above explanations of job demands and burnout, in the below description we will postulate individual TS creators as job demands that lead to burnout.

The first dimension of TS creators, *techno-overload (TO)* describes situation where ICTs force employees to work faster and longer [36]. With the availability of multiple data channels such as internet, smart phones, internal company sources etc., employees are exposed to unlimited information at a faster pace that they can handle and use effectively [14]. This essentially leads to the problem of information overload where it becomes difficult to identify relevant information and to set practical cut-offs and priorities regarding new information [44, 9]. Studies also show that information overload has a substantial influence on the experiencing of stress, working overtime, taking work home, and loss of job satisfaction [23, 5].

Techno-invasion (TINV), the second TS creator describes the invasive effect of ICTs in situations where employees can be reached anytime and feel the need to be constantly connected [45]. This essentially blurred the boundary between work and home as employees work odd hours and perceive the loss of privacy [25, 9]. Thus, techno-invasion leads to work-family conflict which triggers work-exhaustion [1, 16].

Techno-complexity (TCOM) describes situations where the complexity associated with ICTs leads users to feel inadequate with regard to their computer skills and forces them to spend time and effort in learning and understanding ICTs [36]. In today's world organizations are always under pressure to implement latest technologies for competitive advantages which lead to frequent ICTs update [14]. This leads to problems like systems crashes, data getting lost, and lack of technical help at all times and employees have to cope with it [9]. As modern ICTs are complex it creates "skill discrepancy" where employees have to spend much of their time learning how to use the new ICTs as existing skills are not sufficient [31]. On the other hand use of systems like ERP, CRM etc., creates interdependencies that required interactions and collaborative efforts between different functions and organizational branches across the globe. This forces employees to go beyond the traditional silo management which creates role conflict based on culture, perspectives, and competencies [45]. The literature extensively showed that role conflict and role overload leads to stress and burnout among employees [41, 19, 52].

Techno-insecurity (TINS) and *techno-uncertainty (TUNC)* are the fourth and final dimensions of TS creators. The former one associates with situations where users feel threatened about losing their jobs, either because of automation from ICTs or to other people who have a better understanding of ICTs while the later refers to contexts where continuing ICTs change and upgrade unsettle employees and create uncertainty [45]. Because of ever evolving ICTs in organizations, employees often find it difficult to develop a base of knowledge or a meaningful pattern and their existing knowledge became obsolete [24, 50]. Due to this even employees who are keen about learning new applications eventually get frustrated which leads to stress and interpersonal conflicts [12, 54]. Also implementation of certain ICTs like ERP systems required significant process and configuration changes to offer best practices which may not be accepted by all the employees [36]. Thus, they may feel threatened due to the lack of control on their jobs which the technology imposes, thus reducing the job satisfaction and limiting their effectiveness and efficiency [9].

Hence, we proposed that characteristics like techno-overload, techno-invasion, techno-complexity, techno-insecurity, and techno-uncertainty act as job demands which need greater degree of efforts from the employees to deal with. In the absence of suitable situational or individual coping mechanisms, these demands gradually exhausts her/him physically and/or mentally leading to burnout [36, 43].

Accordingly we hypothesized

H1a: Techno-overload is positively associated with burnout.
H1b: Techno-invasion is positively associated with burnout.
H1c: Techno-complexity is positively associated with burnout.

H1d: Techno-insecurity is positively associated with burnout.
H1e: Techno-uncertainty is positively associated with burnout.

3.2. Control Variables

Existing literature suggests that the measure of dependent variables may be confounded by factors that are not considered in the hypothesized model. Therefore, in the research model, we included suitable control variables such as age, gender, educational qualification, work experience, and extent of ICT use measured as the number of average hours of ICT use per week.

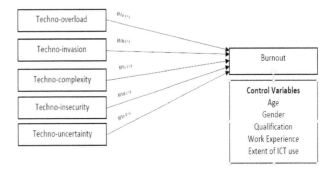

Figure 1: Proposed Research Model

4 RESEARCH METHODOLOGY

4.1. Subjects and Procedure

We used an online survey method for collecting data and testing the proposed hypotheses. Executive education participants [N = 168] enrolled in a two-year EMBA programmer in a public management institute located in India formed the principal respondents for the study. We contacted them over an email explaining the purpose of this research and invited them to respond to the online survey in case they regularly use ICTs for their professional work. Towards limiting the effect of common method bias, we explicitly assured the participants on the confidentiality of their responses [35]. We also encouraged the participants to remain anonymous, if they wished to [35]. We received a total of 133 usable responses. To increase the sample size, we also forwarded the survey to employees across sectors through our acquaintances and received only 30 usable responses. In summary, 163 responses were used for the study. The demographics of the survey respondents are given in Table 1.

Table 1. Demographics of survey respondents

Measures	Items	Frequency	%
Gender	Male	129	79.14
	Female	34	20.85
Age	21 to 30	76	46.62
	31 to 40	70	42.94
	> 40	17	10.42
Educational	Bachelors	114	69.93
Qualification	Master's	45	27.6
	Other	4	2.45
Work	<=10 years	106	65.03
experience	>10 & <= 20	51	31.28
	> 20 years	6	3.68

4.2. Measurements

In this study validated scales from existing literature were adapted to formulate the questionnaire.

To measure the five dimensions of technostress creators, we borrowed items from Srivastava et al. [2015]. The respondents were requested to respond on a seven point Likert continuum [1 = Strongly disagree to 7 = Strongly agree]. Burnout was assessed using a 10 items short scale developed by Malach-Pines [2005]. The participants were to respond on a seven point Likert scale [1 = Never to 7 = Always].

The mentioned control variables were collected as part of the survey. Multiple regression analysis was used to investigate the study hypotheses. The statistical software SPSS 21.0 was used for data analysis, including factor analysis and regression to test the proposed hypotheses.

5. DATA ANALYSES

Prior to performing any regression analysis, we first checked for possible common method bias. Common method variance can either inflate or deflate observed relationships between constructs [35]. Therefore, we performed Harman's one factor test [34] and it showed the single factor explained only 30.901% of the total variance, indicating that common method bias does not affect the data, and by implication the results.

We checked for two types of validity for the measures used in the study: convergent validity and discriminant validity. Convergent validity ascertains whether the measures for a construct are more correlated with one another than with the measures of another construct [33]. Towards that we estimated the factor loadings for each item, which indicates the strength of the correlation between each item and the corresponding construct. An item-factor loading of 0.7 or more is desirable [29].

The construct of techno-insecurity was the most affected with many of the items cross loading with other factors. Finally based on face validity, we retained only one item [i.e. "Because of new ICTs, I feel constant threat to my job security"] to represent the construct. As the loadings within the construct are higher than those across constructs, this demonstrates convergent validity [15]. Table 2 contains the factor loadings as well as the descriptive statistics of each items while Table 3 shows the Cronbach's Alpha values.

We adhered to the recommendation of Fornell & Larcker [1981] to investigate discriminant validity [15]. Accordingly, the average variance explained [AVE] for each factor was compared with the squared correlation [SQ-COREL] between that factor and another factor [except Techno Insecurity]. Table 4 details the evidence and for each factor AVE > SQ-COREAL, thus discriminant validity is satisfied.

Table 2: Descriptive Statistics and Factor Loadings

Factors	Items	Mean	Std. Dev.	Factor Loadings
Techno-overload	TO1	4.75	1.573	.853
	TO2	4.36	1.655	.853
	TO3	4.74	1.602	.832
Techno-invasion	TI1	4.15	1.930	.738
	TI2	4.98	1.841	.803
	TI3	4.28	1.877	.855
	TI4	4.40	1.824	.849
Techno-complexity	TC1	3.23	1.694	.738
	TC3	3.21	1.643	.903
	TC5	3.09	1.569	.878
Techno-insecurity	TIS1	3.33	1.842	N/A
Techno-uncertainty	TU1	4.66	1.626	.817
	TU2	4.49	1.592	.895
	TU3	3.95	1.640	.860
	TU4	4.64	1.502	.830
Burnout	BO2	3.85	1.605	.735
	BO3	3.28	1.642	.820
	BO4	3.46	1.754	.812
	BO5	3.15	1.741	.837
	BO6	2.96	1.653	.816
	BO7	2.88	1.585	.736
	BO8	2.49	1.604	.781
	BO10	3.26	1.684	.734

Note: The table contains only those items having loadings > 0.7. In our analysis we only used these items.

Table 3: Instrument Reliability and Validity

Factors	TO	TINV	TCOM	TUNC	BO
Cronbach's Alpha	0.861	0.885	0.823	0.892	0.918

Table 4: Analysis for Discriminant Validity

Factors	1	2	3	4	5
1.TO	**0.727**	0.175	0.042	0.075	0.041
2.TINV		**0.66**	0.05	o.121	0.101
3.TCOM			**0.71**	0.014	0.040
4.TUNC				**0.724**	0.024
5.BO					**0.616**

Note: The values written in bold are the Average Variance Explained (**AVE**) for the corresponding factor. The other values are the squared correlation among the factors.

6. RESULTS

Multiple regression analysis was conducted to investigate evidence concerning the individual impacts of TS creators on burnout. The results are reported in Table 5, which indicate that among the five TS creators, only techno-invasion [β = 0.212, p < 0.05] and techno-insecurity [β = 0.262, p < 0.01] are significantly related to burnout among employees.

We further wanted to check if the significant TS creators can act as mediator between the non-significant ones and burnout. It will imply that a TS creator may not be directly related to burnout, but it can give rise to another TS creator which will lead to burnout. To test this, we used hierarchical multiple regression analysis where the control variables are entered in the 1st step, techno-overload, techno-complexity and techno-uncertainty in the second step, and finally techno-insecurity in the 3rd step [Results: Table 6]. We conducted the same regression again with techno-invasion as a mediator entered in the 3rd step [Results: Table 7]. It can be observed that in both the cases only techno-complexity [β = 0.212, p < 0.01] reported a significant association with burnout in step-2. The mediation requirement is that the mediator variable should be associated with the outcome variable, while controlling for the causal variables [20]. It may be noted from step 3 of the results that, techno-invasion [β = 0.261, p < 0.01] and techno-insecurity [β = 0.308, p < 0.01] are positively associated with burnout. Further, in presence of techno-insecurity, relationship between techno-complexity and burnout became insignificant [β = 0.055, n.s.], hence full mediation is present. For techno-invasion, it is a case of partial mediation between techno-complexity and burnout.

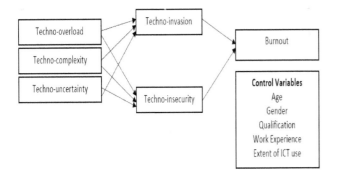

Figure 2: Mediation Model

Table 5: Regression Output

Variable	β	ΔR²
Gender	.222	
Age	-0.088	
Education	0.009	
Work Experience	0.081	
ICT Use per Week	.028	
TO	0.040	0.192**
TINV	0.212*	
TCOM	0.050	
TINS	0.262**	
Techno-Uncertainty	0.022	

Note: *p < 0.05, **p < 0.01, Dependent variable: Burnout

Table 6: Techno-insecurity as a mediator

Variable	β	ΔR²
Step 2		
Gender	.223	
Age	-.075	
Qualification	-.046	
Work Exp.	.092	
ICT Use per Week	.027	0.102**
Techno-Overload	.130	
Techno-Complexity	.210**	
Techno-Uncertainty	.125	
Step 3		
Gender	.213	
Age	-.078	
Qualification	-.002	
Work Exp.	.092	
ICT Use per Week	.036	0.059**
Techno-Overload	.107	
Techno-Complexity	.055	
Techno-Uncertainty	.061	
Techno-Insecurity	.308**	

Table 7: Techno-invasion as a mediator

Variable	β	ΔR²
Step 2		
Gender	.223	
Age	-.075	
Qualification	-.046	
Work Exp.	.092	
ICT Use per Week	.027	0.102**
Techno-Overload	.130	
Techno-Complexity	.210**	
Techno-Uncertainty	.125	
Step 3		
Gender	.232	
Age	-.088	
Qualification	-.024	
Work Exp.	.078	
ICT Use per Week	.019	0.05**
Techno-Overload	.042	
Techno-Complexity	.176*	
Techno-Uncertainty	.066	
Techno-Invasion	.261**	

7. DISCUSSION

The primary objective of our study is to identify the TS creators that contribute to burnout among employees who regularly use ICTs for their professional responsibilities in India. During the analysis we further expand our initial model to understand weather there exist any interaction among these TS creators. Towards that the paper provided a much needed technological component to the existing JD-R model [40]. It posited individual TS creators as job demands that contribute to burnout among the employees. Specifically, our results suggest that in an Indian context techno-invasion and techno-insecurity lead to burnout.

Interestingly, though techno-complexity is not related to burnout directly, techno-insecurity fully mediates the relationship, while techno-invasion partially mediate the same. This results make sense because due to *Techno-complexity*, users feel inadequate with regard to their computer skills which in turn generates *techno-insecurity* where they feel constant threat to their job by new technologies as well as co-workers with new technical skills. Similarly as they have to invest more time to understand the complex technology, it will hamper their private lives thus causing techno-invasion. Below we list the contributions from our study as well as elaborate implications for research and practice.

Our study contributes substantially to the understanding of TS creators and their implications. The literature on organizational stress is rich with evidence suggesting a significant relationship between job stressors and undesirable job outcomes. Situated within this stream of literature, researchers had investigated the role of TS creators towards heralding unwanted organizational outcomes such as diminished job satisfaction [36], lessened productivity and innovation [44]. Further, Srivastava et al. (2015) provide evidence supporting the positive relationship between TS creators and burnout [43]. Our study findings are thus in tune with the literature. However, to the best of our knowledge previous research treated TS creators as a second order factor [36, 44, 43], which we believe reduced the explanatory power of the construct. Accordingly, we positioned each of the TS creators [i.e. techno-overload, techno-invasion, techno-complexity, techno-insecurity, and techno-uncertainty] as a distinct causal variable, in an attempt to understand their unique contribution towards burnout. This is the first contribution of our study. Second, the inclusion of TS creators also helped expand the list of job demands [see 40 for a comprehensive list of job demands identified in literature]. These job demands are reflective of job characteristics in contemporary workplaces, whose association with other organizational outcomes may be studied. Third, our finding that techno-invasion and techno-insecurity explain maximum variance in burnout [in comparison to other technostress creators] is a contribution to the burnout literature. Finally, using the lens of JD-R we conceptualize the interaction of different TS creators. It highlights that techno-insecurity and techno-invasion mediate the relationship between techno-complexity and burnout.

Our study findings present significant insights for the organizations in a digital economy. While "coping with rapid change in IT" [6] has been acknowledged as an ongoing challenge, organizations must learn to address the issues of their employees. Else these may result in burnout and attrition which in turn can burgeon their cost. The results of our study suggested that not all the TS creators, but techno-invasion and techno-insecurity are associated with burnout. Keeping this in mind, managers can take necessary steps to reduce this negative impacts. Specifically, insecurity due to rapid technology changes is one of the major reasons of burnout among the employees. Hence, managers should conduct regular training and knowledge transfer sessions to reduce the negative impacts of techno-insecurity among employees.

8. LIMITATIONS

Like every research, our work too has certain limitations. First, the data were self-reported and thus may be subject to respondents' personal memory and biases whilst answering the questions. Also the study was cross sectional, and the respondents' perceptions and intentions were measured at a single point in time. These limitations can lead to problems of bias – specifically common method bias. Although, we had conducted statistical tests and inferred that common method bias did not affect the study findings, yet in future a longitudinal study with similar objectives may be designed to complement the findings from this research. Second, many items of individual TS creators poorly loaded or cross loaded in their corresponding constructs. The problem was acute for techno-insecurity, where we had to satisfy ourselves by taking a single item for statistical analysis. Future studies may be designed to improve the items of TS creators. Third, the study was conducted employing a sample of Indian workforce. Hence, researchers must exercise caution in generalizing the study findings. Thus future researchers may only take the insights from this study, while investigating evidence for their support in different occupational and national contexts. Finally, this study has a limited focus on only one job-related outcomes [job burnout] inline with JD-R framework. Future studies may incorporate more or different outcomes for research.

References

[1] Ahuja, M. K., Chudoba, K. M., Kacmar, C. J., McKnight, D. H., & George, J. F. (2007). IT road warriors: Balancing work-family conflict, job autonomy, and work overload to mitigate turnover intentions. *MIS Quarterly*, 1-17.

[2] Akinci, B., Kiziltas, S., Ergen, E., Karaesmen, I. Z., & Keceli, F. (2006). Modeling and analyzing the impact of technology on data capture and transfer processes at construction sites: a case study. *Journal of construction engineering and management*, *132*(11), 1148-1157.

[3] Ayyagari, R., Grover, V., & Purvis, R. (2011). Technostress: technological antecedents and implications. *MIS quarterly*, *35*(4), 831-858.

[4] Bakker, A. B., Demerouti, E., De Boer, E., & Schaufeli, W. B. (2003). Job demands and job resources as predictors of absence duration and frequency. *Journal of vocational behavior*, *62*(2), 341-356.

[5] Bawden, D., & Robinson, L. (2009). The dark side of information: overload, anxiety and other paradoxes and pathologies. *Journal of information science*, *35*(2), 180-191.

[6] Benamati, J., & Lederer, A. L. (2001). Coping with rapid changes in IT. *Communications of the ACM*, *44*(8), 83-88.

[7] Bharadwaj, A. S. 2000. A resource-based perspective on information technology capability and firm performance: an empirical investigation. *MIS Quarterly*, 24(1), 169-196.

[8] Broos, A. (2005). Gender and information and communication technologies (ICT) anxiety: Male self-assurance and female hesitation. *CyberPsychology & Behavior*, *8*(1), 21-31.

[9] Chandra, S., Srivastava, S. C., & Shirish, A. (2015). Do Technostress Creators Influence Employee Innovation?. In *PACIS* (p. 93).

[10] Chandra, S., Srivastava, S. C., & Theng, Y. L. (2012). Cognitive absorption and trust for workplace collaboration in virtual worlds: An information processing decision making perspective. *Journal of the association for information systems*, 13(10), 797-835.

[11] Chen, A. J., & Karahanna, E. (2011). Personal life interrupted: Understanding the effects of technology mediated interruptions from work to personal life. In *Proceedings of the International Conference on Information Systems*

[12] C. Brod. (1984). Technostress: The human cost of the computer revolution. Addison Wesley Publishing Company.

[13] Demerouti, E., Bakker, A. B., Nachreiner, F., & Schaufeli, W. B. (2001). The job demands-resources model of burnout. *Journal of Applied psychology*, *86*(3), 499.

[14] Fisher, W., S. Wesolkowski. 1999. Tempering technostress. *IEEE Technology Society Magazine* 18(1) 28-33

[15] Fornell, C., & Larcker, D. F. 1981. Evaluating structural equation models with unobservable variables and measurement error. *Journal of Marketing Research*, 18(1), 39-50.

[16] Gaudioso, F., Turel, O., & Galimberti, C. (2017). The mediating roles of strain facets and coping strategies in translating techno-stressors into adverse job outcomes. *Computers in Human Behavior, 69*, 189-196.

[17] Ghislieri, C., Emanuel, F., Molino, M., Cortese, C. G., & Colombo, L. (2017). New technologies smart, or harm work-family boundaries management? Gender differences in conflict and enrichment using the JD-R theory. *Frontiers in psychology, 8*, 1070.

[18] Hunton, J. E., Lippincott, B., & Reck, J. L. (2003). Enterprise resource planning systems: comparing firm performance of adopters and nonadopters. *International Journal of Accounting information systems*, 4(3), 165-184.

[19] Jawahar, I. M., Stone, T. H., & Kisamore, J. L. (2007). Role conflict and burnout: The direct and moderating effects of political skill and perceived organizational support on burnout dimensions. *International Journal of Stress Management, 14*(2), 142.

[20] Kenny, David A., Deborah A. Kashy, and Niall Bolger (1998), "Data Analysis in Social Psychology," in Handbook of Social Psychology, 4th ed., Vol. 1, ed. Daniel Gilbert, Susan T. Fiske, and Gardner Lindzey, New York: McGraw-Hill, 233–65.

[21] Khan, A., & Mahapatra, M. (2017, June). The Impact of Social Media as Technostress Inhibitor on Employee Productivity. In Proceedings of the 2017 *ACM SIGMIS Conference* on Computers and People Research (pp. 113-116). ACM.

[22] Khan, Z., & Jarvenpaa, S. L. (2010). Exploring temporal coordination of events with Facebook. com. *Journal of Information Technology, 25*(2), 137-151.

[23] Klausegger, C., Sinkovics, R. R., & "Joy" Zou, H. (2007). Information overload: a cross-national investigation of influence factors and effects. *Marketing Intelligence & Planning, 25*(7), 691-718.

[24] Kupersmith, J. 1992. Technostress and the reference librarian. *Reference Services Rev.* 20(2) 7- 14

[25] Mandel, M. 2005. The real reasons you're working so hard. Business Week (Oct. 3) 60-67.

[26] Maslach, C., Schaufeli, W. B., & Leiter, M. P. (2001). Job burnout. *Annual review of psychology, 52*(1), 397-422.

[27] Melville, N., Kraemer, K., & Gurbaxani, V. 2004. Information technology and organizational performance: An integrative model of IT business value. *MIS Quarterly*, 28(2), 283-322.

[28] Molla, A., & Heeks, R. (2007). Exploring e-commerce benefits for businesses in a developing country. *The Information Society, 23*(2), 95-108.

[29] Morris, M. G., & Venkatesh, V. (2010). Job characteristics and job satisfaction: understanding the role of enterprise resource planning system implementation. *MIS Quarterly*, 143-161.

[30] Mwakaje, A. G. (2010). Information and communication technology for rural farmers market access in Tanzania. *Journal of Information Technology Impact,* 10(2), 111-128.

[31] Parson, C.K.; Liden, R.C.; O'Conner, E.J.; and Nagao, D.H. Employee responses to technologically-driven change: The implementation of office automation in a service organization. *Human Relations,* 44, 12 (1991), 1331–1356.

[32] PETER, M. (2001). Occupational stress: Toward a more integrated framework. Handbook of Industrial, Work & Organizational Psychology: Volume 2: Organizational Psychology, 93.

[33] Petter, S., Straub, D., & Rai, A. (2007). Specifying formative constructs in information systems research. *MIS Quarterly,* 623-656.

[34] Podsakoff, P. M., & Organ, D. W. (1986). Self-reports in organizational research: Problems and prospects. *Journal of management, 12*(4), 531-544.

[35] Podsakoff, P. M., MacKenzie, S. B., Lee, J. Y., & Podsakoff, N. P. (2003). Common method biases in behavioral research: a critical review of the literature and recommended remedies. *Journal of applied psychology, 88*(5), 879.

[36] Ragu-Nathan, T. S., Tarafdar, M., Ragu-Nathan, B. S., & Tu, Q. (2008). The consequences of technostress for end users in organizations:

Conceptual development and empirical validation. *Information systems research, 19*(4), 417-433.

[37] Rao, N. H. (2007). A framework for implementing information and communication technologies in agricultural development in India. *Technological Forecasting and Social Change, 74*(4), 491-518.

[38] Sardeshmukh, S. R., Sharma, D., & Golden, T. D. (2012). Impact of telework on exhaustion and job engagement: A job demands and job resources model. *New Technology, Work and Employment, 27*(3), 193-207.

[39] Schaufeli, W. B., & Bakker, A. B. (2004). Job demands, job resources, and their relationship with burnout and engagement: A multi-sample study. *Journal of Organizational Behavior,* 25, 293–315.

[40] Schaufeli, W. B., & Taris, T. W. (2014). A critical review of the Job Demands-Resources Model: Implications for improving work and health. In *Bridging occupational, organizational and public health* (pp. 43-68). Springer Netherlands.

[41] Sethi, V., Barrier, T., & King, R. C. (1999). An examination of the correlates of burnout in information systems professionals. *Information Resources Management Journal (IRMJ), 12*(3), 5-13.

[42] Shu, Q., Tu, Q., & Wang, K. 2011. The impact of computer self-efficacy and technology dependence on computer-related technostress: A social cognitive theory perspective. *International Journal of Human-Computer Interaction, 27*(10), 923-939.

[43] Srivastava, S. C., Chandra, S., & Shirish, A. (2015). Technostress creators and job outcomes: theorising the moderating influence of personality traits. *Information Systems Journal, 25*(4), 355-401.

[44] Tarafdar, M., Tu, Q., & Ragu-Nathan, T. S. (2010). Impact of technostress on end-user satisfaction and performance. *Journal of Management Information Systems, 27*(3), 303-334.

[45] Tarafdar, M., Tu, Q., Ragu-Nathan, B. S., & Ragu-Nathan, T. S. (2007). The impact of technostress on role stress and productivity. *Journal of Management Information Systems, 24*(1), 301-328.

[46] Vranjes, I., Baillien, E., Vandebosch, H., Erreygers, S., & De Witte, H. (2017). The dark side of working online: Towards a definition and an Emotion Reaction model of workplace cyberbullying. *Computers in Human Behavior, 69*, 324-334.

[47] Wang, K., Shu, Q., & Tu, Q. (2008). Technostress under different organizational environments: An empirical investigation. *Computers in Human Behavior, 24*(6), 3002-3013.

[48] Wang, W., Daneshvar Kakhki, M., & Uppala, V. (2017). The Interaction Effect of Technostress and Non-Technological Stress on Employees' Performance.

[49] Wang, K., & Shu, Q. (2008, September). The moderating impact of perceived organizational support on the relationship between technostress and role stress. In *Database and Expert Systems Application, 2008. DEXA'08. 19th International Workshop on* (pp. 420-424). IEEE.

[50] Weil, M.M., and Rosen, L.D. Technostress: Coping with Technology @work @home @play. New York: John Wiley, 1997.

[51] Xia, Q., Zhao, X., Philip, Q. T. E., Chang, X., & Huang, W. (2016, June). An Empirical Research on Technostress Creators and End-User Performance: the Mediating Roles of Affective Attitudes. In *PACIS* (p. 196).

[52] Yip, B., Rowlinson, S., & Siu, O. L. (2008). Coping strategies as moderators in the relationship between role overload and burnout. *Construction Management and Economics, 26*(8), 871-882

[53] van Zoonen, W., Verhoeven, J. W., & Vliegenthart, R. (2017). Understanding the consequences of public social media use for work. *European Management Journal,* 35(5), 595-605.

[54] Zorn, T. E. (2003). The emotionality of information and communication technology implementation. *Journal of Communication Management,* 7(2), 160-171.

[55] Maslach, C., Schaufeli, W. B., & Leiter, M. P. (2001). Job burnout. *Annual review of psychology, 52*(1), 397-422.

[56] Maslach, C., & Leiter, M. P. (2016). Understanding the burnout experience: recent research and its implications for psychiatry. *World Psychiatry, 15*(2), 103-111.

The Flip Side of the Coin: Employer Social Networking to Find Job Seekers

Bruce C. Herniter
Louisiana Tech University
502 W. Texas, P.O. Box 10318
Ruston, LA 71272
herniter@latech.edu

Michael L. Faulkner
DeVry University
630 U.S. Highway One
North Brunswick, NJ 08902
mfaulkner@devry.edu

Thomas F. Stafford
Louisiana Tech University
502 W. Texas, P.O. Box 10318
Ruston, LA 71272
stafford@latech.edu

ABSTRACT

Employers are more concerned than ever with effective hiring. Business competes for personnel in a dynamic employment market; securing the best prospective employee requires dedicated use of parallel networking channels to identify applicants of interest. One channel is interpersonal and is highly favored, carrying the power of interpersonal trust in the form of recommendations from "known others." Applicants and employers, alike, favor strong personal connections when it comes to evaluating opportunities and prospects. The other channel is intermediated, and characterizes the confused conventional knowledge notion that online social media are effective channels through which applicants can influence employers. The true state of this channel's effect lies more in the employer's ability to use online social media as a filtering and qualifying mechanism to vet employees in advance of considering whether to engage in further interactions toward employment.

KEYWORDS

ACM proceedings, candidate search, job search, model, networking, social network

[1]ACM Reference format:

B. Herniter, M. Faulkner and T. Stafford. 2008. SIG Proceedings Paper in word Format. In *Proceedings of ACM SIGMIS-CPR '18, June 18–20, 2018, Buffalo-Niagara Falls, NY, USA*, 8 pages. https://doi.org/10.1145/3209626.3209719

1 INTRODUCTION

Hiring and job search are two sides of the same coin. When workers seek new employment, they use a variety of techniques to look for positions including searches of print and electronic media, submitting resumes or formal applications, an "elevator speech" during fortuitous chance encounters, and networking. Meanwhile, the role of the employer in networking is understated in the literature. Employers have options for identifying good candidates, such as placing advertisements, using their human resources department, hiring a search firm, and -- just as is the case with job seekers -- networking. For both the job seeker and the employer, networking "involves contacting friends, acquaintances, and referrals to obtain information and leads about job opportunities" [24]. Intermediated social media networking is typically thought to provide a public face from the employee to the employer [1]. Estimates are that up to half of jobs are found using such online social networks [15]. Social media research shows that employers often use social media for background research on job candidates in order to clear them for hiring [4,5]. At the same time, other research shows that organizations also place great value on referrals to persons well-known to their own employees [3,17].

Weak ties networks, popularly noted in the literature as the key venue of influence and information in such circumstances (in view of Granovetter's conclusions on influence and social network effects), are actively used by job seekers to explore job prospects and influence company personnel who might have the ear of the hiring decision maker [11,12]. On the flip side, employers using weak tie networks might uncover talent heretofore unknown to them. The literature suggests that while weak tie networks are more useful for job seekers in identifying heretofore unknown job prospects, strong tie networking appears to be greatly favored by employers as they seek known, influential and reliable sources of information on whom to consider for job openings [16]; in contrast to the Granovetterian view, this is what might be thought of as the "strength of strong ties." Meanwhile, the entirely distinct case of social media networking is a factor that must be reconciled with the interpersonal sources of influence that job seekers and employers utilize to meet their job market needs.

The purpose of this study is to explore social networking from the employer's point of view. If networking is an effective way for job seekers to contact employers, why should networking not also be effective for employers to contact quality candidates as well? Do employers perceive networking to be an effective way for job seekers to contact them?

SIGMIS-CPR '18, June 18–20, 2018, Buffalo-Niagara Falls, NY, USA
© 2018 Association for Computing Machinery.
ACM ISBN 978-1-4503-5768-5/18/06...$15.00
https://doi.org/10.1145/3209626.3209719

1.1 Conceptual Framework

Our conceptual framework of the elements involved in employer-job seeker contact, developed from Faulkner et al. [8], is illustrated in Figure 1. This framework illustrates a three-dimensional intersection of search skills, employer roles, and search methods, aligned toward the identification of qualified employees identified in the job search/employee identification process, via information channels. All of these are intended to gather information about searching for job candidates by employer, as opposed to the customary research focus of searching for a job by the job seeker.

In the networking processes we study, the three dimensions that converge on candidate identification include 1) the characteristics of the manager/firm, 2) the skills the manager is seeking in job candidates (communications versus technical skills), and 3) the channel by which information about the candidate reached the manager (either through a formal application to the company or through an informal approach, which would be via networking channels). The use of "head hunters" (*i.e.,* corporate recruiters) could potentially part of either the formal or informal process. As we shall see, it emerged in the analysis.

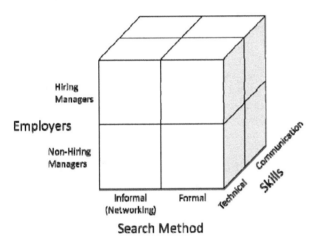

Figure 1: Conceptual Framework

1.2 Rational for Employer Networking

The rationale for social network use by employers for finding/qualifying job candidates (use of informal search methods in the framework, connoting both personal and intermediated network channels) is represented in our conceptual framework as the interaction with company insiders knowledgeable about employee prospects in the job market (personal) and as the leveraging of online social media to examine candidates for suitability (intermediated). The rationale for job seekers using social networks (both personal and intermediated) is represented as the distinction between the interpersonal channel of contact (through both strong and weak ties networks) versus the intermediated channel of online social media.

As we seek to reconcile three parallel sources of information and influence in the job market dynamics of seeker and employer contact models (strong and weak social networks, and online social media), several important questions are raised for consideration and addressed in this paper:

- What preferences do employers have for use of networking to find employees for open positions?
- If used, how does employer networking mirror the job seeker perception that networking contacts are the most productive venue to useful job leads?
- To what extent is employer and job seeker networking interpersonal, mediated, or combined, in the process of seeking solutions to the staffing problem?
- Do networking channels have a formal role in employer hiring systems?

The authors explored these questions via a qualitative case study format formed through interviews with a select group of top managers knowledgeable about corporate hiring. Analysis is conducted for purposes of generating theoretical considerations leading to hypotheses about the role of networking channels in bringing job-seekers and employers together in the staffing process. The paper proceeds thus: first we review literature related to the use of networking sources in the hiring process; we then report on our case study of top managers interviews about the hiring process and networking channels; this is followed by initial discussion of the relative influence of networking sources, with conclusions indicating fruitful avenues for further inquiry.

2 LITERATURE REVIEW

For learning about job opportunities, there are formal routes (official job posting and application processes with companies) and informal routes (networking; finding out about opportunities from people you know, either in person or intermediated). Much is known about how job seekers find out about jobs they might want to apply for; less is known about how the employer identifies promising job applicants. On the company side of candidate search and acquisition, the formal route consists of various procedures that employers use to attract applications to positions; this can include posting jobs in traditional media such as newspapers, as well as digital media, such as job boards such as Monster.com). It also includes direct candidate application, résumé review and the personal interview process. Human Resources plays an active role in implementing these steps.

Networking is the second broad strategy used by employers for finding suitable job candidates who do not self-identify through the HR department. The economic rationale for networking is that the market for employment is inefficient. Job seekers have limited information concerning positions beyond their immediate employer and/or geographical area, and employers must expend resources (advertisements, HR personnel salaries, search firms, etc.) to gather information on job prospects. Networking is a way to gather information at a cost lower than formal job application channels, and it leverages human contact either directly or through inter-mediated means. Granovetter, who is best known for describing the power of loosely tied interpersonal networks of acquaintances in prior decades (e.g., Granovetter [11], and "the strength of weak ties"), now positions social networking nicely in terms of today's digital intensive communications, reckoning that technology and social change are fully intertwined [12].

2.1 Networking as Promotion: Findings Job Openings

The use of strong ties is what we often think of as "networking" in the job market sense: people we know well and trust for leads on things we want to find out about. Strong networks are social networks made up of acquainted humans and the close connections between them. Where weak ties networks of loosely affiliated individuals are useful for diffusing information about opportunities not well-known to in-group members [11], strong tie networks come with the power of trust and certainty arising from long standing personal knowledge and experience with network members [16]. Plainly put, it's likely the case that persons with access to better social resources (i.e., more robust strong ties networks) will obtain better workplace outcomes [17]. Murray, Rankin, and Magill [19] also found that strong ties were about seven times more likely than weak ties to serve as an effective source of job information. This serves as an indication that strong-ties interpersonal networks might work better for job seekers than weak ties networks, which might typically be expected to be intermediated.

In line with that strong ties notion, data from the 1981 Youth Cohort of National Longitudinal Survey or NLS (and now called the National Longitudinal Survey of Youth or NLSY) has been used by researchers [27]. Holzer [14, p.10], working from NLSY data reports that friends and relatives (35%) and direct application to the employer (30%) were the two most successful methods associated with job offers that were accepted. Despite the seeming conventional wisdom that online social media can help job seekers find opportunities, evidence points toward the notion that (at least among students entering the job market in the current times) professional online social media (LinkedIn, specifically) are far preferred over casual online social media (Facebook, for example) among job seekers [13]. Meanwhile, a negative relationship between the number of contacts and job search success via online social networks has been observed [6]. It appears that strong interpersonal links help student job seekers, and weak intermediate links probably do not help.

2.2 Networking as Filtration: The Case of Vetting Applicants

The orthodox, received view of social networks in job searches is that they are promotional platforms useful for presenting information about job availabilities or for learning about such availabilities. Over half of job seekers indicate that they found jobs using social networking of some sort [15]. Yet, the emerging view – at least on the employer side – is that both interpersonal and intermediated social networks serve as effective checks used by employers to screen potential hires. Employers do "electronic background checks" with online social media and conduct "real time reality checks" through interpersonal links to trusted company insiders who have personal contacts with prospective applicants. This is illustrated in Figure 1, above, through the parallel information paths traveling outward from organizations to interpersonal and intermediated information sources about applicants.

In the online space, the use of social networking is increasingly popular with employers for a number of reasons [23,24]. Some think it is a matter of due diligence, to avoid negative factors that might not arise from review of applicant materials or formal background checks [5]. There is some question as to whether information gleaned from screenings of online social media of prospective applications is accurate enough to serve such employer vetting purposes in an objective manner [4]. There is also some concern that using seemingly actionable information gleaned from person social networking sites of job applicants could backfire by providing grounds for discrimination complaints [22], even when seemingly undesirable traits related to substance abuse are identified in such online screenings of personal social networking sites.

To that end, it might be no surprise that employers would use interpersonal networks and be highly influence by them. There is an indication that interpersonal sources of networking are considered more effective than intermediated sources of networking by employers [3]. Direct personal referrals from known and favored associates provide a hugely preferred source of candidate bona fides, as reported by 96% of companies willing to express a preference in one survey [18]. In another, nearly half of company insiders admitted using their position to help a "close-ties" individual with their job application at their firm [2].

3 PROPOSED MODEL

Guiding our data collection and analysis process, we conceptualize the three parallel information sources accessed by employers (everything aside from the formal application process through corporate HR departments) in a proposed model of effects. Weak and strong social networks are useful for company insiders advising the firm on attractive candidates, and these channels comprise two of the three ways in which employers informally learn about employees. In the third channel, job seekers utilize online social media to provide information that employers might access and to learn about employment opportunities, while companies access the online social media in a filtration process designed to vet employees as to suitability, prior to initiating direct personal contact for interview discussions. We illustrate this conceptual process in Figure 2.

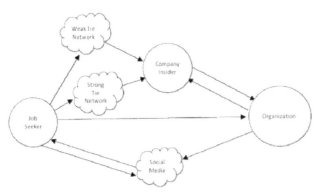

Figure 2: Conceptual model of hiring networking channels

3.1 Methodology

In the process of gathering data to assess our conceptual model of the information channels and networking resources used by employers to identify and screen job candidates, we utilized a case study of a group of 6 highly-placed managers who were identified professional colleagues in Direct Marketing Association regional chapters in the Eastern United States. These individuals were all employed at the level of Vice President or better, serving as senior executives, chief executives, or company board members. All the managers at some time supervised the people they hired and all played some role in the hiring process. Face-to-face interviews utilizing a structured interview guide were conducted with field recorders for purposes of later transcription and analysis, and ranged in time from 45 minutest to a little more than an hour, each.

Analysis was conducted in accordance with accepted grounded theory methods (e.g., Charmaz [7]; Glaser & Strauss [9]), leveraging the well-accepted sequence of initial open coding followed by thematic axial coding of our transcribed interviews, and as warranted, process coding to indicate sequence and actions (e.g., Saldana [26]). This was performed using the Nvivo analysis tool [21] in which the transcribed interviews were stored and analyzed for coding purposes.

Initially, each of the six transcribed interviews in our case study were parsed by two of the researchers (collocated at the same institution), acting together as a consensus team in coding analysis. That is, as each point of data was considered for meaning or import, the authors worked together on the same computer and contemporaneously determined codes of meaning that were commonly agreeable as they went forward.

3.2 Initial Analysis – Open Coding at Level One

In parsing the transcribed interviews with the managers, we identified 49 distinct terms (shown in Appendix A) in initial coding, which is often called "open coding" in the grounded theory process [26,28]. In second level coding of these 49 initial open code terms (basic groupings of meaning in a first pass at interpreting the transcripts), we derived a series of axial, or "second level" codes which are considered a way to processes initial codes into categories of meaning for subsequent theoretical consideration [28]. Our criteria for consideration of axial coding inclusion was frequency of occurrence for the initial open codes in the transcripts. By considering terms that had at least five references in the transcripts to the code, we found 22 distinct nodes of meaning to analyze.

As can be seen (Appendix A), a number of these terms related to qualities of a desirable employee (desirable characteristics, employee skills, communication and management skills, internal candidate, and experience matters). Some considerable number more related to the process of seeking and hiring employees (CEO involvement, headhunter, hiring process model, HR, interviewing, trial and error, referrals, target of opportunity, and tricks of the trade). The remaining open code terms (direct contact, formal approach, informal, networking, pass-along contact, strong tie networking, and social media) all seemed to reference channels of communication between companies and employees. Considered at the second level of coding analysis (e.g., Yin [28]), it appeared that qualifications, processes and channels best characterized the thematic groupings in initial analysis.

3.3 Level Two: Axial and Process Coding

We returned to the interview data, as recommend by Glaser and Straus [9] in a "constant comparative approach," in order to take advantage of the possibly of a jointly occurring coding and analysis process. Our hope was that this might lead to theoretical insights as we considered our initial open code results and what they might imply for the ongoing second and third order coding and analysis, particularly thematic axial coding [9, p. 109]. In doing so, we were mindful that the grounded theory process, as interpreted by modern writers, involved threes specific coding types and potentially four different levels of coding complexity leading right up to candidate theoretical constructs [28, p. 191]. The three code types are open codes, axial codes and process codes, and having recursively identified a wide range of 49 open codes, we distilled 22 key nodes of meaning in frequency analysis, all of which appeared to code axially on three thematic nodes (qualifications, processes and channels), we sought first to understand the meaning inherent in the employee recruitment process. Given that one of the key axial codes derived regarded process, specific consideration of subsequent process coding seemed called for. This was achieved through a word search query using the SQL functionality of the Nvivo tool [21], which resulted in a handy visual heuristic for quick and meaningful interpretation in the form of a tag cloud of words specific to the hiring process, as noted in Figure 3.

Figure 3: Process coding of interview data presented in tag cloud

3.4 Level Three Coding: Thematic Considerations

In process coding, aided by the word search tag cloud, we had the clear sense that the key to understanding how managers came to find desirable job candidates in the market place was largely a function of the people involved in the hiring process. On the notion of "taking two to tango," this clearly implied further consideration of the two major types of people in the job search networking process: applicants and employers. Our further consideration of employee characteristics that might lead to job seekers being noticed by employers provided a useful third level of thematic coding. This third level was beginning to show potential theoretical constructs for ongoing consideration. Carefully considering our respondent interview data in regard to mapping desirable employee traits gave us a consideration best characterized visually in Figure 4:

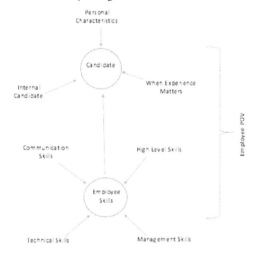

Figure 4: Employee viewpoint – desirable job applicant characteristics

It seemed, based on third level coding of the data (specifically for the employee side of the equation, that is) that potential applications were seen first and foremost as candidates for a given job, in which some key characteristics mattered more to employers than others: first, internal candidates were a known quantity and were highly prized for that reason (much easier to learn about and understand given their proximity, it appeared), yet when candidates were external, factors such as their personal characteristics (which had a strong implication for yet further analysis, discussed below), and a notable degree of job-specific experience and expertise were differentiating factors. Skill-wise (another third-order node of coding), the hiring employer nearly always wanted communications skills packaged along with managerial capabilities in an ideal employee, and to the degree that job-related skills were further considered, technological capabilities were important.

In regards to the employer side of the job search networking equation, the nuances were more complex at the third level of analysis, shown in Figure 5:

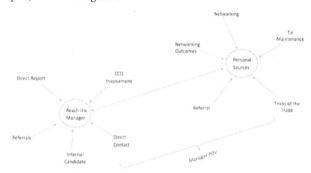

Figure 5: Employee viewpoint – the job-search networking process

From the point of view of hiring managers, it was clear that personal sources of influence were important, carrying with them the "strong-tie power" of credibility. Mangers expected that canny job applicants would know this, too, and that the most effective job applications would utilize personal strong-tie sources to connect with the company and put forward their case for consideration. "Reaching the manager" is what social networking seemed to be all about, in the manager's expectation.

3.5 Fourth Level Coding: Theoretical Considerations

We now turn to the fourth level of analysis, where theoretical expectations may be expressed and so return to the theoretical basis of the study found in our review of the social networking literature. In consideration of our conceptual underpinnings as we approached the data collection process for this study (e.g., Faulkner et al., [8]), our integrative syntheses at the fourth level of coding and analysis required that we consider the synergistic merger of all sources of job applicant and employer social networking channels to convey meaning as to which channels might have more efficacy, and how they might be used.

Returning one last time to our interview transcripts to parse the notions of our respondents in recursive consideration of the ongoing levels of coding analysis, we generated a holistic theoretical view of the interaction of employer and application, noted in Figure 6.

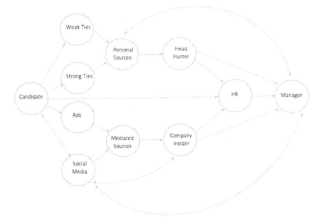

Figure 6: Holistic fourth stage coding and theoretical model

What we discerned in fourth stage coding, supporting a prospective theoretical model of employer social networking for job applicant evaluation, is that there are two distinct and parallel channels through which an application might gain a manager's attention. Much in keeping with the conceptual model that guided our data collection and analysis, there are strong personal channels of social influence that employers attend to and which applicants seek to leverage to gain attention. These are represented at the top portion of Figure 6, where it can be seen that the orthodox route to being noticed at a company comes from weak and strong tie personal contacts. Emerging from this channel is the association of recruiters (or "head hunters"). The recruiters mirror the role of the company insider in the formal channels. The power of personal influence being what it is, a "known" personal source can jump a candidate past several layers in the application and evaluation process, and it is the utilization of social networks, particularly those comprised of strong and influential ties that have the ability to do this for applicants.

In contrast, there is the potent role of online social networking to consider in the other parallel channel of information; this is the mediated channel of networking, and while we have to consider the potential impact that employment advertising (primarily online) has in the process, our interpretive analysis indicates to us that the point from the literature on the efficacy of online social networking in employment hiring processes is correct: social media online is something that runs both ways in the hiring process. Applicants might consider using it to identify opportunities and present a "face" to the company, but company officials (including both "known" insiders and key decision makers) will very likely access online social media to "vet" candidates, informally but no less influentially, as a part of evaluating potential prospects.

As we see in the previous research, casual online social media such as Facebook, are far less influential as a positive "push" to get candidate information in front of decision makers (when compared to "professional" online social media such as LinkedIn) and these casual social media have far greater potential to expose application characteristics that one might wish to keep private from prospective employers. The fact that it's not right to use information about one's private life in making employment screening decisions does not obviate the reality of its potent influence.

4 CONCLUDING THOUGHTS

We started this research asking a simple question: does the employer experience of networking match that of job-seeker? The literature examining the job seeker point of view clearly emphasizes the value of networking. The literature on the employer's side emphasizes skills and use of social media. To bring these sides together, we needed to go back to the source, the employers themselves. Structured interviews were conducted with high-level executives to discover what factors go into the job candidate search. Coding methodology, with its inductive approach, is a productive tool to analyze interview data. Interview data is "messy" and interviewers express their thoughts in the language of their experience. Starting with organizing comments into codes, proceeding to develop categories and then themes, coding is well-suited to producing rich models. The theoretical model presented in this paper captures two main pathways. The path of personal sources captures the strong and weak networks so often used by job seekers. The path of mediated sources captures both the advertising outreach to potential candidates as well as the use of social media. Recruiters emerged as network mediators. By combining the two sources in a single model, we see a synthesis of the previous approaches into a coherent whole that is a useful starting point for researchers. Further work exploring the separate channels, the roles of company insider, and the recruiters is warrented.

A INITIAL CODING TERMS

Name	Sources	References
Broken System	1	3
CEO Involvement	**2**	**6**
Desirable Characteristics	**2**	**10**
Direct Contact	**5**	**6**
Direct Report Source	2	4
Efficacy	1	3
Employee Skills	**2**	**6**
Communication Skills	**3**	**6**
Management Skills	**2**	**5**
Technical Skills	2	2
Feeder	1	2
Formal as Labor	1	4

Saver		
Headhunter	4	12
High Level Skills	2	4
Hire 'n Fire	1	1
Hiring Biases	1	2
Hiring Process Model	4	12
Formal Approach	6	20
Assessment Tests	2	2
HR	5	10
Interviewing	4	5
Informal	4	10
Trial and Error	2	5
Qualifications	1	1
Implicit Knowledge of the Business	1	3
Internal Candidate	6	17
Involvement	1	1
Jump Start Network	1	2
Know your Limitations	2	4
Marketing	2	4
Meetings	1	1
Networking	5	22
Pass-Along Contact Network	3	5
Strong Tie Networking	3	8
Tie Maintenance	3	4
Networking Outcomes	1	4
Networking for Dollars	1	1
Planning ahead	2	2
Prerogative of the Direct Report	3	3
Referrals	3	5
Right Place and Time	1	1
Schools are Screwing Up	1	1
Social Media	4	8
Target of Opportunity	2	10
Things that I used to do	1	3
Tricks of the Trade	4	12
Value of Education	3	3
Experience Matters	3	9
Hands off	1	2

REFERENCES

[1] S. Aral, C. Dellarocas, and D. Godes. 2013. Introduction to the special issue – social media and business transformation: A framework for research. Information Systems Research, 14(1), 3-13.

[2] L. Beaman and J. Magruder. 2012. Who gets the job referral? Evidence from a social networks experiment. American Economic Review, 102(7), 3574-93.

[3] J. C. Berkshire. 2005. Social network recruiting. HR Magazine, 50(4), 95-98.

[4] S. L. Black, D. L. Stone, and A. F. Johnson. 2015. Use of social networking websites on applicants' privacy. Employee Responsibilities and Rights Journal, 27(2), 115-159.

[5] V. R. Brown and E. D. Vaughn. 2011. The writing on the (Facebook) wall: The use of social networking sites in hiring decisions. Journal of Business and Psychology, 26(2), 219.

[6] R. Buettner, 2016. "Getting a Job via Career-Oriented Social Networking Sites: The Weakness of Ties," 2016 49th Hawaii International Conference on System Sciences (HICSS), Koloa, HI, 2016, 2156-2165. doi: 10.1109/HICSS.2016.272

[7] K. Charmaz. 2014. Constructing grounded theory. Los Angeles: Sage.

[8] M. L. Faulkner, B. C. Herniter, and T. F. Stafford. 2017. Job seekers and social networking in the networked age. SIGMIS-CPR '17, June 21-23, 2017, Bangalore, India, 2017, 169-170. doi: 10.1145/3084381.3084416

[9] B. G. Glaser and A. L. Strauss. 1999. The discovery of grounded theory: Strategies for qualitative research. Piscataway NJ: Transaction Publishers.

[10] M. Granovetter. 1973. Strength of weak ties. American Journal of Sociology, 78(6), 1360-1380.

[11] M. Granovetter. 1995. Getting a Job: A Study of Contacts and Careers. University of Chicago Press, Chicago IL.

[12] J. Herbold, and B. Douma. 2013. Students' use of social media for job seeking. The CPA Journal, 83(4), 68-71.

[13] H. J. Holzer. 1988. Search method use by unemployed youth. Journal of Labor Economics, 6(1), 1-20.

[14] Y. M. Ioannides, and L. D. Loury. 2004. Job information networks, neighborhood effects, and inequality. Journal of Economic Literature, 42(4), 1056-1093.

[15] D. Krackhardt, N. Nohria, and B. Eccles. 2003. The strength of strong ties. In R. Cross, A. Parker, and L. Sasson (Eds.). Networks in the knowledge economy. UK: Oxford University Press.

[16] Lin, N., Ensel, W., and Vaughn, J. 1981. Social resources and strength of ties: Structural factors in occupational status attainment. American Sociological Review 46, 393-405.

[17] R. Maurer. 2017. The challenge of building support for human resource programs. Strategic HR Review, 16(3), 131-135.

[18] S. O. Murray, J. H. Rankin, and D. W. Magill. 1981. Strong ties and job information. Sociology of Work and Occupations, 8(1), 119-136.

[19]   I. Nikolaou. 2014. Social networking Web sites in job search and employee recruitment. International Journal of Section and Assessment, 22(2), 179-189. QSR. 2017. NVivo 11 for Mac. Doncaster, Victoria Australia: QSR International Pty Ltd.

[20]   R. W. Reinsch, W. H. Ross, and A. B. Hietapelto. 2016. Employer's use of social media in employment decisions: risk of discrimination lawsuits. In A. Rahim (Ed.). Intelligence, sustainability, and strategic issues in management: Current topics in management. New York: Routledge.

[21]   L. D. Rosen. 2012. iDisorder: Understanding our obsession with technology and overcoming its hold on us. New York: Palgrave Macmillan.

[22]   N. Roulin. 2014. The influence of employers' use of social networking websites in selection, online self-promotion, and personality on the likelihood of faux pas postings. International Journal of Selection and Assessment, 22(1), 80-87.

[23]   M. Saks. 2005. Job search success: A Review and Integration of the predictors, behaviors, and outcomes. In S. D. Brown and R. W. Lent (Eds.). Career development and counseling: Putting theory and research to work. Hoboken, NJ: John Wiley.

[24]   J. Saldana. 2016. The coding manual for qualitative researchers. Los Angeles: Sage.

[25]   United States Bureau of Labor Statistics. (2018, April 6). National Longitudinal Surveys. Retrieved from Unites States Bureau of Labor Statistics: https://www.bls.gov/nls/#overview

[26]   R. K. Yin. 2011. Qualitative research from start to finish. New York: The Guilford Press.

User Experiences with Personal Intelligent Agents: A Sensory, Physical, Functional and Cognitive Affordances View

Sara Moussawi
Carnegie Mellon University
Information Systems
Pittsburgh, PA USA
smoussaw@andrew.cmu.edu

ABSTRACT

The interaction between users and their personal intelligent agents like Apple's Siri, Amazon's Alexa, and Google Home is getting more personal, therefore raising questions about the ethical obligations of technology companies. Thus, a thorough examination of users' experiences with these agents is indispensable. After all, it is merely the interaction between the human actor and the system that enables the artifact to be of consequence. This study uses an affordances lens to explore such use patterns. We qualitatively analyze 232 interviews with personal intelligent agents' users. The results reveal sensory affordances that support functional ones (hands-free and eyes-free use, familiarity and emotional connection) and dominate the users' experience with these agents. We also detect cognitive (personalization and learning from interactions), functional (speedy assistance and usefulness), and physical affordances (potential improvement). These findings have implications for researchers and practitioners alike seeking to understand usability patterns and challenges resulting from the integration of Apple's Siri, Google Now, Amazon's Echo and Microsoft's Cortana into users' everyday life.

Keywords

Personal intelligent agents; Sensory affordances; Cognitive affordances; Physical affordances; Functional affordances; Usability; Ethical implications.

ACM Reference format:
Sara Moussawi. 2018. User Experiences with Personal Intelligent Agents: A Sensory, Physical, Functional and Cognitive Affordances View. In Proceedings of ACM SIGMIS-CPR '18, June 18–20, 2018, Buffalo-Niagara Falls, NY, USA, 7 pages. https://doi.org/10.1145/3209626.3209709

1. INTRODUCTION

Personal Intelligent Agents (PIAs) such as Apple's Siri, Amazon's Alexa, Google Home, and Microsoft Cortana have been gaining wider popularity recently. As of July 2017, Verto Analytics reported 48.4 million American monthly active users of Siri (41.4 million), Alexa (2.6 million), Google Home (4.7 million) and Cortana (0.7 million) [25].

An intelligent agent is a system that acts intelligently and in the place of a human to perform a given task [15]. The agent is considered personalized when it operates within a specific user's context and hence is capable of formulating more precise queries when interacting with the user [15]. Therefore, we define a PIA as a personalized system that operates autonomously, is aware of its environment, anticipates the user's needs, learns and adapts to change, communicates with the user, and is timely in finding the necessary information and delivering the output while aiming to maximize its chance of success [15, 27, 30, 31, 35].

Artificially intelligent systems including PIAs possess specific capabilities that allow them to exhibit general intelligence including but not limited to natural language processing abilities, knowledge representation, automated reasoning, and machine learning [27]. On one hand, natural language processing abilities enable such systems to communicate successfully with the user. On the other hand, knowledge representation allows the systems to convert and store what it knows and hears. As for automated reasoning, it gives the system the capability to use stored information to answer questions. And machine learning makes it capable of adapting to new circumstances that it might face.

Artificial Intelligence (AI) is perceived as the art of creating functional systems that can necessitate human intelligence or that use computational models to exhibit mental faculties and intelligent behavior. In other words, AI can either emulate human-like reasoning and behavior or display rational faculties [13]. To date, most AI research has adopted the design research paradigm and focused on the development of complex algorithms, artifacts, and representations [20]. A multitude of similar artifacts are eventually incorporated into IT applications, and hence become subject for behavioral style research [20, 7].

The impact of such AI-enabled systems is impossible to predict without gaining more understanding of the way humans perceive and interact with these systems. A plethora of IS research indeed suggests that the success of IT applications can only be determined through their actual use and user interactions with them [16].

This premise holds true especially if the adoption of the system is voluntary [2]. Usability analyses (i.e. examining the extent to which a system enables users, in a given context of use, to efficiently and effectively accomplish goals while promoting feelings of satisfaction [10] become indispensable thus to assess the success of these systems [2].

Given the unique characteristics of these systems (intelligence, natural language processing and production abilities, learning behavior, awareness of the environment) and their novelty in the individual use space, understanding usability patterns is of key importance. Hence, this study aims to explore use trends among active PIAs' users. We seek to understand how users perceive their agents, interact with them, and integrate them in their everyday life. The theoretical underpinnings are grounded in the affordances literature, while the data analysis specifically builds on an affordances' typology adapted from Hartson [9]. To this extent, we empirically collect and qualitatively analyze interviews with 232 PIAs' users, specifically users of Apple's Siri, Amazon's Alexa, Google Now, and Microsoft's Cortana.

An exploration of prior research reveals that very few papers focus on the user interactions with personal intelligent agents [20, 17]. These papers explored data privacy related topics [17], compared reviews of assistant and non-assistant apps using a latent semantic analysis, examined the impact of gender and demeanor on the user's emotions when interacting with a special purpose embodied conversational intelligent agent with environmental sensors [23], or studied the users' reactions to an intelligent travel advisory agent with human-like appearance and speech capabilities [12].

In the next section, we present a review of the affordances literature, and then we discuss Hartson's [9] typology. Following that, we elaborate on our research design, data analysis, results, and discussion. We conclude with a contributions and implications section.

2. THEORETICAL BACKGROUND

2.1 The Affordances View

The affordances lens helps explain the increasingly symbiotic relationship between the technology artifact and the human actor as well as evaluate usability. An ecological psychologist, Gibson [5], coined the term in 1986 to refer to what an environment offers an organism (animal or human). Gibson used the noun 'affordance' to imply a complementarity between the organism and the environment. Based on Gibson's work, an affordance is a physical relationship between an actor and physical artifacts in the world [5].

Norman [21] appropriated the term to the context of human-computer interaction. According to Norman, affordances are properties of the artifact, and their presence suggests functionality and use through perceived or real action possibilities [22]. A real affordance is about physical characteristics while a perceived affordance is about characteristics in the appearance of a device or a system that provide clues for operation.

Hartson [9] built on Norman's work and proposed four kinds of affordances in the context of interaction design. Norman's perceived affordances became cognitive affordances that help users with cognitive actions. Norman's real affordances became physical affordances, which aid users with their physical activities. Hartson also added two new types of affordances: sensory and functional. Sensory affordances help users with their sensory actions, while functional affordances connect usage to usefulness.

In Information Systems (IS) research, the affordance lens supports a deeper understanding of the relationship between the IT artifact and the human actor [32]. In the IS literature, affordances are either viewed as goal-directed actions offered by a system to its user, or as socially and culturally emerging relationships between users and artifacts [11, 14, 16]. In IS, the affordances lens has been used to explore the interaction between the human actor and the technology artifact in organizations [26, 36], virtual worlds [29], eHealth [6], and most recently at the individual level with fitness tracking devices [2].

For the purpose of this study, we build on Hartson's typology as it better aligns with the characteristics of the users' interactions with PIAs.

2.2 Physical, Functional, Cognitive, and Sensory Affordances

Hartson [9] defined four complementary types of affordances in the context of interaction design and evaluation: physical, functional, cognitive, and sensory affordances.

A physical affordance is a design feature that facilitates physically performing an action [9]. The home button on an iPhone device or the two buttons at the top of the Amazon's Echo device have a good size relative to the device's size and thus enable users to easily interact with the button.

A cognitive affordance is a feature that supports and enables thinking or knowing about something [9]. In the context of PIAs, a clear explanation of a command communicated by voice or also displayed in text on the screen, is an example of a cognitive affordance because it helps the user understand how to use the command for functionality purposes.

In the world of non-computer devices, a doorknob is a cognitive and physical affordance for operating the door. The physical affordance implies that the doorknob can be grasped and turned in order to invoke the mechanism. The door itself is a functional affordance that allows passage. The visual design of the doorknob conveys a cognitive affordance, a message implied by convention in this case [9].

Considering both the user and the purpose of the affordance, a functional affordance helps the user in doing something. In an IT context, functional affordances refer to potential usage of an IT artifact [16]. Usage potentials exist for any user who intend to and has the ability of taking advantage of the IT artifact, even when the user is not aware of the usage potential [28]. For instance, a smart phone's camera feature affords the user the ability to take pictures and the user may not perceive this functionality. When the users interact with an IT artifact, they develop a mental image of its capabilities and constraints, and then act based on that image. An example of a functional affordance in a PIA context is making phone calls. The command: "Hey Siri, call Liz" is a functional affordance that helps the user make the call.

A sensory affordance is a feature that aids and enables the user in sensing something. Sensory affordances include features or devices associated with visual, auditory, tactile, or other sensations. In interaction design, sensory affordances play a supporting role to cognitive and physical affordances. Hartson [9] proposes that users must be able to sense cognitive and physical affordances for them to aid the user's cognitive and physical actions. In the context of PIAs, sensory affordances are abundant given the PIAs' natural language processing and production capabilities. A system like Amazon's Echo is designed to integrate seamlessly into the environment and be available for the user through voice commands. Hence, the user initiates the interaction by speaking to Alexa. The user knows that the agent is available to help either by hearing Alexa reply with voice or by seeing the colorful light on the top of the physical Echo device. Depending on the context of use, it is possible that every interaction with a PIA is conducted by voice communication only. In this case, sensory affordances are dominant and help reinforce other perceived affordances. For example, if wanting to send a text message, the user can talk to the agent to do so. Such an interaction is driven by voice, and the text on the screen could play a supporting role. In either case, the sensory affordance (i.e. voice feature) is boosting the functional one (i.e. texting feature).

3. RESEARCH DESIGN

Our objective in this study is to better understand how users perceive their intelligent agents, and interact and connect with them. The goal is to explore the research issues in a natural context in order to maintain the richness of information [4]. We use an interpretivist perspective and aim to understand the users' perceptions of their PIAs through the meanings that users assign to them [19]. While Eisenhardt [4] argues that qualitative research needs to start with a clean theoretical plate, Paré [24] states that it is nearly impossibly to achieve that, and that theory can play a significant and essential role in guiding research. Therefore, we use our review of the literature, and the affordances lens to guide the interview process. We follow an inductive reasoning approach to analyze the data. Two researchers worked on collecting the data through structured open-ended interviews with PIAs' users. The questions were posted as part of a larger research study for students at a large Northeastern university in the U.S.. The description of the questions was informal and participants could take the time needed to answer them. We aimed to make sure participants felt comfortable with no pressure of time. The participation was voluntary, and students received course credit upon completion of the study. The course credit awarded was constant among all subjects and was not subject to performance or other factors.

We filtered participants by asking them about their prior use of PIAs. Only participants who reported using a PIA at least twice in the previous month were considered eligible for this study. If they chose to participate, users were presented with an informed consent where they were assured anonymity and confidentiality. The study was available for completion over few months during fall 2016.

3.1 Data Analysis

A total of 252 subjects qualified to participate. We excluded 20 data records from the data analysis due to incomplete responses. The resulting final sample consisted of 232 respondents, a satisfactory number to achieve saturation in qualitative interviewing [8].

Around 78% of the subjects were Apple's Siri users, 16% were Google Now users, 4% were Microsoft's Cortana users, and 2% were Amazon's Echo users. Around 60% of users were using their agent for more than a year. About 51% of the subjects were 18 to 20 years old, 27% were 21 to 23 years old, and 57% were female. Descriptive statistics are presented in Table 1.

Table 1. Subject Demographics

Variable	Frequency (%)
Age	
18-20	119 (51.3%)
21-23	62 (26.7%)
24-26	26 (11.2%)
27-29	6 (2.6%)
30-32	9 (3.9%)
33-35	3 (1.3%)
36 or above	7 (3%)
Gender	
Male	132 (56.9%)
Female	98 (42.2%)
Prefer not to say	2 (0.9%)
Year	
Freshman	19 (8.2%)
Sophomore	102 (44%)
Junior	94 (40.5%)
Senior	17 (7.3%)
PIA Type	
Apple's Siri	180 (77.6%)
Microsoft's Cortana	9 (3.9%)
Google Now	38 (16.4%)
Amazon's Echo, Alexa	4 (1.7%)
Other	1 (0.4%)
Times of Use on Average	
Once a month	16 (6.9%)
2-3 times a month	64 (27.6%)
Once a week	26 (11.2%)
2-3 times a week	58 (25%)
Once a day	26 (11.2%)
Twice a day	10 (4.3%)
More than twice a day	32 (13.8%)
Period of Use	
Less than a month	4 (1.7%)
1-2 months	10 (4.3%)
3-4 months	22 (9.5%)
5-6 months	21 (9.1%)
7-8 months	8 (3.4%)
9-10 months	15 (6.5%)
11-12 months	12 (5.2%)
More than a year	140 (60.3%)

We conducted several rounds of coding. Our interpretation of the text relied mostly on the users' own terms. The first step was a pre-coding phase where we highlighted, and circled interesting parts of the text. The following step was an open coding stage where we assigned in vivo codes to transcripts. The next two stages involved analyzing the codes in order to identify categories, and then extract themes.

4. RESULTS

Eight main categories emerged from the data analysis. We identified sensory affordances that supported functional affordances (hands-free and eyes-free use, familiarity and emotional connection), cognitive (personalization and learning from interactions), functional (speedy assistance and usefulness), and physical affordances (potential improvement).

We discuss the results in detail next and present them in Table 2.

4.1.1 Hands-Free and Eyes-Free Use

An overwhelming majority of users expressed satisfaction with the PIA's availability at all times and with the ability to use the agent without reaching out to the device. The PIA's ability to process natural language, while not referred to directly, was a common theme.

Participants indicated that they used their PIA when they could not reach out to their phone. They reported asking for the PIA's help when both their hands were busy. A recurring instance described using the PIA to make calls and send texts while driving or to make calls while wearing the headphones. One user indicated:

I really think the command texting is the most important to prevent people from texting and driving, which is a large portion as to why accidents are happening with teenagers and young adults.

For many users, being able to get assistance without having to type or to reach for their phone was very important. The PIA in this case helped get the job done, allowed multitasking, and increased efficiency.

4.1.2 Personalization and Learning from Interactions

Some users reported that the PIA can provide answers based on their specific preferences and interactions. A few users perceived the PIA to be learning over time while other reported that the agent certainly did not learn from interactions. One user indicated:

I feel that the personal intelligence agent can be personalized to feel like it is mine. It can learn my name and can track down my activities that I have set and remind me when I need to do something that I otherwise may forget. Although I don't religiously use it like some people may, I enjoy its presence as a feature on my tablet and would be upset if it was ever removed.

4.1.3 Speedy Assistance

Based on the participants' responses, time saving seemed to be a common reason for use and satisfaction with use. Users reported that they used the PIA because it was fast in providing answers and completing tasks. Their agent saved them time especially when they were in a hurry. As one user put it:

... my interaction with Apple Siri has saved me a lot of time. Apple Siri has helped me find information quickly and efficiently.

Users also reported enjoying the interaction and considering the agent to be more useful when it was swift in providing assistance. One user indicated:

I give Siri a lot of gratitude. It saves time for me because I never have to type ... since I can just ask it. I feel happy using this agent because [it's] enjoyable, funny, and interesting.

Another reported:

I feel like it helps me search things up faster because I can talk to it instead of [typing] into google.

4.1.4 Usefulness

Users overwhelmingly stated that their PIA was helpful and useful. For most users, the PIA made difficult tasks easier and helped simplify their everyday routines. A group of users explained that while the PIA was useful, it was not central to their daily life. Another group of users elaborated on the convenience aspect. As one user put it:

It is a useful piece of software that really speeds up the time in doing [simple] tasks like setting the alarm, and doing a [Google] search. At times I wish it were able to understand more complex commands.

Another indicated:

I would say that it was surprisingly useful [,] useful and intelligent ... I was especially surprised by its ability to understand different accents... It also works very fast and gives basic but useful [information] about what it's being asked.

However, a small group of users stated that the agent was useful only at times. Some reported that they perceived their agent to be less competent than they initially expected. Others expressed that the agent can be annoying when it does not understand the question.

4.1.5 Emotional Connection

A large group of users felt an emotional connection towards their PIA. Users reported feelings of comfort just from having the PIA around. One user indicated:

Siri is fun to use, sometimes it gives the comfort I need at the moment, and other times it help to find nearest restaurant when in need.

Another user stated:

...it is very helpful and friendly. it sometimes cheer me up when I am feeling sad. I consider siri my friend.

Other users reported feelings of gratitude for the PIA's existence and help. Participants explained how the agent made their life easier, caused them to laugh, and was available to assist them. Some users even referred to the PIA as 'her' or 'she'. Users also described how the agent was always friendly and nice to them. A Siri user indicated:

I would not like to replace "My Siri" because she knows everything about me. If I have a new Siri, I have to start all over again to introduce myself. I feel like we are friends.

While a Google Now user indicated:

I really appreciate it..I really do appreciate the fact that it always seems to provide information that is relevant to me even before I had ever thought of it. My Google Now may not know who I actually am, but boy does it have a handle on who the 'online' me is.

4.1.6 Familiarity and Potential Improvement

The respondents expressed familiarity with the agent. When asked if they would replace the agent that they have been using, a large majority of users communicated that they would not be willing to replace their PIA. However, a smaller group of users stated that they would substitute the PIA for a better one. Overall, users recognized that the PIAs did not reach their full potential yet. As one user put it:

I would be okay with it being upgraded, but not completely changed. Although I would get used to it eventually, I have already gotten used to Siri and if anything is changed that I may not agree with I would be upset. I am not against improvements of course as long as it does not remove anything I currently use.

4.1.7 Emerging Tensions: Satisfaction and Disappointment

Participants also reported emerging tensions during their interactions with the PIAs. That is, a significant number of users seemed to be very pleased when their PIA understood what they wanted, but felt annoyed when they had to repeat the command several times. Other users reported feeling frustrated when the PIA did not live up to their expectations. One user was describing an instance where s/he asked the PIA to set a reminder:

...Siri recognized the command, and I felt very pleased. However, to my disappointment, the reminder never came.....after realizing this, I went in to my device and surely the reminder was there. Apparently, Siri had noted the reminder and date and time, but the reminder never happened. I was quite disappointed, for it was not the first time that Siri did not complete the task it was intended to do.

A few users were irritated when the PIA seemed inconsistent. They expressed frustration as a result of getting different answers or reactions to similar requests. As one user put it:

...It's a new experience when you're able to speak with your phone to do something. It feels as though you have a friend with you. Though sometimes it is frustrating when the agent does not comprehend the words I say.

For a group of users, satisfaction with the PIA seemed to depend on the level of control the user had and the perceived reliability. One user indicated:

...I am satisfied when it does exactly as I say. I am [angry] when it doesn't recognize my voice.

Another user stated:

When using the intelligent agent it can be useful at times in answering my questions or completing tasks but it can also become a waste of time when their is a [miscommunication] between myself and the agent turning simple tasks in to longer complex ones.

Table 2: Interview Questions and Codes

Interview Question	Codes (total number of occurrences)
In your own words, how would you describe the personal intelligent agent[1] you have been using?	Multitasking, hands-free use, communication abilities (55); personalization and learning from interactions (12); speedy assistance (40); helpfulness/ usefulness (99); emotions and connection (37); potential improvement (14); inconsistency, conditional satisfaction, reliability (19); interaction, presence, enjoyment (20); control (7)
In your own words, how do you feel about the personal intelligent agent you have been using?	Helpful (41); emotions and connection (46); quality vs. cost (5); task completion (11); hands-free use (19); speedy assistance (20); ease of use and usefulness (33); personalization (8); communication abilities (9); intelligence (8); learning (4); potential improvement (18); sense of humor (4); inconsistency, conditional satisfaction, reliability (15); control (13)
Would you be willing to replace the personal intelligent agent you have been using? Why or why not? Explain.	Familiarity/ accustomed to agent (49); willingness to replace the agent for a better one (48); willingness to replace the agent if it had major improvements / while retaining original functionality (8 /3); not willing to replace the agent (134); the agent is not irreplaceable for me (53); willingness to try new aagent (12); does not matter (15); prefer just because it is on the phone/ a particular brand (31)
Do you have other comments you would like to share about your interaction with the personal intelligent agent you have been using?	Hands-free and eyes-free use (17); personalization and learning from interactions (7); speedy assistance (5); usefulness /helpfulness (16); emotions and connection (24); potential Improvement (18); inconsistency, conditional satisfaction, reliability (8); control (3)

[1]An explanation of what a personal intelligent agent is and a list of examples were provided to participants at the beginning of the study.

5. DISCUSSION

Our results uncovered sensory affordances that support functional ones: hands-free and eyes-free use, familiarity and emotional connection. Users were satisfied by the ability to use the agent without having to reach for their device. The natural language processing and production abilities played a supporting role in assisting the users to complete their every day tasks. Additionally, our results showed that the continuous interaction via voice helps users satisfy other non-utilitarian needs, in particular any needs for a connection. This result is supported by recent numbers disclosed by the Amazon Alexa team which revealed that 50% of the interactions with Alexa are non-utilitarian or entertainment-related, and include declarations of love to the agent, proclamations of loneliness and requests for jokes [1].

We also detected cognitive affordances: personalization and learning from interactions. These cognitive affordances aided the user to perceive the agent as able to adapt to a learning curve and provide answers based on the user's preferences. Such affordances improved the usability of the agent by boosting the user's efficiency and satisfaction. Cognitive affordances of personalization and learning from interactions emerged as a result of clear cues communicated over time.

Sensory affordances, mainly voice, could play a supporting role for these specific cognitive affordances if the interaction was solely voice-based. Additionally, we identified a physical affordance: potential improvement. A physical affordance is a design feature that facilitates physically performing an action [9]. The potential improvement of the agent is a physical characteristic that is related to features of the agent that can improve the speed and quality of every interaction.

Furthermore, we detected functional affordances: speedy assistance and usefulness. Functional affordances help the user execute a task, and hence enhance usefulness. Users reported using the agent when their goal was to save time. The agent in this case acted fast to provide answers and complete tasks, especially when users were in a hurry. In addition, users reported that the PIA helped simplify life and made difficult tasks easier. The PIA in this case was useful to complete everyday tasks such as making phone calls, sending texts, setting reminders and getting directions. It is possible that every interaction with the PIA is conducted with voice communication only, leading to the emergence of sensory affordances that could play a supporting role to functional affordances.

6. CONTRIBUTIONS AND IMPLICATIONS

While functional and physical affordances have been investigated in prior IS research, sensory and cognitive affordances have received less attention. This paper emphasizes the relevance and applicability of Hartson's typology to a PIA context. We built on this typology to guide our exploration of users' interaction with PIAs in their everyday life, which constitutes a contribution to both PIA and affordances research in IS. The features that these agents possess are presenting the users with multiple ways of action whether functional, cognitive, physical or sensory related. Our results suggest that while PIAs were initially designed as tools to achieve the users' goals, they are being adapted to extend beyond their initial design. With agents more and more commonplace, this study interestingly reveals that users are actually developing an emotional connection with PIAs as these agents are offering the illusion of companionship to their users.

In relation to usability, we find that these agents are not consistently able to efficiently and successfully help users accomplish their goals, and, as a result, are creating mixed feelings of satisfaction and disappointment. With the continuous and fast development of these systems, and with the increasing number of users adopting them, our results provoke some reflection. This connection between users and PIAs seems to be blending the boundaries between the real and virtual for many users. Hence, it is necessary to look into ways to protect users in the relationships that they establish with these systems [33].

Beyond usability, few additional examples of similar applications and what users are sharing with agents shed the light on the associated ethical ramifications. That is, an increasing number of users are reporting feelings of loneliness and depression, even abuse instances to their agents [1] with the agents' responses in these cases being inadequate [18]. Additionally, various recent applications emphasize the need for some ethical guidelines. For instance, Microsoft's Tay is a chatbot that learned from Twitter feed and turned into a racist while NamePrism is a tool that uses machine-learning algorithms to make ethnicity and nationality predictions [3, 34]. There seems to be a need to reflect on what these systems can do to us rather than for us. It is important to consider how these systems and the relationships we develop with them can impact our self-identity, sense of being human, and perceptions. If we accept that PIAs have an impact on users, then this raises vital questions around the responsibility of PIA creators (i.e. companies, software engineers, designers) to design and modify agents to improve the well-being of users.

While a set of ethical rules was developed a few years ago to guide building robots [37], no ethical rules exist for developing PIAs and similar systems. As a matter of fact, only a few companies started working on building mechanisms that could potentially tackle the need for ethically grounded design, e.g. Google's internal AI ethics board [37]. Technology companies have ethical obligations to consider, particularly in what relates to products development for the betterment of their users' lives. These companies have the responsibility to create an atmosphere where their product designers, software engineers, and developers are encouraged to value users' welfare. Taking active steps in that direction is especially important since these agents are not merely a collection of useful features. Understanding the impact of the employees' choices and the companies' decisions and fully considering their effects on people's lives could help promote such an atmosphere.

7. ACKNOWLEDGMENTS

We thank Dr. Raquel Benbunan-Fich for providing theoretical advice.

8. REFERENCES

[1] Andres, H. (2017). Alexa, Can You Prevent Suicide? How Amazon trains its AI to handle the most personal questions imaginable. *The Wall Street Journal*. Retrieved from https://www.wsj.com/articles/alexa-can-you-prevent-suicide-1508762311

[2] Benbunan-Fich, R. (2017). *Usability of Wearables without Affordances*. Paper presented at the Twenty-third Americas Conference on Information Systems, Boston.

[3] Chen, S. (2017). AI Research Is In Desperate Need Of An Ethical Watchdog *Wired*. Retrieved from https://www.wired.com/story/ai-research-is-in-desperate-need-of-an-ethical-watchdog/

[4] Eisenhardt, K. M. (1989). Building theories from case study research. *Academy of Management Review, 14*(4), 532-550.

[5] Gibson, J. J. (1986). *The ecological approach to visual perception*. Hillsdale, NJ: Erlbaum.

[6] Goh, J. M., Gao, G., & Agarwal, R. (2011). Evolving work routines: adaptive routinization of information technology in healthcare. *Information Systems Research, 22*(3), 565-585.

[7] Gregor, S., & Benbasat, I. (1999). Explanations from intelligent systems: Theoretical foundations and implications for practice. *MIS quarterly*, 497-530.

[8] Guest, G., Bunce, A., & Johnson, L. (2006). How many interviews are enough? An experiment with data saturation and variability. *Field methods, 18*(1), 59-82.

[9] Hartson, R. (2003). Cognitive, physical, sensory, and functional affordances in interaction design. *Behaviour & Information Technology, 22*(5), 315-338.

[10] Ivory, M. Y., & Hearst, M. A. (2001). The state of the art in automating usability evaluation of user interfaces. *ACM Computing Surveys (CSUR), 33*(4), 470-516.

[11] Kaptelinin, V., & Nardi, B. (2012). *Affordances in HCI: toward a mediated action perspective.* Paper presented at the Proceedings of the SIGCHI Conference on Human Factors in Computing Systems.

[12] Knijnenburg, B., & Willemsen, M. C. (2014). *Inferring Capabilities of Intelligent Agents.* Paper presented at the Special Interest Group on Human-Computer Interaction.

[13] Kurzweil, R., Richter, R., & Schneider, M. L. (1990). *The age of intelligent machines* (Vol. 579): MIT press Cambridge.

[14] Leonardi, P. M. (2011). When flexible routines meet flexible technologies: Affordance, constraint, and the imbrication of human and material agencies. *MIS quarterly*, 147-167.

[15] March, S., Hevner, A., & Ram, S. (2000). Research commentary: an agenda for information technology research in heterogeneous and distributed environments. *Information Systems Research, 11*(4), 327-341.

[16] Markus, M. L., & Silver, M. S. (2008). A foundation for the study of IT effects: A new look at DeSanctis and Poole's concepts of structural features and spirit. *Journal of the Association for Information Systems, 9*(10/11), 609.

[17] Mihale-Wilson, C., Zibuschka, J., & Hinz, O. (2017). *About User Preferences And Willingness To Pay For A Secure And Privacy Protective Ubiquitous Personal Assistant.* Paper presented at the Twenty-Fifth European Conference on Information Systems (ECIS), Guimarães, Portugal.

[18] Miner, A. S., Milstein, A., Schueller, S., Hegde, R., Mangurian, C., & Linos, E. (2016). Smartphone-based conversational agents and responses to questions about mental health, interpersonal violence, and physical health. *JAMA internal medicine, 176*(5), 619-625.

[19] Myers, M. D. (2013). *Qualitative research in business and management* (Second ed.): SAGE Publications.

[20] Nguyen, Q. N., & Sidorova, A. (2017). *AI capabilities and user experiences: a comparative study of user reviews for assistant and non-assistant mobile apps.* Paper presented at the Twenty-third Americas Conference on Information Systems, Boston.

[21] Norman, D. A. (1988). *The Psychology of Everyday Things.* Basic Books: New York.

[22] Norman, D. A. (1999). Affordance, conventions, and design. *interactions, 6*(3), 38-43.

[23] Nunamaker, J. F., Derrick, D. C., Elkins, A. C., Burgoon, J. K., & Patton, M. W. (2011). Embodied conversational agent-based kiosk for automated interviewing. *Journal of Management Information Systems, 28*(1), 17-48.

[24] Paré, G. (2004). Investigating information systems with positivist case research. *The Communications of the Association for Information Systems, 13*(1), 57.

[25] Perez, S. (2017). Siri usage and engagement dropped since last year, as Alexa and Cortana grew. Retrieved from https://techcrunch.com/2017/07/11/siri-usage-and-engagement-dropped-since-last-year-as-alexa-and-cortana-grew/

[26] Robey, D., Anderson, C., & Raymond, B. (2013). Information technology, materiality, and organizational change: A professional odyssey. *Journal of the Association for Information Systems, 14*(7), 379.

[27] Russell, S., & Norvig, P. (2010). *Artificial Intelligence: A modern approach* (Third ed. Vol. 25). New Jersey: Pearson Education.

[28] Savoli, A., & Barki, H. (2013). Functional Affordance Archetypes: a New Perspective for Examining the Impact of IT Use on Desirable Outcomes.

[29] Schultze, U. (2010). Embodiment and presence in virtual worlds: a review. *Journal of Information Technology, 25*(4), 434-449.

[30] Shoham, Y. (1993). Agent-oriented programming. *Artificial intelligence, 60*(1), 51-92.

[31] Steels, L., & Brooks, R. A. (1995). *The artificial life route to artificial intelligence: Building embodied, situated agents*: L. Erlbaum Associates Hillsdale, NJ.

[32] Stendal, K., Thapa, D., & Lanamäki, A. (2016). *Analyzing the concept of affordances in information systems.* Paper presented at the System Sciences (HICSS), 2016 49th Hawaii International Conference on.

[33] Turkle, S. (2012). *Alone together: Why we expect more from technology and less from each other*: Basic books.

[34] Vincent, J. (2016). Twitter taught Microsoft's AI chatbot to be a racist asshole in less than a day. Retrieved from http://www.theverge.com/2016/3/24/11297050/tay-microsoft-chatbot-racist

[35] Wooldridge, M., & Jennings, N. R. (1995). Intelligent agents: Theory and practice. *The knowledge engineering review, 10*(02), 115-152.

[36] Zammuto, R. F., Griffith, T. L., Majchrzak, A., Dougherty, D. J., & Faraj, S. (2007). Information technology and the changing fabric of organization. *Organization science, 18*(5), 749-762.

[37] Zeng, D. (2015). AI Ethics: Science Fiction Meets Technological Reality. *IEEE Intelligent Systems, 30*(3), 2-5.

Social Support in Online Health Communities: A Social-Network Approach

Srikanth Parameswaran
State University of New York
at Buffalo
sparames@buffalo.edu

Rajiv Kishore
State University of New York
at Buffalo
rkishore@buffalo.edu

1 INTRODUCTION

Online health communities (OHC) provide patients and healthcare providers an avenue for affective and health related communication [1]. As digitized hubs of user-powered health information, OHCs bridge the urban-rural divide by enabling ubiquitous online content, empower patients with stigmatized diseases who may live in isolation, and provide social support for better mental and behavioral health outcomes [2, 3]. From the user-generated content (UGC) in online health communities, patients find emotional, experiential and informational support [3]. What makes OHCs more interesting is, in the support seeking\providing process, community members willingly or unwillingly become embedded in a "web-of-support". Threaded discussions allow members to see other contributing members, thereby making members aware of each other. With the passage of time and as a consequence of participation in several threads, members become part of a network of OHC members who are connected by their common participation in thread(s). Potentially, the community member's social network position in the web-of-support (WOS) could alter the nature and extent of a community member's perception of the "other" members and hence could have implications on how the member provides social support.

The objective of this study is to examine how OHC member's social network position in the WOS affects the extent and characteristics of member generated social support. We explore how social network position influences extent of social support (the extensiveness of the member's content) and the linguistic features of social support text - we study self-absorption.

ACM Reference Format:
Srikanth Parameswaran, and Rajiv Kishore. 2018. Social Support in Online Health Communities: A Social-Network Approach. In Proceedings of ACM *SIGMIS-CPR, June 18–20, 2018, Buffalo-Niagara Falls, NY, USA* ACM, NY, NY, USA, 2 pages. https://doi.org/10.1145/3209626.3209725

We focus on the occurrence of a) self-focused content with words such as 'i', 'me', or 'myself' versus, b) socially-focused content with words such as 'you', 'ur', or 'y'all' [4]. We ask the following research question: *How does social network position affect UGC (social support), in terms of extent, the exhibition of self-absorbed language, and use of socially-focused language?*

2 THEORETICAL FOUNDATIONS

By using arguments from the social presence and the social network theory, we propose hypotheses relating member social network position to the extent of social support and linguistic features in online social support. In OHC context, social presence is the extent to which a focal member is aware of other community members [5]. High social presence makes members communicate better. First, in our paper, by integrating the social network theory, we extend the social presence idea and argue that based on their position in the WOS network, users would differ in the extent as well as the nature of their perceived social presence, and hence would differ in their content shared. We further posit that, member's different dimensions of their network positions, brokerage and influence, will have differential impacts on the extent of online social support.

Second, there is a dearth of studies explaining the linguistic features in UGC (social support) in the OHC context, while there are studies explaining UGC in contexts like social commerce [6] and e-learning [7]. The OHC context gives rise to the importance self-absorption in UGC because a right balance of the "self" and the "other" is crucial for OHC content quality [8]. Given the OHC context, we make a distinction between self-focused content versus social-focused content in UGC in OHC. Different social network dimensions can afford different manifestations of social presence and hence could impact self-absorption in their UGC.

In the OHC context, social capital denotes the resources accumulated by a member as a result of his\her relationship with other users in the OHC [9]. The research on social capital quantifies users on their importance in their social network using various measures of centrality – each measure captures a different aspect of importance in the network. In this paper, we focus on two such centrality measures namely brokerage and influence. In the OHC context, high brokerage means that members are connected to a network of users who are not connected. Brokers achieve the information and control benefits by spanning the structural holes in the WOS [10]. These members also benefit from the diversity of information because the members in their network are not connected and hence there is less likelihood of redundant information. On the other hand, influence measures the extent to which members interact with other users who are well connected [11]. A member could be connected to just one other member. If the other member is in turn connected to several members then the focal member is said to have higher influence compared to another member who has connection with one member who is not well connected. In the social network literature, betweenness centrality and eigenvector centrality are considered as proxies for brokerage and influence, respectively.

3 RESEARCH MODEL AND HYPOTHESES

Higher centrality in the WOS means that the focal member interacted with other users by means of participation in threads. So, both centralities imply that the focal members are more aware of other members signaling an increase in their social presence. Increased social presence would entail better understanding of other members and increased future content contribution due to awareness, gratifications, altruism and reputation benefits [12]. Another line of argument in the social network literature establishes curvilinear effects due to central positions in social networks [13]. Combining these arguments, we take a stand that both brokerage and influence would improve the extent of social support, but with curvilinear effects. We argue for a network-based explanation enabled by different dimensions of online social network position – brokerage would enable a "diverse others" perception and influence would enable an "others as opinion leaders" perception. Due these different perceptions, the curvilinear effects pan out differently for the two dimensions of social network position of our interest. Also, these perceptions entail that OHC members are better able to define the social context in the OHC, and focus attention towards others (versus the self). However, there is a ceiling unto which the two dimensions are needed to establish the social context. Once the social context is defined by the user, the social context shifting due to the social network position reduces. Thus, brokerage and influence would impact the exhibition of self-focused and socially-focused language, but with curvilinear effects.

4 RESULTS AND DISCUSSION

We empirically tested our model using text and social network data collected from an online health community for diabetes patients. Variables were operationalized using text mining and social network analyses. Using panel data modeling we show statistically significant relationships between online social network positions and extent of social support, and online social network positions and linguistic features. We found support for all of our hypotheses. We will present the full results at the conference.

5 CONTRIBUTIONS AND IMPLICATION

Our paper makes two contributions to literature on OHC, UGC, social presence and social networks. One, we build a social network position based model of extent of social support in OHCs. By doing so, we extend the current social presence based explanations, and argue that as users spend more time they also form a WOS based on which they create content. Two, we build two social network based models of linguistic features, one with self-focused content as the outcome and the other with social-focused content as the outcome. By doing so we extend the research on the predictors of linguistic features to the OHC context. Our results have important implications for design of OHC, building recommender systems, framing OHC policies, and moderating content and networks in OHC.

REFERENCES

[1] Merolli, M., Gray, K., and Martin-Sanchez, F. (2013). Health outcomes and related effects of using social media in chronic disease management: a literature review and analysis of affordances. *Journal of Biomedical Informatics*, 46(6), 957-969.

[2] Goh, J. M., Guodong (Gordon) Gao, and Agarwal, R. (2016). The Creation of Social Value: Can an Online Health Community Reduce Rural-Urban Health Disparities? *MIS Quarterly*, 40(1), 247-263.

[3] Yan, L., and Tan, Y. (2014). Feeling blue? Go online: an empirical study of social support among patients. *Information Systems Research*, 25(4), 690-709.

[4] Pennebaker, J.W., Booth, R.J., Boyd, R.L., and Francis, M.E. (2015). *Linguistic Inquiry and Word Count: LIWC2015*. Austin, TX: Pennebaker Conglomerates

[5] Short, J., Williams, E., and Christie, B. (1976). The Social Psychology of Telecommunications. London: John Wiley & Sons.

[6] Goes, P. B., Lin, M., and Au Yeung, C. M. (2014). "Popularity effect" in user-generated content: evidence from online product reviews. *Information Systems Research*, 25(2), 222-238.

[7] Lowenthal, P. R. (2009). The Evolution and Influence of Social Presence Theory on Online Learning. *Social Computing: Concepts, Methodologies, Tools, and Applications: Concepts, Methodologies, Tools, and Applications*, 113.

[8] Garrison, D. R., Anderson, T., and Archer, W. (1999). Critical inquiry in a text-based environment: Computer conferencing in higher education. *The internet and higher education*, 2(2), 87-105.

[9] Coleman, J. S. (1988). Social capital in the creation of human capital. *American journal of sociology*, 94, S95-S120.

[10] Burt, R. S. 1992. Structural holes: The social structure of competition. Cambridge, MA: Harvard University Press.

[11] Borgatti, S. P. (2005). Centrality and network flow. *Social networks*, 27(1), 55-71.

[12] Wasko, M. M., and Faraj, S. (2005). Why should I share? Examining social capital and knowledge contribution in electronic networks of practice. *MIS quarterly*, 35-57.

[13] Zhou, J., Shin, S. J., Brass, D. J., Choi, J., and Zhang, Z. X. (2009). Social networks, personal values, and creativity: evidence for curvilinear and interaction effects. *Journal of applied psychology*, 94(6), 1544.

Cloud Computing and Firm Innovation:
The Role of Scalability and Heterogeneity in the face of IT Resource Uncertainties

Laxmi Gunupudi
Indian Institute of Management,
Bangalore, India
laxmi.gunupudi@gmail.com

Rajiv Kishore
State University of New York at
Buffalo, Buffalo, NY, USA
rkishore@buffalo.edu

Akie Iriyama
Waseda Business School,
Tokyo, Japan
airiyama@gmail.com

1. Introduction

Cloud computing is an innovation that has gathered a huge amount of interest in the information technology (IT) industry [1]. With its unique characteristics of scalability, consumption based pricing, heterogeneity and standardized services [2, 3], cloud computing is a new procurement model which influences the provision and consumption of IT services in organizations. Capabilities provided by cloud have the potential to support innovations in organizations. Managerial understanding and perceptions about capabilities offered by cloud markets enhances their confidence in engaging in innovative activities. Possibility of anytime access to scalable, heterogeneous IT resources provides safeguards by reducing risks related to innovation. In order to understand the role of cloud in supporting innovative behaviours of firms, we explore prior research on types of innovative activities taken up by firms and conditions under which firms engage in such activities.

Strategic innovative actions emerged as a strong underlying theme researched in various streams including organizational learning and strategy [4, 5], innovation [6] and entrepreneurship [7]. However, there is still a need to understand the antecedents of these activities in organizations [8]. Environmental characteristics such as dynamism has been identified as important factors that influence innovation related activities in firms [8-10].

ACM Reference format:
Laxmi Gunupudi, Rajiv Kishore, and Akie Iriyama 2018. Cloud Computing and Firm Innovation: The Role of Scalability and Heterogeneity in the face of IT Resource Uncertainties. In Proceedings of ACM SIGMIS-CPR '18, June 18–20, 2018, Buffalo-Niagara Falls, NY, USA. 8, 2 pages. https://doi.org/10.1145/3209626.3209722

Global competition and dynamic environment is driving organizations to reduce costs, increase profitability and enhance productivity [11]. This environmental dynamism or uncertainty can be characterized by changes in technologies, variations in customer preferences and fluctuations in product demand. Since IT is an integral part of any organizations and supports all the business processes of modern organizations, the uncertainties in the environment percolate to the business processes of the organizations and ultimately impact the IT resource requirements of these business processes. Hence the demand uncertainties in the market translate to the IT resource demand uncertainties at the business process level and the technological uncertainties in the environment correspond to IT resource technological uncertainties at the business process level. Organizations have to thrive in this ever changing and dynamic environment. They have to keep up with the pace of changing technology and continuously innovate to survive in this environment. This imposes enormous pressure on organizations to continuously innovate so as to reduce costs, sustain competitive advantage and improve the bottom line [12]. Specifically research suggests that a reduction in variance-increasing activity within the firm prevents it from registering and/or responding to environmental uncertainty [13]. Organizations have to manage these uncertainties at the business process level and engage in innovation related activities in order to remain competitive and profitable. While we know that environmental uncertainties drive innovative behaviors in firms, we seek to understand how IT supports these innovative behaviors. In this study, we address the following research question:

What is the role of demand and technological uncertainties of IT resources in shaping the firms innovative behaviors? And how do services provided by cloud computing enable or support these innovative behaviors?

2. Theoretical Background

Cloud markets are based on multi-tenant[1] architecture and cater to several customers. They pool their resources and provide a variety of IT resources. Hence, they are more efficient in handling demand and technological uncertainties and provide more flexibility for the firm. It is posited that highly variable and unpredictable workloads are more suitable for cloud-based services [11]. Cloud service's ability to add and remove resources at a fine-grain and with a very small lead time helps firms manage their variable workloads more efficiently [2]. Similarly, the burden of managing and providing heterogeneous, state-of-the-art IT resources falls on the shoulders of the cloud service provider, and this protects the organizations from the risk of technological obsolescence [14]. Hence the cloud capabilities of scalability and heterogeneity have the potential to help organizations tackle IT resource uncertainties and engage in innovation. To address this research question, we focus on how cloud capabilities of scalability and heterogeneity help organizations tackle these uncertainties in the environment and engage in innovation related activities.

Through an empirical study of business process across firms from different sectors, we aim to provide a more nuanced understanding of the influence of IT resource uncertainties on innovative behaviors of firms and the role of services provided by cloud computing in promoting these behaviors. Through our study, we intend to extend innovation literature in the context of cloud computing by demonstrating how cloud services further enhance firm capabilities and enable them to engage in innovative behaviors under conditions of IT resource uncertainties.

3. Implications

Through this study, we intend to extend literature on antecedents of innovation behavior of firms. Prior research suggests that environmental characteristics such as dynamism has been identified as important factors that influence innovation related activities in firms [8-10]. Organizations have to thrive in this ever changing and dynamic environment. This imposes enormous pressure on organizations to continuously innovate so as to reduce costs, sustain competitive advantage and improve the bottom line [12]. Specifically research suggests that a reduction in variance-increasing activity within the firm prevents it from registering and/or responding to environmental uncertainty [13]. The uncertainties in the environment ultimately impact the IT resources requirements of these business processes. Hence the demand uncertainties in the market translate to the IT resource demand uncertainties at the business process level and the technological uncertainties in the environment correspond to IT resource technological uncertainties at the business process level. Organizations have to manage these uncertainties at the business process level and engage in innovation related activities in order to remain competitive and profitable. Firms engage in activities to understand customers better and to introduction of new and creative products under uncertain environmental conditions in order to stay competitive. Managerial understanding and perceptions about capabilities offered by cloud markets enhances their confidence in engaging in innovative activities. In this context of cloud computing adoption by firms, we seek to understand how demand and technological uncertainties of IT resources influence firm's innovative behaviors.

Through this research we would like to make an important contribution to existing literature on innovation, in the context of cloud computing, by demonstrating how cloud services further enhance firm capabilities and enable them to engage in

innovative behaviors under conditions of IT resource uncertainties. We intend to examine this using the two important capabilities offered by cloud – scalability and heterogeneity. We will examine the role of cloud capabilities in the relationship between IT resource uncertainties and innovation in organizations.

4. References

[1] Martens, B., J. Poeppelbuss, and F. Teuteberg. *Understanding the cloud computing ecosystem: results from a quantitative content analysis.* in *Proceedings of the 10th International Conference on Wirtschaftsinformatik WI.* 2011.

[2] Armbrust, M., et al., *Above the Clouds: A Berkeley View of Cloud Computing.* UC Berkeley Reliable Adaptive Distributed Systems Laboratory, 2009.

[3] Vaquero, L.M., et al., *A break in the clouds: towards a cloud definition.* ACM SIGCOMM Computer Communication Review, 2008. **39**(1): p. 50-55.

[4] Levinthal, D.A. and J.G. March, *The myopia of learning.* Strategic management journal, 1993. **14**(S2): p. 95-112.

[5] Benner, M.J. and M.L. Tushman, *Exploitation, exploration, and process management: The productivity dilemma revisited.* Academy of management review, 2003. **28**(2): p. 238-256.

[6] Danneels, E., *The dynamics of product innovation and firm competences.* Strategic management journal, 2002. **23**(12): p. 1095-1121.

[7] Shane, S. and S. Venkataraman, *The promise of entrepreneurship as a field of research.* Academy of management review, 2000. **25**(1): p. 217-226.

[8] Jansen, J.J., F.A. Van Den Bosch, and H.W. Volberda, *Exploratory innovation, exploitative innovation, and performance: Effects of organizational antecedents and environmental moderators.* Management science, 2006. **52**(11): p. 1661-1674.

[9] Song, M. and M.M. Montoya-Weiss, *The effect of perceived technological uncertainty on Japanese new product development.* Academy of Management journal, 2001. **44**(1): p. 61-80.

[10] Lavie, D., U. Stettner, and M.L. Tushman, *Exploration and exploitation within and across organizations.* The Academy of Management Annals, 2010. **4**(1): p. 109-155.

[11] Misra, S.C. and A. Mondal, *Identification of a company's suitability for the adoption of cloud computing and modelling its corresponding Return on Investment.* Mathematical and Computer Modelling, 2011. **53**(3): p. 504-521.

[12] Demirkan, H., et al., *Service-oriented technology and management: Perspectives on research and practice for the coming decade.* Electronic Commerce Research and Applications, 2009. **7**(4): p. 356-376.

[13] Burgelman, R.A., *Fading memories: A process theory of strategic business exit in dynamic environments.* Administrative Science Quarterly, 1994: p. 24-56.

[14] Glaser, J., Cloud computing can simplify HIT infrastructure management. Healthcare financial management: journal of the Healthcare Financial Management Association, 2011. **65**(8): p. 52-55.

Will Users of Process Management Systems Be More Innovative? A Study on Process Innovation and Process Orientation in the Financial Industry

Michael Leyer
University of Rostock
Germany
michael.leyer@uni-rostock.de

Daniel Beimborn
Frankfurt School of Finance & Management
Germany
d.beimborn@fs.de

Janina Kettenbohrer
University of Bamberg
Germany
janina.kettenbohrer@uni-bamberg.de

1 INTRODUCTION

Process innovation – defined as the creation of new processes or the substantial improvement of existing processes – has become essential for the competitiveness of a firm [4]. However, many companies struggle with establishing a holistic process innovation approach, involving all their employees, who are the main resource for generating, championing and implementing process innovation ideas [1]. In our study, we analyze how BPM systems (BPMS) can help getting people engaged in process innovation. BPMS support activities of business process management (BPM) such as process modeling & documentation, process simulation, or workflow management. Will employees who are regularly using BPMS think and act in a more process-oriented manner and will they show more process innovation behavior?

Applying the four-factor theory of work group innovation and using survey data, we show that employees who make regular use of a BPMS will exhibit a process-oriented attitude and thus contribute to process innovation. Thus, we contribute to the IS literature on understanding drivers for individual process innovation behavior and on the value contribution of knowledge-based IT systems for process innovation.

2 MODEL DEVELOPMENT

Contributions to process innovation exhibited by employees – *individual process innovation behavior* – is the outcome variable of our model. Performing a business process in a way that it is effective, efficient, and leading to satisfied customers, represents

ACM Reference format:
Michael Leyer, Daniel Beimborn, and Janina Kettenbohrer. 2018. Will Users of Process Management Systems Be More Innovative? A Study on Process Innovation and Process Orientation in the Financial Industry. In Proceedings of ACM SIGMIS-CPR, June 18–20, 2018, Buffalo-Niagara Falls, NY, USA, 2 pages.
https://doi.org/10.1145/3209626.3209727

a competitive advantage for companies. Introducing such a process innovation requires the generation, championing, and implementation of new ideas [5]: *idea generation* describes the recognition of problems in a process and the articulation of ideas that change the process radically; *idea championing* refers to championing activities, as adoption is triggered by promoting innovation ideas across colleagues and supervisors. *Idea implementation* covers then the subsequent activities related to introducing the idea successfully and sustainably in an organization so that the process innovation becomes part of the organizational routine.

To exhibit process innovation behavior, employees need to have a process-oriented mindset, i.e., they take the larger process, of which their work is part of, into account when performing their daily work [3]. This *individual process orientation* consists of three dimensions, too; first, it requires *knowledge* regarding the design of the overall process; second, employees have to be *aware* of how their work influences the overall process; third, *process coordination* refers to teamwork and connectedness across departments with colleagues involved in a process. Overall, such a process orientation makes it easier to develop ideas, champion them among colleagues involved in the same process and successfully implement them. Thus, we hypothesize:

H1: *The higher the process orientation of employees involved in a process, the higher is their individual process innovation behavior.*

BPM systems contain information that is relevant for employees' daily work (visual process models, information about working procedures etc.). Each time, employees want to receive information about their tasks and therefore access the BPM system, they get a process-oriented view of their work environment [2]. Consequently, knowledge regarding the design of the process is explicitly or implicitly acquired. Process visibility also increases situation awareness in process operations and helps to identify bottlenecks in the course of process improvement. The employees become aware of interdependencies between their own and their colleagues' tasks as well as of their tasks' impact on the overall process. Due to the interdependencies between the different tasks within a process, employees have to coordinate with their colleagues. BPMS support this coordination and enable personal exchange because these interdependencies and the corresponding colleagues are made transparent. Thus, we hypothesize:

H2: *The usage of a BPM system by employees leads to higher individual process orientation (knowledge, awareness, coordination).*

Turning the argumentation around, process orientation serves as mediator of the impact of BPMS usage on innovation behavior.

H3: *Individual process orientation positively mediates the relationship between BPMS usage and process innovation behavior.*

Figure 1 shows the research model at a glance.

Figure 1: Research Model

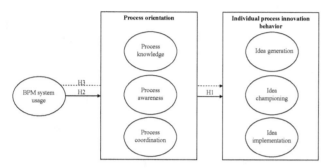

3 METHODOLOGY AND RESULTS

To test our research model, we used a survey-based approach and collected data from employees in the German financial industry. We targeted process workers (i.e., no leadership positions) via a university mailing list and gathered 1,054 responses. Of these participants, 296 agreed to answer a second questionnaire. They were contacted two months later with a shorter questionnaire, containing measures for the dependent variable only; in this second stage, we received 171 responses; from those 135 were usable because they did not show any missing values. We tested our research model using partial least squares (PLS). Process orientation and Individual process innovation behavior have been implemented as second-order constructs reflecting the three dimensions each, as introduced above. Figure 2 shows the results of testing our model. All three hypotheses can be supported.

Figure 2: Results (*: .05; **: .01; ***: .001; n = 135)

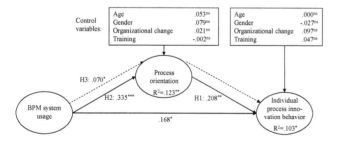

4 DISCUSSION AND CONCLUSION

Using a BPM system has a positive effect on individual process innovation behavior with process orientation being an important mediator. The BPMS allows employees to see processes in one place, to understand relationships and to trace potential influencing factors for operational problems. Hence, creative processes among employees are triggered by having process information present in one's mind and creating ideas from daily work.

Similarly, the BPMS helps to convince colleagues and to champion new ideas throughout the organization by informing employees which of their colleagues are relevant in processes, assuring employees having an idea that it is beneficial for the whole process, or discussing interdependencies between activities and processes affected by an idea.

Moreover, BPMS makes project members more aware of the dependencies of activities and processes given the influence and consequences of a change of processes. This makes it easier to follow a joint vision in the sense of process orientation and facilitates to inform and integrate affected employees with potentially less resistance, i.e., supporting ideal implementation.

Overall, the introduction of a BPMS is an important lever for process innovation. It does not only contribute positively to employees' process orientation, which is relevant for an efficient process execution, but also supports individual process innovation behavior through this mindset. Hence, process innovation in an organization can be fostered by supporting individual employees with a BPMS. Accordingly, organizations should be more aware of the enablers and drivers to foster innovation activities next to daily operational work. Implementing a BPM system that is actually and regularly used by the employees shows to be beneficial to foster their innovation behavior.

KEYWORDS

Process innovation; process orientation; BPM system usage; individual innovation behavior

REFERENCES

[1]   ANDERSON, N., POTOCNIK, K., and ZHOU, J., 2014. Innovation and creativity in organizations. A state-of-the-science review, prospective commentary, and guiding framework. *Journal of Management 40*, 5, 1297-1333.

[2]   KETTENBOHRER, J., BEIMBORN, D., and LEYER, M., 2016. Examining the impact of BPM system usage on employees' process orientation. In *Proceedings of the International Conference on Information Systems 2016* (Dublin2016), Association for Information Systems, 1-18.

[3]   LEYER, M. and WOLLERSHEIM, J., 2013. How to learn process-oriented thinking. An experimental investigation of the effectiveness of different learning modes. *Schmalenbachs Business Review 65*, 4 (October), 454-473.

[4]   PIENING, E.P. and SALGE, T.O., 2015. Understanding the antecedents, contingencies, and performance implications of process innovation. A dynamic capabilities perspective. *Journal of Product Innovation Management 32*, 1, 80-97.

[5]   SCOTT, S.G. and BRUCE, R.A., 1994. Determinants of innovative behavior. A path model of individual innovation in the workplace. *The Academy of Management Journal 37*, 3, 580-607.

A Predictive Method to Determine Incomplete Electronic Medical Records

Amir Talaei-Khoei
University of Nevada Reno
1664 N. Virginia Street,
Reno 89557 USA

University of Technology Sydney
15 Broadway, Ultimo NSW
2007 Australia
atalaeikhoei@unr.edu

Luvai F. Motiwalla
University of Massachusetts Lowell
220 Pawtucket St, Lowell,
MA 01854 USA
luvai_Motiwalla@uml.edu

S. Farzan Kazemi
University of Nevada Reno
1664 N. Virginia Street,
Reno 89557 USA
farzan.kazemi@nevada.unr.edu

ABSTRACT

This paper is utilizing predictive models to determine missing electronic medical records (EMR) at general practice offices. Prior research has addressed the missing values problem in the EMRs used for secondary analysis. However, health care providers are overlooking the missing records problem that stores the patients' medical visits information in EMRs. Our study provides a technique to predict the number of EMR entries for each practice based on their past data records. If the number of EMR entries is less than predicted, it warns the occurrence of missing records with the 95% confidence interval. The study uses seven years of EMRs from 14 general practice offices to train the predictive model. The model predicts EMR data entries and accordingly identified missing EMRs for the following year. We compared the actual visits illustrated by de-identified billing data to the predictive model. The study found auto-correlation method improves the performance of identifying missing records by detecting the period of prediction. In addition, artificial neural networks and support vector machines perform better than other predictive methods depending on whether the analysis aims at detecting missing EMRs or when identifying complete EMRs with no missing records. Results suggest that clinicians and medical professionals should be mindful of the potential missing records of EMRs prior any secondary analysis.

KEYWORDS

Data Completeness, Missing Records, Electronic Medical Records

ACM Reference format:

Amir Talaei-Khoei, Luvai F. Motiwalla, and S. Farzan Kazemi 2018. A Predictive Method to Determine Incomplete Electronic Medical Records. In Proceedings of ACM SIGMIS-CPR '18, June 18–20, 2018, Buffalo-Niagara Falls, NY, USA, 8 pages. https://doi.org/10.1145/3209626.3209706

1 INTRODUCTION

Policy makers and healthcare professionals have sought to overhaul the daily extract-transform-load (ETL) approaches which generated the electronic medical records (EMRs) data warehouses, which can be used for auditing, continuous quality improvement, health service planning, epidemiological studies, and evaluation research [21,62]. Although integrating of this increasing amount of data in the EMR warehouse is essential [27], the biggest barrier for their successful use has been the missing data problem [39,47,61]. Weiskopf and Weng (2013) [60] have found missing data in EMRs as the biggest issue for its' lack of use. Unfortunately, existence of EMRs and utilizing them in general practice offices does not necessarily mean that EMRs have sufficient information to be used in medical and healthcare analysis [16]. It has been reported that practice offices, clinics, and hospitals miss values and records when entering EMRs [27]. The quality of epidemiologic studies that depend on data from EMRs vary widely due to missing data. Read et al. (2017) in their study of missing health data found, regardless of recent improvements in EMRs, incomplete data was a huge barrier for medical research and stated that 25% of Type-2 diabetes patients' records collected between 2004-11were missing data that was relevant for cardiovascular disease and cancer outcomes.

These studies highlight the difficulty of using EMRs because most health-care providers cannot trust the accuracy and validity of information stored in these databases. Therefore, identification of missing records and improving their information transparency are critical for successful use of EMR for epidemiology or clinical research.

1.1 Missing Records versus Missing Values: Why is it important to study missing records?

In the field of information processing, missing data refers to the extent to which necessary data for a specific task or decision is not available [31,37]. Research in statistics has also focused on the inference techniques to solve the missing data problem [7,49,49].

However, the EMRs magnifies the missing data problem because they include extensive narrative texts, redundancies, and complex longitudinal information. This make them complex than common research datasets in the way that they are collected, stored, and structured [10,59].

There is a body of research on assessment of missing data in EMRs. Arts et al. (2002) defined minimum data requirements for EMRs in respect to either intrinsic expectations or extrinsic use of EMRs. Defining EMRs data requirements based on extrinsic use of EMRs refers to the fit-to-purpose definition given by Ziegel (1990). In a systematic literature review, Weiskopf and Weng (2013) have defined four dimensions of missing data for EMRs: *breadth, density, predictive,* and *documentation.* Breadth indicates that a record in an EMR misses values for one or multiple attributes. For instance, clinicians interested in clinical outcomes may need values for more than one attributes of a patient's medical record to understand her clinical conditions [3]. When this multi-attribute data is missing, compromises the breadth dimension. Density refers to the insufficient frequency of longitudinal data points for the

values of an EMR attributes [51]. For instance, EMRs utilization partially focused on occurrence frequency of the same examination tests, medication, or diagnoses [24]. The predictive dimension of missing data in EMRs is defined as using a particular mathematical model to predict a healthcare or medical outcome such as clinical phenomenon, disease status, and risk [11,55,63]. Finally, the documentation dimension of EMRs is related to recording of all observations about a patient care during the clinical process [18].

Breadth, density, and predictive dimensions focus mainly on the missing values in records. However, documentation focuses on missing records (all values) of a patient in a clinical encounter [59]. For instance, when a physician does not document a visit by a patient completely does not have any record about her diagnosis or treatment. In this example, while the breadth, density, and predictive fail to identify missing data, the documentation shows that the problem is not about missing values but it is about missing records. This in our opinion is a much bigger problem in epidemiological studies. Therefore, our focus is on the documentation dimension and missing records.

Table 1: Comparison of Different Dimensions of Missing Data in EMRs

	Definition	Missing Values or Missing Records	Assessment at Repository or Data Entry Points
Breadth	Breadth refers to unavailability values for the attributes in a record of a patient's EMR [3].	Missing Values	Repository
Density	Density refers to the insufficient frequency of longitudinal data points for the values of an EMR attributes [51].	Missing Values	Repository
Predictive	Predictive refers to unavailability of values for required EMR attributes to use a particular predictive model to predict a healthcare or medical outcome [11,55,63].	Missing Values	Repository
Documentation	Documentation refers to unavailability a record in a patient's EMR for her medical visit [18].	Missing Records	Data entry point

The concept of missing values has been the topic of research in statistic and formal computing [5,6,22,23,44,45]. There is a huge body of research on identifying missing values in EMRs presented in a survey conducted by Liu et al. (2017) [31], but not much on missing records. Although missing records are an important dimension of missing data, they can be only assessed in association with data entry points at the clinicians' offices. Literature has proposed three methods to assess missing records in EMRs:

- Through a benchmark reference that can be obtained by contacting the clinician who has entered the records. However, this has been often considered to be practically challenging as such benchmarks may not be available [25].
- Through crosschecking EMRs with an alternative trusted data source. For instance, the data entry practice maintains paper records [46], which may not necessarily be the case. Similarly, Logan et al. [32] compared clinical visits with EMR entries. This is often operationalized by mapping billing data to

EMRs. However, this approach requires access to billing data of practice offices.

Researchers in the field of information processing have proposed mathematical-based methods that identify missing records. Motro and Rakov (1997) use database views to identify missing records in a table that has a reference in another table used in the view. [40] identify missing records when integrating a table to another. Liu et al. (2016) [31] identified missing records by investigating the dependencies among tables. All of these methods are based on the assumption that a record in a table is missed for technical reasons, however, a reference to it can be found in another tables in the same database. Since physicians may miss to record the entire medical encounter during a patient visit, there will not be any dependencies or reference available for the record.

1.2 This Study

This paper proposes the use of predictive models to address the aforementioned shortfalls associated with missing records in EMRs. The main objectives of this paper are:

- Predictive models extract non-trivial patterns in the number of data entries at general practice office. This study utilizes time-stamped data that present the number of data entries for EMRs, and subsequently uses predictive models to identify incidence of missing records when the number of entries obtained by predictive models is less than expected. The time-stamped data used in this paper refers to the number of EMRs entered by a physician in each particular.

- Performance of predictive models may vary from one dataset to another [58]. Therefore, the present study develops an evaluation method to test if the choice of predictive models influences the performance of the proposed method in terms of identify missing EMRs.

- Periodicity is the repetition of a pattern at regular periods [43] in predictive models. Detecting the period in a predictive analysis can assist making better predictions, as well as helping the identification of structural similarities [50,57]. Although the data presenting EMR entries generally focus on the missing number of EMR entries per day, this study examines whether identifying the prediction period could improve the performance of missing EMRs detection. For instance, a physician's weekly schedule may vary from one week to another. Therefore, predicting the number of daily entries for a week will not necessarily be the best approach due to the weekly changes in the schedule. In such situations, the analysis period may be extending.

This paper compares the performance period detection (i.e., using a day, a week or a month as the period of prediction). Since a physicians' schedule does not extend to a year, one-year period was not included in the comparison. Commonly used methods to detect prediction period were used, specifically, *Autocorrelation* [36] and *Fourier Transform* [34]. The current study attempts to answer the following research questions with these methods:

1. How can predictive analytics identify missing records in EMRs using time-stamped data entries at general practice offices?

2. Does the choice of predictive models impact the performance of identifying missing EMRs?

3. Does the period detection of time-stamped entries of EMRs influence the performance of identifying missing EMRs?

To address these questions, we have utilizes seven years of EMRs from 14 general practice offices to train the predictive methods. These methods predicted EMR data entries and accordingly identified missing EMRs for the following year. The results were compared to the actual number of visits obtained by the de-identified billing data. The performance measures such as area under curve (AUC), Sensitivity, and Specificity were calculated for these results. The predictive methods being evaluated were Artificial Neural Networks (ANN), Support Vector Machine (SVM), Decision Trees (DT), and Logistic Regression (LR). The paper also looked if auto-correlation or Fourier Transform improved the performance of detecting missing records. The remainder of this paper is organized as follows: Section 2 presents the methodology of data collection,

preparation, and analysis for the approach. Section 3 presents the analysis results. Section 4 discusses the findings of the paper, and finally, Section 5 summarizes and concludes the article.

2 METHODS

Figure 1 provides an overview of the methodology of our study. As shown in this figure, the proposed method consists of three elements: (1) data collection, (2) data cleaning and, (3) missing EMRs detection. Different elements of the methods depicted in Figure 1 are discussed under this section.

2.1 Data Cleaning

To clean the data, a four step procedure was utilized. When number of EMR entries is greater than the actual number of entries, we declare that as occurrence of missing records. Third, we have adopted outlier detection algorithms in STATISTICA- II software in order to eliminate entry errors and duplicated data.

2.2. Predictive Methods

The following predictive methods were used in this study.

- *Artificial Neural Networks(ANN)* [1,20,56] are a learning method that learns by identifying patterns in the data as opposed to traditional classification methods such as decision trees discussed below. ANN is organized in layers. Layers are made up of a number of interconnected 'nodes' which contain an 'activation function'. In this study, a multi-layer perceptron-based ANN (MLP-ANN) [41] has been adopted. In our preliminary analysis, MLP-ANN has been shown the most suitable ANN to our data structure. MLP-ANN consists of a series of fully interconnected layers of nodes, where there are only connections between adjacent layers [17].

- *Support Vector Machine (SVM)* is a supervised machine learning algorithm that can be used for binary classification [53,54]. For instance, in this study, T2D_status is used to develop a predictive model for developing T2D. In this algorithm, each data item is made of n features. The value of each feature corresponds to the value of a particular coordinate. Support vectors are simply the co-ordinates of an individual observation. SVM is a frontier which best segregates the two classes.

- *Logistic Regression* (LR) is a statistical method for analyzing a dataset based on the independent variables that predict a dichotomous outcome variable with only two possible values [4,35]. In logistic regression, the log odds of the dependent variable are modelled as the linear combination of the predictors.

- *Decision Tree (DT)* is a supervised learning algorithms (having a pre-defined target variable) that is mostly used in classification problems [42]. The entire dataset is in the root when split in different layers based on the predictors to subset of dataset. Based on the outperforming results in our preliminary analysis, this study has used classification and regression trees (C&RT) [52] to generate DTs as suggested by De'ath and Fabricius (2000).

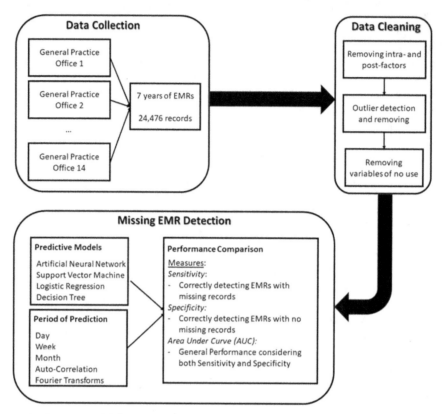

Figure 1: Steps to Use Predictive Methods to Identify Missing Records through Predictive Analytics in Data Entry Point

2.3 Period Detection

The predictive models described in the previous section require specifying a time period that represents the rate at which the data is recorded. Therefore, the predictive models assume that we either know the prediction period or we use period detection methods to identify the period rate of the data [14]. Autocorrelation explained in [36] and Fourier Transforms presented in [34] are commonly used methods for period detection [43]. Autocorrelation demonstrates a good performance for detecting short and long periods, but cannot accurately identify the true period because the multiples of the true period will have the same power as the true period. On the other hand, Fourier Transforms are not able to detect long periods because of low frequency regions and data sparseness [26].

The data presenting the number of daily EMR entries for each physician in general practice offices was presented in a daily format. As mentioned earlier, there is a prior knowledge that the physicians' schedules do not extend to a year. As such, current work compares the performance of the above-mentioned predictive models to identify missing EMRs: (1) using a day as the prediction period, (2) using a week as the prediction period, (3) using a month as the prediction period, (4) using autocorrelation to detect the period of prediction, and (5) using Fourier Transform to detect period of prediction.

2.4 Comparison of Performance

The predictive models under the comparison are to predict the number of EMR entries. However, the period detection whether we use the domain knowledge to use a day, week, month or utilize Autocorrelation and Fourier Transform can also influence the performance of the predictive models [14]. Therefore, this study taki these two perspectives into account compares the twenty methods given in Table 2.

2.5 Measures for Comparison of Performance

As mentioned earlier, performance of the prediction methods in this study was measured and compared using Sensitivity, Specificity, and Area Under Curve (AUC) [12]. *Sensitivity* measures the proportion of positives that are correctly identified. For instance, in this study, sensitivity represents a portion between 0.0-1.0 for occurrence of missing EMRs that are correctly identified. *Specificity* measures the proportion of negatives that are correctly identified. For instance, in this study, specificity represents a portion of 0.0-1.0 of non-occurrences of missing EMRs that are correctly identified. *AUC* is a summary measure of the accuracy considering both sensitivity and specificity for the quantitative prediction conducted by each of the methods presented in Table 2. A test with no better performance than chance has the Sensitivity, Specificity or AUC of 0.5, but a perfect test has them as 1.0.

Table 2 Summary of Methods.

Predictive Models	Prediction Period				
	Day	Week	Month	Auto-correlation	Fourier Transform
ANN	*ANN-D*	*ANN-W*	*ANN-M*	*ANN-A*	*ANN-F*
SVM	*SVM-D*	*SVM-W*	*SVM-M*	*SVM-A*	*SVM-F*
LR	*LR-D*	*LR-W*	*LR-M*	*LR-A*	*LR-F*
DT	*DT-D*	*DT-W*	*DT-M*	*DT-A*	*DT-F*

A confidence interval of 95% was selected, meaning that there is only 5% chance of observing EMR entries outside of the predicted number.

3 RESULTS: MISSING ELECTRONIC MEDICAL RECORDS AT GENERAL PRACTICE OFFICES

In January 2011, we developed a system to link the EMRs from 14 general practice offices in real-time. The system aimed to enhance the diabetes management through forecasting predication of patients at risk of diabetes by continuous analysis of daily-generated Electronic Medical Records (EMR). The dataset used to train the methods is the EMR data entries from these 14 practices from the November 2008 – November 2015. The method predicted EMR data entries and accordingly identified missing EMRs for the following year. We compared the results to the de-identified billing data from November 2015 - November 2016.

Table 3 presents the results of the comparison for the 20 predictive methods over the different predictive periods in terms of performance as measured by AUC, Sensitivity and Specificity.

3.1 Auto-correlation improves the performance.

The results show that period detection improves the performance of prediction methods. Auto-correlation shows better performance compared to Fourier Transform. For instance, while period detection improves the AUC, Sensitivity and Specificity always to be more than 0.5, these measures stay below 0.5 when period detection was not implemented. Auto-correlation has demonstrated better performance compared to Fourier Transform. For instance, when ANN uses AUC, Sensitivity, and Specificity of 0.851, 0.872 and 0.841, Fourier Transform generates 0.791, 0.803, and 0.786, respectively. Therefore, in this paper, only compares auto-correlation and Fourier Transform.

3.2 ANN improves the general performance.

Comparing different predictive models, ANN showed a better performance as measured by AUC. Regardless of period of prediction, ANN demonstrated a better AUC followed by SVM. For instance, ANN generated an AUC of 0.851 for period of prediction detected by auto-correlation and 0.791 for period of prediction detected by Fourier Transform, while SVM had values of 0.839 and 0.778 for these measures, respectively.

Table 3 Comparison of Results.

	Method	AUC	Sensitivity	Specificity
Day	ANN-D	0.291	0.301	0.285
	SVM-D	0.227	0.209	0.293
	LR-D	0.193	0.201	0.189
	DT-D	0.190	0.188	0.193
Week	ANN-W	0.204	0.227	0.193
	SVM-W	0.198	0.153	0.207
	LR-W	0.188	0.199	0.176
	DT-W	0.195	0.197	0.186
Month	ANN-M	0.317	0.387	0.279
	SVM-M	0.289	0.248	0.314
	LR-M	0.191	0.196	0.185
	DT-M	0.172	0.167	0.189
Auto-Correlation	ANN-A	0.851	0.872	0.841
	SVM-A	0.839	0.807	0.911
	LR-A	0.579	0.592	0.544
	DT-A	0.601	0.588	0.625
Fourier Transform	ANN-F	0.791	0.803	0.786
	SVM-F	0.778	0.693	0.887
	LR-F	0.582	0.590	0.542
	DT-F	0.523	0.573	0.502

3.3 ANN improves the detection of missing EMRs.

ANN followed by SVM has demonstrated a better performance to detect missing EMRs. The measure of sensitivity presents the performance of prediction when correctly identifying a missing EMR. For instance, when ANN generated sensitivity of 0.872 for period of prediction detected by Auto-correlation and 0.803 for period of prediction detected by Fourier Transforms, SVM had values of 0.807 and 0.693 for these measures, respectively.

3.4 SVM improves the detection of no missing EMRs.

SVM followed by ANN had a better performance to detect no missing electronic medical records. The measure of specificity showed that the performance of prediction when correctly identifying no missing EMRs. For instance, when SVM provides specificity of 0.911 for period of prediction detected by auto-correlation and 0.887 for period of prediction detected by Fourier Transforms, ANN generated values of 0.841 and 0.786 for these measures, respectively.

4   DISCUSSION

Weiskopf and Weng (2013) [59] believed that missing data occurs in electronic medical records when either a value for variable is missing a whole record. For instance, missing values encounters when the value for a variable in a patient record is missing; e.g. there have not been sufficient tests for the particular conditions, or some variables of EMRs required for a predictive analysis are not available. There have been a number of studies in medical informatics addressing this issue [19,28,29,48]. However, EMRs may also miss a record in which, a patient may have visited a general practice office but no record of her visit was entered in EMR. While there have been limited number of solutions proposed in literature for missing EMRs, the shortfalls presented in Section 1, motivated this work to employ predictive analytics in order to detect missing records. We present the answers to the research questions below.

The differences in physicians served, settings, workflows, data procedures, and regulations may result in changes in the choice of methods. Yet, the overall steps to detect missing EMRs provided in this studycan be used in any settings. The conceptual idea of identifying missing EMRs using the prediction of the number of entries in each general practice offices is generalizable.

4.1 How can predictive analytics identify missing records in EMRs using time-stamped data entries at general practice offices?

The current study evaluated the use of predictive methods such as Artificial Neural Networks (ANN), Support Vector Machine (SVM), Logistic Regression, and Decision Trees (DT) to predict the number of EMR entries in each physician office. Therefore, if the number of entries is less than the predicted number of EMR entries, this can be used as an indicator for missing EMRs.

Our results show that depending on the period of prediction and the predictive model used, different predictive methods can be used to identify missing electronic medical records. This is in agreement with the findings of Endler et al. (2015) [15] that use predictive analytics to measure the quality of billing data at general practice offices. However, our findings advance results of Camdeviren et al. (2007) [8] that only compare the application of LR and DT in the medical domain. As a matter of fact, the current study shows that ANN and SVM, not being compared by

Camdeviren et al. (2007) [8] can improve the results in identifying missing EMRs. Although our findings demonstrated promising results in some cases, particularly, the choice of the method and the period of prediction, which influenced the performance of detecting missing records.

4.2 Does the choice of predictive models impact on the performance of identifying missing electronic medical records?

Our results present some difference in performance when using different predictive methods. While logistic regression and decision tree do not show AUC, sensitivity and specificity to be more than 0.5, we therefore used ANN and LR for the purpose of this study. They were subject to the use of auto-correlation or Fourier Transform that will be discussed in the next section. Our results acknowledge the comparison of performance for predictive methods presented in Caruana and Niculescu-Mizil (2006) [9]. In this comparison, ANN and SVM methods provided good performance. In the same study, Caruana and Niculescu-Mizil (2006) [9] believe LR and DT require calibration to perform well, however, this is not possible in our dataset.

Although the performance of ANN and SVM are similar and close, the comparison of their best utility depends on the purpose of analysis. For instance, if the objective is to identify missing EMRs, ANN improves the performance measured by sensitivity. However, if the objective is to detect complete EMRs with no missing records, SVM relatively demonstrates better performance.

4.3 Does the period detection of time-stamped entry of EMRs influence the performance identifying missing electronic medical records?

The findings of this study demonstrate that period detection methods such as auto-correlation and Fourier Transform substantially improve the performance of predictive methods to identify missing EMRs. Our results demonstrate better performance in auto-correlation compared to Fourier Transform. This is similar to what stated in Li et al. (2012) and Otunba and Lin (2014) [26,43]. Auto-correlation has some difficulties in identifying the exact period of prediction due to the fact that the multiples of the true period will have the same power as the exact period. However, this may not provide any shortfall for the performance of Auto-correlation for the purpose of this study, as multiple of true period perform similarly as good as the true period. On the other hand, Fourier Transform suffer from poor estimation of long periods due to issue of frequency regions or sparseness in data.

4.4 Limitations

The results for the choice of methods of prediction and period detection are primarily illustrative and not exhaustive list. We may have failed to take into account the needs of potential data consumers or practice office. For instance, we did not investigate into the relationship between the choice of the methods and the level of tolerance for missing records that an EMR consumer may have for a particular secondary analysis. More work is necessary for a thorough and robust model to identify the missing records as it relates to the secondary use of EMR data.

5 CONCLUSIONS

Since the implementation of the 2015 Affordable Health-Care Act (ObamaCare), the U.S. health providers have adopted EMRs to improve patient care quality and efficiency. These goals have been compromised due to the missing data, which is a recognized problem in EMR research [33]. While most of prior research has focused on the problems of missing values with database query tool in EMRs, our study proposes the use of predictive methods to estimate the missing records in EMR of each general practitioner's office. Whenever the actual number of entries is less that the predicted one, our approach warns them of the occurrence of missing records. This helps them to realize the validity of clinical findings coming out of statistical analysis of daily-generated EMRs. Our results show that for this approach to be successful, auto-correlation method is better in detecting the period of prediction. However, the success of the approach to provide reliable detection also depends on the predictive method used. While ANN and SVM provide good detections, the choice between these two are based on whether the analysis aims at detection missing EMRs or identifying entries with no missing records. If the objective is to identify missing EMRs, use ANN. Otherwise, use SVM to improve the performance without identifying missing records.

It is difficult to determine precisely the clinical cost-benefit analysis of any analytics effort identifying EMRs with missing records. As researchers and clinicians continue the use of daily generated EMRs for secondary use, it is important to know how many records are missing in the EMR and determine whether to conduct the study or not. There is no point conducting a study whose outcomes will be inaccurate. We urge EMR data consumers to be mindful of the potential limitations of a dataset prior to committing to its use, explicit in their choice of missing records and transparent about it when reporting results.

REFERENCES

[1]   Filippo Amato, Alberto López, Eladia María Peña-Méndez, Petr Vaňhara, Aleš Hampl, and Josef Havel. 2013. *Artificial neural networks in medical diagnosis*. Elsevier.
[2]   Danielle GT Arts, Nicolette F. De Keizer, and Gert-Jan Scheffer. 2002. Defining and improving data quality in medical registries: a literature review, case study, and generic framework. *J. Am. Med. Inform. Assoc.* 9, 6 (2002), 600–611.
[3]   Carl Asche, Qayyim Said, Vijay Joish, Charles Oaxaca Hall, and Diana Brixner. 2008. Assessment of COPD-related outcomes via a national electronic medical record database. *Int. J. Chron. Obstruct. Pulmon. Dis.* 3, 2 (2008), 323.
[4]   Steven C. Bagley, Halbert White, and Beatrice A. Golomb. 2001. Logistic regression in the medical literature:: Standards for use and reporting, with particular attention to one medical domain. *J. Clin. Epidemiol.* 54, 10 (2001), 979–985.
[5]   P. Baraldi, F. Di Maio, D. Genini, and E. Zio. 2015. Reconstruction of missing data in multidimensional time series by fuzzy similarity. *Appl. Soft Comput.* 26, Supplement C (January 2015), 1–9. DOI:https://doi.org/10.1016/j.asoc.2014.09.038
[6]   Roelof K. Brouwer and Witold Pedrycz. 2003. Training a feed-forward network with incomplete data due to missing input variables. *Appl. Soft Comput.* 3, 1 (July 2003), 23–36. DOI:https://doi.org/10.1016/S1568-4946(03)00003-6
[7]   José M. Cadenas, M. Carmen Garrido, and Raquel Martínez. 2013. Feature subset selection Filter–Wrapper based on low quality data. *Expert Syst. Appl.* 40, 16 (November 2013), 6241–6252. DOI:https://doi.org/10.1016/j.eswa.2013.05.051
[8]   Handan Ankarali Camdeviren, Ayse Canan Yazici, Zeki Akkus, Resul Bugdayci, and Mehmet Ali Sungur. 2007. Comparison of logistic regression model and classification tree: An application to postpartum depression data. *Expert Syst. Appl.* 32, 4 (May 2007), 987–994. DOI:https://doi.org/10.1016/j.eswa.2006.02.022
[9]   Rich Caruana and Alexandru Niculescu-Mizil. 2006. An empirical comparison of supervised learning algorithms. In *Proceedings of the 23rd international conference on Machine learning*, 161–168.
[10] Federico Cismondi, André S. Fialho, Susana M. Vieira, Shane R. Reti, João MC Sousa, and Stan N. Finkelstein. 2013. Missing data in medical databases: Impute, delete or classify? *Artif. Intell. Med.* 58, 1 (2013), 63–72.
[11] Ali Dag, Asil Oztekin, Ahmet Yucel, Serkan Bulur, and Fadel M. Megahed. 2017. Predicting heart transplantation outcomes through data analytics. *Decis. Support Syst.* 94, (2017), 42–52.
[12] Ali Dag, Kazim Topuz, Asil Oztekin, Serkan Bulur, and Fadel M. Megahed. 2016. A probabilistic data-driven framework for scoring the preoperative recipient-donor heart transplant survival. *Decis. Support Syst.* 86, (2016), 1–12.
[13] Glenn De'ath and Katharina E. Fabricius. 2000. Classification and regression trees: a powerful yet simple technique for ecological data analysis. *Ecology* 81, 11 (2000), 3178–3192.
[14] Mohamed G. Elfeky, Walid G. Aref, and Ahmed K. Elmagarmid. 2005. Periodicity detection in time series databases. *IEEE Trans. Knowl. Data Eng.* 17, 7 (2005), 875–887.
[15] Gregor Endler, Philipp Baumgärtel, Andreas M. Wahl, and Richard Lenz. 2015. ForCE: Is Estimation of Data Completeness Through Time Series Forecasts Feasible? In *East European Conference on Advances in Databases and Information Systems*, 261–274.
[16] Benjamin A. Goldstein, Ann Marie Navar, Michael J. Pencina, and John Ioannidis. 2017. Opportunities and challenges in developing risk prediction models with electronic health records data: a systematic review. *J. Am. Med. Inform. Assoc.* 24, 1 (2017), 198–208.
[17] Elham Heidari, Mohammad Amin Sobati, and Salman Movahedirad. 2016. Accurate prediction of nanofluid viscosity using a multilayer perceptron artificial neural network (MLP-ANN). *Chemom. Intell. Lab. Syst.* 155, (2016), 73–85.
[18] William R. Hogan and Michael M. Wagner. 1997. Accuracy of data in computer-based patient records. *J. Am. Med. Inform. Assoc.* 4, 5 (1997), 342–355.
[19] Zhen Hu, Genevieve B. Melton, Elliot G. Arsoniadis, Yan Wang, Mary R. Kwaan, and Gyorgy J. Simon. 2017. Strategies for handling missing clinical data for automated surgical site infection detection from the electronic health record. *J. Biomed. Inform.* 68, Supplement C (April 2017), 112–120. DOI:https://doi.org/10.1016/j.jbi.2017.03.009
[20] Turker Ince, Serkan Kiranyaz, Jenni Pulkkinen, and Moncef Gabbouj. 2010. Evaluation of global and local training techniques over feed-forward neural network architecture spaces for computer-aided medical diagnosis. *Expert Syst. Appl.* 37, 12 (December 2010), 8450–8461. DOI:https://doi.org/10.1016/j.eswa.2010.05.033
[21] Mirjana Ivanović and Zoran Budimac. 2014. An overview of ontologies and data resources in medical domains. *Expert Syst. Appl.* 41, 11 (September 2014), 5158–5166. DOI:https://doi.org/10.1016/j.eswa.2014.02.045
[22] José M. Jerez, Ignacio Molina, Pedro J. García-Laencina, Emilio Alba, Nuria Ribelles, Miguel Martín, and Leonardo Franco. 2010. Missing data imputation using statistical and machine learning methods in a real breast cancer problem. *Artif. Intell. Med.* 50, 2 (2010), 105–115.
[23] Sergio Jurado, Àngela Nebot, Fransisco Mugica, and Mihail Mihaylov. 2017. Fuzzy inductive reasoning forecasting strategies able to cope with missing data: A smart grid application. *Appl. Soft Comput.* 51, Supplement C (February 2017), 225–238. DOI:https://doi.org/10.1016/j.asoc.2016.11.040
[24] Abel N. Kho, M. Geoffrey Hayes, Laura Rasmussen-Torvik, Jennifer A. Pacheco, William K. Thompson, Loren L. Armstrong, Joshua C. Denny, Peggy L. Peissig, Aaron W. Miller, and Wei-Qi Wei. 2011. Use of diverse electronic medical record systems to identify genetic risk for type 2 diabetes within a genome-wide association study. *J. Am. Med. Inform. Assoc.* 19, 2 (2011), 212–218.
[25] James D. Lewis and Colleen Brensinger. 2004. Agreement between GPRD smoking data: a survey of general practitioners and a population-based survey. *Pharmacoepidemiol. Drug Saf.* 13, 7 (2004), 437–441.
[26] Zhenhui Li, Jingjing Wang, and Jiawei Han. 2012. Mining event periodicity from incomplete observations. In *Proceedings of the 18th ACM SIGKDD international conference on Knowledge discovery and data mining*, 444–452.

[27] Siaw-Teng Liaw, Alireza Rahimi, Pradeep Ray, Jane Taggart, S. Dennis, Simon de Lusignan, B. Jalaludin, A. E. T. Yeo, and Amir Talaei-Khoei. 2013. Towards an ontology for data quality in integrated chronic disease management: a realist review of the literature. *Int. J. Med. Inf.* 82, 1 (2013), 10–24.

[28] Jau-Huei Lin and Peter J. Haug. 2008. Exploiting missing clinical data in Bayesian network modeling for predicting medical problems. *J. Biomed. Inform.* 41, 1 (February 2008), 1–14. DOI:https://doi.org/10.1016/j.jbi.2007.06.001

[29] Wen-Yang Lin, Lin Lan, Feng-Hsiung Huang, and Min-Hsien Wang. 2015. Rough-set-based ADR signaling from spontaneous reporting data with missing values. *J. Biomed. Inform.* 58, Supplement C (December 2015), 235–246. DOI:https://doi.org/10.1016/j.jbi.2015.10.013

[30] Caihua Liu, Amir Talaei-Khoei, Didar Zowghi, and Jay Daniel. 2017. Data Completeness in Healthcare: A Literature Survey. *Pac. Asia J. Assoc. Inf. Syst.* 9, 2 (2017).

[31] Yong-Nan Liu, Jian-Zhong Li, and Zhao-Nian Zou. 2016. Determining the Real Data Completeness of a Relational Dataset. *J. Comput. Sci. Technol.* 31, 4 (2016), 720–740.

[32] Judith R. Logan, Paul N. Gorman, and Blackford Middleton. 2001. Measuring the quality of medical records: a method for comparing completeness and correctness of clinical encounter data. In *Proceedings of the AMIA Symposium*, 408.

[33] Jeanne M. Madden, Matthew D. Lakoma, Donna Rusinak, Christine Y. Lu, and Stephen B. Soumerai. 2016. Missing clinical and behavioral health data in a large electronic health record (EHR) system. *J. Am. Med. Inform. Assoc.* 23, 6 (2016), 1143–1149.

[34] Alan G. Marshall and Francis R. Verdun. 2016. *Fourier transforms in NMR, optical, and mass spectrometry: a user's handbook.* Elsevier.

[35] Thomas Mazzocco and Amir Hussain. 2012. Novel logistic regression models to aid the diagnosis of dementia. *Expert Syst. Appl.* 39, 3 (February 2012), 3356–3361. DOI:https://doi.org/10.1016/j.eswa.2011.09.023

[36] Amy McQuillan, Suzanne Aigrain, and Tsevi Mazeh. 2013. Measuring the rotation period distribution of field M dwarfs with Kepler. *Mon. Not. R. Astron. Soc.* 432, 2 (2013), 1203–1216.

[37] Sandra de F. Mendes Sampaio, Chao Dong, and Pedro Sampaio. 2015. DQ2S – A framework for data quality-aware information management. *Expert Syst. Appl.* 42, 21 (November 2015), 8304–8326. DOI:https://doi.org/10.1016/j.eswa.2015.06.050

[38] Amihai Motro and Igor Rakov. 1997. *Not all answers are equally good: Estimating the quality of database answers.* Springer.

[39] Loris Nanni, Alessandra Lumini, and Sheryl Brahnam. 2012. A classifier ensemble approach for the missing feature problem. *Artif. Intell. Med.* 55, 1 (2012), 37–50.

[40] Felix Naumann, Johann-Christoph Freytag, and Ulf Leser. 2004. Completeness of integrated information sources. *Inf. Syst.* 29, 7 (2004), 583–615.

[41] Kais Ncibi, Tarek Sadraoui, Mili Faycel, and Amor Djenina. 2017. A Multilayer Perceptron Artificial Neural Networks Based a Preprocessing and Hybrid Optimization Task for Data Mining and Classification. *Int. J. Econom. Financ. Manag. Int. J. Econom. Financ. Manag.* 5, 1 (March 2017), 12–21. DOI:https://doi.org/10.12691/ijefm-5-1-3

[42] Z. Omiotek, A. Burda, and W. Wójcik. 2013. The use of decision tree induction and artificial neural networks for automatic diagnosis of Hashimoto's disease. *Expert Syst. Appl.* 40, 16 (November 2013), 6684–6689. DOI:https://doi.org/10.1016/j.eswa.2013.03.022

[43] Rasaq Otunba and Jessica Lin. 2014. APT: Approximate Period Detection in Time Series. In *SEKE*, 490–494.

[44] Amit Paul, Jaya Sil, and Chitrangada Das Mukhopadhyay. 2017. Gene selection for designing optimal fuzzy rule base classifier by estimating missing value. *Appl. Soft Comput.* 55, Supplement C (June 2017), 276–288. DOI:https://doi.org/10.1016/j.asoc.2017.01.046

[45] Erkki Pesonen, Matti Eskelinen, and Martti Juhola. 1998. Treatment of missing data values in a neural network based decision support system for acute abdominal pain. *Artif. Intell. Med.* 13, 3 (July 1998), 139–146. DOI:https://doi.org/10.1016/S0933-3657(98)00027-X

[46] Jolt Roukema, Renske K. Los, Sacha E. Bleeker, Astrid M. van Ginneken, Johan van der Lei, and Henriette A. Moll. 2006. Paper versus computer: feasibility of an electronic medical record in general pediatrics. *Pediatrics* 117, 1 (2006), 15–21.

[47] Miriam Seoane Santos, Jastin Pompeu Soares, Pedro Henriques Abreu, Hélder Araújo, and João Santos. 2017. Influence of Data Distribution in Missing Data Imputation. In *Conference on Artificial Intelligence in Medicine in Europe*, 285–294.

[48] Murat Sariyar, Andreas Borg, and Klaus Pommerening. 2011. Missing values in deduplication of electronic patient data. *J. Am. Med. Inform. Assoc.* 19, e1 (2011), e76–e82.

[49] Joseph L. Schafer and John W. Graham. 2002. Missing data: our view of the state of the art. *Psychol. Methods* 7, 2 (2002), 147.

[50] Mohammad Ali Shafia, Seyed Jafar Sadjadi, Amin Jamili, Reza Tavakkoli-Moghaddam, and Mohsen Pourseyed-Aghaee. 2012. The periodicity and robustness in a single-track train scheduling problem. *Appl. Soft Comput.* 12, 1 (January 2012), 440–452. DOI:https://doi.org/10.1016/j.asoc.2011.08.026

[51] Matthew Sperrin, Sarah Thew, James Weatherall, William Dixon, and Iain Buchan. 2011. Quantifying the longitudinal value of healthcare record collections for pharmacoepidemiology. In *AMIA Annual Symposium Proceedings*, 1318.

[52] Dan Steinberg and Phillip Colla. 2009. C&RT: classification and regression trees. *Top Ten Algorithms Data Min.* 9, (2009), 179.

[53] Ruxandra Stoean and Catalin Stoean. 2013. Modeling medical decision making by support vector machines, explaining by rules of evolutionary algorithms with feature selection. *Expert Syst. Appl.* 40, 7 (June 2013), 2677–2686. DOI:https://doi.org/10.1016/j.eswa.2012.11.007

[54] Shan Suthaharan. 2016. Support vector machine. In *Machine Learning Models and Algorithms for Big Data Classification.* Springer, 207–235.

[55] Navdeep Tangri, Lesley A. Stevens, John Griffith, Hocine Tighiouart, Ognjenka Djurdjev, David Naimark, Adeera Levin, and Andrew S. Levey. 2011. A predictive model for progression of chronic kidney disease to kidney failure. *Jama* 305, 15 (2011), 1553–1559.

[56] Michal Tkáč and Robert Verner. 2016. Artificial neural networks in business: Two decades of research. *Appl. Soft Comput.* 38, Supplement C (January 2016), 788–804. DOI:https://doi.org/10.1016/j.asoc.2015.09.040

[57] Michail Vlachos, Philip Yu, and Vittorio Castelli. 2005. On periodicity detection and structural periodic similarity. In *Proceedings of the 2005 SIAM International Conference on Data Mining*, 449–460.

[58] Akbar K Waljee, Peter D R Higgins, and Amit G Singal. 2014. A Primer on Predictive Models. *Clin. Transl. Gastroenterol.* 5, 1 (January 2014), e44. DOI:https://doi.org/10.1038/ctg.2013.19

[59] Nicole G. Weiskopf, George Hripcsak, Sushmita Swaminathan, and Chunhua Weng. 2013. Defining and measuring completeness of electronic health records for secondary use. *J. Biomed. Inform.* 46, 5 (2013), 830–836.

[60] Nicole Gray Weiskopf and Chunhua Weng. 2013. Methods and dimensions of electronic health record data quality assessment: enabling reuse for clinical research. *J. Am. Med. Inform. Assoc.* 20, 1 (2013), 144–151.

[61] Adam Wright, Allison B. McCoy, Thu-Trang T. Hickman, Daniel St Hilaire, Damian Borbolla, Watson A. Bowes, William G. Dixon, David A. Dorr, Michael Krall, and Sameer Malholtra. 2015. Problem list completeness in electronic health records: a multi-site study and assessment of success factors. *Int. J. Med. Inf.* 84, 10 (2015), 784–790.

[62] Faramak Zandi. 2014. A bi-level interactive decision support framework to identify data mining-oriented electronic health record architectures. *Appl. Soft Comput.* 18, Supplement C (May 2014), 136–145. DOI:https://doi.org/10.1016/j.asoc.2014.01.001

[63] Di Zhao and Chunhua Weng. 2011. Combining PubMed knowledge and EHR data to develop a weighted bayesian network for pancreatic cancer prediction. *J. Biomed. Inform.* 44, 5 (2011), 859–868.

[64] Eric R. Ziegel. 1990. *Juran's Quality Control Handbook.* Taylor & Francis Group.

Using Reputation to Predict Online Psychological Counselor Appointment: Evidence from a Chinese Website

Junjie Zhou
Henan University of
Economics and Law
jjzhou@huel.edu.cn

Laura Amo*
State University of New
York at Buffalo
lccasey@buffalo.edu

Cheng Ye
GuangZhou Bmind Psychological
Research and Application
yecheng@cug.edu.cn

Sun Kai
Renmin University
of China
sun_kai@ruc.edu.c
n

1 INTRODUCTION

With the rapid growth of social networking in the health industry, the online health community (OHC) has become an important channel for people to conduct mental health care activities. People can seek psychological knowledge to self-educate, communicate with other patients like them to look for support, or interact with psychological counselors for mental health care services. Online health services belong to credence goods.[1] In the credence market, experts not only provide professional services but also act as the experts who determine how much treatment is necessary, due largely to information asymmetry.[2] Thus, doctors usually know more about a patient's condition and the appropriate treatment a patient needs than the patient.[3] The question we address herein is: How do clients choose counselors for online- based mental therapy?

Reputation is effective in helping people to identify the quality of credence goods in an online market. For example, practitioners in e-commerce have designed the reputation systems such as online rating and online reviews to help consumers.[4, 5] Consumers can use the reputation systems to identify sellers' individual reputation, and look for the products that best match their idiosyncratic use conditions.[6, 7] The reputation systems in e-commerce environments provide information on the sellers' online reputation, yet tend to overlook offline reputation.[8, 9] As a result, researchers have appealed to take both doctors' online and offline reputation into consideration to understand patients' online doctor appointment.[3]

Reputation is a reflection of a person's past actions. Considering people live in a blended environment composed of both offline and online world, we divide a counselor's reputation into offline

ACM Reference format:
J. Zhou., L. Amo, C. Ye, and S. Kai. 2018. Using Reputation to Predict Online Psychological Counselor Appointment: Evidence from a Chinese Website. In Proceedings of ACM SIGMIS-CPR, June 18–20, 2018, Buffalo-Niagara Falls, NY, USA, 2 pages. https://doi.org/10.1145/3209626.3209724

reputation and online reputation, because the technical competence a counselor uses online is obtained via offline activities. Specifically, offline reputation refers to the personal reputation earned via past offline activities, e.g., titles or professional training experience. Online reputation refers to the personal reputation obtained via past online activities, e.g., online help behaviors or capabilities displayed online. As prior studies show, sellers' individual reputation positively promotes consumers' buying behavior and improves sellers' performance.[4, 10] We thus hypothesize,

1) *Both a counselor's offline and online individual reputation positively influence people's online psychological counselor appointment.*

Different from online reputation, a counselor's offline reputation is earned via offline activities. Because of information asymmetry, people in OHCs do not have enough knowledge to judge how a counselor earned his offline reputation (e.g., professional titles or trainings). They have to use other online information to verify the quality of a counselor's offline reputation. For example, people can use a counselor's online reputation to check whether his/her online reputation (e.g., online professional performance) is consistent with his/her offline reputation (e.g., titles), and then decide which counselor they should choose. Therefore, the effects of a counselors' offline reputation on people's online counselor appointment will be changed by the counselor's online-reputation factors. We thus hypothesize,

2) *A counselor's online reputation moderates the effect of his/her offline reputation on people's online psychological counselor appointment.*

2 METHODS

We collected the data from a Chinese online psychological community (www.xinli001.com). The community is one of the pioneers in China's online psychological counseling market. It was set up in July 2011, has more than seven million registered members and more than six thousands recognized counselors, and is one of the biggest and most famous online psychological counseling communities in China. The community aims to provide an online platform for counselor-patient interaction. After checking some basic personal information, the community will add counselors to its community-recognized-expert list.

Each counselor has a home page to display his/her personal information. Counselors can upload their offline information such as titles, education background, characteristics of counseling etc. They can use the columns provided by the community for self-display (e.g., posting articles) or interacting with patients (e.g., answering patients' online questions). Patients can look for counselors in the expert list, and view a counselor's detailed information in a new page. They can ask counselors questions and wait for free answers, or pay money to make appointment for direct counseling. A counselor's column information will be updated automatically. For example, once a counselor writes an article, answers a question, or completes a prepaid appointment, the total numbers of his/her articles, answers, or appointment will automatically add one.

We coded the data and got five variables: volume of online appointments a counselor received, professional titles the counselor has and his/her counseling characteristics as offline reputation, articles published, and answers the counselor posts in the community as online reputation (see Table 1).

Table 1. Variables and Coding Method

Variables	Meaning	Classification	Coding method
Online appointment	Numbers of online counseling appointments completed	Dependent variable	System-generated
Titles	Numbers of professional titles, training or achievement	Offline reputation	Manual
Counseling characteristics	Numbers of characteristics a counselor delivers his/her counseling	Offline reputation	Manual
Articles	Numbers of column articles	Online reputation	System-generated
Q&As	Numbers of answers to patients' questions	Online reputation	System-generated

We built a linear regression model (see Equation 1) and then tested it with hierarchical regression analysis via SPSS 20 (see Table 2).

$$Online\ appointment = \beta_1 * Titles + \beta_2 * Characteristics + \beta_3 * Articles + \beta_4 * Q\&As + \beta_5 * Articles * Titles + \beta_6 * Articles * Characteristics + \beta_7 * Q\&As * Titles + \beta_8 * Q\&As * Characteristics + e \ldots\ldots\ldots\ldots (1)$$

3 RESULTS AND DISCUSSION

The results supported our hypotheses. Exception of the three hypotheses relative with Articles, all of others are significant. We will present the full results at the conference.

Our empirical results have shown two significant theoretical contributions. First, we have verified the effects of counselors' offline reputation and online reputation on people's online psychological counselor appointment. Compared with prior research only focusing on online reputation,[4, 10] this paper has

taken both offline reputation and online reputation into consideration, and provided a comprehensive perspective in understanding people's online doctor appointment. Second, our empirical results indicate that clients' online mental health information seeking behavior belongs to the exploitation learning. The effects relative with articles are insignificant, while the effects relative with Q&As are significant. Namely, when people face health problems (e.g., psychological problems), they would turn to ask questions rather than reading articles, because the payoff of asking questions is more direct and certain while the payoff of reading articles is uncertain. This is a typical kind of exploitation learning behavior.

4 CONCLUSION

Few studies have addressed the factors influencing people's online psychological counselor appointment. We treat online psychological counseling as credence goods and use reputation to predict people's online counselor appointment. Our empirical results show that counselors' titles and counseling characteristics as offline-reputation factors, and their online Q&A behavior as online-reputation factor have positive effects on people's online psychological counselor appointment. Counselors' online Q&A behavior alleviates the effect of titles and enhances the effect of counseling characteristics. Therefore, when people try to choose psychological counselors in OHCs, both counselors' offline-reputation factors and online-reputation factors are influential, but online-reputation factors are more effective. OHC managers should direct psychological counselors carefully operating their offline and online reputation in OHCs.

ACKNOWLEDGEMENTS

This work was supported by National Natural Science Foundation of China (71501062).

REFERENCES

[1] Liu, X., et al. The impact of individual and organizational reputation on physicians' appointments online. International Journal of Electronic Commerce, 20, 4, (2016), 551-577.
[2] Emons, W. Credence goods and fraudulent experts. The RAND Journal of Economics, 28, 1, (1997), 107-119.
[3] Liu, X., et al. The impact of individual and organizational reputation on physicians' appointments online. International Journal of Electronic Commerce, 20, 4, (2016), 551-577.
[4] Ye, Q., et al. In-depth analysis of the seller reputation and price premium relationship: a comparison between eBay US and Taobao China. Journal of Electronic Commerce Research, 14, 1, (2013), 1-10.
[5] Ba, S. and P.A. Pavlou. Evidence of the effect of trust building technology in electronic markets: price premiums and buyer behavior. MIS Quarterly, 26, 3, (2002), 243-268.
[6] Chen, Y. and J. Xie. Online consumer review: word-of-mouth as a new element of marketing communication mix. Management Science, 54, 3, (2008), 477-491.
[7] Resnick, P., et al. The value of reputation on eBay: a controlled experiment. Experimental Economics, 9, 2, (2006), 79-101.
[8] Yang, H., et al. Exploring the effects of patient-generated and system-generated information on patients' online search, evaluation and decision. Electronic Commerce Research and Applications, 14, 3, (2015), 192-203.
[9] Detz, A., A. López and U. Sarkar. Long-term doctor-patient relationships: patient perspective from online reviews. Journal of Medical Internet Research, 15, 7, (2013), e131.
[10]Chevalier, J.A. and D. Mayzlin. The effect of word of mouth on sales: online book reviews. Journal of Marketing Research, 43, 3, (2006), 345-354.

Knowledge Sharing by Older Adults: An Empirical Study

Ruochen Liao
State University of New York at Buffalo
rliao2@buffalo.edu

Rajiv Kishore
State University of New York at Buffalo
rkishore@buffalo.edu

Junjie Zhou
Henan University of Economics and Law
jjzhou@huel.edu.cn

1 INTRODUCTION

With the increasing proportion of aging population worldwide, online communities that supports knowledge sharing* among older adults have received special attention for the host of psychological benefits they could bring [1-4]. However, despite the above-mentioned beneficial outcomes of using online knowledge sharing virtual communities (KSVCs) for older adults, the two types of user activities, i.e. knowledge contribution (KC) and knowledge seeking (KS), are often examined together as "social interactions" in the context of older adults [5]. There is a paucity of literature that examines how each type of activity affects older adults' satisfaction in its respective way. Moreover, older adults may react to the aging process differently, and accordingly differ in their psychological and emotional states based on their individual coping strategy [6-8]. It is possible that KC and KS activities have different effects on older adults' satisfaction, depending on their emotional states. Therefore, the aim of this study is to address the key research question: *How do socioemotional aspects pertinent to the aging phenomenon influence older adult's satisfaction derived from knowledge contribution and knowledge seeking activities in knowledge sharing virtual communities?*

2 THEORETICAL FOUNDATIONS

We address the above research question by adopting Socioemotional Selectivity Theory (SST) from the aging and longevity literature [9-11] that examines how age-related social and emotional changes affects older adults' preferences, priorities,

---

* For clarity, throughout this paper, "sharing" refers to mutual, bi-directional sharing behavior between entities that both contribute and receive knowledge. "Knowledge contribution" and "knowledge seeking" are used, respectively, to denote the directional flow of knowledge from/to the focal individual.

ACM Reference Format:
Ruochen Liao, L. Rajiv Kishore, and Junjie Zhou. 2018. Knowledge Sharing by Older Adults: An Empirical Study. In Proceedings of ACM *SIGMIS-CPR, June 18–20, 2018, Buffalo-Niagara Falls, NY, USA* ACM, NY, NY, USA, 2 pages. https://doi.org/10.1145/3209626.3209726

and goals in life, and lead to a more selective use of their time and energy [12]. We posit that at different stage of the aging process, older adults prioritize different goals in life based on their perception of time remaining. Knowledge-oriented goals, such as acquiring new knowledge, developing new contacts, or building social capital, are primarily pursued by individuals who perceive future to be expansive and open ended are more likely to be future-oriented. They are likely to put in more effort in maximizing their future utility and believe that their long-term gains would outweigh their short-term investments [13, 14].

On the contrary, the appeal of future payoffs in knowledge-related goals diminishes for individuals who perceive their remaining time to be limited. In this case, individuals tend to be present-oriented and focus on goals that provide positive experiences occurring in the moment [15, 16]. Social interactions geared towards emotion-related goals, such as spending time with friends and family, altruistic behaviors that bring gratitude from other people, and sharing their life stories with others to develop a sense of meaning in life, will be prioritized. Knowledge-related goals and emotion-related goals coexist with each other throughout our lives, but are simply assigned different priorities according to their salience at different stages of our life cycle, which could help explain the behavioral changes observed in older adults, and patients who are terminally ill, or people migrating to other countries [9].

3 RESEARCH MODEL AND HYPOTHESES

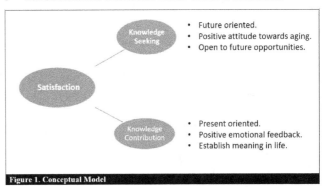

Figure 1. Conceptual Model

Rooted in SST, we posit that the behavioral change of older adults is the reprioritization of emotion-related goals over knowledge-related goals based on a cost-benefit analysis. And this change should also be reflected in their preference of activities while using KSVCs, and the amount of satisfaction they can derive.

We hypothesize that knowledge seeking activities are primarily focused on the acquisition of information for personal development and improvement of future perspective [14, 17]. On the other hand, older adults derive emotional satisfaction from their KC activities through other people's gratitude, and the feeling that they are doing something useful and meaningful. As a result, while both activities could bring satisfaction to older adults using KSVCs, they appeal to different socioemotional states that older adults may have at different stages of the aging process.

Therefore, for older adults, they generally understand their place in the cycle of life, and thus perceive their future time as limited. They regard future as largely irrelevant to them, and are reluctant to waste their limited time on activities that involved uncertainty in the reward. Free from the burden of future, older adults are more likely to prioritize emotion-related goals that bring them immediate emotional satisfaction. As a result, KC activities are more likely to bring higher satisfaction for older adults than KS activities do.

In addition, according to SST, knowledge-related and emotion-related goals are two sets of competing goals [11]. Seeking knowledge carries emotional risks in frustration, rejection and criticism, while emotional-related goals guide individuals to avoid unpleasant experiences. We posit that due to the physiological and cognitive decline caused by aging, older adults are more likely to display a stronger selective preference in allocating time and energy in choosing these two sets of goals in order to derive satisfaction from them. Therefore, we hypothesize that KC and KS substitute each other's effect on satisfaction.

Lastly, we take into consideration the different socioemotional status of individual older adults as a result of their reaction to the aging process. Older adults who are able to maintain a positive attitude toward aging (ATA) are more likely to stay optimistic and open to future opportunities, and may thus be more willing to pursue KS activities. And for those older adults who have a stronger desire to develop a sense of meaning in life (MIL) and philosophy to guide their life, as well as attain a sense of fulfillment [18], they may derive more emotional satisfaction from their KC activities by helping others and sharing their life's stories.

4   RESULTS AND DISCUSSION

We collected data through online survey from three online knowledge sharing communities targeting older adults who were born before or during the 1950s in China supported by www.baidu.com. We used covariance-based SEM method to test our model. We found support for all of our hypotheses except for H3. This suggests that older adults derive their satisfaction from KC and KS activities based on different goals in life, and their prioritization of goals changes depending on their socioemotional status in the aging process.

5   CONTRIBUTIONS AND IMPLICATION

The findings of this study make a significant contribution to the literature on knowledge-sharing virtual communities, and also that of geriatric studies by expanding our understanding about how older adults derive satisfaction from their knowledge seeking and knowledge contribution activities in KSVCs. Consistent with SST, our study shows that it is not chronological age, but rather older adults' emotional states in response to their perceptions of remaining time in life that ultimately influence the satisfaction they derive from their KS and KC activities. While future-oriented and present-oriented goals coexist throughout the adulthood, older adults derive more satisfaction from the type of activity that meets their psychological needs and socioemotional states. This finding leads us to focus on the socioemotional affordance function in the design of virtual communities for older adults, so that older adults would not feel overwhelmed and disoriented in the online space.

REFERENCES

[1]   Melenhorst, A.-S., Rogers, W.A., and Caylor, E.C. The use of communication technologies by older adults: exploring the benefits from the user's perspective. *Proceedings of the Human Factors and Ergonomics Society Annual Meeting*: SAGE Publications Sage CA: Los Angeles, CA, 2001, pp. 221-225.

[2]   Cairney, J., and Krause, N. The social distribution of psychological distress and depression in older adults. *Journal of Aging and Health*, 17, 6 (2005), 807-835.

[3]   Cotten, S.R., Ford, G., Ford, S., and Hale, T.M. Internet use and depression among older adults. *Computers in Human Behavior*, 28, 2 (2012), 496-499.

[4]   Lubben, J., and Gironda, M. Centrality of social ties to the health and well-being of older adults. *Social work and health care in an aging society* (2003), 319-350.

[5]   Lee, G.R., and Ishii-Kuntz, M. Social interaction, loneliness, and emotional well-being among the elderly. *Research on aging*, 9, 4 (1987), 459-482.

[6]   Markus, H.R., and Kitayama, S. Culture and the self: Implications for cognition, emotion, and motivation. *Psychological Review*, 98, 2 (1991), 224.

[7]   Sheldon, K.M., and Kasser, T. Getting older, getting better? Personal strivings and psychological maturity across the life span. *Developmental Psychology*, 37, 4 (2001), 491.

[8]   Carstensen, L.L., Fung, H.H., and Charles, S.T. Socioemotional selectivity theory and the regulation of emotion in the second half of life. *Motivation and Emotion*, 27, 2 (2003), 103-123.

[9]   Carstensen, L.L. Evidence for a life-span theory of socioemotional selectivity. *Current directions in Psychological science*, 4, 5 (1995), 151-156.

[10] Charles, S.T., and Carstensen, L.L. Social and emotional aging. *Annual review of psychology*, 61 (2010), 383-409.

[11] Carstensen, L.L., Isaacowitz, D.M., and Charles, S.T. Taking time seriously: A theory of socioemotional selectivity. *American psychologist*, 54, 3 (1999), 165.

[12] Baltes, P.B. On the incomplete architecture of human ontogeny: Selection, optimization, and compensation as foundation of developmental theory. *American psychologist*, 52, 4 (1997), 366.

[13] Melenhorst, A.-S., Rogers, W.A., and Bouwhuis, D.G. Older adults' motivated choice for technological innovation: evidence for benefit-driven selectivity. *Psychology and aging*, 21, 1 (2006), 190.

[14] Inkpen, A.C., and Tsang, E.W. Social capital, networks, and knowledge transfer. *Academy of management review*, 30, 1 (2005), 146-165.

[15] Fung, H.H., Lai, P., and Ng, R. Age differences in social preferences among Taiwanese and Mainland Chinese: the role of perceived time. *Psychology and aging*, 16, 2 (2001), 351.

[16] Charles, S.T., Mather, M., and Carstensen, L.L. Aging and emotional memory: the forgettable nature of negative images for older adults. *Journal of Experimental Psychology: General*, 132, 2 (2003), 310.

[17] Kankanhalli, A., Tan, B.C.Y., and Wei, K.K. Contributing knowledge to electronic knowledge repositories: An empirical investigation. *Mis Quarterly*, 29, 1 (2005), 113-143.

[18] Krause, N. Longitudinal study of social support and meaning in life. *Psychology and aging*, 22, 3 (2007), 456-469.

Building an Honest and Capable Crowd Workforce

Yi Wang
Department of Software Engineering, Rochester Institute of Technology
yi.wang@rit.edu

ABSTRACT

One of the major challenges of crowdsourcing is to build a labor force that is not only capable but also honest. Prior research on crowdsourcing-mechanism design mostly focuses on motivating individual worker's effort, while neglecting the importance of building highly trustworthy crowd labor force who tends to honestly report the quality of the microwork. To fill this gap, we propose a novel mechanism in this paper. The proposed mechanism combines the principal-agent model and signaling game to enable the information exchange from crowd workers to a requester, and to provide dynamic financial incentives/punishments to honest/dishonest behaviors identified in random quality inspections. To evaluate our proposed mechanism, we perform extensive simulations. Our results suggest that the proposed mechanism is effective and efficient to motivate workers who are capable but less honest to change their behavior when sending signals to indicate their finished microwork, while the extra cost of implementing the proposed mechanism could be minimal. With the behavioral changes of the "liars", a highly capable and honest labor force of crowd workers may be developed. The model is also useful as a foundation for theoretical and empirical studies of information exchanges from worker to a requester in the crowdsourcing market.

CCS CONCEPTS

• **Information systems** → **Crowdsourcing**; • **Theory of computation** → *Algorithmic game theory and mechanism design*;

KEYWORDS

Crowdsourcing; principal-agent model; signaling game; worker's integrity; incentives

ACM Reference Format:
Yi Wang. 2018. Building an Honest and Capable Crowd Workforce. In *Proceedings of 2018 Computers and People Research Conference, Buffalo-Niagara Falls, NY, USA, June 18–20, 2018 (SIGMIS-CPR '18),* 8 pages.
https://doi.org/10.1145/3209626.3209713

1 INTRODUCTION

It is hard to find a capable, trustworthy population of crowd workers [4, 22, 39]. A requester usually may not be able to precisely evaluate her crowd workers' capability and integrity. She often

has no choice but "believes" those anonymous workers are capable and honest for exhaustively inspecting the thousands of submitted microworks is neither realistic nor worth. However, many studies in psychology, economics, and management have proven that simply assuming employees are trustworthy is risky, e.g., [5, 11, 27] even in traditional work environments. In crowdsourcing markets, requesters (as employers) are more limited to control the worker's dishonest behaviors which may potentially lead to severe problems. Considering the following scenario:

Catherine, a computer vision researcher, wants crowd workers to help her annotating the outlines of the human body in a large chunk of images. After publishing her tasks on Mturk and receiving some submissions, she realized that the quality of the submitted microwork varies. Excluding the low-quality microwork is costly and time-consuming, because she has to manually check every submitted microwork. She thinks: I would like my workers to tell me the quality of their submissions! After some quick hacking, she updates her crowdsourcing platform to ask her workers to provide a self-assessment of their submissions. However, Catherine soon finds that she is in another dilemma: "Should I believe that they tell the truth rather than lie for higher payment?"

If all crowd workers are honest, Catherine's dilemma is no longer a problem. Unfortunately, it is impossible. For example, Paolacci & Chandler found that at least 45% crowd workers lied to pass a pre-screen question [33]. Crowd workers can be classified into four categories according to their capability and integrity (Figure 1). For requesters, workers high in both capability and integrity (the first quadrant) are always favorable, but they may only account for a small proportion of the crowd labor force. There might be many incapable but honest workers (the second quadrant), incapable liars (the third quadrant), and capable liars (the fourth quadrant). Incapable but honest workers are harmless. Because they always tell requesters the true quality of their submitted microworks, then requesters can simply exclude their submissions and republish the microworks if they report low quality. Dealing with incapable liars is also easy. As their capability can be learned through various methods, a request can simply kick them out and block them for future microworks. The tricky part is how to deal with "capable liars." Simply kicking them out from the crowd worker pool is not a wise choice for they are capable of providing good results for the majority of microwork. Apparently, motivating them to behave like ideal workers is a better solution.

To motivating "capable liars" to behave like ideal workers hence develop a stable population of capable and "honest" crowd workforce, we design a dynamic mechanism by combining principal-agent model and signaling game. In this process, a crowd worker is required to send her self-assessment on the quality of each microwork she submitted as a signal in repeated interaction with the requester. Based on the signal, the requester randomly inspects the submitted microwork with a small probability of p. We performed extensive simulations based on this process. The results indicate:

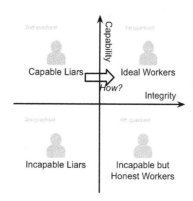

Figure 1: Four types of crowd workers according to their capability and integrity.

(1) The proposed mechanism is able to facilitate the behavioral changes of crowd workers, motivating "capable liars" behaves like "capable and honest" ideal workers.
(2) The proposed mechanism is effective to help a requester generate competitive total payoff while keeping individual crowd worker's contribution at a fairly high level.
(3) For a requester, the cost of enabling the behavioral changes through proposed mechanism is minimal.

Compared with the popular crowdsourcing mechanisms, the advantages of proposed mechanism are four-fold. First, the proposed mechanism is effective in developing a stable workforce consists of workers who are capable and honest (at least from a behavioral perspective). Second, by allowing the information exchange (in the form of the signal of "quality of the submitted microwork"), a large proportion of low-quality work could be automatically excluded without extra inspections. Third, the proposed mechanism goes beyond performance-based payments and incentive models, e.g., [20, 36, 37], by paying incentives for worker's integrity to enable behavioral changes of crowd workers without relying on external reputation systems [42]. Last but not least, we avoid the simple assumption of a homogeneous pool of workers by allowing them to be different in their capability and integrity.

The rest of this paper proceeds as follows. Section 2 introduces the backgrounds of this work. Section 3 presents the model. Section 4 introduces the simulation design, while the simulation results are reported in Section 5. Section 6 discusses related issues. Section 7 and section 8 briefly introduces related work and concludes the paper respectively.

2 BACKGROUND

The proposed mechanism build on two well-known models, which are principal-agent model and signaling game. We are going to introduce them and how we adapt them in our model.

2.1 Principal-Agent Problem

Crowdsourcing has long been known as a multi-round, multi-worker version of the classic principal-agent model in contract theory [20, 21, 29]. However, different from the prior literature of classic principal-agent model such as [18], we discard the notion of worker's unobservable decision on the level of "effort" (moral

hazard) in the classic principal-agent model. This decision is based on two considerations. First, the level of effort is unobservable and hard to be learned even in a multi-round game. Second, given the fact that a single crowdsourcing task may involve thousands of workers and a large number of small pieces of microwork, optimizing contract to incentivize individual worker's effort on so many small tasks is trivial and not cost-effective. Moreover, many typical tasks may be not effort-responsive–exerting more effort leads to better quality [20]. Besides, focusing on the observable quality of submissions also makes our mechanism become output-contingent and hence reduces the potential threats of crowd worker's biases.

In crowdsourcing, crowd worker's integrity is critical. For a requester like Catherine, she may prefer her workers tell her that the microwork they finished is not good. Then she can simply pay a small sum of money to reward honest workers while discarding their submissions. For her, avoiding to include wrong results into her training data is more important than simply collect all submissions. To reflects this, we adapt and extend the "*adverse selection*" variation of the principal-agent problem. Here, a crowd worker's type (ability & integrity) is unknown at the early rounds of the process. In repeated settings, it is very likely that worker's ability can be learned. To learn worker's "integrity" is impossible without allowing them to make some claims about their work.

Accordingly, our technique is different from those employed in contract theory, and performance-based payments (PBPs). Based on above discussions, "integrity" implies that there are some information exchanges from worker to the requester. We use the signaling game to conceptualize this type of exchanges in next subsection.

2.2 Signaling Game

The standard principle-agent model neglects the transmission of information from the agent to the principal. The transmission of information in interactions depends on signals. Hence, it is a natural choice to incorporate the principal-agent model with another type of games, i.e., signaling game. For a crowd worker, the quality of her finished task is largely a piece of private information for it is impossible for the requester to painstakingly examine all finished tasks. When allowing information flows from workers to the requester, the signal sent by a worker may be true or fake depending on the integrity of the worker. The requester may take actions according to the received signal. We can use simple two-player signaling game [38] (figure 2) to describe this type of information exchange.

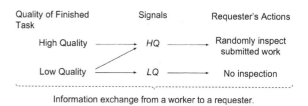

Information exchange from a worker to a requester.

Figure 2: Signaling game between a worker and a requester.

A submitted microwork can be either in *high quality* or in *low quality*. There are two possible signals: {*High-Quality (HQ), Low-Quality (LQ)*}. Ideally, a worker should send *HQ* for microworks she finishes in high quality and *LQ* for the others. However, since the quality of her work is largely private, she may send *HQ* even when her work is not that good.When a requester receives a *HQ* signal, she is in a dilemma of judging the integrity of the worker who sends the signal, so she may randomly inspect the submitted work and dynamically adjust the payoff according to the results of the inspections. When she receives a *LQ* signal, she can simply exclude the submitted work. In this case, she just needs to distribute the plain payoff to the worker. We will introduce the details of the payoff structure in the next two sections. Apparently, there is no separating equilibrium for the game described in figure 2, i.e., the requester would never have systematic knowledge about whether a worker sends a fake signal because the signal itself carries misinformation. However, by enforcing some incentives/punishments, it is possible to make a liar behave more honestly [8, 24]. This forms the rationale of motivating "capable liars" to behave like "ideal workers."

3 THE MODEL

3.1 Players

The game has two types of players, a requester (principal) and many crowd workers (agents). Let's suppose there are initially m workers in total. There is no interaction among agents, so each round can be viewed as a two player (requester vs. one worker) game. A worker's game contains multiple periods from 0 to n_i (period n denoted the last microwork finished by crowd worker i). Using j to index each period for worker i, we can use ij to index each unique submitted microwork and each period. A typical microwork may take the form of annotating the outlines of the human body in 10 images (doing 1 image is an *atom task*). However, we have no restrictions on this. The only requirement is that a microwork should allow the quality variance.

3.2 Modeling Players

Modeling requester is straightforward. We only need to specify the probability p to describe the chance of inspection when a requester receives a "*HQ*" signal. Modeling worker is a little bit complex. A worker is characterized by two attributes: her capability and honesty. Based on literature in psychology (e.g., [32], we assume both attributes follows normal distribution over the whole population of m workers. These two attributes jointly determine the chances that a crowd worker provides high-quality submissions and sends dishonest signals. The probability of sending a faked *HQ* signal for a microwork can be expressed as:

$$P = \varphi(cap, hon) \tag{1}$$

In our model, we assume φ is a linear function of the joint distribution of (cap, hon) though it may take more complex forms. We also assume the distribution of cap and hon are independent. Basically, the increase of cap or hon will cause the decrease of P.

Another important issue we need to consider in modeling a worker is their behavioral change results from the changes of payment in each round after they were caught lying. Of course, we can simply assume that a caught worker will automatically become an honest worker after being caught and get experience some monetary loss. However, this may not true. Honesty is widely accepted as a basic personality trait that is not easy to change in short period

[1]. So we take an indirect way by adjusting the probability of a crowd worker's decision on "lying" in future rounds according to the worker's monetary loss [40].

$$P' = \varphi(cap, hon) - \Delta(\theta)$$
$$\text{where } \theta \text{ represents the monetary loss.} \tag{2}$$

3.3 Process

For a specific worker i, figure 3 depicts the whole process of her interaction with the requester. In period 0, the requester offers an employment contract to her. Then, she starts working on the first microwork in period 1. She will continue work for the requester until some event triggers the "termination" in period n_i. There are two events can trigger the "termination," which are: (1) no microwork is available; (2) the worker is kicked out and blocked by the requester. In a period j where $0 < j \leq n_i$, the interactions between the requester and the crowd worker i are depicted in the right part of figure 3. The interactions begin as normal crowdsourcing process: the requester publishes a task, then, worker i accepts it and working on it. However, worker i is asked to send a signal to indicate the quality of the microwork she just finished. Obviously, worker i may not always tell the truth. As we discussed in section 2.2, she may send "*HQ*" even when her submission's quality is low. The requester, upon receives the signal, is in "Catherine's dilemma".

However, the proposed mechanism allows the requester to do a little bit extra things. If the signal is "*LQ*", she can simply ignore the submission and pay a small amount of money (V_L) to the worker i to reward worker i's honesty. If the signal is "*HQ*", there is a possibility that worker i tells lie. Since it is impossible to exhaustively inspect every submission, the requester may decide whether or not to inspect the submission with a probability p. If she decides not to inspect, worker i will receive a normal payment for high-quality submission (V_H). If she decides to inspect, the payment becomes dynamical according to the inspect results and the learned "type" of crowd workers. Let's write this payment as V_D. The details of the payment structure will be introduced in next subsection.

3.4 Payoff Structure

Given the dynamic nature of the proposed mechanism, the worker's payoff structure is complex. As we pointed out in section 2, worker's unobservable decision on her effort level is not our concern. Therefore, we simply suppose there is a universal effort e to finish a single microwork for all m workers. Hence, worker i's payoff in a round j can be expressed as:

$$P_{ij} = g(i, j) - e \tag{3}$$

In 3, $g(i, j)$ refers the monetary payment worker i received from the requester for the microwork ij. $g(i, j)$ is defined as follows:

$$g(i, j) = \begin{cases} (V_L), & \text{Signal is "LQ", no inspection is needed} \\ (V_H)_n, & \text{Signal is "HQ", and no inspection} \\ (V_H)_y, & \text{Signal is "HQ", confirmed by inspection} \\ (V_F), & \text{Signal is "HQ", rejected by inspection} \end{cases} \tag{4}$$

The punishment for lying does not only influence the payoff of the current period, but also potentially leads to liars' behavioral adaptation in future periods.

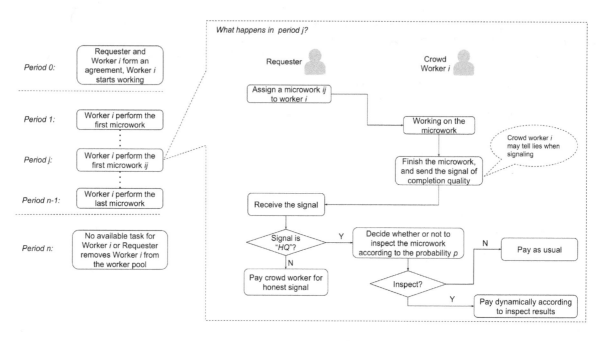

Figure 3: The process of the proposed mechanism. The right part is the overview of all periods, and the right part is the details of interactions in each period.

For a requester, her total payoff is the utility she received from all high-quality microworks, minus the payment she pays to crowd workers and the cost of administrating inspections to a sample of submitted microworks. Let's suppose she will get a fixed utility u for each submitted microwork that assumes to be high quality, and let:

$$u(i,j) = \begin{cases} u & \text{if microwork } ij \text{ assumes to be high quality} \\ 0 & \text{if microwork } ij \text{ is low quality} \end{cases} \quad (5)$$

We assume the cost of a inspection is c, and let:

$$c(i,j) = \begin{cases} c & \text{if inspect microwork } ij \\ 0 & \text{if not inspect microwork } ij \end{cases} \quad (6)$$

Hence, a requester's total payoff U_R can be expressed as:

$$U_R = \sum_{i=1}^{m} \sum_{j=1}^{n_i} [u(i,j) - g(i,j) - c(i,j)] \quad (7)$$

4 SIMULATION EXPERIMENT DESIGN

We carry out extensive simulation experiments to understand the practical performance of proposed mechanisms on simulated crowd worker distributions. We begin by describing our benchmarks, parameters and experimental setup in this section.

4.1 Benchmarks

We compare our mechanism against the following three benchmarks. Please note that, throughout this paper, we use the term **"report"** to refer a **"finished atom task"**.

BENCHMARK 1: SIGNAL-NO-TOLERANCE (S-N-T)

Benchmark 1 is to simulate the simplest mechanism, which will directly kick out the liars immediately after any dishonest behaviors are detected. Under this mechanism, the requester will sample some

feedback signals and manually diagnose the details. If she finds any dishonest behavior, the requester will kick out the liar immediately and will pay nothing for this working round.

BENCHMARK 2: REPORT-NO-TOLERANCE (R-N-T)

Benchmark 2 is similar to the Signal-No-Tolerance. Under this mechanism, the requester will require the crowd workers to submit the finished atom tasks directly. They will sample some finished atom task from each worker to diagnose. If any harmful dishonest behavior is detected, the requester will kick out the liar immediately and will pay nothing for this working round.

BENCHMARK 3: REPORT-SAMPLE-AND-PAY (R-S-P)

Benchmark 3 is relatively mild. The requester will require the crowd workers to submit the finished atom tasks and conduct the same sampling and inspection. But the requester will not kick out any workers, instead, she will pay the workers based on based on the manually diagnose result and worker claimed quality.

4.2 Parameters Choices

4.2.1 Parameters Related to Players. As we discussed in section 3.1, each worker is characterized by two attributes: capability (*cap*) and honesty (*hon*). Based on psychology literature on the distribution of individual's cognitive ability and integrity (e.g., [13, 32]), each attribute is randomly assigned from a normal distribution. For *cap*, we set *mean* = 0.5 and *Std.* = 0.2; for *hon*, *mean* = 0.7 and *Std.* = 0.2. Again, we performed sensitive analyses to examine the results over variations over these two distributions. The sensitive analyses indicate the results are robust when the distributions allow enough variance on these two attributes.

4.2.2 Parameters Related to Payoffs. In our simulation, there are some key parameters should be elaborated. As we stated above, we defined the net utility gain in equation 7. The noteworthy point is that in this experiment, we need to numerically present the value changes, so we should further detail the cost of an inspection and payment cost of the microworks. Firstly, we define the (V_F) = 0, which means there will be not any payment for the detected dishonest behavior. Furthermore, given we used u in equation 5 to denote the utility gain of a high quality microwork and c in equation 6 to denote the inspection cost, we define $(V_H)_n = \alpha u$, $(V_H)_y = \beta u$, $(V_L) = \gamma u$ and $c = \sigma u$ respectively.

Empirical studies of profit distribution between employees and their employer have consistently shown that it is rare for employees to share more than 50% of the total profit in modern capitalism [9]. In the less regulated crowdsourcing labor market, it is reasonable to assume that an employer's share of the "profit" of a microwork should less than 50%. Since the highest pay arrangement is $(V_H)_y$ and inspection is necessary for receiving this payment, $(V_H)_y + c = (\beta + \sigma)u$ should no more than 50%. So we simply set β = 0.45, and σ = 0.05 in the simulation experiment. Also, we assumed α = 0.3 and γ = 0.1. We performed sensitive analysis over these parameters and found the results are consistent if there relative numerical relationship ($\beta > \alpha >> \gamma = 0.1 > \sigma$) holds.

4.3 Experimental Setup

Our simulation implements 4 conditions: three benchmarks defined in section 4.1, and our mechanism. Each simulation instance (mapping to each condition) contains 50 periods. We run each simulation instance for 20 times. The results reported in next section is based on the aggregated results.

In each simulation instance, we assumed that there are 1000 crowd workers for each mechanism. Some of the workers may be kicked out in each period, and the remaining workers will automatically include in the next period. At the beginning of each period, we assign a microwork containing a fixed number of atom tasks (e.g., labeling an image) to each available worker. To avoid the bias on microwork's difficulty, i.e. being too difficult or too easy for the crowd workers, we generate the difficulty values randomly following the same distribution as we assign the capability to workers. In this experiment, each microwork contains 10 atom tasks.

As soon as a crowd worker receives the microwork, she evaluates her capability of successfully finishing the microwork. For each atom task in a microwork, if crowd work's capability is higher than the difficulty, she can finish it successfully, and vice versa. Furthermore, we define a submitted microwork is in high-quality if 80% of its atom tasks are finished successfully.

Since a crowd worker is *rational*, she always sends a *HQ* signal as the self-estimation of their work to the requester if she finished a high-quality microwork. However, if she failed to reach a high-quality performance, she may honestly send a *LQ* signal to the requester, and receive the *LQ* payment; or send a *HQ* signal (cheating) to the requester and hope her cheating would never be detected by the requester. To simulate the dishonest behavior, we will randomly generate a *cheatingwillingness* value from the same distribution that was used to generate the honesty for the workers. If the *cheatingwillingness* is smaller than the worker's honesty, she chooses to send honest "LQ" signal, otherwise, she decides to cheat.

For the requester, because it is impossible to inspect all of the reports, she uses randomly sampling to evaluate the workers' performance. Then, based on different mechanisms, the requester applies different methods to kick out the less favorable workers. Please note that to compare the effectiveness of kicking out the less favorable workers, we set a fixed *sampleratio* = 0.1 for all of the mechanisms. That is, in all 4 mechanisms, a requester inspects the same number of microwork in the initial period.

5 RESULTS

There are two main goals of our mechanism: to improve the net utility gain and to build up a stable and capable workforce. Based on these goals, we will evaluate the population composition of different types of crowd workers, requester's payoff, as well as the extra cost of implementing our mechanism.

5.1 Population Composition of Different Types of Crowd Workers

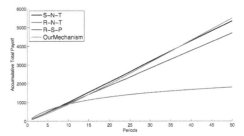

(a) Requester's accumulative payoff over 50 periods.

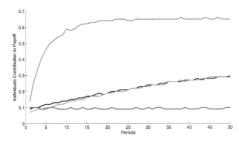

(b) Individual contribution to requester's payoff in each period.

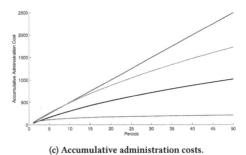

(c) Accumulative administration costs.

Figure 4: Experiment Results (averaged over 20 runs)

Table 1: The composition workforce after 50 periods (averaged over 20 runs), Report-Sample-and-Pay is excluded because it does not kick out any workers.

Mechanism	Total Remaining	High Capability		High Integrity		Ideal Workers		Converted Capable Liars
		before	after	before	after	before	after	
Signal-No-Tolerance	353.10	102.40	98.50	181.10	137.10	16.75	16.55	336.55
Report-No-Tolerance	17.60	99.65	17.55	183.15	3.30	17.55	3.30	14.30
Our Mechanism	393.15	102.40	102.10	180.40	137.10	18.65	18.60	374.55

For the main goal of this study is to develop a mechanism that is able to identify and increase the population of "ideal" crowd workers, we first examine the population dynamics of different types of crowd workers.

The column 'High Capability' of table 1 describes the number of workers having capability larger than 0.75 in BENCHMARK 1, 2 and our mechanism[1], of which, 'before' denotes the original workforce, 'after' denotes the workforce after 50 periods. Similarly, the column 'High Integrity' shows the number of workers having honesty larger than 0.85, and the column 'Ideal Workers' shows the number of workers having honesty larger than 0.85 and capability larger than 0.75 at the same time.

The last column suggests that our mechanism keeps most *converted* "capable liars" in the worker pool. Although we know these workers' honesty is not that high, we cannot differentiate them from their behaviors after a specific period of time. No matter what is in their mind, at least, they start to behave like an ideal worker. In contrast, BENCHMARK 1 are not only less effective in motivating "capable liars" to behave like ideal workers, but also more likely to kick out some of the ideal workers.

BENCHMARK 2 works very bad in retaining good workers (and bad ones). In total, only 1.8% workers left after 50 periods. With the progress of the crowdsourcing process, it almost kicks out all workers. Obviously, it has systematic disadvantage on keeping the workforce above a certain level. We summarized the change of the number of individuals of *high capability* and *high integrity* before and after the running the simulations on three different mechanisms. In table 1, it is straightforward to conclude that signaling based mechanisms, (BENCHMARK 1 and our mechanism, works especially well on keeping the honest worker in the workforce. Therefore, signaling based mechanism should be considered if market designers want to promote honest culture.

5.2 Requester's Total Payoff

Figure 4.1 describes the requester's total payoff dynamics over the 50 periods. Figure 4.1.a focuses on the accumulative net total payoff in all 50 periods. First of all, our mechanism consistently outperforms BENCHMARK 2 which take different actions to kick out crowd workers. Second, our mechanism also achieves better payoff gain against BENCHMARK 3 which keeps all 1000 workers in each round. ForBENCHMARK 1, our mechanism is lower in the early periods, but slowly outperform in later periods.

Figure 4.2 depicts the dynamics of each worker's contribution in each round. Our mechanism beats BENCHMARK 3 again. In the later periods, each individual contributes thrice the amount a worker contributes under BENCHMARK 3. For BENCHMARK 2, our mechanism achieves comparable (indeed, slightly higher in later periods)

individual contributions. Although BENCHMARK 2 does yield highest individual contribution, this increase is at the price of kicking out the majority of workers (see row 2 in table 1), which eventually hurts the total payoff. This suggests that our mechanism achieves an outstanding trade-off between keeping more "capable" workers and avoiding the harm of their dishonesty.

Both the total payoff and individual worker's contribution become stable in our mechanism. This result indicates another favorable attribute of our mechanism, i.e., the requester will have more precise knowledge about her expected payoff. This helps her to better manage the whole process of the crowdsourcing.

5.3 Requester's Extra Cost

Our mechanism does incur some extra cost. The extra cost comes from two sources: 1. bonus for crowd workers' honesty, and 2. cost of administrating of inspection. Although we have shown that the total payoffs under our mechanism are significantly better than the three benchmarks, we still want to examine the extra cost to ensure that the extra cost is not excessive in specific periods which potentially threats the payment ability of the requester. Figure 4.3 describes the accumulative extra cost in 50 periods. Apparently, the total cost of our mechanism is higher than BENCHMARK 1 AND 2 but less than BENCHMARK 3. At least, we can say the extra cost is no more than the mechanism without kicking out unqualified work, and the total cost increase is around 70% compared with BENCHMARK 1 (1725.50 vs. 1019.05). Moreover, the growth of the extra cost is pretty smooth, hence the requester will not face any payment crisis in any periods. We also calculated the individualized administration cost for our mechanism. Given that our mechanism keeps more workers than BENCHMARK 1 AND 2, the differences become trivial (0.06 vs. 0.05).

6 DISCUSSION

6.1 Intrinsic Honesty vs. Behavioral Honesty

In many situations, intrinsic honesty must be combined with [15] social institutions to avoid cheating at the behavioral level. In current crowdsourcing market, only intrinsic honesty keeps crowd workers from cheating and violating rules. Psychology literature has concluded that rule violations and cheating does not only have direct adverse economic consequences, but might also impair individual intrinsic honesty, and vice versa [31, 34]. This suggests, by reducing the behavioral level dishonesty, it is may be possible to positively influence crowd worker's intrinsic honesty. If so, it would help to build a value system in current crowdsourcing market where systematic administrations are in absence. Hence, in a much broader perspective, researchers, including ourselves, perhaps need to pay more attention to motivating behavioral honesty as well as incentivizing more efforts from crowd workers.

---

[1] BENCHMARK 3 IS EXCLUDED BECAUSE IT DOES NOT KICK OUT ANY WORKERS.

6.2 Effort Responsive Tasks

One assumption of our mechanism is that the effort level does not influence the quality of the work. When the task is effort responsive, our mechanism may still work. For we provide incentives according to the outcome of crowd worker's submissions, it may be still able to identify and increase those who are motivated to contribute more effort. However, this requires an additional characteristic to deal with the willingness of contributing more effort when modeling the crowd workers. This addition is not side-effect free, there would be $2 \times 2 \times 2 = 8$ types of work, and the interactions between an individual's capability and effort could be very complex. To validate the effectiveness of effort responsive tasks, we need to conduct further theoretical and empirical analyses.

7 RELATED WORK

This paper is related to two different areas: optimal contract design in labor economics, design, and operation of payment scheme for crowdsourcing. Below we outline connections and differences of our work to each of these two areas.

7.1 Optimal Contract Design

Designing optimal contract has been well studied in labor economics [7]. Obviously, our work can be viewed as an extension and adaptation of classic principal-agent model. As we mentioned in section 2, we do not consider the unobservable effort level of crowd workers, since the performance (quality of work) is more explicit for requesters and workers to jointly form the realization of the specific choice in a contract dynamically. Our mechanism also adapts the idea in [2] where principal may only observe the total outcome which is a function of all agents' effort levels while replacing the effort levels with easily detectable quality of work.

Multi-Armed Bandit (MAB) and Dynamic Pricing have also been used in crowdsourcing mechanism design. The MAB problem focuses on settings where an agent repeatedly chooses among behaviors with uncertain payoffs and must consider exploration (learn the details of payments) and exploitation (maximizing rewards obtained). It has been well studied by operation researchers and economists. Gittins et al. [17] presents an overview of this type of models. There are also a whole bunch of work applying MAB model in optimal contract design for crowdsourcing such as [6, 14, 21, 26, 37, 41]. We did not put our work under MAB framework since we are more interested in the influence of information exchanges from a worker to a requester. Dynamic pricing deals with the situation that principal offers a different contract to workers who are available over the time. In crowdsourcing, its implementation is that a worker may select accept or reject the contract offered by a requester. For a comprehensive survey of related work, please refer [10]. For the online market, an example of dynamic pricing is Badanidiyuru et al.[3] in which a principal's buying is an abstraction of a requester's solicitation of finished microworks. However, most of the dynamic pricing research of online market is more concerned with restricting a principal's budget in a specific level [28]. Our mechanism does not enforce such a restriction.

Recently, researchers also begin applying some behavioral economic theories to design optimal contract in crowdsourcing market as a reaction to the fact that workers often deviate from the standard economic rationality assumption. For instance, Easley & Ghosh [12] suggests to use Behavior Economics theory, specifically, prospect theory in their paper, in crowdsourcing mechanism design. We plan to explore how heterogeneity in crowd workers' preferences influences our mechanism's effectiveness and efficiency in future research through designing mechanisms allowing alternative workers' beliefs-preferences-constrains models [16] and conducting empirical behavioral experiments.

7.2 Payment Scheme for Crowdsourcing

There has been a fast-growing body of work in understanding the right payment scheme for workers in online labor markets. Horton and Chilton [22] present a model of workers and introduce methods to estimate workers' appropriate wages. The "hagglebot" introduced in [23] is able to negotiate payment rates for an image-labeling task with workers on Amazon MTurk. In real-world crowdsourcing market, a requester may have a certain budget restriction. To tackle this problem, Sigla & Krause [37] design a payment scheme that maximizes budgeted requester's utility while keeping incentive compatible with workers.

There have also been empirical studies focusing on how workers' behavior changes based on the financial incentives offered to them. For example, Manson & Watt [30] studied the influence of performance-independent financial incentives on worker's behavior. In their study, increasing financial incentives increase the number of tasks workers complete, but not the quality of their work. Shaw et al. [35] argued the financial incentives may need to be combined with other non-monetary mechanisms in order to improve the quality of work. In general, whether or not financial incentives have a positive influence on the quality of submitted microworks may heavily depend on the context and settings of the task. For example. Harris' MTurk experiments on resume screening show that the quality of work is better with performance-based payments than with uniform payments [19]. Recent work such as [25] also suggested that paying for batch may encourage worker's participation, which indicates studying the crowd worker's cognition/interpretation of the payment scheme should be promising.

To sum up, the previous literature demonstrates that crowd workers in the crowdsourcing market respond to the change of financial incentives, but maybe in various ways. Our work distinguishes itself from prior research is that we are trying to use financial incentives/punishments as an intervention to identify and increase the population of "ideal" crowd workers, while provides a way to transfer information from crowd workers to requesters.

8 CONCLUSIONS

We designed a mechanism for building honest and capable crowd workforce in the online crowdsourcing market. We start with adaptations of the classic principal-agent problem, and extend it to a new mechanism by integrating it with the signaling game which allows information transfer from a crowd worker to a requester. We performed extensive simulations to demonstrate the effectiveness and efficiency of our mechanism without incurring excessive extra costs. Our mechanism is the first work aiming to help the requester identify and increase the population of both capable and honest crowd workers. We believe that our results provide an important step towards developing practical and easily implemented techniques for increasing the effectiveness and efficiency of crowdsourcing.

There are some natural extensions for future work. We have planned to perform randomized behavioral experiments on the popular crowdsourcing platform Amazon Mechanical Turk with the goal of validating the proposed mechanism with real crowd workers. We will empirically validate the effectiveness and efficiency of our mechanism in real-world crowdsourcing market where the stochastic assumptions may not hold. Experiment on Mturk will also offer us an opportunity to explore when, where, and why the proposed mechanism helps build a highly capable and honest workforce. In this study, we considered a simple additive utility function for the requester. It would be useful to extend our approach to more complex and realistic utility functions, for example, considering the diminishing marginal utility. Additionally, it would be more practical to design mechanisms which considers different utility values of workers, according to their individual preferences.

REFERENCES

[1] Michael C Ashton, Kibeom Lee, and Chongnak Son. 2000. Honesty as the sixth factor of personality: Correlations with Machiavellianism, primary psychopathy, and social adroitness. *European Journal of Personality* 14, 4 (2000), 359–368.

[2] Moshe Babaioff, Michal Feldman, and Noam Nisan. 2006. Combinatorial Agency. In *Proceedings of the 7th ACM Conference on Electronic Commerce (EC '06)*. ACM, New York, NY, USA, 18–28. https://doi.org/10.1145/1134707.1134710

[3] Ashwinkumar Badanidiyuru, Robert Kleinberg, and Yaron Singer. 2012. Learning on a Budget: Posted Price Mechanisms for Online Procurement. In *Proceedings of the 13th ACM Conference on Electronic Commerce (EC '12)*. ACM, New York, NY, USA, 128–145. https://doi.org/10.1145/2229012.2229026

[4] Amin Ranj Bar and Muthucumaru Maheswaran. 2013. *Confidentiality and integrity in crowdsourcing systems*. Springer Science & Business Media.

[5] Thomas E Becker. 1998. Integrity in organizations: Beyond honesty and conscientiousness. *Academy of Management Review* 23, 1 (1998), 154–161.

[6] Arpita Biswas, Shweta Jain, Debmalya Mandal, and Y Narahari. 2015. A truthful budget feasible multi-armed bandit mechanism for crowdsourcing time critical tasks. In *Proceedings of the 2015 International Conference on Autonomous Agents and Multiagent Systems*. International Foundation for Autonomous Agents and Multiagent Systems, 1101–1109.

[7] Patrick Bolton and Mathias Dewatripont. 2005. *Contract theory*. MIT press.

[8] David Catteeuw, The Anh Han, and Bernard Manderick. 2014. Evolution of Honest Signaling by Social Punishment. In *Proceedings of the 2014 Annual Conference on Genetic and Evolutionary Computation (GECCO '14)*. ACM, New York, NY, USA, 153–160. https://doi.org/10.1145/2576768.2598312

[9] Frank Cowell. 2011. *Measuring inequality*. Oxford University Press.

[10] Arnoud V den Boer. 2015. Dynamic pricing and learning: historical origins, current research, and new directions. *Surveys in operations research and management science* 20, 1 (2015), 1–18.

[11] Brian R Dineen, Roy J Lewicki, and Edward C Tomlinson. 2006. Supervisory guidance and behavioral integrity: relationships with employee citizenship and deviant behavior. *Journal of Applied Psychology* 91, 3 (2006), 622.

[12] David Easley and Arpita Ghosh. 2015. Behavioral Mechanism Design: Optimal Crowdsourcing Contracts and Prospect Theory. In *Proceedings of the Sixteenth ACM Conference on Economics and Computation (EC '15)*. ACM, New York, NY, USA, 679–696. https://doi.org/10.1145/2764468.2764513

[13] Christopher Eppig, Corey L Fincher, and Randy Thornhill. 2010. Parasite prevalence and the worldwide distribution of cognitive ability. *Proceedings of the Royal Society of London B: Biological Sciences* 277, 1701 (2010), 3801–3808.

[14] Peter Frazier, David Kempe, Jon Kleinberg, and Robert Kleinberg. 2014. Incentivizing Exploration. In *Proceedings of the Fifteenth ACM Conference on Economics and Computation (EC '14)*. ACM, New York, NY, USA, 5–22. https://doi.org/10.1145/2600057.2602897

[15] Simon Gächter and Jonathan F Schulz. 2016. Intrinsic honesty and the prevalence of rule violations across societies. *Nature* (2016).

[16] Herbert Gintis. 2009. *The bounds of reason: Game theory and the unification of the behavioral sciences*. Princeton University Press.

[17] John Gittins, Kevin Glazebrook, and Richard Weber. 2011. *Multi-armed bandit allocation indices*. John Wiley & Sons.

[18] Sanford J Grossman and Oliver D Hart. 1983. An analysis of the principal-agent problem. *Econometrica: Journal of the Econometric Society* (1983), 7–45.

[19] Christopher Harris. 2011. You're hired! an examination of crowdsourcing incentive models in human resource tasks. In *Proceedings of the Workshop on Crowdsourcing for Search and Data Mining (CSDM) at the Fourth ACM International*

Conference on Web Search and Data Mining (WSDM) (CSCW '11). 15–18.

[20] Chien-Ju Ho, Aleksandrs Slivkins, Siddharth Suri, and Jennifer Wortman Vaughan. 2015. Incentivizing High Quality Crowdwork. In *Proceedings of the 24th International Conference on World Wide Web (WWW '15)*. ACM, New York, NY, USA, 419–429. https://doi.org/10.1145/2736277.2741102

[21] Chien-Ju Ho, Aleksandrs Slivkins, and Jennifer Wortman Vaughan. 2014. Adaptive Contract Design for Crowdsourcing Markets: Bandit Algorithms for Repeated Principal-agent Problems. In *Proceedings of the Fifteenth ACM Conference on Economics and Computation (EC '14)*. ACM, New York, NY, USA, 359–376. https://doi.org/10.1145/2600057.2602880

[22] John Joseph Horton and Lydia B. Chilton. 2010. The Labor Economics of Paid Crowdsourcing. In *Proceedings of the 11th ACM Conference on Electronic Commerce (EC '10)*. ACM, New York, NY, USA, 209–218. https://doi.org/10.1145/1807342.1807376

[23] John J Horton and Richard J Zeckhauser. 2010. Algorithmic wage negotiations: Applications to paid crowdsourcing. (2010).

[24] Simon Huttegger, Brian Skyrms, Pierre Tarres, and Elliott Wagner. 2014. Some dynamics of signaling games. *Proceedings of the National Academy of Sciences* 111, Supplement 3 (2014), 10873–10880.

[25] Kazushi Ikeda and Michael S. Bernstein. 2016. Pay It Backward: Per-Task Payments on Crowdsourcing Platforms Reduce Productivity. In *Proceedings of the 2016 CHI Conference on Human Factors in Computing Systems (CHI '16)*. ACM, New York, NY, USA, 4111–4121. https://doi.org/10.1145/2858036.2858327

[26] Shweta Jain, Balakrishnan Narayanaswamy, and Y Narahari. 2014. A Multiarmed Bandit Incentive Mechanism for Crowdsourcing Demand Response in Smart Grids. In *Proceedings of AAAI (AAAI'14)*. 721–727.

[27] Deborah L Kidder. 2005. Is it 'who I am','what I can get away with', or 'what you've done to me'? A Multi-theory Examination of Employee Misconduct. *Journal of Business Ethics* 57, 4 (2005), 389–398.

[28] Robert Kleinberg and Tom Leighton. 2003. The Value of Knowing a Demand Curve: Bounds on Regret for Online Posted-Price Auctions. In *Proceedings of the 44th Annual IEEE Symposium on Foundations of Computer Science (FOCS '03)*. IEEE Computer Society, Washington, DC, USA, 594–. http://dl.acm.org/citation.cfm?id=946243.946352

[29] Jean-Jacques Laffont and David Martimort. 2009. *The theory of incentives: the principal-agent model*. Princeton university press.

[30] Winter Mason and Duncan J Watts. 2010. Financial incentives and the performance of crowds. *ACM SIGKDD Explorations Newsletter* 11, 2 (2010), 100–108.

[31] Nina Mazar, On Amir, and Dan Ariely. 2008. The dishonesty of honest people: A theory of self-concept maintenance. *Journal of marketing research* 45, 6 (2008), 633–644.

[32] Deniz S Ones and Chockalingam Viswesvaran. 1998. Gender, age, and race differences on overt integrity tests: Results across four large-scale job applicant datasets. *Journal of Applied Psychology* 83, 1 (1998), 35.

[33] Gabriele Paolacci and Jesse Chandler. 2014. Inside the Turk: Understanding Mechanical Turk as a participant pool. *Current Directions in Psychological Science* 23, 3 (2014), 184–188.

[34] Shaul Shalvi, Jason Dana, Michel JJ Handgraaf, and Carsten KW De Dreu. 2011. Justified ethicality: Observing desired counterfactuals modifies ethical perceptions and behavior. *Organizational Behavior and Human Decision Processes* 115, 2 (2011), 181–190.

[35] Aaron D. Shaw, John J. Horton, and Daniel L. Chen. 2011. Designing Incentives for Inexpert Human Raters. In *Proceedings of the ACM 2011 Conference on Computer Supported Cooperative Work (CSCW '11)*. ACM, New York, NY, USA, 275–284. https://doi.org/10.1145/1958824.1958865

[36] Yaron Singer and Manas Mittal. 2013. Pricing Mechanisms for Crowdsourcing Markets. In *Proceedings of the 22Nd International Conference on World Wide Web (WWW '13)*. ACM, New York, NY, USA, 1157–1166. https://doi.org/10.1145/2488388.2488489

[37] Adish Singla and Andreas Krause. 2013. Truthful Incentives in Crowdsourcing Tasks Using Regret Minimization Mechanisms. In *Proceedings of the 22Nd International Conference on World Wide Web (WWW '13)*. ACM, New York, NY, USA, 1167–1178. https://doi.org/10.1145/2488388.2488490

[38] Brian Skyrms. 2010. *Signals: Evolution, learning, and information*. Oxford University Press.

[39] Aleksandrs Slivkins and Jennifer Wortman Vaughan. 2014. Online Decision Making in Crowdsourcing Markets: Theoretical Challenges. *SIGecom Exch.* 12, 2 (Nov. 2014), 4–23. https://doi.org/10.1145/2692359.2692364

[40] Kenneth E Train. 2009. *Discrete choice methods with simulation*. Cambridge university press.

[41] Long Tran-Thanh, Sebastian Stein, Alex Rogers, and Nicholas R Jennings. 2012. Efficient crowdsourcing of unknown experts using multi-armed bandits. In *European Conference on Artificial Intelligence*. 768–773.

[42] Yu Zhang and Mihaela van der Schaar. 2012. Reputation-based incentive protocols in crowdsourcing applications. In *INFOCOM, 2012 Proceedings IEEE*. IEEE, 2140–2148.

The Impact of E-Mentoring on Information Technology Professionals

John Cotton
Department of Management
Marquette University
Milwaukee, WI - USA
john.cotton@marquette.edu

Monica Adya
Department of Management
Marquette University
Milwaukee, WI - USA
monica.adya@marquette.edu

ABSTRACT

Our research examines the impact of virtual mentoring, or E-mentoring. We surveyed 133 IT professionals as to their experiences as protégés. We asked them about their mentoring relationships, as well as job and career outcomes, and the extent to which they interacted with the mentor virtually. We predicted that E-mentoring would lead to less effective mentoring relationships, less mentoring satisfaction, and lower career outcomes, and that these effects would be moderated by age (millennial protégés versus older protégés). We found few effects, other than lower satisfaction with E-mentoring relationships. The results suggest that E-mentoring can be as effective as face-to-face mentoring. However, few in our sample had completely virtual mentoring relationships, so it may still be possible that E-mentoring with almost no face-to-face interaction may be less effective.

CCS CONCEPTS

• Social and professional topics → Computing profession →Employment Issues; Computing occupations

KEYWORDS

Mentoring; Virtual Communications; Millennials

ACM Reference format:

J. Cotton, M. Adya 2018. The Impact of E-Mentoring on Information Technology Professionals. In Proceedings of ACM SIGMIS-CPR '18, June 18–20, 2018, Buffalo-Niagara Falls, NY, USA, 4 pages. https://doi.org/10.1145/3209626.3209715

1 INTRODUCTION

The topic of mentoring has developed into a rich research area, demonstrating how mentoring relationships can have an impact on a variety of career outcomes. Mentoring is found to promote

salaries, promotions, improved work performance, new career roles, and enhanced skills. Mentorship eases socialization and acculturation of new employees [14] and expands social and professional networks [9]. At the firm level, mentoring increases job satisfaction, organizational commitment, and employee retention [16]. Whereas similar benefits are expected to accrue for information technology (IT) professionals, the benefits of mentoring in such individuals has only been examined as a peripheral issue.

1.1 E-Mentoring

E-mentoring can be thought of as a continuum, from completely face-to-face interactions to completely virtual interactions, where the mentor and protégé never physically meet. Given the technology of today's environment, completely face-to-face interaction is probably rare. Even close relationships will involve email, texting or other communication technologies. However, most mentoring relationships have a significant face-to-face component. But, what happens as this component shrinks, or disappears entirely? Is a mentor and his/her impact the same when the relationship occurs via Skype, e-mail and other technologies? There have been a number of instances where virtual relationships have been found to be unsatisfactory, or at least less efficient than face-to-face interactions.

For example, Grenny and Maxfield [7] reported a survey of 1,100 on-site and remote employees. They found that remote employees were more likely than onsite employees to report feeling left out and less supported. The conclusion has been that virtual relationships are more difficult to develop and maintain but can be successful.

What about virtual mentoring or e-mentoring? Because protégés are not geographically restricted in finding mentors, e-mentoring allows potential protégés to expand the potential pool of mentors [8]. Research has demonstrated that e-mentoring can increase knowledge [2][4], communication skills [1], and teamwork skills [5]. However, this research has generally compared e-mentoring with no mentoring. How does e-mentoring compare with face-to-face mentoring? Does e-mentoring affect the mentoring relationship? If so, how?

1.2 Protégé Demographics

A demographic of interest with e-mentoring is age. The millennial generation (born between 1985 and 2000) has consistently demonstrated a greater understanding and talent with technology in comparison to older workers. Twenge and colleagues [15] argued that "the constraints of time, space and physicality that previous generations were raised with do not exist for Millennials in the same way". In a conceptual paper on E-mentoring, Neely, Cotton and Neely [10] hypothesized that Millennials should be more likely to attempt e-mentoring and should also be more effective in managing mentoring in this fashion. (Other demographics were also examined in this study, but we have not finished those analyses, and because of space limitations, we are only reporting age effects. The findings thus far for other demographics are similar.)

1.3 Hypotheses

The discussion above leads to the following hypotheses related to the adoption of E-mentoring:

H1: E-mentoring will be as effective as face-to-face mentoring with regard to career-oriented mentor relationships, but less effective than face-to-face mentoring with regards to psychosocial mentor relationships.

H2: E-mentoring will be less effective than face-to-face mentoring with regards to satisfaction with the mentor relationship.

H3: E-mentoring will be less effective than face-to-face mentoring with regards to job and career outcomes.

H4: Millennials in IT careers are more likely to benefit from e-mentoring than other generations.

2 METHODS

2.1 Respondents

The authors employed a Qualtrics survey of their own design. To be included in the sample the respondent must have had an IP address within the United States, be currently employed (not retired or seeking employment) as an IT professional and have a mentor currently or in the past. In addition, several questions were inserted into the survey designed to indicate if the respondents were paying attention to the questions or simply answering at random. A total of 139 responses met these requirements. However, six respondents did not answer the question regarding e-mentoring, so 133 responses were utilized for the analyses involving this variable.

2.2 Questionnaire

2.2.1 Demographics
Respondents were asked which range encompassed their current age (18-25, 26-35, 36-45, 46-55, 56-65, above 65). Ages ranged from 26 to more than 65, with a median of 36-45 years and a mode of 36-45 years (33%). In terms of gender, 56% were male, 43% female and 1% (1 respondent) indicating another identity. In terms of race, 71% reported themselves as Caucasian, 10.8% African American, 8.6% Hispanic, 8.6% Asian/Pacific Islander, and 1% (1 respondent) American Indian. Respondents were asked their level of education, ranging from high school diploma to doctorate. Of the sample, 7.2% had high school diplomas, 13.7% had associate degrees, 55.4% had bachelor's degrees, 20.1% had master's degrees, 2.9% had doctorates and 1 respondent indicated "other".

2.2.2 E-Mentoring
In the questionnaire, respondents were asked, "to what extent do you and your mentor meet face-to-face as opposed to virtually (e.g., using videoconferencing, e-mail, phone call or other technology mediated communications)?" The respondents could indicate their mentoring interactions on a scale from 0-100, where 0 indicated completely face-to-face interactions and 100 indicated completely virtual interaction. The sample varied across the entire scale, with 12 respondents (7.8%) reporting complete face-to-face interaction, and 4 respondents (2.6%) indicating complete virtual interaction and the rest in between. However, interaction tended to skew towards the face-to-face extreme, with the mean and median both around 37. We created a variable where the responses were broken into quartiles, with the breaks occurring at 15, 37 and 53, indicating that the distribution was skewed towards the face-to-face extreme but there was a significant amount of virtual mentoring as well. This 4-level variable was employed in the regression analyses.

2.2.3 Mentoring Relationship
The mentoring relationship was assessed through a series of scales designed to assess various functions completed by the mentor. These functions included six psychosocial functions (being a role model, social, counseling, friendship, acceptance, acting like a parent) and five career functions (sponsorship, challenging assignments, providing protection, giving exposure, coaching). In addition, there was a four-item measure of mentor satisfaction. These measures of mentor functions have been employed previously [13]. The reliability of the psychosocial scales was reasonable, with Cronbach alphas of 0.85 (Role Model), 0.92 (Social), 0.93 (Acting like Parent), .73 (Counseling), 0.82 (Friendship), 0.89 (Acceptance). The reliability of the career functions was also acceptable, with Cronbach Alphas of .80 (Sponsorship), 0.89 (Challenging Assignments), 0.73 (Providing Protection), 0.85 (Giving Exposure), and 0.88 (Coaching). The mentor satisfaction scale had a reliability of 0.80.

2.2.4 Job and Career Outcomes
The dependent variables assessed included Occupational Commitment, Organizational Commitment, Turnover Intentions, Career Satisfaction and Job Satisfaction. Occupational Commitment was assessed using scales from [11], measuring affective commitment (six items) and continuance commitment (six items). The reliability coefficients for these scales were 0.86 and 0.81, respectively. Organizational commitment was assessed using scales from [11], measuring affective organizational

commitment (six items) and continuance organizational commitment (six items). The reliability coefficients for these scales were 0.79 and 0.78, respectively. Turnover intentions were measured with a three-item scale from [10]. Its Cronbach alpha was 0.79. Career satisfaction was assessed by a five-item scale developed by [6]. The reliability of that scale was 0.93. Job satisfaction was assessed by agreement or disagreement with a single item, "Overall, I am satisfied with my job".

3 FINDINGS

Because an interaction was predicted between E-mentoring and age, the hypotheses were tested by regressing the mentoring functions and other outcomes on both the e-mentoring scale (broken into the four quartiles) and whether the protégé was a millennial (under 35) or older. We predicted that the career-oriented mentoring functions would be unaffected by e-mentoring, but the psychological support functions would suffer with e-mentoring in comparison to more of a face-to-face environment. Only one of the five career-oriented functions were marginally related to e-mentoring, age, or the interaction of these. The function of "protecting the protégé" was marginally significant ($F=2.77$, $p<.07$). Examining the individual predictors shows that this effect was due to age ($t=2.34$, $p<.03$) and not E-mentoring. Of the psychological support functions, being social ($F=3.95$, $p<.03$), being a parent ($F=4.25$, $p<.02$), and showing acceptance ($F=5.39$, $p<.01$) all had significant effects. With the first two, age was the significant predictor ($t=2.68$, $p<.01$; $t=2.62$, $p<01$), while for showing acceptance, E-mentoring had the significant effect ($t=3.24$, $p<.01$).

In regard to satisfaction with the mentoring relationship, the regression was highly significant ($F=8.71$, $p<.001$). The individual betas showed that this effect was due to the E-mentoring variable ($t=4.17$, $p<.001$). As mentoring became more virtual, satisfaction with the mentoring relationship went down.

In terms of other career outcomes (job satisfaction, commitment, etc.), E-mentoring had no impact. This suggests that the influence of E-mentoring is only on the mentoring relationship and has little carry-over to other outcomes.

Across all the analyses, the interaction of E-mentoring and age was not significant.

4 CONCLUSIONS

In terms of our hypotheses and examination of E-mentoring, significant effects were infrequent. As academics looking to prove our hypotheses, this lack of significance is disappointing. However, for mentors and protégés thinking of virtual mentoring, these effects are both positive and exciting. The results suggest that E-mentoring provides essentially the same mentoring relationship quality, and equal effects with regards to job and career outcomes. Since it would seem unlikely for E-mentoring to be *more* effective than face-to-face mentoring, these results are about as positive as one could expect.

The one area in which E-mentoring was less effective was in terms of satisfaction with the mentoring relationship. Even though the E-mentoring appeared to provide similar support for protégés, they were not as satisfied with the virtual relationship. It may be that there are other outcomes we did not assess that are less effective with E-mentoring. Or, it may be that E-mentoring is successful, but is more work, or intrinsically less satisfying than face-to-face relationships.

One concern with the findings is that we examined the entire continuum of E-mentoring, and not just the extreme, which would be completely virtual E-mentoring. We divided our range of E-mentoring into four equal parts, and the most extreme quartile included the scores of 54-100 on the 100-point scale. It may be that we need a stronger, more refined comparison where primarily virtual E-mentoring is examined. As an ad hoc analysis we tried comparing the top 25% with the remaining 75% and found few effects. It might be possible to find effects looking at the top 10%, but we had too few respondents to perform statistical tests. Future research could see if E-mentoring becomes less effective if it is almost entirely conducted virtually.

A limitation of the current study is that it examines the responses of IT professionals. If any employee group would be ready and able to conduct E-mentoring, this would be the group. Surveying members of other professional groups might find that E-mentoring is less effective in a variety of ways.

Overall, at this point, the evidence suggests that E-mentoring is an effective approach to mentoring IT professionals. Given the ability to expand the potential pool of mentors for professionals, these results suggest that E-mentoring should be encouraged.

REFERENCES

[1] Adams, G., & Crews, T. B. (2004). Telementoring: A viable tool. *Journal of Applied Research for Business Instruction, 2*(3), 1–4.

[2] Allen, T.D., Eby, L.T., Poteet, M.L., Lentz, E., & Lima, L. (2004). Career benefits associated with mentoring of protégés: A meta-analysis. *Journal of Applied Psychology, 89,* 127-136.

[3] Carmel, E. & Agarwal, R. (2001). Tactical approaches for alleviating distance in global software development. *IEEE Software*, 18, 22-29.

[4] de Janasz, S. C., & Godshalk, V. M. (2013). The role of e-mentoring in protégés' learning and satisfaction. *Group and Organization Management, 38*(6), 743–774.

[5] Gajendran, R. S., & Harrison, D. A. (2006). The good, the bad, and the unknown about telecommuting: Meta-analysis of individual consequences and mechanisms of distributed work. *Academy of Management Proceedings, 2006,* (1) D6.

[6] Greenhaus, J.H., Parasuraman, S, & Wormley, W.M. (1990). Effects of Race on Organizational Experiences, Job Performance Evaluations, and Career Outcomes. *Academy of Management Journal, 33,* 64-86.

[7] Grenny, J., & Maxfield, D. (2017). A study of 1,100 employees found that remote workers feel shunned and left out. *Harvard Business review,* November 2.

[8] Fodeman, D. (2002). Telementoring. *Technology and Learning, 23*(4), 28-30.

[9] Headlam-Wells, J., Gosland, J., & Craig, J. (2005). "There's magic in the web": e-mentoring for women's career development. *Career Development International, 10*(6/7), 444–459.

[10] Irving, P.G., Coleman, D.F., & Cooper, C.L. (1997). Further assessments of a three-component model of occupational commitment: Generalizability and differences across occupations. *Journal of Applied Psychology, 82,* 444-452.

[11] Meyer, J.P., Allen, N.J., & Smith, C.A. (1993). Commitment to organizations and occupations: Extension and test of a three-component conceptualization. *Journal of Applied Psychology, 78,* 538-551.

[12] Neely, A., Cotton, J.L., & Neely, A. (2017). E-mentoring: A model and review of the literature. *AIS Transactions on Human-Computer Interaction, 9,* 220-242.

[13] Ragins, B.R., & Cotton, J.L. (1999). Mentor functions and outcomes: A comparison of men and women in formal and informal mentoring relationships. *Journal of Applied Psychology, 84,* 529-550.

[14] Single, P. B., & Single, R. M. (2005). E-mentoring for social equity: Review of research to inform program development. *Mentoring and Tutoring: Partnership in Learning, 13*(2), 301–320.

[15] Twenge, J.M., Campbell, S.M., Hoffman, B.J., & Lance, C.E. (2010). Generational differences in work values: Leisure and extrinsic values increasing, social and intrinsic values decreasing. *Journal of Management, 36,* 117-142.

[16] Wood, P., & Leck, J. (2008). Dysfunctional mentoring. *International Journal of Diversity in Organisations, Communities & Nations, 8*(4), 19-26.

The Development of a Conversational Agent Mentor Interface Using Short Message Service (SMS)

Leron Julian
Morehouse College
Department of Computer Science
Atlanta, GA, USA
leron.julian@morehouse.edu

Kinnis Gosha
Morehouse College
Department of Computer Science
Atlanta, GA, USA
kinnis.gosha@morehouse.edu

Earl W. Huff, Jr.
Clemson University
School of Computing
Clemson, SC, USA
earlh@clemson.edu

ABSTRACT

Previous studies have investigated the role of embodied conversational agents in providing mentoring advice in faculty-student relationships. One limitation is the need for the protege to visit a specific website to access the agent (mentor). This paper presents the design and development of a conversational agent mentor that uses a more pervasive application for dialogue, short message service (SMS). The SMS conversational agent has been constructed to be used as a virtual mentor, to mentor undergraduate computer science majors at a Historically Black College (HBCU) who are considering pursuing a graduate degree in computing. This study has been designed to compare the effectiveness of the SMS conversational agent to the original conversational agent, an embodied conversational agent (ECA).

CCS CONCEPTS

• **Human-centered computing** → **Interaction design**; *Human computer interaction (HCI)*;

KEYWORDS

Embodied Conversational Agent (ECA), Conversational Agent, Short Message Service (SMS), Virtual Mentorship

ACM Reference Format:
Leron Julian, Kinnis Gosha, and Earl W. Huff, Jr.. 2018. The Development of a Conversational Agent Mentor Interface Using Short Message Service (SMS). In *SIGMIS-CPR '18: 2018 Computers and People Research Conference, June 18–20, 2018, Buffalo-Niagara Falls, NY, USA.* ACM, New York, NY, USA, 4 pages. https://doi.org/10.1145/3209626.3209721

1 INTRODUCTION

Several publications have mentioned the importance of mentoring. One study, for example, states that "a recent meta-analysis indicated that former protegees tend to be paid more, promoted more often, and are more positive about their careers than those who have never been mentored" [2]. One enhancement to mentoring is the addition of virtual mentoring. In 2013, Kinnis Gosha conducted a between-group study with 37 African American male undergraduate computer science majors in which it was discovered that mentoring can be done using an embodied conversational agent. An embodied conversational agent (ECA) is an effective way to represent an intelligent conversation between humans and artificially intelligent software by conversing with humans using the same verbal and nonverbal means [3]. Although the study conducted by Gosha [6] showed positive results, it required that a user had to open up a standalone website to interact with the virtual mentor. A limitation with this approach is that a user would have to interact with a tool that they do not normally use on a mobile device, which would potentially cause the user to interact with the mentor less. One widely used phone application for most people is short message service (SMS), commonly known as "text messaging". The goal of this study is to compare the level of effectiveness between the original embodied conversational agent mentor and a new conversational agent mentor with an SMS interface. For this study, effectiveness will be measured through qualitative and quantitative methodologies and techniques. It is hypothesized that there will be no significant difference between the effectiveness of the mentorship provided by the SMS conversational agent, the standalone website, and a human mentor.

2 LITERATURE REVIEW

Mentoring is a "partnership between two people (mentor and mentee) normally working in a similar field or sharing similar experiences. It is a helpful relationship based on mutual trust and respect" [1]. Mentorship is necessary, especially for students considering graduate school. It is stated by James Blackwell that by mentoring at the undergraduate level, students can "foster a continuing interest in education and may lead to a decision to undertake graduate work" [4]. Therefore, developing a conversational agent as a virtual mentor can help foster undergraduate students to pursue graduate studies in the STEM fields and by using SMS, it can make this mentorship more accessible.

Based on previous research [8], three mentoring functions have been identified: career, psychosocial, and a third, networking help [13]. One type of mentoring relationship is faculty-student mentoring. This type of mentoring "benefit students in numerous ways, which include increased employment opportunities (Bova 2000; Cameron 1978), development of professional skills (Bova and Phillips 1984), and professional growth (Harris and Brewer 1986), among others" [9].

One may confuse virtual mentoring with telementoring. Telementoring is the same as traditional mentoring; with the exception

SIGMIS-CPR '18, June 18–20, 2018, Buffalo-Niagara Falls, NY, USA
© 2018 Association for Computing Machinery.
ACM ISBN 978-1-4503-5768-5/18/06...$15.00
https://doi.org/10.1145/3209626.3209721

that the mentor and mentee may communicate using a medium such as a telephone, email or video call [10]. Virtual mentoring is not traditional mentoring because two humans are not involved; only one human and a computer agent.

Short message service (SMS) "is the most successful data service in the mobile telecommunications environment and it is one of the few mobile data services that have so far achieved extensive diffusion" [5]. Based on research, Corrocher states that the market for SMS has significantly grown after 1999. Around the world, the mobile messaging industry was worth $130 billion in 2008 and grew to $224 billion in 2013. SMS accounts for many revenues and is expected to continue being the most dominant mobile messaging format (2013). Therefore, with SMS being widely used as a form of communication today, using SMS as a virtual mentoring platform will be beneficial. SMS is what we use daily to interact with each other, therefore by using SMS to create a virtual mentor, it will humanize the mentor; making it seem as if the user is actually receiving mentorship by a human.

Moura and Carvalho [11] states that "The evolution of wireless communication has created a new educational paradigm called mobile learning (m-learning)" (2014) which includes the use of mobile devices in education and mentoring. SMS is a reliable and popular communication feature for mobile devices and it has become a trend to use SMS as the basis of communication.

Despite having the many benefits of interacting via SMS, it is also important to note the implication of using it where it seems to create a 'shrinking world' where individuals do not need to occupy the same physical space. Mobile communication allows people to interact regardless of their location and there are many social problems that come along with the use of SMS and mobile communication. Spagnolli and Gamberini [12] states that "Social presence seems characterized by a sense of constant availability, symmetric commitment and shared understanding" (2006). Interacting via SMS can create a seemingly noticeable divide as opposed to interacting face-to-face. Along with that divide comes the issue of the missing psychosocial component that two individuals lack when interacting via SMS as opposed to an in-person interaction. This is one difference that will be noticed when comparing the SMS conversational agent to Gosha's study [6].

The original virtual mentor was developed in the form of an embodied conversational agent [6]. ECAs are virtual representations of humans through speech and visual cues. An ECA has been programmed to have a sense of understanding what is being said to it and it can also produce facial expressions, speech, and gestures as a response. A well-known researcher in ECA's, Timothy Bickmore, discusses [3] his findings at the SIGCHI Conference on Human Factors in Computing in 2001. He discusses ECA's and the importance of building the type of relationship that the designer of the ECA wants. In summary, he states that ECA's are particularly well suited to the task of relationship building to emulate the experience of human face-to-face interaction. He also states that the nonverbal channels are important for conveying information and for regulating the flow of the conversation. These nonverbal channels are also especially crucial for relational conversation since they can be used to provide such social cues as attentiveness, positive affect, liking and attraction, and to mark shifts into and out of relational activities [3]. Instead of utilizing an embodied conversational agent, for this study, a conversational agent was developed. A conversational agent was developed in place of an embodied conversational agent because an embodied conversational agent would mean that the virtual mentor would need to have visual representations of human features and qualities. A conversational agent lacks the visual representations of humans and utilizes just the interaction through verbal or text means only; which ties into the SMS application for this study.

Other conversational agents that some of us interact with on a daily basis are smart speakers such as Google Home. This device assists humans with everyday tasks simply through conversation with the smart speaker. "While Amazon pioneered the internet-connected speaker (smart speaker) that responds to voice commands, it now has plenty of competition from other tech heavyweights. [The] digital assistants on these speakers - Amazon's Alexa, Google Assistant, Microsoft's Cortana and soon Apple's Siri" [7] are known in the literature as conversational agents.

3 TOOL DEVELOPMENT

For this research, an SMS conversational agent was developed to serve as a virtual mentor. The main programming language used for the algorithm was Javascript, Node.Js in particular, which enables Javascript code on the server-side. To enable an automated reply to the user's question through the use of SMS and the Javascript algorithm, the Twilio API was used. The Twilio API allows programmers to send and receive SMS text messages, phone calls, and more. A phone number was given through the Twilio service which will be used as the number that the user will text to contact the SMS agent. Within the tool, TwiML, a Twilio markup language, was used to dictate what the Twilio API should do when an incoming message is received. To host the program on a server and make it accessible to all users, it was decided that the program and its files will be hosted on Heroku which is a cloud application platform that allows Node.js programs to be deployed on its servers. Heroku was used because of its compatibility, ease of use, and overall price of service (free). All of the program files were stored in a Github repository.

The goal was to make the interaction between the conversational mentor agent and the mentee as simple and convenient as possible. The steps taken for the interaction between the virtual mentor and the mentee goes as follows: 1) A user will text the number of the conversational agent with their question being in the message body, 2) The question asked is saved in a variable and that question is copied to another variable which will be parsed, stripping it of all punctuations and numbers, 3) The algorithm then replaces the words that are in their past tense or plural to its base tense, 4) Each word in the question is compared to an array of synonyms to see if any words have synonyms and if they do, then the words are swapped out for their synonyms, 5) Non-keywords are stripped from the question (an array of keywords is given) and any remaining words are stored in an array, 6) If three or more words are remaining in that array, then they are compared to sets of three keywords that assume a certain question. If there is a match within these three words, then the highest ranked answer is returned to the user via SMS text message, 7) If there is no match with any of the sets of keywords and at least two words are left in the array, then the remaining two words in the array are sequentially compared to sets of two keywords that assume a certain question. If there is a match within this two-keyword set, then the highest ranked answer is returned to the user via SMS text message, 8) If there is not a match with any of the sets of the two keywords, then the question copy string is sequentially compared to individual keywords that assume a question was asked in a certain category. If there is a match with a single keyword, the highest ranked response for that single keyword is returned to the user via SMS, assuming it has identified the category of the question sent to the system, 9) If there are no categories in which the sets of words fall under, then the agent replies "I don't understand your statement", 10) The conversational agent then returns a text message back to the mentee with the original question asked to the conversational agent and under it, the answer to that question. Figure 1 shows a sample interaction between a mentee and the virtual mentor.

To be noted, in order to remain consistent with Gosha's study, the knowledge base for the virtual mentor was derived from Gosha's study [6]. The knowledge base includes the synonym bank, keywords, and the answers that will be replied to the user based on their question. The knowledge base is designed to answer two categories of questions: funding graduate school and career options.

4 EXPERIMENTAL DESIGN

The type of research design that will be used for this study is a mixed methods research design. Mixed methods research designs include both qualitative and quantitative methods. For this research, the quantitative strand will include pre and post-survey instrument tools while the qualitative strand will include the interview

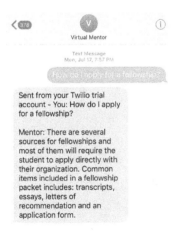

Figure 1: Screenshot of SMS conversational agent mentor interaction

of the participants rating their experience with their mentor and any problems/improvements with the mentors. In evaluating the effectiveness of the mentoring, the only mentoring function that will be taken into consideration is career mentoring since it is the only mentoring function (so far) where virtual mentoring has been shown to be comparable to traditional mentoring [6].

The participants for this research will consist of only undergraduate computer science majors from historically black colleges (HBCUs). Also, the participants needed to have at least an interest in attending graduate school. These participants will be the ones utilizing the SMS conversational agent as a virtual mentor to receive mentorship on considering graduate school.

The procedure for this study will remain consistent with the procedure in Gosha's study [6]. However, the SMS virtual agent will be used in place of the ECA implemented through the website or a human mentor.

There will be two survey instruments given to the participants at their institution. Both survey instruments will include open and close-ended questions with a combination of amplitude and questionnaire style questions. The first survey instrument will be given and collected before the initial mentorship is received by the virtual agent. The second survey instrument will be given to the participants and collected in less than five days after receiving the initial mentorship. The rationale behind collecting the second survey instrument in no more than five days is to prevent the participant from forgetting their mentorship experience.

The participants will begin by completing the first survey instrument. After the first survey instrument is completed, the participant will be sat down in a room and with their own personal cell phone, given that they have one, will be given the phone number of the SMS virtual mentor. The participants will be told that the virtual mentor only knows questions based on the topics of career options and graduate school funding but the participants will be allowed to ask any question that they would like to the virtual mentor. There is no time limit nor is there a limit on the number of questions that the participant can ask the virtual mentor. After each mentoring session is complete, the participant will then fill out the second post-survey instrument.

The data collected in this research will be received from pre and post-survey instrument tools given to the participants. This survey tool will be used to measure the effectiveness of the SMS conversational agent. This pre and post-survey tool will include a series of questions asked to the participant, which will overall rate the effectiveness of the mentorship received.

The data collected from the SMS conversational agent will be compared to the results from Gosha's study [6]. The pre and post-survey evaluations will be used to measure the effectiveness. A paired sample t-test from the SMS conversational agent and Gosha's study [6] will be used in order to test for any major differences in the scores from the pre to post-survey evaluation. In the case of this research study, the SMS conversational agent mentor is compared to Gosha's study [6], which compares an ECA virtual mentor to a human mentor. Therefore, a repeated measures analysis of variance will be used. This is because there is a comparative analysis of three groups.

5 RESULTS

The results of this research have not yet been received nor has data been compiled. This research focuses on the design, development, and the planning for the SMS conversational agent as a virtual mentor. The SMS conversational agent virtual mentor has already been developed and tested, however it has not been used to mentor as of yet.

REFERENCES

[1] n.d.. What is Mentoring? http://www.mentorset.org.uk/what-is-mentoring.html
[2] Tammy D Allen, Lillian T Eby, Mark L Poteet, Elizabeth Lentz, and Lizzette Lima. 2004. Career benefits associated with mentoring for protégés: A meta-analysis. *Journal of applied psychology* 89, 1 (2004), 127.
[3] Timothy Bickmore and Justine Cassell. 2001. Relational agents: a model and implementation of building user trust. In *Proceedings of the SIGCHI conference on Human factors in computing systems.* ACM, 396–403.
[4] James E Blackwell. 1989. Mentoring: An action strategy for increasing minority faculty. *Academe* 75, 5 (1989), 8–14.
[5] Nicoletta Corrocher. 2013. The Development of Short Message Services. *Revue économique* 64, 1 (2013), 149–163.
[6] Kinnis Gosha. 2013. *The application of embodied conversational agents for mentoring African American STEM doctoral students.* Clemson University.
[7] Anick Jesdanun. 2017. Buyers' Guide: Choosing a smart speaker for your home.
[8] Kathy E Kram. 1983. Phases of the mentor relationship. *Academy of Management journal* 26, 4 (1983), 608–625.
[9] Vicente M Lechuga. 2011. Faculty-graduate student mentoring relationships: Mentors' perceived roles and responsibilities. *Higher Education* 62, 6 (2011), 757–771.
[10] Christina Ligadu and Patricia Anthony. 2015. E-Mentoring 'MentorTokou': Support For Mentors and Mentees During The Practicum. *Procedia-Social and Behavioral Sciences* 186 (2015), 410–415.
[11] Adelina Moura and Ana Amélia Carvalho. 2010. Mobile learning: using SMS in educational contexts. In *Key competencies in the knowledge society.* Springer, 281–291.
[12] Anna Spagnolli and Luciano Gamberini. 2007. Interacting via SMS: Practices of social closeness and reciprocation. *British Journal of Social Psychology* 46, 2 (2007), 343–364.
[13] Harriet R Tenenbaum, Faye J Crosby, and Melissa D Gliner. 2001. Mentoring relationships in graduate school. *Journal of Vocational Behavior* 59, 3 (2001), 326–341.

Identifying and Discussing Drivers and Barriers of a Job System for the Virtual Agile Workforce of the Future

David Richter
Tourlane GmbH
Jaegerstrasse 71
10117 Berlin - Germany

david@cdrichter.de

Victoria Reibenspiess
German Graduate School of
Management & Law
Bildungscampus 2
74076 Heilbronn - Germany
victoria.reibenspiess@ggs.de

Andreas Eckhardt
German Graduate School of
Management & Law
Bildungscampus 2
74076 Heilbronn - Germany
andreas.eckhardt@ggs.de

ABSTRACT

Agile software development, such as Scrum, and more recently agile project management have been topics that have been part of management literature over recent years. The further development towards agile work systems and with it the necessary changes to an agile workforce of the future is at the scope of this work. A structured literature review, based on articles published in peer-reviewed Management and Information Systems (IS) journals, is performed to find out in how far scientific research has already covered this development and to further analyze, what aspects play the most important roles in the advancement of agility. The key findings focus on the presence of flexible working arrangements, used by organizations and employees, virtual work, the necessary knowledge management measures as well as the vital role that leadership plays in the organization.

CCS CONCEPTS

• **Social and professional topics** → **Project and people management**

KEYWORDS

Agile Workforce; Agile Work Systems; Leadership; Virtual Work; Flexible Working Arrangements; Knowledge Management

ACM Reference format:
D. Richter, V. Reibenspiess, and A. Eckhardt 2018. SIG Proceedings Paper in word Format. In *Proceedings of ACM SIGMIS-CPR'18, Buffalo-Niagara Falls, NY, USA, June 2018*, 7 pages.
https://doi.org/10.1145//3209626.3209710

1 INTRODUCTION

Since the beginning of modern employer-employee relationships, the very environments, in which they existed, have always been developing and changing. All this in line with the society or more precise the needs of the individuals the society consists of [1]. Biernacki [2] argues, that the drivers of these changes can be

grouped into several subsections. Among these are on the one side, considered rather "hard" facts, technical advances and progress, legal developments or social advances. The other side consists of rather "soft" facts; trends that are subject to the changing values, expectations and disposition of the employees.

Just like society is always developing and thus changing, the work environment cannot stop or reach the end of its development with the ever-stronger importance the Internet has for the economy (resulting both in necessities and opportunities) driving changes in the needs and interests of employees and employers alike. Both have been looking for more flexibility, reducing boundaries and improving efficiency. While this sounds like both parties involved look for the same thing, the actual "form" this flexibility is supposed to take can be vastly different for employers from what employees look for [3]. As a result, the security both sides were originally longing for, is not a given anymore. It can be, but it no longer has to be. From the classic white-collar office worker with a 9-5 job to the highly skilled and highly paid freelancer expert, which is only hired for a very specific project, a lot of different employment scenarios are possible [4].

Breaking down the expression at the core of this work, agile workforce, it is interesting to see, where the term "agile" comes from and the meaning it has taken. Richards [5] explains in his article, that the modern use of the term agility originally stems from a range of aspects that resulted in fighter planes beating their combatants. The reason though, was not only superior technology or maneuverability, but also found in the pilots by being observant and, due to being well oriented, able to adjust in a timely and effective manner. The term made its way into business strategy at the start of the 1990s when it was first used, usually to describe a certain type of manufacturing company [5].

Of course, the agile concept is not exclusive to manufacturing or production companies. In recent years, the main sector that was attributed with agility was the service industry, more precisely the IT sector. The term agile software development is characterized by team members' interaction and organization, the constant creation of working software bits, the ongoing communication with the customer and keeping an open mind to be able to respond to change quickly [6]. Kautz et al. [7] outline Scrum, probably the best-known agile software development technique in use today, as also usable as general project management method. Due to the fact, that in the Scrum methodology constant interaction with the customer, along with the underlying assumption that customer's demands most certainly will change in the course of a project, means adaptability is immanent [7]. Denning [8] takes it further and defines agile as a term that is used for a set of management practices (including Scrum, Kanban and Lean) with the goal of providing solutions through the use of cross-functional, self-organizing teams. A further look at the practices used in agile project management emphasizes, that constant review, anticipation, and reorganization are vital parts of agility.

The key term of this review was at first introduced by Shafer et al. [9], who used agile workforce to describe a workforce that is primarily trained to do multiple jobs in one company. Looking at the features outlined in the project management practice, it seems, that more emphasis than just cross training needs to be on the skills and capabilities of the employee. Breu et al. [10] used workforce agility already in a more elaborate way and described the fact, that companies, aiming to be agile, need the company's workforce to be skilled and capable in certain aspects.

Summarizing some of the key characteristics, that the above articles and authors mentioned, agility can be outlined as being observant, anticipating, adaptable, flexible and decisive. What has been missing so far has been a look at the general agile features and interests of the aggregated workforce. Younger and Smallwood [4] start with a wide-scope approach to the agile workforce, as they include all non-traditional work relationships and alternative forms of employment. Their focus though is on external knowledge workers that mainly work on project basis for their contracting partners. Thus, the term agile workforce has to be taken a step further. It should include all members of the workforce, whether traditional employees or what is sometimes referred to as the "extended workforce" (for example contractors, freelancers or outsourcing partners) [11]. Hence, we define the agile workforce as *"the part of the workforce (internal, external, extended and potential) that follows agile principles both in an organization's as well as in its own interest."*

According to a recent study from practice by the USA division of Randstad [12] that focused on the agile workforce (term used referring to external labor), currently about 11% of workforce consists of agile workers. While the study claims, that by 2019 up to 50% of workers could belong to the agile workforce, executives expect 69% of their workforce to be agile by the year 2025 [12]. Hoffman et al. [13] argue that, what they call, a new compact, a self-understanding of the cooperation between employer and employee is necessary. Further, Tripp et al. [14] encourage others in their study on job satisfaction in agile teams, to take a closer look at workplace characteristics in this particular field.

As the current literature is not specifically focusing on the topic of an agile workforce in the outlined meaning, there is a need to advance in this field. The focus will be on the consequences for companies and organizations employing this future agile workforce. Thus, we review the current research on the agile workforce and closely related topics, trying to answer the question: **How can companies prepare for, sustainably react on and work with the agile workforce?**

To answer the research question, we apply a literature review. The remainder of this work is as follows. At first, we provide a quick overview on related work. Then, we describe the methodology of our work in detail. The results of a detailed content analysis are shown in the fourth section. The last section discusses key topics identified in the analysis in regard to their relevance for the research question and provides a comprehensive conclusion of the work.

2 RELATED WORK

With this article offering a structured overview of the topics relating to the agile workforce, this related work sections casts a look over literature reviews that have focused on the agile workforce before. Just two reviews were touching similar topics.

In his 2013 structured literature review on workforce agility, Muduli [15] tries to shed light on the general attributes of the agile workforce and fitting management practices. Muduli bases his results on a total of 38 scientific articles. They have been published over a period of 37 years between 1972 and 2008. Taking a closer look at the distribution, of the articles over time reveals, that 57% of articles identified as relevant by Muduli were published up until the year 2000 and only two focused explicitly on workforce agility. This is an especially interesting find, as it can be argued, that these articles certainly do take the agile production or agile manufacturing approaches into account, but lack the rapid development taken after the year 2000, for example regarding virtual work. Muduli derives seven key attributes of an agile workforce, namely adaptiveness, flexibility, having a positive attitude towards development, speed, collaboration, competence and informative (in the sense of both looking for information as well as providing information) [15]. The review ultimately defines workforce agility as *"a well-trained and flexible workforce that can adapt quickly and easily to new opportunities and market circumstances"* [15]. While this is a very comprehensive take, it still leaves a lot of questions about the agile workforce, for example such as its composition, nature, capabilities, or motivation untouched.

Some of these aspects are part of the second literature review by Qin and Nembhard [16]. While their focus is on the meanings and implications of workforce agility regarding operations management, it does cover a wide range of topics and characteristics generally relevant to the agile workforce. The authors base their review on a total of 115 articles released over a period of 61 years between the years 1955 and 2015. The authors make the point, that workforce agility is still scarce in the available literature on agile business practices and that the usual parameters referring to agile are not necessarily the same for the agile workforce. This is justified by referring to the complex human mindset, factors and behaviors. The authors also outline, how literature on agility uses several attributes to characterize agility and applies them also to the workforce. Qin and Nembhard [16] go on to explain a range of attributes used in agile literature and compare them for their applicability to workforce agility. The authors go on to use the data from their analysis to show how workforce agility can be achieved and that different approaches to reach workforce agility coincide with certain attributes. Although the authors focus on operations management aspects regarding workforce agility, they covered a wide range of topics, at least briefly, that are generally applicable to the agile workforce.

3 METHODOLOGY

3.1 Approach chosen

For the purpose of conducting a scientifically sound structured literature review, we follow the approach suggested by Webster and Watson [17], which is a three-staged process of identifying relevant literature, structuring the review and finally contributing to theoretical development [17]. Manhart and Thalmann [18] develop a visualization of the literature review process that is accurate and offers an overview of the different steps involved and the links between them. As illustrated in the preceding figure, the review process is not a one-way road, but includes several review cycles. Most notable is this in the first stage, the identification of relevant literature. The process starts with a search term, that is derived from the underlying problem and thus the initial research question. Through the literature search process, reading and re-reading the identified articles a kind of "feedback loop" develops, that can lead to expanding the set of search terms used. Another loop exists between the concluding content analysis and the prior step of the development of a concept matrix. Here the later step and outcomes can possibly influence the selection criteria for the concept matrix.

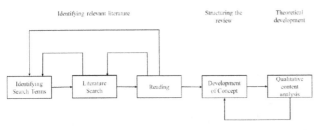

Figure 1. Procedure of the Literature Review (adapted from Manhart and Thalmann [18].

3.2 Literature Basis

To ensure the review is based on scientifically sound literature, only articles were considered, that were peer-reviewed and published in journals reaching a certain quality standard as suggested by Webster and Watson [17]. To ensure only articles of the desired quality were selected, VHB-JOURQUAL3 was used to determine the quality. The German Academic Association for Business Research (VHB) developed this rating system. It depicts the most recent rating system published in the academic field. Over 1,100 VHB members were part of the evaluation process. Overall 934 scientific journals were reviewed. 651 of these received 25 or more evaluations and were thus given a rating [19]. VHB-JOURQUAL3 has 22 subsections or partial ratings, relating to different scientific fields. As the research question proposed is applicable to different management fields, 429 journals were chosen as basis for the review.

3.3 Search Terms

To identify potentially suitable articles, a set of search terms had to be defined. Due to the chosen topic and research question, the initial search terms were agile, workforce, and management; agile describing the characteristics of the group researched, workforce for the main subject being investigated and management for the organizational aspect of dealing with the initially described phenomenon. Through the first search processes, further terms were added, resulting in the following list of search terms being used for identifying articles (see Table 1).

Table 1. Search Terms Used

Initial Search Terms	Added Terms
Agile	Agility, Flexible, Flexibility
Workforce	Employee, Staff, Labor, Labor Market
Management	Manager, Leadership

These search terms were used for a Boolean search in the format ISSN AND agile (or added related terms) AND workforce (or added related terms) AND/OR management (or added related term). After a first search run, defining that the search terms needed to be part of title, abstract or subject terms that did not lead to a satisfying number of results, no restricting parameters were defined on where in an article the selected search terms were to be found.

3.4 Article Inclusion Criteria

The abstracts of the results of the described search were scanned and evaluated for a concrete applicability to the research topic. Reason for exclusion was if the reviewed articles only focused on agility as a side note in software development techniques without expanding at least into the field of project management (or even further). No limiting parameters were applied to the facts of where the papers were published, what regions or countries were investigated. Due to the fact, that the literature reviews mentioned in section 2 were relatively limited in their analysis and applicability, the year of publication was not set as a fixed criterion. Date of publication of the articles did play a role (due to the changing circumstances around the understanding of agility and workforce agility) but was not necessarily a reason for exclusion. Also, the subject of who was being researched (employees, freelancers, managers, companies, organizations, etc.) was not used as an exclusion criterion, as the research question tries to set up a bigger picture including all possibly relevant parties. Articles had to be in English language, as is the lingua franca of today's science [20].

After applying the aforementioned classification, a total of 266 published articles remained that met all outlined criteria. In the detailed review process several articles were eliminated from the selection, as their research topics were too far from a useful application in the sense of this paper. After reviewing the remaining articles, assessing the articles' sources for further relevant articles and repeating the process [17], the total number of articles considered relevant for this review shrunk to 191.

3.5 Structuring the Review

The structure of this review is concept-centric. The analysis is divided into two sections. The first is the individual analysis of each article meeting the selection criteria. The analysis is performed on a quantitative level and a qualitative level. The qualitative approach relies primarily on the development of a concept matrix as proposed by Webster and Watson [17]. Each article is being assessed for its most dominant topics in relation to the agile workforce, underlying concepts, contents and focus [17]. The identified main topics then were grouped into relevant core domains as follows and shown in the preceding Table 2.

Further aspects were added to the matrix describing the articles in general, as suggested by DeLone and McLean [21]. The criteria used are the published format, type of article and research method as well as a short evaluation of each article's importance and relevance in regard to the agile workforce. To ensure the thematic fit with computer personnel research, we only focus on the domains of agile work systems, flexible organization, leadership, and virtual work within this paper.

Table 2. Core Domains and Topics of the Concept Matrix

Core Domain	Agile Work Systems	Flexible Employment (work time & space)	Flexible Organization	Flexibility Strategy	Intl. Organizational Agility Concepts & Culture	Leadership	Virtual Work
	Agile Company	Compressed Workweek	Contingent Labour	HR Strategy	Company Values	Change	Data Security
	Agile Mgmt	Empowerment	Contractor	Knowledge Mgmt	Corporate Culture	Communication (Obstacles)	Virtual Company
	Agile Project Mgmt	Expats	Crowdsourcing	Skill Development	Cross-Cultural Cooperation	Conflict Management	Virtual Team
	Agile Workforce	Flex Time	Downsizing	Strategic Mgmt	Cross-National Cooperation	Control	
Relevant Topics	Scrum	Flex-Shift	Offshoring		Globalization	Employee Loyalty	
		Flexible Work (FWA)	Open Source		Intercultural Aspects	Entrepreneurial	
		Gradual Return to Work	Outsourcing		Multinational Company	Leadership Style	
		Overtime	Temp Work		Process Mgmt	Network	
		Remote Work			Project Mgmt	Paradox	
		Work-Life / Family				Team Functionality	
						Trust	

4 RESULTS

4.1 Research Topics

The following sub-subsections show the identified topics relevant for this approach that could be identified by evaluating the journal articles. As outlined in subsection 3.5 the topics present in the articles were clustered to core domains relating to the agile workforce. Oftentimes articles touched topics relating to more than one of these domains. All topics relevant identified in the articles, were attributed to the specific articles and contributed to the evaluation, even if the article was placed as primarily belonging in a different domain. The following keyword cloud (see Figure 2) contains all topics identified and assigned in the evaluation of articles and gives an overview of relevant topics and their importance in the literature. The font size and intensity correlates with the number of articles a topic has been assigned to.

Figure 2. Research topics by occurrence in articles.

4.2 Agile Work Systems

As outlined in the introduction, the term workforce agility has, so far, not been used in a distinct way, but rather used by different authors, at different times with a different meaning. Having this in mind, some articles considered relevant and claiming to be about the agile workforce will be listed in a different cluster. Although agile work stands at the center of this work, the number of articles relating to the concept is rather low. Only 7.3% of articles about agile work systems focus primarily on this domain. Among topics in the domain, agile company and agile project management stand out as most important. Due to the history of the economical term agility and the application of agile measures to the nature of companies, the relatively high frequency the term agile company is found, can be explained [9]. Similarly, as the adoption of agile software development measures first happened in the field of project management [22], agile project management, simply put, had more time to be researched, compared to the other mentioned topics. Only one article focused completely on the agile workforce. This article by Breu et al. [10] has its focus on enabling an existing workforce to act in an agile way.

An interesting aspect is a look at articles including topics of, but not being primarily assigned to the agile work systems cluster. Apart from the fact, that again the topic agile company is the most dominant, all six articles relating to this topic have their core domain in flexibility strategies. As the agile cluster of topics certainly is future-oriented, it does make sense that articles focusing on strategy topics in regard to flexibility show a trend towards agility.

4.3 Flexible Organization

Relating to Elchardus and Heyvaert [23], the flexible organization is the core domain for topics that focus on the flexibility of employees to the organization's benefit. The most important topic observable in the articles is outsourcing. Regarding the original concept of outsourcing, more recent years brought a shift of outsourcing not only of manufacturing tasks, but also of IT projects, whole engineering tasks or other services [24]. There is no more distinction between outsourcing in the home country of an organization and outsourcing to different parts of the world, which in literature is labeled as offshoring [25]. With 14 total articles relating to this topic, 7.3% of articles had an outsourcing topic. The second important topic in this domain is contingent labor, a term used for "non-standard" employment practices, such as temp work, outsourcing or contracting [26]. Ten articles (5.2%) had a distinct relation to this topic that is especially relevant in regard to some older definitions of workforce agility. The topic of temp work is also a stand-alone, as six articles took a closer look at this phenomenon. Crowdsourcing, observed in five articles (2.6%), is a topic with a potentially higher relevance for the future and in the context of workforce agility. The expression stands for the phenomenon of offering, most times by comparison simple, knowledge work to a crowd of knowledge workers, willing to work on the topic for a set remuneration [27]. Although mentioned in only one article, open sourcing is another possible "future topic" (currently mainly IT-related), that is also relevant for the concept of the agile workforce. The basic idea is that an engaging community of developers helps to boost the attractiveness of a core product by developing complementing products [28].

The total 29 articles relating to the flexible organization seem small for the sheer size of the topic, but this can be explained by the selection of articles focusing on workforce agility and not primarily on the topics relevant in this domain.

4.4 Leadership

The domain leadership is the cluster for topics that heavily rely on leadership to achieve successful results.

In general, this cluster's topics have far more mentions in articles from different core domains (83) than it has articles that focus mainly on leadership topics. The most dominant topic in this cluster is the leadership style (67 total articles). The application is far-reaching. Leadership styles are vital in how to manage change processes and lead change to a successful and sustainable implementation of new processes, models, or structures [29]. The topic with the second most articles assigned is team functionality (48 overall articles, 25%). Similar to the leadership style argument, the functioning of teams and a healthy relationship among team members is a prerequisite for the successful implementation of changes [30]. With this only outline nature of the team functionality, again the occurrence in articles from different core domains makes sense. The topic of networks has been placed in this cluster, as in the predominant context here, it is mainly driven by leaders and their creation of or enabling access to business networks [31]. Further, the cluster trust is a multi-faceted topic that can be applied, for example, in the complex and challenging case of virtual team members, especially in the creation phase [32]. Another example on a different level is that employers need to have trust in their employees when empowerment practices are implemented [33]. Articles (8 in total) related to communication (obstacles) are all placed in other core domains. The communication aspect is vital and always of great importance to make sure the wanted outcomes can be achieved and performance can be enhanced [34]. The remaining three topics paradox (6 articles total), entrepreneurial (5 articles) and change (4 articles) play all significant roles in the development towards agile companies or the achievement of agile practices. Paradox stands for the situation, that in a dynamic and competitive environment contradictory demands occur that a company needs to fulfill. These demands, especially from leaders, make coping mechanisms necessary, that either allow for a solution of paradox tensions or enable the leader to sustainably handle the paradox [35]. The entrepreneurial topic features articles, that either concentrate on entrepreneurship in the classical sense often found in regard to start-ups and their attitudes and articles, that entrepreneurial approaches are needed within companies and departments and the entrepreneurial mindset is pictured as a driver to achieve agile innovation [36]. Change has been mentioned across all domains, but is often treated as implicit.

4.5 Virtual Work

Virtual work is the final core domain identified for the agile workforce. Although this domain holds the second-fewest articles, it is one of the future topics that will have a substantial impact on the future of working arrangements and the structure of organizations [37]. The dominating topic in this cluster is that of virtual teams (26 articles in total). The oldest article relating to this topic, Qureshi and Vogel [38] already outlined that there were three different areas of controversy, when implementing virtual teams. These issues could be either of technological, work-related or social nature [38]. While the technological issues are mainly solved, questions in regard to the integration of virtual teams into existing work processes or topics relating to the social factor, such as communication between team members, cross-cultural issues or knowledge sharing are still of ongoing importance. A phenomenon that, in part, can only exist thanks to virtual teams is that of virtual companies (3 articles). Kratzer [37] argued, that a complete virtualized organization cannot exist, and while Mullenweg [39] and his company Automattic are considered a prime example of a virtual company, it does still have a postal address and an "automattic lounge" in San Francisco. A topic that is connected especially with work in the virtual space is that of data security (1 article). Due to the focus of this review on workforce agility, not many articles have yet connected the topics for data security and the requirements of a future agile workforce. Still, this topic holds significant value for future research and developments in this field.

5 DISCUSSION AND OUTLOOK

As the agile characteristics provide the necessary tools to take on the challenges, that an ever-quicker, ever-more dynamic and ever-more demanding business environment asks for, the focus on delivering tailor-made solutions to the customer, or rather developing these in cooperation with the customer (through his input) is a competitive advantage still today, but will soon be a bare necessity in the competition for customers.

Agile practices are already a reality in software development and currently rapidly spreading out in the context of project management. The first multi-national companies have adapted agile work processes for whole departments, while some medium sized software companies are completely based on agile management practices [8]. Most likely, this development will rather gather pace over the coming years and thus make agility a more important topic in the general management focus.

The aim of this research was to identify ways and means of companies to prepare for, deal with and react to the future agile workforce. Several topics have emerged as being vital in companies preparing for their agile future. For the nearer future, the companies that can benefit from agility are service sector companies, working on project basis.

While it may sound like a platitude, companies will only be able to attract the top talent of the agile workforce, if they become agile themselves. Inflexible hierarchical constructs that do not allow for the necessary freedom of top knowledge workers to own and drive projects of their interest will only result in these workers leaving the organization. This means that foremost companies need to be willing to change and adapt at least parts of their operation to new work systems, providing self-organized teams of knowledge workers with the tools, freedom, and support to pursue projects, that are as close to customers' needs as possible. For many organizations, this is much to ask, as a perceived loss of control is involved in this restructuring. Quite the opposite is the case. Agile measures always contain thorough observation and anticipation of the surroundings, coupled with preparation, development of answers and the freedom for the worker to act on opportunities and threats they identify. This rather results in lower risks to a company than before. The responsibility for business success is spread across all workers, as all workers are also empowered to contribute.

A key task for organizations will be acquiring the talent needed to work towards becoming an agile company. While the globalization, and more specific the rise of virtual work, has opened new employment markets and access to previously unreachable talent, this is also true for an organization's competitors. Thus, preparing for the agile workforce is also coupled with the need for strong employer branding. Research on the Digital Natives has shown, that sharing employees' values has already become more important for their employment decision than the amount of their salary. The young generation has already arrived in organizations, but more workers sharing their attitudes and values are still to come, meaning they will make up a sizable percentage of the future workforce. Ignoring their needs will result in organizations not being able to acquire needed talent and thus missing out on developing their business. A further aspect is, that companies need to be able to explain, what their goal is and what they want to achieve with the knowledge workers they are trying to acquire. Additionally, not providing a meaningful task is another barrier.

HR departments in organizations need to be more involved in the strategic processes and empowered to take the necessary measures to attract, develop and retain the highly sought for talent. This means also, that the management of the total agile workforce, not only the core workforce, needs to be newly organized. HR needs to be able to deal with freelancers, contractors, and internal workers alike, allowing also for the creation of personalized contract arrangements, when necessary.

Another key factor, that companies need to invest in, is functioning, easy to use knowledge management systems, that are able to provide not only the knowledge that is considered necessary, but upgrade this functionality through network features, that allow the direct connection, communication and potentially even forming of (virtual) teams, if topics need to be covered, that are not yet part of the knowledge system.

A major enabler of all practices above is to be found in the leadership function. The role includes aspects spreading into all mentioned subjects so far. The role will go further away from the strong and controlling leader of today. Instead leadership in agile environments needs to follow the principle, that *"people are an organization's most valuable resource and [...] a manager's job is to prepare and free people to perform"* [40].

Looking at the literature that formed the basis of this review, it needs to be pointed out, that in general there is only scarce scientific literature to be found focusing on the topic of agility outside the field of software development or the agile companies of the 1990s yet. As just one example, only one article could be found that covered the field of legal implications connected with company flexibility. As this article dated back to 1998 (thus prior the emergence of virtual work) we found, that the challenges outlined were outdated. Instead a fully new review is needed that addresses the requirements and tasks for both decision- and policy-makers in organizations and public institutions, alike. This situation is true for the vast majority of aspects covered in the review, as the agile workforce, agile measures and flexibility seem to be a vital part of research, but hardly ever standing at the core of it. As we tried to show in this article, research on the future agile workforce, drivers and barriers should not be treated as a side-note, but rather be at the core of organizations and scientific researchers alike.

REFERENCES

[1] Kocka, J. 2000. Arbeit frueher, heute, morgen: Zur Neuartigkeit der Gegenwart, Geschichte und Zukunft der Arbeit. *Konferenz, die vom 4. bis zum 6. Maerz 1999 unter dem Titel … vom Wissenschaftskolleg zu Berlin … veranstaltet wurde.* Campus-Verlag, Frankfurt/Main, 476-492.

[2] Biernacki, R. 2000. Arbeitsmarkt zwischen Kontingenz und Kontinuitaet: Kommentar zu Hansjoerg Siegenthaler, Geschichte und Zukunft der Arbeit. *Konferenz, die vom 4. Bis zum 6. Maerz 1999 unter dem Titel … vom Wissenschaftskolleg zu Berlin … veranstaltet wurde.* Campus-Verlag, Frankfurt/Main, 110-116.

[3] Alis, D., Karsten, L., and Leopold, J. 2006. From Gods to Goddesses: Horai management as an approach to coordinate working hours. *Time & Society.* 15,1, 81-104.

[4] Younger, J., and Smallwood, N. Aligning Your Organization with an Agile Workforce; https://hbr.org/2016/02/aligning-your-organization-with-an-agile-workforce, 11 Feb 2016, 27 January 2018.

[5] Richards, C. W. 1996. Agile manufacturing: beyond lean? *Production & Inventory Management Journal.* 37, 2, 60-64.

[6] Beck, K., Beedle, M., van Bennekum, A., Cockburn, A., Cunningham, W., Fowler, M., Grenning, J., Highsmith, J., Hunt, A., Jeffries, R., Kern, J., Marick, B., Martin, R. C., Mellor, S., Schwaber, K., Sutherland, J., and Thomas, D. Manifesto for Agile Software Development; http://agilemanifesto.org/, 2001, 27 January 2018

[7] Kautz, K., Johanson, T. H., and Uldahl, A. 2014. The Perceived Impact of the Agile Development and Project Management Method Scrum on Information Systems and Software Development Productivity. *Australasian Journal of Information Systems.* 18, 3, 303-315.

[8] Denning, S. 2016. How to make the whole organization "Agile". *Strategy & Leadership.* 44, 4, 10-17.

[9] Shafer, R. A., Dyer, L., Kilty, J., Amos, J., and Ericksen, J. 2001. Crafting a Human Resource Strategy to Foster Organizational Agility: A Case Study. *Human Resource Management.* 40,3, 197-211.

[10] Breu, K., Hemingway, C. J., Strathern, M., and Bridger, D. 2002. Workforce agility: The new employee strategy for the knowledge economy. *Journal of Information Technology.* 17,1, 21-31.

[11] Silverstone, Y., Tambe, H., and Cantrell, S. M. The Rise of the Extended Workforce; https://www.accenture.com/t20150827T020600__w__/us-en/_acnmedia/Accenture/Conversion Assets/DotCom/Documents/Global/PDF/Strategy_7/Accenture-Future-of-HR-Rise-Extended-Workforce.pdf, 27 January 2018.

[12] Randstad. Workplace 2025: Embracing Disruption in a Post-Digital World. http://experts.randstadusa.com/hubfs/Randstad_Workplace_2025_Executive_Summary.pdf, December 2016, 27 January 2018.

[13] Hoffman, R., Casnocha, B., and Yeh, C. 2013. Tours of duty: The new employer-employee compact. *Harvard Business Review.* 91, 6, 49-58.

[14] Tripp, J. F., Riemenschneider, C., and Thatcher, J. B. 2016. Job Satisfaction in Agile Development Teams: Agile Development as Work Redesign. *Journal of the Association for Information Systems.* 17, 4, 267-307.

[15] Muduli, A. 2013. Workforce agility: A review of literature. The IUP. *Journal of Management Research.* 12, 3, 55-65.

[16] Qin, R., and Nembhard, D. A. 2015. Workforce Agility in Operations Management. Surveys in *Operations Research and Management Science.* 20, 55-69.

[17] Webster, J., and Watson, R. T. 2002. Analyzing the Past to Prepare for the Future: Writing a Literature Review. *MIS Quarterly.* 26, 2, 13-23.

[18] Manhart, M., and Thalmann, S. 2015. Protecting organizational knowledge: A structured literature review. *Journal of Knowledge Management.* 19, 2, 190-211.

[19] Hennig-Thurau, T., Sattler, H., Dyckhoff, H., Franke, N., and Schreyoegg, G. VHB-JOURQUAL3; http://vhbonline.org/en/service/jourqual/vhb-jourqual-3/, 27 January 2018.

[20] Gordin, M. D. 2015. *Scientific Babel: The language of science from the fall of Latin to the rise of English.* Profile Books, London.

[21] DeLone, W. H., and McLean, E. R. 1992. Information Systems Success: The Quest for the Dependent Variable. *Information Systems Research.* 3,1, 60-95.

[22] Stettina, C. J., and Hoerz, J. 2015. Agile portfolio management: An empirical perspective on the practice in use. *International Journal of Project Management.* 33, 1, 140-152.

[23] Elchardus, M. and Heyvaert, P. 1990. *Soepel, flexibel en ongebonden. Een vergelijking van twee laat-moderne generaties.* VUBPress, Brussel.

[24] Gupta, A. 2009. Deriving mutual benefits from offshore outsourcing. *Communications of the ACM.* 52, 6, 122.

[25]   Kalaignanam, K., and Varadarajan, R. 2012. Offshore outsourcing of customer relationship management: Conceptual model and propositions. *Journal of the Academy of Marketing Science.* 40, 2, 347-363.

[26]   Bolton, S. C., Houlihan, M., and Laaser, K. 2012. Contingent Work and Its Contradictions: Towards a Moral Economy Framework. *Journal of Business Ethics.* 111, 1, 121-132.

[27]   Deng, X. N., Joshi, K. D., and Galliers, R. D. 2016. The duality of empowerment and marginalization in microtask crowdsourcing: Giving voice to the less powerful through value sensitive design. *MIS Quarterly.* 40, 2, 279-302.

[28]   Ågerfalk, P. J., and Fitzgerald, B. 2008. Outsourcing to an unknown workforce: Exploring opensourcing as a global sourcing strategy. *MIS Quarterly.* 32, 2, 385-409.

[29]   Nadler, D. A., and Tushman, M. L. 1990. Beyond the charismatic leader: *Leadership and organizational change, Managing strategic innovation and change: a collection of readings.* Oxford Univ. Press, New York, NY.

[30]   Blatt, R. 2009. Tough love: How communal schemas and contracting practices build relational capital in entrepreneurial teams. *The Academy of Management Review.* 34,3, 533-551.

[31]   Mainemelis, C., Kark, R., and Epitropaki, O. 2015. Creative Leadership: A Multi-Context Conceptualization. *The Academy of Management Annals.* 9, 1, 393-482.

[32]   Dennis, A. R., Robert, L. P., Curtis, A. M., Kowalczyk, S. T., and Hasty, B. K. 2012. Research Note -Trust Is in the Eye of the Beholder: A Vignette Study of Postevent Behavioral Controls' Effects on Individual Trust in Virtual Teams. *Information Systems Research.* 23, 2, 546-558.

[33]   Langfred, C. W., and Rockmann, K. W. 2016. The Push and Pull of Autonomy. *Group & Organization Management.* 41, 5, 629-657.

[34]   Sarker, S., Ahuja, M., Sarker, S., and Kirkeby, S. 2011. The Role of Communication and Trust in Global Virtual Teams: A Social Network Perspective. *Journal of Management Information Systems.* 28, 1, 273-310.

[35]   Smith, W. K., and Lewis, M. W. 2011. Toward a theory of paradox: A dynamic equilibrium model of organizing. *The Academy of Management Review.* 36, 2, 381-403.

[36]   Wilson, K., and Doz, Y. L. 2010. Agile innovation: A footprint balancing distance and immersion. *California Management Review.* 53, 2, 6-26.

[37]   Kratzer, N. 2005. Employment organization and innovation- Flexibility and security in 'virtualized' companies. *Technology Analysis & Strategic Management.* 17, 1, 35-53.

[38]   Qureshi, S., and Vogel, D. 2001. Adaptiveness in virtual teams: Organisational challenges and research direction. *Group Decision and Negotiation,* 10, 1, 27-46.

[39]   Mullenweg, M. 2014. The CEO of Automatic on holding "auditions" to build a strong team. *Harvard business review,* 92, 4, 39-42.

[40]   Drucker, P. F., Collins, J., Kotler, P., Kouzes, J., Rodin, J., Rangan, V. K., and Hesselbein, F. 2008. *The Five most important Questions you will ever ask about your organization: An inspiring tool for organizations and the people who lead them* (3rd ed.). Chichester: John Wiley. Jossey-Bass; San Francisco, California.

The Role of Historically Black Colleges and Universities in American STEM Education

Curtis C. Cain, Ph.D.
Howard University
2600 6th St. NW., Washington, D.C.
United States of America
Curtis.Cain@Howard.edu

Allison J. Morgan Bryant, Ph.D.
Howard University
2600 6th St. NW., Washington, D.C.
United States of America
Allison.Bryant@Howard.edu

Carlos D. Buskey, Ph.D.
Howard University
2600 6th St. NW., Washington, D.C.
United States of America
Carlos.Buskey@Howard.edu

ABSTRACT

This paper positions the discussion of leveraging Historically Black Colleges and Universities in the effort to increase diversity in STEM Education. STEM Education can be prominently featured at HBCUs with the outcome of producing STEM graduates that enter into technical fields. As HBCUs shift from their initial founding and look to achieve strategic success in other areas, STEM Education would seem to be a natural fit. However, as with many well-intentioned goals at HBCUs, the ability to be successful in STEM Education hinges on several criteria, including funding, external corporate partnerships and internal collaborations. Given the roadblocks that HBCUs face and have been able to overcome, thus far, anchoring themselves as a cornerstone in STEM Education could prove to be a shift they could master. We conclude with five research questions that should further be explored by HBCUs as an extension of their STEM Education goals. HBCUs are unique institutions that will continue to play a pivotal role in America's postsecondary educational system. Participation in STEM education is just one of the many ways their role will continue to be solidified.

ACM Reference format:

Cain, C.C., Morgan Bryant, A.J. and Buskey, C.D. 2018. The Role of Historically Black Colleges and Universities in American STEM Education. In Proceedings of ACM SIGMIS-CPR, June 18–20, 2018, Buffalo-Niagara Falls, NY, USA, 4 pages.
https://doi.org/10.1145/3209626.3209712

KEYWORDS

Diversity, STEM education, Historically Black Colleges & Universities, HBCU, intervention, Google, corporate alliance, Silicon Valley climate, corporate culture, educational partnership.

1 INTRODUCTION

In the United States[9], a country where heavy emphasis is often placed on the concept of social mobility, education is critical.

Postsecondary education is now essential for participation in an increasingly competitive technical labor market. The overall number of minority individuals in higher education is steadily increasing, although still not equivalent to the level of participation of White students. Black, Asian, and Latino students have experienced significant increases in postsecondary education participation in the past 10 years. The data on the growth rates of Black students, however, indicate more of a good news/bad news conundrum. Even though the total number of Black students is increasing, the gender gap between Black men and Black women in higher education has grown wider[8]. While Black women students are experiencing notable growth in enrollment and graduation, the participation of Black men is declining and is the lowest of all demographic groups[8]. In spite of barriers and roadblocks, Black students are choosing careers in Science, Technology, Engineering, and Math (STEM). As a result, there is a prime opportunity for Historically Black Colleges and Universities (HBCUs) to become the torch bearers in STEM Education for Black students by building coalitions internally, seeking external federal funding, and developing corporate partnerships and programs.

2 STEM EDUCATION

STEM Education[10,11] is broadly defined as an interdisciplinary approach to teaching the different, rather broad, subjects of Science, Technology, Engineering and Mathematics using methods and techniques that simulate practical application. In the recent past, and perhaps even today, the aforementioned subjects were taught in a vacuum whereby one subject rarely, if ever, treaded onto the next. However, in practice, these subjects often intersect and overlaps in countless and significant ways.

In 2015, the U.S. Department of Education[10,11,12,13] stated that only sixteen percent of high school students were interested in STEM careers and had significant proficiency in mathematics that would denote success in a STEM field. They also indicated that nearly thirty percent of high school freshmen had a stated interest in a STEM related field, but over fifty percent of those students would lose interest by the time that they graduate from high school. According to STEMconnector, a search company comprised of companies and nonprofit associations in STEM within the United States, there is a projected need for 8.65 million workers in STEM jobs by 2018. As an example, Cloud Computing alone has created over 2 million jobs between 2011 and 2015. The U.S. Bureau of Labor Statistics projects that in 2018, over 70 percent of STEM careers will be in computing. These daunting statistics paint a bleak picture of the United States' continued dominance in STEM fields when there are not enough students finding STEM as a field they choose to enter.

While addressing the National Education Association in 2010, President Barack Obama said, "We understand that our nation's prosperity is tied to innovation spurred on by students' engagement in STEM". He continued by saying, "For America to be technologically competitive in the future, our students must become more fluent in complex science and math." If the United States is to meet the demand for world class talent in science, technology, engineering, and mathematics, it is essential that a diverse population be attracted to engineering and other technical fields[6]. In support of that notion, research states that innovation is more creative, more relevant, and has farther reach when produced by diverse individuals or teams[17]. Given that the Black population has remained steady in the United States of America, we must begin to understand why there are relatively few Blacks in IT and how they identify with the field [16, 1,2,3,4,5,18].

According to the U.S. Census Bureau, in 2012[7,8], 13.1 percent of the United States population was comprised of Black people. Blacks trail behind the national average in terms of degree completion. The 4-year graduation rate for Black students is 63.6 percent compared to the overall U.S. graduation rate of 80.6 percent. The U.S. Department of Education (2010) states that there are more than 8 million Black public-school students, 76 percent attend schools inside urbanized areas that include both city and suburban districts. The majority of Black public schools have fewer certified teachers with degrees in the subjects they teach, which has contributed to many school closings in urban areas. For example, in non-Black public schools more than 75 percent of math teachers had math as their major in college as opposed to 56 percent of teachers in majority Black schools. Of that 56 percent, fewer number of the teachers were certified [7,8,18]. There is an opportunity for HBCUs to leverage STEM Education, but first, it is necessary to understand how HBCUs came into existence and the numerous hurdles they have had to overcome.

3   HISTORICALLY BLACK COLLEGES AND UNIVERSITIES (HBCU)

HBCUs[12] were founded on the premise of providing Black Americans a place to receive a quality higher education at time when the educational system in the United States of America was still segregated. Prior to the establishment of HBCUs, Blacks were typically denied admission to traditionally White institutions. As a result, HBCUs were birthed, not from an aspect of choice, but one of need. During the Civil War, there was no system for higher education available for Black students. Antiquated laws prohibited Blacks, in some parts of the country, from receiving any type of education. The first HBCU was the Institute for

Colored Youth, now Cheney University, was founded in 1837. Following Cheney were Lincoln University (1854) and Wilberforce University (1856)[12].

Although the aforementioned schools were called universities, it was not until the 1900s that HBCUs offered curriculum at the postsecondary level[12]. Prior to the 1900s, HBCUs existed to teach Black students who, up until that time, had been barred any formal education. The 1896 United States Supreme Court ruling in Plessy v. Ferguson established the precedent, in public education, that racially segregated schools did not violate the Fourteenth Amendment and therefore Black schools were deemed "separate, but equal" to White schools, despite the preponderance of evidence that Black schools lacked access to the same resources. It was not until the 1954 ruling by the United States Supreme Court in Brown v. Board of Education where the "separate but equal" doctrine was rejected on the basis of Black children not having access to equal protection as afforded by the Fourteenth Amendment of the United State Constitution. Despite the ruling in Brown v. Board of Education, HBCUs are still needed today. There are 101 HBCUs in the United States, which account for 3 percent of colleges and universities, yet, they produce twenty-seven percent of Black students with bachelor's degrees in Science, Technology, Engineering and Mathematics (STEM) fields.

In the 21st Century, HBCUs have experienced a fundamental shift from the origin of their founding. Today, while only accounting for 3 percent of colleges, HBCUs play a critical role in producing twenty-seven percent of Black STEM graduates, thereby producing a vast majority of disproportionate Black STEM graduates. Even though Black students are deciding to major in IT and Engineering, the racial demographic of the IT and Engineering industry lacks significant Black representation creating a situation where Blacks are woefully underrepresented[19,20]. By this account, a two-fold issue is revealed: a problem in academia, by which 3 percent of the colleges and universities produce twenty-seven percent of Black STEM graduates, and a problem in society, whereby STEM, and in particular IT and Engineering, fields continue to lack racial diversity[19,20].

4   STEM EDUCATION + HBCU

HBCUs are in a unique position to operate as a catalyst to address many of the issues in the United States workforce, and specifically the state of STEM overall. Most HBCUs are collegial in nature and small enough as to where a blending of the four discrete subjects in a practical setting to increase diversity in STEM would bode well for all parties - students, educators, corporations, and the United States workforce overall. For example, Howard West[14,15] is a joint venture between Google Inc., in Mountain View, CA and Howard University, a HBCU in Washington, D.C., whereby a campus was created at Google's Headquarters.

Howard West was staffed by Google Engineers and Howard University Faculty. The mission of Howard West is to bring rising-Juniors from Howard University to Google, building upon the instruction received at Howard University, to better equip these students with the necessary skillset to not only become a Software Engineer at Google but ultimately enter the technical field.

During the pilot of the Howard West program in the summer of 2016, about thirty students were chosen to participate and spend their summer at Google. While at Google, students took 4 courses, were immersed in the Silicon Valley culture, routinely visited other Silicon Valley corporations, as well as participated in mock interviews and technical interview preparation. The courses the students took were Software Engineering, Fundamentals of Algorithms, Machine Learning and Mobile Application Development. The courses were taught by a Howard University faculty member in conjunction with a Google Engineer. There was an emphasis on project-based learning initiatives as well as practical application.

The partnership between Google and Howard University presents a unique glimpse into how one top Silicon Valley company has decided to invest in and approach its diversity initiatives while jostling with shifting the organizational climate to be more receptive to people of different backgrounds. Additionally, Howard University is building the foundation of establishing solid corporate partnerships in a growing industry that would desperately benefit from the ethnic makeup of its student body population. While the two organizations certainly have common goals, they also have divergent views which then lead to competing goals.

5 DISCUSSION

There are several issues which have the potential to be explored by researchers on the horizon of HBCUS and STEM education, one of which is the access to resources. By resources, we can begin an analysis of basic, publicly available and accessible information, such as university endowments. If we declare the assumption that endowments are for the long term fiscal solvency and growth of the university, and not for spending on any one program and that endowments are not necessarily easily accessible monetary reserves, we can see large discrepancies in terms of access to capital, even if for long term growth and solvency. For example, Howard University, in Washington, D.C., as of June 2016, had the largest endowment of any HBCU with $578 million. That ranks Howard University 160th among all schools. If we contrast the endowment of Howard University with Harvard University, the difference is staggering. Harvard University, which is the wealthiest institution, at the same time frame, June 2016, had an endowment of $35.7 billion. To put those numbers in context, Harvard University has an endowment that is about 62 times that of Howard University, the wealthiest HBCU. Essentially, what we are beginning with is a place of 160th for the top HBCU that has an endowment that is roughly 2 percent of Harvard University,

the wealthiest institution of higher education. While Harvard University is the wealthiest, we need not look to Harvard to see stark differences. Howard University's endowment equates to around $57,000 for each student while Vanderbilt University's endowment equates to an excess of $300,000 per student. Even though Howard University has the largest endowment of all HBCUs, beginning from a place of 160th would mean that HBCUs simply do not have the assets to gain investments of those schools with multibillion-dollar endowments. In fact, if we were to sum the top ten HBCU endowments we would not eclipse 2 billion dollars. It is the access to capital and resources that allow programs like Howard West to come to fruition. Additionally, it is companies like Google that have the potential to bridge shortfalls in funding for HBCUs if there are benefits to all parties involved.

STEM Education initiatives, which seek interdisciplinary approaches to teaching with an emphasis on practical applicability, should be explored and integrated across the curriculum. In conjunction with STEM Education, an avenue of research worth investigation is the notion of STEM fatigue. For example, there may be students who may have been pushed in the direction of STEM, perhaps by guidance counselors, parents, teachers, media and by virtue of attending specific mathematics and science centric high schools (i.e. Preparatory/Magnet Programs) whereby once they arrive to college, they simply no longer wish to purse STEM as other career options become available to them. Frameworks that show STEM partnerships across different schools and colleges within universities should be developed to denote the subject matter overlap and expectation for project based and practical application. Regardless of the obstacles, HBCUs are capable of working together, pooling their resources and creating an understanding that harkens back to the original conception of HBCUs, and that is to ensure their students have level footing to fully participate in the national and global economy. Research questions that emanate from this topic are:

- What characteristics and strategies utilized by HBCUs increase recruitment or retention in STEM programs?
- Does teaching STEM topics in a culturally inclusive way affect student interest or learning at HBCUs?
- Have HBCU alliances with tech corporations influenced minority student career choice for STEM fields?
- What elements of the HBCU culture can be positively attributed to success in STEM disciplines and career fields?
- How are HBCUs uniquely positioned to combat STEM fatigue among minority students?

All of these questions enter into the heart of addressing the unique environment of HBCUs and their role in providing the proper climate for minority students to thrive in STEM. By investigating these questions, the attributes of HBCUs which facilitate student engagement in STEM can be unpacked. In addition, the opportunities for growth of these Universities in terms of development of programs and creation of interventions to foster interest and support for STEM education, is both relevant and necessary. Once we begin to have a fuller understanding of the role of STEM Education, we can begin to explore the role corporations should play, outside of internships, in student engagement at the undergraduate level for preparation to enter their respective fields. Presently, universities have goals as do corporations, and those goals often times do not dovetail. However, STEM Education may create an avenue for these goals among different entities to become mutual.

4 CONCLUSIONS

As the demand for talent in STEM fields continues to increase exponentially, the need for diverse perspectives and representation in those areas grows also. In order to continue interest and innovation in those areas, especially for minority students, HBCUs are well positioned to take a leadership role in the creation of STEM scholars. HBCUs already benefit from an inclusive culture, and legacy of achievement which make them an excellent environment to facilitate education in the STEM disciplines. While there is a concerning underrepresentation of Black students, specifically Black males, in STEM fields, this research seeks to understand how to make STEM education more fertile for these populations. Also, the examination of the partnerships and programs at these Universities will provide a better understand of how to facilitate successful engagement of minorities in STEM areas to yield greater participation and success overall.

ACKNOWLEDGMENTS

Pursuing this research would not be possible without the contributions of Howard University and the National Science Foundation (Grant No. DGE-0750756), we are grateful for your continued support and commitment to this research.

REFERENCES

[1]   Cain, C.C., Trauth, E.M. (2017). Black Men in IT: Theorizing an Autoethnography of a Black Man's Journey into IT within the United States of America. The Data Base for Advances in Information Systems ,48, 2 (April 2017), 35-51. DOI: https://doi.org/10.1145/3084179.3084184

[2]   Cain, C.C., Trauth, E.M. (2016). " Black Lives Matter: The Journey of a Black IT Scholar," Proceedings of the ACM SIGMIS Computers and People Research Conference (Washington, D.C.).

[3]   Cain, C.C., Trauth, E.M. (2015). "Theorizing the Underrepresentation of Black Males in Information Technology (IT)," Proceedings of the 21th Americas Conference on Information Systems (Puerto Rico).

[4]   Cain, C.C., Trauth, E.M. (2013). "Stereotype Threat: The Case of Black Males in the IT Profession," Proceedings of the ACM SIGMIS Computers and People Research Conference (Cincinnati, OH).

[5]   Cain, C.C., Trauth, E.M. (2012) "Black Males in IT Higher Education in The USA: The Digital Divide in the Academic Pipeline Re-visited," Proceedings of the 18th Americas Conference on Information Systems (Seattle, WA).

[6]   Chubin, D. E., May, G. S., and Babco, E. L. "Diversifying the Engineering Workforce." Journal of Engineering Education, 2005, 94(1), 73-86.

[7]   U.S. Census Bureau. 2013 State and County QuickFacts. Data derived from Population Estimates, Census of Population and Housing, Small Area Income and Poverty Estimates, State and County Housing Unit Estimates, County Business Patterns, Non-employer Statistics, Economic Census.

[8]   National Center for Education Statistics. 2003. The Condition of Education, U.S. Department of Education, Institute of Education Sciences. June 2003.

[9]   Wilkins, R.D. 2006. "Swimming Upstream: A Study of Black Males and the Academic Pipeline". Ph.D. dissertation, Georgia State University, 2006.

[10] "Science, Technology, Engineering and Math: Education for Global Leadership." Science, Technology, Engineering and Math: Education for Global Leadership | U.S. Department of Education, www.ed.gov/stem.

[11] "World Class Collaboration to Enable the STEM Economy." STEMconnector, www.stemconnector.com/.

[12] "Historically Black Colleges and Universities and Higher Education Desegregation." Home, US Department of Education (ED), 15 Oct. 2015, www2.ed.gov/about/offices/list/ocr/docs/hq9511.html.

[13] Bureau of Labor Statistics, U.S. Department of Labor, The Economics Daily, 8.8 million science, technology, engineering, and mathematics (STEM) jobs in May 2016 on the Internet at https://www.bls.gov/opub/ted/2017/8-point-8-million-science-technology-engineering-and-mathematics-stem-jobs-in-may-2016.htm (visited January 27, 2018).

[14] Weller, Chris. "A Historically Black College Just Opened a Campus at Google Headquarters - Here's What It's like Inside." Business Insider, Business Insider, 28 June 2017, www.businessinsider.com/inside-howard-university-google-west-campus-2017-6.

[15] Guynn, Jessica. "Google Opens Howard University West to Train Black Coders." USA Today, Gannett Satellite Information Network, 24 Mar. 2017, www.usatoday.com/story/tech/news/2017/03/23/howard-university-google/99518020/.

[16] Carter, M & Grover, V (2015). Me, my self, and I (T): Conceptualizing Information Technology Identity and its Implications. MIS Quarterly. Volume 39. Issue 4. pp. 931-958

[17] Tröster, C, Mehra, A, van Knippenberg, D.L, 2014. Structuring for team success: The interactive effects of network structure and cultural diversity on team potency and performance. Organizational Behavior and Human Decision Processes 124, 245–255.

[18] Cain, C.C. (2016). "Swimming Upstream: The Case of Black Males in Information Technology (IT) Higher Education". Ph.D. Dissertation, The Pennsylvania State University, 2016.

[19] National Science Foundation, Division of Science Resources Statistics, Women, Minorities, and Persons with Disabilities in Science and Engineering: 2009, NSF 09-305, (Arlington, VA; January 2009). Available from http://www.nsf.gov/statistics/wmpd/

A Day in the Life: An Interactive Application to Introduce IT Students to the Workplace

Leigh Ellen Potter
Idea Lab, Griffith University
Kessels Rd, Nathan, 4111
QLD, Australia
+617 3735 5191
L.Potter@griffith.edu.au

ABSTRACT

Students can enter IT degrees with only a general idea of available career pathways and career options. Students often select an IT degree based on intrinsic interest in IT [8], however their career decisions can be based on misconceptions about the industry. The 'Day in the Life' application seeks to provide industry and career knowledge to first- and second-year IT students through an informative resource detailing the daily activities of various IT professionals, with a focus upon individual video interviews and organisation-related content. Usability testing was conducted to answer the question: to what level does this site alone change students' perspectives or understanding of day-to-day work in the IT industry? While revisions are recommended, overall student feedback indicates that the application has a positive effect on student knowledge, understanding, and career confidence.

Keywords

Student experience; user centred design; IT profession; career preparation.

ACM Reference format:

Leigh Ellen Potter. 2018. A Day in the Life: An Interactive Application to Introduce IT Students to the Workplace. In Proceedings of ACM SIGMIS-CPR, June 18–20, 2018, Buffalo Niagara Falls, NY, USA, 5 pages. https://doi.org/10.1145/3209626.3209712

1. INTRODUCTION

In 2015, I spoke to a second year student taking my User Interface Design course. He came into the second workshop for the course, brimming with enthusiasm! One of the 'homework' activities in week one had tasked the students with finding a job advertisement for their personal, dream job. This student told me he had been on the verge of dropping out of the degree, because he didn't really know what he was doing. That glimpse into industry and the career options that were available changed his view, and finding a career to aim for gave him a new focus and enthusiasm. He said that NOW he knew what he wanted, and it affected his course selections and major completion moving on from that point.

Employers prefer graduates who are broadly prepared for the numerous responsibilities they will face in the modern workplace [5, 11], however Information Technology (IT) students can be unsure about their career options. When asked, they know they want to work with technology, but are less sure of what kind of role or job would suit them best.

Individual interests and industry experience are key influences for student career choices [9]. At present, students frequently enter IT degrees with only a general idea of the available career pathways and their subsequent career options. Students often select an IT degree based on intrinsic interest in IT [8], however their career decisions can be based on misconceptions about the industry. Additionally, they have a poor understanding of the day-to-day reality of a chosen career role and whether or not this role is a suitable fit for their specific skills, interests and personality.

This lack of clarity influences both their choice of subjects and their degree progress, with some students dropping out of their degree as a result. It also influences their acquisition of employability skills, through a lack of understanding of what industry requires from them and which direction they need to take. Some students have some practical experiences in work, enabling them to use their existing knowledge and experiences to build new knowledge, and many undergraduate degree programs include Work Integrated Learning (WIL) components where students work with an industry partner. We need to reach those students who do not yet have industry experience and have not had an opportunity to complete WIL. They need exposure to industry workplaces and practicing IT professionals.

Current approaches to inform students about their career have been developed by academics and student support teams, and include information sessions and online information. Engagement with this information is at the discretion of the student, heightening the importance of using techniques that will resonate with students. In some cases, students are not aware of the services that are available for them to support their career preparation. It is critical that any career resources are delivered through student accessible mediums.

This paper presents the development of the Day in the Life project, aimed at supporting students in both learning about their career path options and in selecting courses to support their career development. It will describe the participatory design approach that was used to create a product designed by students, for students, and the evaluation and revision stages undertaken to support the product for release to the student cohort.

We will first look at student enrolments in IT courses, and their study approach. We will then consider careers and career information before outlining the Day in the Life application, and the results of student evaluations of the application.

2. CONCEPTS

This paper is focused on career linkage for students, rather than on specific knowledge, skills, or abilities that students need to forge a successful career. Before a student can develop the necessary skills, they must first determine the roles that interest them, and that suit their general aptitude. This knowledge guides their course selection, and course success.

2.1 Student success in Australian IT courses

According to figures from the Department of Education and Training [3], IT courses in Australia have seen a steady increase in enrolments from a low in 2008, however have not as yet returned to their peak level of 79 026 enrolments in 2002. Unfortunately, figures also show that degree completion rates are decreasing across the sector, meaning that fewer students are completing their IT degrees.

Student satisfaction with Australian university education is generally high with 80% of students giving a positive rating for the quality of their educational experience, however the student satisfaction for computing and information systems students is the lowest of all study areas at 73% [15].

Of concern is the number of students considering leaving the higher education sector, with 18% of students considering departure. Students most like to leave are those with the lowest grades, followed by indigenous students, students with disabilities, and older students. Common reasons in these cases for leaving relate to finances, stress, workload, and study/life balance [15].

Of those who finish their study, nearly 72% of students across the higher education sector in Australia are in full-time employment four months after completing their degree, with an overall employment rate of 86.5% [14]. Computing and information systems students fare favourably for employment, with 73% of students employed at four months, and an overall employment rate of 82%.

2.2 IT Student learning

IT is an inherently practical discipline, and IT students respond to tangible examples of course concepts and to the opportunity to reflect on these prior to application in a practical context, which then supports authentic learning. Linking to existing knowledge and using discussion and experiences helps them to challenge existing ideas. This reflective practice supports the development of their professional practice [17]. IT students benefit from a constructivist classroom and an active learning approach to provide an engaging learning experience [1].

2.3 Careers and Career Information

Approaches to career information and career preparation vary between education institutions. Active involvement of industry professionals in courses is increasing. Dillon and Lending [5] describe the development of an IT Consulting class involving industry consultants as mentors and collaborators within the class as a method for preparing students for a career in consulting. WIL courses and components are widely recognised as beneficial for student skills development and career preparation [7]. Career guidance offices and careers services are widely available [4].

In the context of this project, Griffith University has a proactive employability approach that includes real-life industry experience, WIL, internship programs, ePortfolios, mentoring, global mobility, and a Careers and Employment service. It received a higher than average result for graduate satisfaction of 85.5% in the 2017 national Employer Satisfaction Survey [13]. Employing this range of measures does not ensure student engagement: engagement with career preparation outside embedded course work components is at the discretion of the individual.

2.3.1 Career Expectations of the current cohort

A survey of forty first- and second-year students was conducted at the beginning of this project, to explore student perceptions of their career options. Only 10% of respondents identified a specific role that they wished to have in the future, such as software engineer or business analyst. A further 10% nominated roles that they would be unlikely to achieve as initial graduates from an IT degree, such as Project Manager. The majority of students nominated general areas rather than roles, such as "something software", with 30% of respondents unable to nominate a future career. When asked how much research they had conducted into their career options, the majority of students stated between five and ten hours, with a small number of students at opposite extremes – a high of thirty hours, and a low of no research at all. It was interesting in the context of the formal support provided by the university through the careers and employment service and mentoring programs that the majority of students sourced their information online, with favourite websites given as YouTube, Reddit, Facebook, and Google.

All respondents listed qualities they were looking for in their future career, with common responses including stability, security, ability for career progression, and "money and lots of it." They all felt their current degree was suitable for their career aims, however some raised concerns about the application of the material "for day-to-day understanding."

3. The Day in the Life Project

The Day in the Life project was initiated to address an identified need for easily accessible information for students about a range of work roles and workplaces that an IT graduate may encounter. Building on Ma et al. [10], a virtual field trip pedagogy [12] was envisaged, providing both soft (facilitated informally [18]) and embedded (planned into a course [2]) scaffolding for learning. The student experience is core to the application and student engagement with the material is critical if the application is to be a success. Based on these needs, participatory design with two groups of students as active partners [6] was followed to ensure that student voices, values, and preferences were captured. A team of six final year ICT students worked collaboratively with an educational designer, an interaction designer, and a lead academic to develop a first version of the application. A second team of three final year students worked collaboratively with a user experience consultant and a lead academic to evaluate and revise the application, ready for release to the student body.

3.1 The Application

The first student team developed a vision statement to guide their application development:

Day in the Life is:

For: University students studying a degree within Information and Communication Technology

Who: Need a more realistic understanding about the different jobs and associated responsibilities within the IT industry. Day in the Life

Is a: website based virtual industry field trip

That: Will explore different IT industry locations and interviews with a variety of IT professionals.

Our Product: will enable students to explore real life industry locations and access interviews from a variety of IT professions to gain a deeper understanding of working within the IT industry

The final product was to be a platform providing interviews with industry professionals from a range of positions and industries. Students using the platform would be able to search by role and industry, and additional information would be provided detailing degree and course for each role.

3.2 Development

Development was incremental and iterative. A general application description was provided at the beginning of the project: an immersive online application that will allow students to visit different industry sites, learn about the industry and workplace, and hear from people currently working in the industry about their role and responsibilities. The first team worked over a period of eight months, completing six development iterations:

- Iteration one - problem definition: understanding the problem, generating ideas to support a solution, generating user stories, planning the approach

- Iteration two – platform development: developing an initial platform shell and conducting a pilot film shoot

- Iteration three – initial prototype: developing a framework and footage for a single site, evaluation with students

- Iterations four and five - incremental development: filming in four more organisations, addition of footage and supporting material, student evaluation

- Iteration six: completion of version one of product

The second team took handover of the application for formal evaluation and revision, completing two more product iterations over three months:

- Iteration seven – full usability evaluation: completing a formal usability evaluation of the application with currently enrolled first and second year students

- Iteration eight – final revisions and release.

The final product provided information about six IT employers representing consulting, private development houses, independent operators, and the public services, and interviews with people working in a range of roles including design, business analysis, software development, testing, project management, security, networking, and gaming. For each role, specific information is provided including degree and course matches, alternate role names, types of work, and average income.

3.3 Evaluation

Formal evaluation by the second team followed the approach outlined by Rubin and Chisnell [16]. The usability factors focused on were effectiveness (the extent to which the site behaved according to user expectation), usefulness (extent to which the site fulfilled goals of learning), and satisfaction (overall evaluation of user feelings towards to the site). Formal testing was completed using ten students enrolled in a first year subject and ten students enrolled in a second year subject. All students were school leavers (rather than mature age students with work experience). Students were first asked for background information about their current studies and knowledge of career information. They were then given access to the Day in the Life application, and asked to explore, with observations of their approach to the application, noted features, comments and questions recorded. Once familiarised with the application, a series of eight tasks were provided, reflecting anticipated scenarios or activities that a visitor might undertake, such as 'find information about networking and security', and 'use the application to find more about the workplace and culture of design studios'. Participants completed these tasks using the think aloud approach. Observations were recorded of all interactions, including time to complete tasks, difficulties encountered, and comments made by the participant. On completion of the tasks, a short survey was provided asking for specific feedback about the application.

Informal testing was also completed with twenty students from the cohort of the third year WIL course. This involved students exploring the application, and providing verbal feedback about their experience and opinions of the application. Notes were taken about the interactions and feedback was captured in observation records.

4. Initial Outcome

As expected, the evaluation highlighted a number of usability issues relating to the layout and structure of the application itself, and a clear list of recommended revisions was generated to improve the functionality of the site. However, the main focus of this paper is the intervention itself: how useful is the Day in the Life application for students in supporting their career preparation?

4.1 Career Information

Day in the Life presents information about a range of work roles through video interviews with IT professionals and text information about roles.

Watching videos of actual IT professionals made the information "more human, hearing their perspectives." Students valued the personal perspective given, and felt it helped them to "know what to expect." The descriptions of "what they do on a day-today basis, what they enjoy" were highly valued, as it was "real world and applicable, it's like someone is talking to you." Students described this style of presentation as 'motivating' in relation to their own career preparation.

Feedback from participants indicated that they would prefer more written information in support of the videos. The videos were described as providing "a bit of a taste of everything", which then triggered a desire for more specific information including different levels for each role (ie, what is the difference between a junior and a senior business analyst?) and a more specific breakdown of income for each role and level. Many students commented that the income range given for the roles was too broad. The students wanted the information to be "more relatable to me."

Students also requested the addition of video transcripts, so they could go back and search through a written version of what each IT professional had said. While the application provides high level search functionality (by career and organisation), students wanted more detailed search functionality to target their own goals.

The participants reported positively on the usefulness of the information in exploring their own interests, and all participants demonstrated improvements in their understanding of career options outside their interests (for example, a student with an interest in software development looking at business analysis). This suggests that the application is helpful in learning about new career options.

Most students reported an increase in confidence after watching the videos that they could find a role that suited their interests, largely because there were "a lot of options", and "more roles than I realised". Some students recorded no change, and in one case a student responded negatively, stating there was "just not enough information [about] project managers, so nothing interesting and I didn't watch so didn't learn." This reinforces earlier feedback about greater information about different levels of roles. Project management is an unlikely role for a fresh graduate from an undergraduate degree, however is still a goal for some students and an appropriate goal for a Masters level student.

4.2 Organisation Information

Day in the Life presents information about working in a range of different organisations through the IT professional interview videos, 360 videos of physical workplaces, and text information about the organisations.

The videos within the organisations were described as interesting and viewed as "good at seeing what it looks like, but not what it really IS like to work there." Students requested more footage of the workplace, showing a greater range of perspectives (ie deskwork, meeting rooms, studios etc).

Students stated that the video interviews were more helpful with understanding what it was like to work at an organisation than the footage of the workplace itself. They had more requests for revisions to the presentation of organisations than to the presentation of career information, asking for a direct tie to the organisation from the career interview, greater description of the benefits of working for that organisation, a more detailed range of roles that the organisation offered, remuneration packages, career progression, and graduate programs.

All but one student stated that they felt more confident about finding an organisation that would match their own working style after using the application, after see the range of different organisations that employed IT people. One student reported no change in their confidence, based on a need to know more about the organisation than the information provided through the application.

4.3 Overall feedback

The overall feedback on the application was positive. It was described as 'clean cut' and 'nicely structured', and the first hand experience and personal nature of the videos was very helpful. Students did not realise there was such a variety of roles available to them in industry, and hearing about people's day to day working lives was valuable.

The links to degrees and certifications were very useful, both as a reference and a tool. While students wanted to be able to access more detailed information, they appreciated the summary style career information presented with each interview.

The addition of more detailed search functionality would improve the usability of the site, and the ability of students to find information about specific roles. Being able to 'preview' a page would help students navigate the site.

The most important feedback received indicated a positive influence on students' career understanding, course and career choice, and motivation to continue. Several students commented that "this gives me an idea of something to strive for", or that they were "motivated seeing what's out there." For students who came into the evaluation with a clear idea of their career goals, the application gave them a "better idea [of their choice], reinforced my decision."

5. Recommendations

In order to support students, we must allow them a voice. What is obvious to an industry professional, or an academic who has researched IT, is not obvious to a student fresh to the fold. Using participatory design for the development of Day in the Life ensured that student needs and viewpoints were captured within the application. Working directly with students was at times a challenging choice, as they required additional supervision to keep on track of development, however the process has yielded novel views and higher relevance of the chosen structure for student users. This was reflected in the student feedback on the application structure and layout.

While the students gained most benefit from the career information provided through the application, there is still room for improvement. With no industry exposure, students do not necessarily understand the different roles available to them, or the variation in levels between roles and how that affects the work required of a role. Clarification is required explaining the differences between a role at a graduate level, where that role would sit after two years experience in the role, and how the role changes with seniority. Likewise, the progression from a junior role to a senior needs to be explained so that students have realistic expectations.

Students gained great value from the personal presentation of recorded face-to-face interviews. This presentation style made the content feel relevant to them personally, and relatable on a different level from a dry text description. While summary information about a career is useful as a prompt, students would also prefer to have access to more detailed text descriptions in support of the video, to explore at their own pace and to allow them to selectively choose the material that is of interest.

It is apparent that the organisational information supplied through the application, while useful, is insufficient. Having seen that there is a range of different organisations available and that each has their own approach and style, students wished to know more detail to allow them to contrast and compare. Career preparation is twofold, and it is not enough to simply choose a career: it is important to also look for an employer that will be a good match for your own work approach and style.

Students did not realise that there was a large range of options for work and organisations available to them, and felt this information made them more confident in their ability to find a career that would match their needs. Overall feedback indicates that having access to a tool that provides personal information, real-life experiences and situations, and links to resources that connect a student to that real-life outcome is valuable to student career preparation. Students felt that Day in the Life was a useful tool for them as they worked towards their careers.

6. Next steps
The application is in revision to be released to students at first, second, and third year level in 2018. It will be embedded within two specific courses, and will be added to the School's Career Opportunities online resource, which is available to all students in the school.

This release will enable us to evaluate the use of the application 'in the wild'. We will survey students, particularly first year students, to determine the influence of the application on course choice and progress. A broader release will also enable more detailed feedback on potential required revisions to improve the usability of the application.

The application will also be trialled with a high school audience to determine its usefulness in engaging school students with the IT profession.

If successful, the application framework may also be suitable for other disciplines.

7. REFERENCES

[1] Biggs, J.B. and Tang, C. 2011. *Teaching for Quality Learning at University.* Open University Press.

[2] Brush, T. and Saye, J. 2001. The use of embedded scaffolds with hypermedia-supported student-centred learning. *Journal of Educational Multimedia and Hypermedia.* 10, 4 (2001), 333–356.

[3] Department of Education and Training 2017. *Higher Education Statistics.*

[4] Dey, F. and Cruzvergara, C.Y. 2014. Evolution of Career Services in Higher Education. *New Directions for Student Services.* 2014, 148 (2014), 5–18.

[5] Dillon, T.W. and Lending, D. 2014. Using Professional Consultants to Mentor CIS Students on a Simulated Consulting Project. *Proceedings of the 52nd ACM conference on Computers and people research* (2014), 171–175.

[6] Druin, A. and Systems, A.C.M. 1999. Cooperative inquiry: Developing new technologies for children with children. *Proceedings of ACM CHI 99 Conference on Human Factors in Computing.* (1999), 223-230-NaN-0.

[7] Jackson, D. 2015. Employability skill development in work-integrated learning: Barriers and best practice. *Studies in Higher Education.* 40, 2 (2015), 350–367.

[8] Kori, K., Pedaste, M., Niitsoo, M., Kuusik, R., Altin, H., Tõnisson, E., Vau, I., Leijen, Ä., Mäeots, M., Siiman, L., Murtazin, K. and Paluoja, R. 2015. Why do Students Choose to Study Information and Communications Technology? *Procedia - Social and Behavioral Sciences.* 191, (2015), 2867–2872.

[9] Lent, R.W.L., Brown, S.D., Talleyrand, R., McPartland, E.B., Davis, T., Chopra, S.B., Alexander, Michael S. Suthakaran, . and Chai, C.-M. 2002. Career Choice Barriers, Supports, and Coping Strategies: College Students' Experiences. *Journal of Vocational Behaviour.* 60, 1 (2002), 61–72.

[10] Ma, E., Patiar, A. and Cox, R. 2014. Undergraduate Hotel Management Students' Perceptions of a Virtual Field Trip Website. *CAUTHE 2014: Tourism and Hospitality in the Contemporary World: Trends, Changes and Complexity.* (2014), 1005–1008.

[11] Potter, L.E. and Vickers, G. 2015. What skills do you need to work in cyber security? A look at the Australian market. *SIGMIS-CPR 2015 - Proceedings of the 2015 ACM SIGMIS Conference on Computers and People Research* (2015).

[12] Procter, L. 2012. What is it about Field Trips? Praxis, Pedagogy and Presence in Virtual Environments. *Procedia - Social and Behavioral Sciences.* 55, October (2012), 980–989.

[13] QILT 2018. *2017 Employer Satisfaction Survey National Report.*

[14] QILT 2018. *2017 Graduate Outcomes Survey.*

[15] QILT 2018. *2017 Student Experience Survey National Report.*

[16] Rubin, J. and Chisnell, D. 2011. *Handbook of Usability Testing.* John Wiley & Sons.

[17] Schön, D. 1983. *The Reflective Practitioner: how professionals think in action.* Temple Smith.

[18] Simons, K.D. and Klein, J.D. 2007. The impact of scaffolding and student achievement levels in a problem-based learning environment. *Instructional Science.* 35, (2007), 41–72.

Categorization: A Source of Theory and Output of Research

Fred Niederman
Saint Louis University
3674 Lindell Blvd, 404
St. Louis, MO 63108
fred.niederman@slu.edu

Roman Lukyanenko
HEC Montréal
3000 Chemin de la Côte Sainte Catherine
Montréal, Québec H3T 2A7
roman.lukyanenko@hec.ca

ABSTRACT

In a research community, the use of the concept of category and categorization is widespread, generally helpful, but sometimes overly constraining. Despite the wealth of studies that propose new categories, a somewhat static view of categories pervades many disciplines. As we demonstrate on the analysis of a seminal framework by Gregor (2006), a given set of categories can be criticized and challenged in light of potentially valid alternatives. In contrast, we suggest for researchers to adopt the assumption of fluidity of categories, which leads to a different approach to demonstrating the contribution of research that deals with categories.

CCS CONCEPTS
• **Social and professional topics~Management of computing and information systems**

KEYWORDS
Classification, categorization, theory, research method,

ACM Reference format:
F. Niederman, and R. Lukyanenko. 2018. Categorization: A source of theory and output of research. In *Proceedings of ACM SIGMIS-CPR '18, June 18–20, 2018, Buffalo-Niagara Falls, NY, USA.* 8 pages. https://doi.org/10.1145/3209626.3209717

INTRODUCTION

"[o]n those remote pages it is written that animals are divided into (a) those that belong to the Emperor, (b) embalmed ones, (c) those that are trained, (d) suckling pigs, (e) mermaids, (f) fabulous ones, (g) stray dogs, (h) those that are included in this classification, (i) those that tremble as if they were mad, (j) innumerable ones, (k) those drawn with a very fine camel's hair brush, (l) others, (m) those that have just broken a flower vase, (n) those that resemble flies from a distance" (from ancient Chinese encyclopedia 'Celestial Emporium of Benevolent Knowledge') [5].

"[E]xisting typologies are likely to contain inconsistencies, trade-offs, and— perhaps most importantly—irrelevant elements. However, if not all parts of a configuration are equally important, the issue becomes this: Which are the critical aspects in a typology, and which elements are nonessential? The challenge of typologies thus is determining what really matters (and to what degree) in understanding the causal structure of a type." [13].

In a research community, the use of the concept of category[1] and categorization is widespread, generally helpful, but sometimes overly constraining. Recent management literature includes a stream of studies that focus on the actions and processes of "categorizing" rather than on static categories themselves [10, 13]. We believe, underlying the emergence of this stream is the fundamental difference in understanding of categories as fixed and determined (what Barsalou [1] calls "common categories") or whether they are fluid and explicitly constructed (what Barsalou [1] calls "ad hoc categories"), see also [24]. These differences correspond to worldviews that focus on objects and their permanence versus activities and how conceptualizations of objects by humans are in constant change.[2]

---

[1] Regarding terminology, several words, categorization, typology, and taxonomy tend to be used interchangeably in some cases or with distinctions in others. Doty and Glick [10] make a clear but idiosyncratic set of distinctions among the terms. At times one or another term is used pejoratively to suggest something lesser than "theory" at other times rather neutrally. Our preference would be to refer to categorization as what Barsalou calls "ad hoc", typology, and taxonomy as common following the guidelines of static or "common category" types.

[2] Note that objects in this case is a convenient reference to the whole array of entities including the physical and the socially constructed (e.g. a "table" and a "property deed")[3, 26, 43].

SIGMIS-CPR '18, June 18–20, 2018, Buffalo-Niagara Falls, NY, USA
© 2018 Association for Computing Machinery.
ACM ISBN 978-1-4503-5768-5/18/06...$15.00
https://doi.org/10.1145/3209626.3209717

On the one hand understanding the concepts of category and categorization is a rather philosophical and linguistic endeavor, but it also has concrete implications regarding how we interpret collected knowledge. In this paper we will discuss at length the categorization of theory following Gregor [14] – a seminal categorization of theories that may exist in the information systems discipline. At the time of writing the paper was cited more than 2,300 times and serves as a significant reference for IS scholars. The intent is to consider how our interpretation of theory can change with the reconsideration of how to think about the nature of categories. It is our contention that a static view of categories and categorization will lead to different understandings about the nature of the discussion presented as well as our ability to extend them. In an ironic twist, one of the five categories of theory discussed by Gregor (2006) pertains to categorization as a type of theory. In this paper, we will discuss categorization per se using Gregor's typology as an example and further probe her first theory category exploring how categories can BE theory. It depends on which scholar one reads as to whether categorization is theory, implies theory, or sets the stage for further refinement [35, 45]. Not all scholars are completely consistent in their discussions of the nature of categories, which produces further fuzziness in thinking on this topic.

The thrust of our study presented below is to examine the nature of categories and categorization per se. We suggest a more nuanced view of the process by which a set of categories may be proposed and a more detailed description of what a category "is" within a set of categories.

2 NATURE OF CATEGORIES

Much research in IS adopts what we call a "static view" of categories. A static view (sometimes referred to as "classical model") holds that they are permanent, meaningfully differentiated, and mutually exclusive (in that instances to be categorized can be determined to each belong to its underlying category [8, 29]). For example, when a bachelor is defined as "an unmarried man". Any instance (object) that shares these two attributes can be necessarily categorized as a bachelor.

Under this view, a category would simultaneously be describable as a set of rules whereby each new instance can be unambiguously sorted into the right group and where all members of each group share a unique set of attributes relative to the others. In other words, there should be both deductive and inductive access to each category (known in philosophy as intension vs extension, see [44]). If I see a new bird, I should be able to apply some combination of its attributes to determine if it is in the finch family or the jay family [35, 36]. At the same time, I should be able to gather say 100 finches and 100 jays and group them accordingly so that all members of each group share common attributes which are not shared with the other group (note that they may share values on one dimension but not all dimension – dogs and cats share mammalian values, but not common reproduction, for example). As Gregor (2006) implicitly points out this mapping of attributes to groups dates back to the thinking of Aristotle about the nature of things.

In contrast, a fluid or ad hoc view of categories would build categorization on the fly (pun intended). A group of 100 birds, whether finches or jays, might be grouped into those that are fast versus slow (for the purpose of gathering them by a fast worker versus a slow worker), large or small (for purposes of assigning them to cages), or hungry or already fed (for purposes of knowing which to feed next). Applying this to an organizational example, employees might be grouped into blue collar and white collar (for wage versus salary), vested and non-vested (for distribution of investment newsletters), smokers and non-smokers (for differentiating health care contributions) etc. Note that in both the bird and worker examples, such categorization is fluid (individuals move from unfed to fed and back repeatedly rather than staying in one category) and the instances may be difficult to assign (is a first level manager who does 80% of her work on the assembly line blue or white collar?) Note particularly how the categorization itself is purposeful – if we pay the same for health care for smokers and non-smokers, there may no reason to create such a categorization and no one would bother [see also, 32]. It is also fluid as individuals shift between categories over time. Consider that when done with a threshold of care, it can be useful – why pay the extra smoking cost premium for health care for 100% of workers if only 20% are smokers?

The fact that objects do not inherently belong to categories, and that classification schemas are constant in a flux, has been argued repeatedly by psychologists, linguists, philosophers, natural and social scientists [4, 6, 18, 21, 29, 39]. Information systems researchers also begun to propose solutions that are predicated on a more dynamic view of categories [22, 34, 36]. Thus, Parsons and Wand [33], state: "[m]ultiple class structures can be constructed to model a domain of phenomena. Different structures may be useful for different purposes, and there is no inherently "correct" way of classifying the phenomena in a domain".

In information systems, the argument in support of this position is rooted in ontology – a branch of philosophy that studies what exists in reality [12, 23, 25, 34]. Specifically, "substantialist ontology" [11, 37], such as that of Mario Bunge, states that individuals or things are fundamental elements of existence [7]. The things possess properties (or, from the cognitive perspective, attributes).

Classes are then formed based on some purpose by focusing on certain properties of interest, and ignoring others [20, 25, 31]. Thus, classification is an inherently purpose-driven, and therefore, always dynamic and fleeting process.

Consistent with this general perspective is the works of Lawrence Barsalou that extends these arguments in an important direction [1, 2, 29]. From this body of work, it is evident that notwithstanding the general ontological premise, some categories are more stable than others. These Barsalou [1] calls "common categories", and they are typically the categories that describe nature. As psychologists argue, in nature, attributes of things, correlate in bundles [41]. Thus, organisms that fly tend to have wings, organisms that have wings, tend to have low body metabolism, and organisms that have wings, tend to spend considerable time in the air and on high objects (e.g., flying, building nests). This fundamental aspect of reality results in an important function of categories – inferential utility [32, 36, 41]. Inferential utility means that when observing an organism, humans do not need to observe directly every property of this organism. Instead, many of these properties can be inferred from the observable ones. This makes classification fundamentally useful for humans. Building on this argument, researchers, such as Parsons and Wand [32, 36], have argued that sciences need to develop those categorization schemas – they called "classes" that follow the same natural process, and identify those categories that have inferential utility.

However, Barsalou argues that the inferential utility is not universal for categories. In particular, there is an important group of categories, those that are explicitly constructed (what Barsalou [1] calls "ad hoc categories"), see also [24]), which by design do not have many inferences. For example, we may form a category "things to take on vacation", which would contain many dissimilar objects that share only a single goal-oriented property. This "temporary" category would not have the same inferential utility as categories such as "bird" or "tree". That is, having observed some features of a member (e.g., that the passport is made of paper) of this category, it would be difficult to reliably infer additional features that would still be true for all members of this category (i.e., binoculars, walking sticks, swimming goggles, sun lotion, would not be made of paper). Nonetheless, these categories remain useful, but not for understanding reality, rather for communicating goals, perspectives, values as well as for effective social interaction and action. For example, we can use the single unifying property (things that are useful for the vacation), to scan our house for items fitting this criterion, and thus consider putting them in a suitcase.

In summary, based on the arguments in philosophy and psychology, we can conclude that a given object can be a member of multiple categories, that categories are

constructed for a particular purpose. At the same time, some categories are more stable than others. Extrapolating these arguments into the task of creating categories to make a research contribution, we argue the following:

When researchers seek to devise a new categorization scheme, they may face two different scenarios. First, if the aim is to uncover some fundamental regularities in nature, they should seek to develop what Barsalou coined "common categories" or Parsons and Wand called "classes". While these categories would not be definitive and only categories applicable to the phenomena of interest, they should carve the domain at the important areas of discontinuities. As these categories neatly partition reality, they should have as little overlap as possible, and ideally none. For example, such natural categories as trees, birds and snakes (also called "basic-level categories) have very few common, shared attributes [9, 19, 24, 40]. In other words, these categories should exhibit strong internal cohesion, and very loose coupling.

The "common categories" should offer rich inferences – that is be made of inter-correlated and interdependent attributes, such that having identified some phenomena as a member of this category, one could infer additional, unobservable properties. Such categories would be more stable, and more long lasting, as long as the underlying phenomena does not change.

Second, if on the other hand, researchers seek to develop categories that are designed for effective communication about some scientific phenomena and for some specific action (e.g., compartmentalizing research papers into conference tracks), they should instead develop Barsalou's "ad hoc categories". These categories do not have to uncover fundamental regularities in the domain, and their utility is tied more directly to the usefulness and value of the goal behind these categories.

3 EXEMPLAR RESEARCH: GREGOR (2006)

We now apply our arguments to a prominent typology in the information systems discipline, "The nature of theory in information systems" by Shirley Gregor [14].

Gregor's (2006) typology of theory is presented within the static tradition. We are not critical of this whether the choice resulted from simply assuming that the static tradition represents the totality of conceptualizing typology or if it was a conscious decision. There are advantages of a static tradition such as the definitiveness of the categories, the easy recognition of the typology as a style per se, and of the vision of the categories as relatively permanent. However, more than a decade later, viewing the categorization framework from a fluid or ad hoc categorical perspective may suggest helpful new insights and extensions. Re-examining the fundamental assumptions is further timely, as both psychology, and, information systems studies that reference psychology, begin to recognize the value of a more nuanced approach to the nature of categories [24, 28].

The ad hoc perspective raises a number of questions not addressed by the original typology. How are the categories created (addressed briefly in Gregor (2006)? How do instances enter or exit from categories? How are the categories used? Note we do not ask are these the best categories (e.g. the best way to divide up the domain of instances into sub groups) but assume that it is one of many ways. As described by [36] these sorts of questions pertaining to categories open up new avenues of investigation in management broadly and in information systems research as well.

Actually Gregor uses one dimension of "goal" as a basis for developing categories whereas, she points out, Markus and Robey [27] present three dimensions each of which alone or in combination could be used to generate an alternative categorization scheme for theory. These proposed dimensions are: "...the nature of the causal agency (technology, organizational, or emergent); (2) the logical structure (whether *variance* or *process* theory); and (3) the level of analysis. Gregor 2006, p. 621)". It is clear that if the terrain is divided by one, two or all three of these, we will get different groupings of instances than we would derive from Gregor (2006).

Each of these three dimensions upon fine examination have their own limitations and challenges. They are difficult to show as being exhaustive or mutually exclusive. The list of possible causal agents is reasonably illustrative, but difficult to argue that it encompasses all agency possibilities (what about individual will, for example?); variance and process theories would seem to focus on entities in their permanence versus entities in the ways they change, but what about social forces (e.g. network theories); patterns of change (e.g. evolution, dialectics, cycles); complexity theories (e.g. non-deterministic systems), and the like. Moreover, it is not clear that these cannot be mixed and matched [see 15] by defining relationships among combinations of entities that are stable while others change. And finally level of analysis, given the uncountable ways to divide and subdivide hierarchies also seems like a malleable basis for a taxonomy.

Addressing the first issue of how the categories are constructed within Gregor (2006) is in itself interesting. The first step is identifying a dimension on which theories, one presumes instances of theory, can vary. The particular dimension she selects pertains to "goals" of which four (analysis and description, explanation, prediction, and prescription) are presented. In a footnote it is explained that these four goals derive from writing by Aristotle regarding four explanations of any "thing". Frankly, to our thinking, these are a reasonable and intuitive set of goals that would differentiate different types of theory. Interestingly, though a fifth category is derived from the combination of explanation and prediction. However, there is no explanation for why the other 9 logically possible combinations (5 more of pairs; 3 of sets of 3; and 1 of all four) are not equally proposed. Both "explanation and prescription" or "analysis and prediction" would seem likely to generate some instances. I "explain" that giving bonuses makes employees have higher morale, therefore for low morale I "prescribe" giving bonuses. Alternatively, I have "analyzed" that white collar workers have more autonomy (by observation or by definition), therefore I "predict" there will be more variance in how they make decisions or take actions (relative to blue collar workers). The reader can work out whether there are reasonable examples for the other combinations. That said, the fifth category of "explanation and prediction" seems perfectly reasonable. For my students (first author), I illustrate this category with the related theory that taking aspirin will, all else equal, bring down a fever (prediction) and, does this in part by suppressing the normal functioning of platelets, according to Wikipedia (explanation). Note how we could have only a predication or only an explanation in this case, but that the linkage of the two intuitively provides additional value. However, it is worth considering that much prediction, if it doesn't use established categories, may include an analysis or taxonomical component as a stated or unstated precursor to explanation or prediction. The point of this observation though is the probability that Gregor's categories of theory are NOT comprehensive. She acknowledges as much discussing the use of "critical theory" as possibly being considered a type of theory without fitting into any of the five categories but rather aiming at ways to improve people's lives.

Further, there is no clear demonstration that the categories are mutually exclusive. It is not clear why the same theory as a statement cannot be prescriptive and predictive? The wording might be a little unusual, such as you should give raises to productive employees because this will add to morale – which would seem to be both prescriptive and predictive. There is no category for both of these in the given typology.

What is clear from these rather pedantic criticisms is that the value of the Gregor categorization scheme is not dependent on being either comprehensive or mutually exclusive. It neither provides guidelines for assessing a new theory and assigning it to a category nor shows how a set of say 100 theories can be segregated by theory type with clear commonalities among category instances and differences across category instances. Which leaves the question of what, then, is the source of value? Doty and Glick [10] present the idea of ideal types which represent a sort of definitional type with or without any exactly matching instances (like an ideal circle is all points equidistant from a chosen point, but of course there are no instances because points are one dimensional and thus cannot be produced in a three dimensional world). This notion is also similar to the psychological concept of a prototype – a set of ideal attributes for an instance of a category [41]. In this sense Gregor's theory types are ideal types not meant to organize actual sets of theory instances, but rather to highlight differences on one possible dimension and elevate the importance of that dimension.

We do not argue against the wisdom of using goals as a basis for the taxonomy Gregor presents, however, we emphasize that the underlying question is not whether this categorization is true to the way reality is, but rather whether it is useful. In other words, a question of judgment, utility, and preference rather than truth and demonstrability. Those coming after Gregor are free to propose alternate formulations based on the Markus and Robey dimensions or whatever others they can conceive.

Note, though, that Gregor's dimensions can (1) take on a life of their own and come to be viewed as "the categories" rather than as one of a set of possible categories; (2) help guide and shape the thinking for followers who find them logical and "good enough" for their own uses; and (3) relieve others from the burden of having to define the categories anew for every further use.[3]

How should we understand "analysis" as theory?

The second area of examination of this paper pertains to her first theory type entitled "analysis" which highlights the description of a domain of interest and the development of a typology for that domain per se. Interestingly some other scholars, notably Weber [45] do not tend to recognize this category as a type of theory at all suggesting it may at best be a kind of "model" or pre-theoretic construct.

However, the discussion of the Gregor process for arriving at a set of categories is really an exercise in reflexivity, since the first of her categories itself pertains to categorization as a sort of theory. We wish to examine in more detail how the development and use of categorization can enhance research, both in terms of theory building and testing, and also more broadly in terms of knowledge accumulation.

This first of her categories of theory is called "analysis". It is distinguished in the definitional table (p. 62) not by what it is but by what it is not. It is theory that does not specify causal relationships (leaving open the question of whether it specifies other sorts of relationships like correlation, sequence, or probabilistic effects). It also is theory that does not specify prediction – and clearly this would conflict with the Popperian view of the sanctity of falsification in the formulation of theoretical statements as a way to distinguish between those that can and those that cannot be refuted (assuming the gathering of conflicting empirical evidence.)

The discussion emphasizes the use of typology and taxonomy as a central element in such analysis. The illustration of this sort of theory is based on a paper by Iivari, Hirschheim, and Klein [17] which presents a set of four IS development approaches pointing out "similarities and differences between them". (p. 623). Essentially, the four approaches represent a typology suggesting that each characterizes a different way to develop new systems. Presumably each development instance in practice would fall within one or another category, though these days we are seeing the rise of hybrid systems development approaches that combine elements of agile and traditional approaches. Projecting the likely intent of this category of theory is the notion that creating such a categorization scheme may provide significant value in and of itself in terms of its usefulness for understanding the domain. It may also provide input into other categories of theory such as predicting that agile methods will outperform (in cost, time, scope, quality or other measures) traditional methods at least relative to small customer facing applications. Note the symbiotic relationship between the content of the taxonomy as a necessary ingredient for developing the testable theoretical statements pertaining to performance of instances within each category. There is no logical prediction theory of this type without the distinct categories set forth in the taxonomy (or an alternative formulation). It is, of course, possible that the proponent of a testable theory of prediction may base statements on flimsy, ill-conceived and ad hoc categories (or strong ones) that have not been independently a source of reflection. Note further that the prediction test will have to assume (or measure) that each instance actually fits into that particular category in order to test contrasts between categories.

It is likely that the untestable nature of the development of categories is what leads some, notably Weber (2012) not to consider these as theories per se; but it is the utility of separate development and examination of these categories that in our view would lead to considering these as theory. It would seem that it takes little imagination to convert quality categorization schemes into prediction style theory by simply considering the characteristics of each category (e.g.,

---

[3] Gregor (2006) adds an intriguing comment about grounded theory as theory emergent from a grounded process, but having read both process and outcome works of grounded theory it is not clear why the product of such work, if it stands independent of its specific environment, would not be amenable to being treated as analysis, prediction, explanation, or prescription). In other words, once formulated as a theory, would we know (or care) whether it came from a grounded theory process, another inductive process, a deductive process, or extrapolation from another field?

instances in category 1 will be larger, more talented, quieter, etc. relative to those instances in category 2) or considering different productivity levels in using instances from each category.

Having accepted the assumption that "ad hoc categories" are fundamentally untestable with respect to the underlying reality (i.e., the instances they seek to organize), we can consider a different way of ascertaining their scientific utility. What researchers can (and should) test is the utility of categories for the consumer of these categories. In other words, when addressing the question of how "how good a categorization schema is?" one can test the relative benefit the user of the schema accrues as compared to something else. In this conception, categories are artifacts – figments of human imagination intended to serve as mental tools that help reduce complexity of reality. As tools, categories cannot be the sources of an objective truth; instead, they offer a pragmatic utility [38].

The tool perspective on categories leads us to formulate the following question: how can one establish the utility of categories? To address this question, it is important to note that categorization is a fundamental human mechanism. Psychologists argue that our access to reality is invariably mediated by categories – otherwise we would be incapable of dealing with the infinite diversity of the sensory experience - always unique and constantly changing [16, 41]. The implication of this for research in any given domain is that humans always operate on a set of explicit or implicit categories to make sense of this domain. In other words, there is always a benchmark, a reference point, a status quo. A second consequence of the utilitarian, tool view of categories is the need for guidelines for how apply them unambiguously and consistently (i.e., having a manual to accompany the tool). Here, it is noteworthy to consider Gregor's (2006) prescription for formatting theories of the categorization, descriptive, or analytic type:

"The logic for the placement of phenomena into categories should be clear, as should the characteristics that define each category. In addition important categories or elements should not be omitted from the classification system, that is, it should be complete and exhaustive (p. 624)."

We note the term "should" can be interpreted across a range from "must" to "would be nice if". We would be highly sympathetic to the latter but find the former interpretation to be unrealistic. To the extent that phenomena *DO* fit nicely into such categories or where a particular definition is clear and straightforward to apply, this is handy and helpful. Perhaps it is a goal to strive for as categories evolve. However, it is a tough criterion to pass when a field is opening to new and initial scrutiny. We suggest that the theory typology presented in this

paper is extraordinarily useful, worthy of publication, but might not fit within this definition in its most rigorous interpretation. On the other hand, if a classification scheme, for example, rightly classifies a number of instances and defines a central tendency, even if not all instances, it can be of immense utility (as we argue Gregor's (2006) schema does.) Similarly, the criteria of completeness and mutual exclusivity, while a desirable target, are unlikely to be achieved and challenging if not impossible to demonstrate. If we needed to achieve these criteria as a "must" for categorization, we would likely have to do without categories at all – at least in our literature if not in our cognitive lives.

4 CONCLUSIONS

In this paper, we provided a more nuanced exposition of the nature of categories. Specifically, we show that fundamentally, two kinds of contributions can be made in research that seeks to propose new categories. First, researchers may identify natural discontinuities in reality, and propose categories to conceptualize these. If this is the intent of research, researchers need to be forthcoming and explicit in stating this objective. Having committed to this cause, researchers then need to demonstrate how the new categories make "deep" partitions of reality. This can be done by showing that the categories are internally strongly cohesive, but are also loosely coupled. In addition, the categories should offer rich inferences and capture bundles of inter-correlated attributes.

In contrast, other researchers may seek to propose "ad hoc categories". These categories are fundamentally utilitarian, and do not have to exhibit the properties of "common categories". When proposing a new classification schema based on these categories, researchers should be explicit in suggesting the added benefit of the proposed schema with the explicit or implicit schema or schemata that already exists. Such comparisons are most likely to be based on logical argument and presentation of inferred benefits. The generation of new, thought provoking, and potentially useful research questions would indicate utility of the categories in and of themselves. However, empirical data about such categorization based on interview, survey, "applicability check" [42] or observational evidence might also prove useful.

Assuming the demonstration of utility of new categories, any specification of specific and unambiguous rules for assigning individual cases to categories should be presented with humility as they will likely be subject to change over time. Consider the "black swan" and the inability to inductively "prove" exceptions just because none have been observed. In fact, the debate over specific instances and their assignment to categories can show differences in perceptions of that instance leading to greater understanding of particular cases (e.g. discovery or invention of new attributes) as well as the relative importance of identified attributes. To the extent that an abundance of instances exist, another approach to categories would be to demonstrate the population of each category (this is sometimes done with literature reviews assigning each underlying article into one or another category). Although once published such a sorting acquires a halo of acceptance, the discussion about these assignments and the nature of these instances or articles holds the potential for richer and deeper interpretations and elicitation of useful meaning.

Following this logic of fluid or ad hoc categories, future researchers using these categories may (1) find them applicable and create further inference based on them; (2) find "fuzziness" in their boundaries and further refine our understanding of them; (3) discover significant cases (perhaps presenting as "outliers") that populate the ubiquitous "other" category until their volume suggests a new substantial category; or (4) simply present new conundrums and raise innovative new problems or questions.

To be more specific, we see applications for examination of categories throughout the array of topics of relevance to those studying "computer personnel" or "computation and people". For example, recent scientific research calls into question the simplistic categorization of all people by either sex or gender as "male" or "female" without consideration of the many potential variations on the levels of both chromosomes and social roles. Much management and MIS literature particularly pertaining to social inclusion tends to be based on old and often unquestioned categories that do not necessarily account for shades and variations of biological and cultural distinctions.

Another example pertains to IT workers. Recent literature has discussed the decades long movement of the use of computing from the exclusive realm of IT professionals to just about every worker from utility meter readers to robotics specialists directing mechanisms to pour molten metals into molds [30]. Perhaps it is time to rethink differentiations among those who work with computing in different ways that would be meaningful for understanding the evolution of these people and jobs. Such categorization has implications for approaches to train, hire, retain, and make use of their labors.

Thus, we encourage researchers to embrace a more fluid, more fleeting conceptualization of categories as elements of research contribution. As we demonstrated on the analysis of a seminal categorization framework by Gregor (2006), a given set of categories can be criticized and challenged, as many alternative ways to organize phenomena in a domain are possible – even while its initial "common category" presentation also demonstrates usefulness. We suggest for researchers to demonstrate the utility of categories to their consumers, and systematically

and rigorously compare the new categories proposed to those already in existence. At the same time, we recommend for reviewers and editors to (1) treat categories presented as if they were solid and permanent with some skepticism while seemingly paradoxically (2) being open to varied and diverse approaches to categorization within any given domain – especially ones where categories have been accepted and untested for a long period of time. We believe that IS research can meaningfully increase its accumulated knowledge base by considering the character of the categories and instances as well as the relationships between them within IS overall as well as each sub-discipline.

REFERENCES

[1] Barsalou, L.W. 1983. Ad hoc categories. *Memory & Cognition.* 11, (1983), 211–227.

[2] Barsalou, L.W. et al. 1998. Basing categorization on individuals and events. *Cognitive psychology.* 36, 3 (1998), 203–272.

[3] Bergholtz, M. and Eriksson, O. 2015. Towards a Socio-Institutional Ontology for Conceptual Modelling of Information Systems. *Advances in Conceptual Modeling.* Springer. 225–235.

[4] Berlin, B. et al. 1966. Folk Taxonomies and Biological Classification. *Science.* 154, 3746 (1966), 273–275.

[5] Borges, J.L. 1966. *Other inquisitions, 1937-1952.* Washington Square Press,.

[6] Bowker, G.C. and Star, S.L. 2000. *Sorting things out: classification and its consequences.* MIT Press.

[7] Bunge, M. 1977. *Treatise on basic philosophy: Ontology I: the furniture of the world.* Reidel.

[8] Carey, S. 2009. *The Origin of Concepts.* Oxford University Press.

[9] Castellanos, A. et al. 2016. Conceptual Modeling in Open Information Environments. *AIS SIGSAND Symposium* (Lubbock, TX, 2016), 1–7.

[10] Doty, D.H. and Glick, W.H. 1994. Typologies as a unique form of theory building: Toward improved understanding and modeling. *Academy of management review.* 19, 2 (1994), 230–251.

[11] Emirbayer, M. 1997. Manifesto for a relational sociology. *American journal of sociology.* 103, 2 (1997), 281–317.

[12] Eriksson, O. et al. 2018. Institutional ontology for conceptual modeling. *Journal of Information Technology.* (2018), 1–19.

[13] Fiss, P.C. 2011. Building better causal theories: A fuzzy set approach to typologies in organization research. *Academy of Management Journal.* 54, 2 (2011), 393–420.

[14] Gregor, S. 2006. The nature of theory in information systems. *MIS Quarterly.* 30, 3 (Sep. 2006), 611–642.

[15] de Guinea, A.O. and Webster, J. 2017. Combining variance and process in information systems research: Hybrid approaches. *Information and Organization.* 27, 3 (2017), 144–162.

[16] Harnad, S. 2005. To Cognize is to Categorize: Cognition is Categorization. H. Cohen and C. Lefebvre, eds. Elsevier Science. 20–45.

[17] Iivari, J. et al. 2000. A dynamic framework for classifying information systems development methodologies and approaches. *Journal of Management Information Systems.* 17, 3 (2000), 179–218.

[18] Lakoff, G. 1987. *Women, fire, and dangerous things: what categories reveal about the mind.* University of Chicago Press.

[19] Lassaline, M.E. et al. 1992. Basic Levels in Artificial and Natural Categories: Are All Basic Levels Created Equal? *Percepts, Concepts and Categories: The Representation and Processing of Information.* B. Barbara, ed. North-Holland. 328–378.

[20] Lukyanenko, R. et al. 2016. Emerging problems of data quality in citizen science. *Conservation Biology.* 30, 3 (2016), 447–449.

[21] Lukyanenko, R. et al. 2016. Participatory Design for User-generated Content: Understanding the challenges and moving forward. *Scandinavian Journal of Information Systems.* 28, 1 (2016), 37–70.

[22] Lukyanenko, R. et al. 2017. Representing Crowd Knowledge: Guidelines for Conceptual Modeling of User-generated Content. *Journal of the Association for Information Systems.* 18, 4 (2017), 297–339.

[23] Lukyanenko, R. et al. 2014. The IQ of the Crowd: Understanding and Improving Information Quality in Structured User-generated Content. *Information Systems Research.* 25, 4 (2014), 669–689.

[24] Lukyanenko, R. and Samuel, B.M. 2017. Are all Classes Created Equal? Increasing Precision of Conceptual Modeling Grammars. *ACM Transactions on Management Information Systems (TMIS).* 40, 2 (Forthcoming 2017), 1–25.

[25] March, S. and Allen, G. 2015. Classification with a purpose. *Symposium on Research in Systems Analysis and Design* (Richmond, VA, 2015), 1–10.

[26] March, S.T. and Allen, G.N. 2014. Toward a social ontology for conceptual modeling. *Communications of the AIS.* 34, (2014).

[27] Markus, M.L. and Robey, D. 1988. Information technology and organizational change: causal structure in theory and research. *Management science.* 34, 5 (1988), 583–598.

[28] Medin, D.L. et al. 2000. Are there kinds of concepts? *Annual review of psychology.* 51, 1 (2000), 121–147.

[29] Murphy, G. 2004. *The big book of concepts.* MIT Press.

[30] Niederman, F. et al. 2016. On the co-evolution of information technology and information systems personnel. *ACM SIGMIS Database: the DATABASE for Advances in Information Systems.* 47, 1 (2016), 29–50.

[31] Ogunseye, S. et al. 2017. Do Crowds Go Stale? Exploring the Effects of Crowd Reuse on Data Diversity. *WITS 2017* (Seoul, South Korea, 2017).

[32] Parsons, J. and Wand, Y. 2008. A question of class. *Nature.* 455, 7216 (Oct. 2008), 1040–1041.

[33] Parsons, J. and Wand, Y. 2013. Cognitive Principles to Support Information Requirements Agility. *Advanced Information Systems Engineering Workshops* (2013), 192–197.

[34] Parsons, J. and Wand, Y. 2000. Emancipating Instances from the Tyranny of Classes in Information Modeling. *ACM Transactions on Database Systems.* 25, 2 (2000), 228–268.

[35] Parsons, J. and Wand, Y. 2012. Extending Classification Principles from Information Modeling to Other Disciplines. *Journal of the Association for Information Systems.* 14, 5 (2012), 2.

[36] Parsons, J. and Wand, Y. 2008. Using cognitive principles to guide classification in information systems modeling. *MIS Quarterly.* 32, 4 (Dec. 2008), 839–868.

[37] Pentland, B. et al. 2017. Capturing reality in flight? Empirical tools for strong process theory. *ICIS 2017* (Seoul, South Korea, 2017), 1–12.

[38] Purao, S. 2013. Truth or dare: The ontology question in design science research. *Journal of Database Management (JDM).* 24, 3 (2013), 51–66.

[39] Ritvo, H. 1997. *The platypus and the mermaid, and other figments of the classifying imagination.* Harvard University Press.

[40] Rosch, E. et al. 1976. Basic Objects in Natural Categories. *Cognitive Psychology.* 8, 3 (1976), 382–439.

[41] Rosch, E. 1978. Principles of Categorization. E. Rosch and B. Lloyd, eds. John Wiley & Sons Inc. 27–48.

[42] Rosemann, M. and Vessey, I. 2008. Toward improving the relevance of information systems research to practice: the role of applicability checks. *MIS Quarterly.* 32, 1 (2008), 1–22.

[43] Searle, J.R. 1995. *The construction of social reality.* Simon and Schuster.

[44] Smith, L.B. 2005. Emerging ideas about categories. L. Gershkoff-Stowe and D.H. Rakison, eds. L. Erlbaum Associates. 159–175.

[45] Weber, R. 2012. Evaluating and Developing Theories in the Information Systems Discipline. *Journal of the Association for Information Systems.* 13, 1 (2012), 1–30.

The Evolving Emphasis on Hard and Soft Skills in the IT Profession

Tenace Kwaku Setor
Nanyang Technology University
Singapore
tenacekw001@e.ntu.edu.sg

Damien Joseph
Nanyang Technology University
Singapore
adjoseph@ntu.edu.sg

Shaikh Faheem Ahmed
Nanyang Technology University
Singapore
faheemah001@e.ntu.edu.sg

ABSTRACT

Technology IPOs expose Information Technology (IT) firms to significant challenges that are fundamentally different from those faced during the founding or startup stage. To tackle the post-IPO challenges, IT firms pay premium wages to hire professional executives from the external labor market rather than from within. Yet, how the executive pay of external hires compares to that of internal hires when IT firms mark significant milestones in their lifecycle remain understudied. The current study therefore examines the pay of internal and external hires and place it within the context of the IPO timeline i.e. pre- and post-IPO. By analyzing data from multiple sources using a linear mixed effects modelling technique, we find that IT firms pay internal hires significantly higher than external hires in the pre-IPO stage. In the post-IPO stage, IT firms pay external hires significantly higher than internal hires. We discuss the implications of the findings on theory and practice.

CCS CONCEPTS

• **Social and professional topics** → **Computing profession**
→ Employment issues; Computing occupations

ACM Reference format:

Tenace Kwaku Setor, Damien Joseph, and Shaikh Faheem Ahmed. 2018. The Evolving Emphasis on Hard and Soft Skills in the IT Profession Website. In Proceedings of ACM SIGMIS-CPR, June 18–20, 2018, Buffalo-Niagara Falls, NY, USA, 1 page. https://doi.org/10.1145/3209626.3209727

Features Related to Patient Portal User Satisfaction: N-Gram-Based Analysis of Users' Feedback

Mohammad Al-Ramahi
Indiana University East
Hayes Hall 255J
Richmond, IN 47374
moaabdel@iu.edu

Abdullah Wahbeh
Slippery Rock University of PA
1 Morrow Way
Slippery Rock, PA 16057
abdullah.wahbeh@sru.edu

Cherie Noteboom
Dakota State University
820 N Washington Ave
Madison, SD 57042
cherie.noteboom@dsu.edu

ABSTRACT

"U.S. health care spending grew 5.8 percent in 2015, reaching $3.2 trillion or $9,990 per person. As a share of the nation's Gross Domestic Product, health spending accounted for 17.8 percent" [1]. Therefore, an intensive national effort to improve healthcare using information technology (IT) with a focus on reducing costs and increasing quality of service is well underway. In this regard, patient portals, known as personal health records, show promise as tools that patients value and that can reduce healthcare cost and improve health. These Health Information Technology (HIT) are positioned as a central component of patient engagement through the potential to change the physician-patient relationship and enable chronic disease self-management. Patient portals can lead to improvements in clinical outcomes, patient behavior, and experiences. However, portal adoption is still low, due to technological limitations and to the lack of adaptability to primary care practice workflow [2]. Large studies in outpatient settings have found that providing patients with adequate functionalities leads to increases in patient satisfaction and then adherence to patient portal [3]. In fact, patient portal user satisfaction is increasingly recognized as an important component of quality [4]. However, little is known about the different patient portal characteristics that are associated with higher patient satisfaction. It seems there is insufficient evidence to support how portals empower patients and improve quality of care. According to the literature, many studies have addressed the relationship between the use of health information technologies and patients' satisfaction [4-7]. Despite the fact that there is some evidence that such technologies improve and enhance patients' satisfaction, there exist some inconsistencies in the findings and reported results [4]. The literature also highlighted the need for further research that focuses on use of the patient portal and measures of quality indicators such as medical outcomes, medication adherence, and patient satisfaction [5]. In this study, we systematically analyze users' reviews of mobile patient portal to extract features that are associated with patient satisfaction. To this end, we use user rating as a proxy for user satisfaction and adopt word-level n-grams to represent user reviews. We use MyChart reviews as Epic has captured significant market share with at least partial health information for 51% of the US population. It has been described as the default EHR choice not for its superior performance, but because other systems are considered inferior [8]. Specifically, in this research, we aim to identify predictors of patient satisfaction based on a systematic analysis of user feedback from actual use of patient portal. The data were collected using a web crawler. We obtain our data set consisting of 500 reviews. For data preprocessing, we removed stop words and represented user reviews using vectors of word-level n-grams weights. For the word n-grams, we include unigram, bigrams, and trigrams. We perform feature selection using the commonly used Chi-square ($X2$) method. To evaluate the predictive power of the features selected, we chose four evaluation metrics, precision, recall, accuracy, and F1 Score. Results analysis show that the majority of selected features are related to the ease of use of the patient portal, other features are related to specific features and functions the users can use within the application such as scheduling appointments, communication with health providers, using the calendar, etc. Results also report "touch id", fingerprint recognition feature, which is a security related feature that allows users to log in to their portal. The performance results of the features selected in predicting user satisfaction using different classifiers such as decision tree, linear SVC, ridge classifier, logistic regression, Bernoulli Naïve Bayes (NB), and random forest show very good performance with accuracy ranging 73%-80%, F1 ranging 81%-86%, Precision ranging 88%-96%, and Recall ranging 75%-79%.

ACM Reference format:
Mohammad Al-Ramahi, Abdullah Wahbeh, and Cherie Noteboom. 2018. Features Related to Patient Portal User Satisfaction: N-Gram-Based Analysis of Users' Feedback. In Proceedings of ACM SIGMIS-CPR, June 18–20, 2018, Buffalo-Niagara Falls, NY, USA, 1 page. https://doi.org/10.1145/3209626.3209727

REFERENCES

[1]   T. C. f. M. M. S. CMS. (2016, Nov 19, 2017). *National Health Expenditure Data*. Available: https://go.cms.gov/1Jy5kin

[2]   B. Sorondo *et al.*, "Using a Patient Portal to Transmit Patient Reported Health Information into the Electronic Record: Workflow Implications and User Experience," *eGEMs*, vol. 4, no. 3, 2016.

[3]   A. S. McAlearney *et al.*, "High Touch and High Tech (HT2) Proposal: Transforming Patient Engagement Throughout the Continuum of Care by Engaging Patients with Portal Technology at the Bedside," *JMIR Research Protocols*, vol. 5, no. 4, 2016.

[4]   R. Rozenblum *et al.*, "The impact of medical informatics on patient satisfaction: a USA-based literature review," *International journal of medical informatics*, vol. 82, no. 3, pp. 141-158, 2013.

[5]   A. G. Dumitrascu *et al.*, "Patient portal use and hospital outcomes," *Journal of the American Medical Informatics Association*, 2017.

[6]   M. Al-Ramahi and C. Noteboom, "A Systematic Analysis of Patient Portals Adoption, Acceptance and Usage: The Trajectory for Triple Aim?," in *Proceedings of the 51st Hawaii International Conference on System Sciences*, 2018.

[7]   C. Noteboom and M. Al-Ramahi, "What are the Gaps in Mobile Patient Portal? Mining Users Feedback Using Topic Modeling," in *Proceedings of the 51st Hawaii International Conference on System Sciences*, 2018.

[8]   R. Koppel and C. U. Lehmann, "Implications of an emerging EHR monoculture for hospitals and healthcare systems," *Journal of the American Medical Informatics Association*, pp. amiajnl-2014-003023, 2014.

Building Health Information Networks Using Facebook: A Pilot Study with New Mothers in Rural Appalachia

Devendra Potnis
University of Tennessee at Knoxville
Knoxville, Tennessee, USA
dpotnis@utk.edu

Macy Halladay
University of Tennessee at Knoxville
Knoxville, Tennessee, USA
mhallada@vols.utk.edu

ABSTRACT

This qualitative inquiry studies the key factors influencing the process of building, growing, and sustaining a health information network among new mothers on Facebook, who live in Appalachian Tennessee. Grounded theory analysis of in-depth phone interviews reveal that (i) realizing information needs, (ii) turning to the Internet and social media, (iii) joining the Facebook group, (iv) building a community of practice on the group, (v) information practices of users, and (vi) deriving benefits to meet the information needs, help them build the health information network.

KEYWORDS

Facebook, Health, Information network, Appalachia, New mothers

ACM Reference format:

D. Potnis and M. Halladay. 2018. Building Health Information Networks Using Facebook: A Pilot Study with New Mothers in Rural Appalachia. In *Proceedings of ACM SIGMIS-CPR '18, June 18–20, 2018, Buffalo-Niagara Falls, NY, USA*, 1 page. https://doi.org/10.1145/3209626.3209730

1 PROBLEM STATEMENT

Tennessee ranks 44th in the US for overall health of women. Building and strengthening a social support system for new mothers for providing timely, affordable access to information can help Tennessee achieve its topmost health priority. The utility and increasing popularity of Facebook help women access and receive timely, affordable information for addressing the escalating health crisis in Tennessee. The research question was: *What are the key factors enabling new mothers to build, grow, and sustain a health information network over Facebook?*

2 RELEVANT LITERATURE

Online communities of new mothers can help them seek consultations, moral support, and additional information or referrals as well as improve maternal mental health, child outcomes and increased relationship satisfaction [1]. Women join online motherhood groups for a variety of reasons including seeking health information, social support, self-understanding and other commonly experienced challenges during motherhood.

3 METHODS

We conducted this pilot with members of the Knoxville Cesarean and VBAC (Vaginal Birth after Cesarean) Support Group, which is a Facebook group incepted in 2009. Women were recruited by the group administrators using a Facebook announcement. We conducted 8 phone interviews with each interview lasting on average about 35 minutes. We applied grounded theory principles to identify open codes, axial codes, and selective codes, for identifying the key factors influencing the ability of new mothers to form a health information network on Facebook [2].

4 FINDINGS & CONCLUSIONS

We identified the following stages critical for building, growing, and sustaining a health information network over Facebook: (i) realizing information needs, (ii) turning to the Internet and social media for local support and guidance, (iii) joining the Facebook group, (iv) building a community of practice with the help of group administrators, (v) information practices including information searching, using, and sharing, and (vi) deriving tangible and intangible benefits after meeting information needs. This pilot reveals the process of transforming an online social network into a health information network on Facebook.

REFERENCES

[1] Evans, M., Donelle, L., & Hume-Loveland, L. (2012). Social support and online postpartum depression discussion groups: A content analysis. Patient education and counseling, 87(3), 405-410.. DOI:http://dx.doi.org/10.1177/0192513x10375064

[2] Potnis, D., Chengalur-Smith, I., & Mishra, G. (2017). Information networks for bridging information divide in isolated communities of farmers in rural India, Proceedings of the Association for Information Science and Technology, 54(1), 781-783. DOI: https://doi.org/10.1002/pra2.2017.14505401155

Computing Career Exploration For Urban African American Students using Embodied Conversational Agents

Poster Abstract

Kinnis Gosha
Morehouse College
Department of Computer Science
Atlanta, GA, USA
kinnis.gosha@morehouse.edu

Earl W. Huff, Jr.
Clemson University
School of Computing
Clemson, SC, USA
earlh@clemson.edu

Jordan Scott
Morehouse College
Department of Computer Science
Atlanta, GA, USA
jordan.scott@morehouse.edu

CCS CONCEPTS

• **Human-centered computing** → **Web-based interaction**; **Interaction design**; • **Social and professional topics** → *Professional topics*;

KEYWORDS

Computing Careers Now, computing career, embodied conversational agents, virtual computing career exploration fair

ACM Reference Format:
Kinnis Gosha, Earl W. Huff, Jr., and Jordan Scott. 2018. Computing Career Exploration For Urban African American Students using Embodied Conversational Agents: Poster Abstract. In *SIGMIS-CPR '18: 2018 Computers and People Research Conference, June 18–20, 2018, Buffalo-Niagara Falls, NY, USA.* ACM, New York, NY, USA, 1 page. https://doi.org/10.1145/3209626.3209731

1 MOTIVATION AND PROBLEM STATEMENT

Computing jobs are increasingly making up a large portion of the STEM jobs in the workforce; however, very few of those jobs are held by African Americans. A 2008 report by the National Science Foundation [1] revealed that Black computer science bachelor's degree graduates (not just those from HBCUs) are disproportionately likely to NOT go into a science or engineering job or further school. Approximately 29 percent of black graduates were employed in non-science and engineering jobs compared to 13 percent or seven percent for White or Asian graduates, respectively. The study conducted investigated the perception of computing careers of African American high school students using a virtual computing career exploration fair. Students interacted with virtual computing professionals, created with the use of embodied conversational agents (ECAs), through the Computing Careers Now website to learn about different positions in computing.

2 PROCEDURE

The study took place in a large urban city in southeastern United States. We recruited teachers from several urban high schools to participate by allowing us to use their class as part of the study. The teachers discussed the purpose of the website with the students and asked those who were willing to use it. Students were taken to a computer lab where they would use the website to listen to an ECA as it disseminated information about a particular computing profession. After using the website, students were asked to complete an online survey. Questions from the survey asked students about their thoughts of the website itself, the ECA they listened to, the effectiveness of the ECA teaching them about careers in computing, and improvements to the website. Additionally, a focus group interview was conducted with the teachers who participated to obtain their perceptions of the virtual computing career exploration fair and the state of their school in regards to the presence of support for Computer Science.

3 RESULTS

Results from the student surveys revealed the following: 1) the majority of participants (54%) found the website to be useful in learning more about computing careers; 2) most of the participants were somewhat more interested in pursuing a career in computing; however, 52% of them indicated that if they wanted to pursue a computing career, they felt they could achieve it; 3) most of the participants were somewhat likely to interact with an ECA again to learn more information about computing careers but more likely to interact with an ECA to learn about other careers. From the focus group interview, we learned that many of the urban schools in the area of study do not provide adequate support and exposure to the field of computing and more resources are needed to increase interest in CS. Additionally, the teachers felt there needs to be training for the teachers to incorporate computing concepts into their curriculum.

4 IMPLICATIONS

The findings from this study has shown that the Computing Careers Now website can be a useful tool in helping disseminate information about careers in computing. Further improvements to the website interface and functionality of the ECA are needed for better user experience. A future study is being planned in which we will target high school students who already show some interest in computing and/or are taking a high school computing course and additional measuring instruments will be applied to better evaluate the effectiveness of the website.

REFERENCES

[1] Flora Lan. 2012. Characteristics of Recent Science and Engineering Graduates: 2008 General Notes. (2012).

Understanding the Dynamics of Young People's Self-Presentation on Social Media

Wu He
Old Dominion University
Norfolk, VA 23529
1-757-683-5008
whe@odu.edu

Yilin Shan
Cape Henry Collegiate School
Virginia Beach, VA 23454
1-757-481-2446
yshan19@student.capehenry.org

ABSTRACT

Social media sites such as Instagram, Snapchat and Facebook have become an important part of young people's lives. Social media provides a new platform for self-presentation, which is one of the prominent functions used by young people. However, their self-presentations are often skewed towards the idealized description of who they desire to be. The truthfulness of self-presentation may range from selected presentation, ideal self, self-promotion, to twisted, false self (Minas Michikyan, Dennis, & Subrahmanyam, 2015). Research has reported that selective self-presentation on social media may have negative impact on the wellbeing of young people (Chou & Edge, 2012). For example, the idealized self-presentation leads to upward social comparison of others, which causes reduced self-esteem, anxiety and depression (Vogel, Rose, R., & Eckles, 2014; Feinstein et al., 2013). So it is important to examine the factors that influence self-presentation by young people who are more vulnerable to psychological distress.

We argue that the uses and gratifications theory can be used to analyze why and how self-presentation evolves. Uses and gratifications theory presents the media use as a goal directed behavior. The focus of the theory is on what people do with the media (Katz et al., 1974). It assumes that people actively choose and use media channels in response to their specific needs, and obtain gratifications by fulfilling the needs (LaRose, Mastro, & Eastin, 2001). For instance, when an individual has a need for social interaction, the individual choose Facebook to gratify this need.

We seek to apply this theory to help understand what needs young people seek to gratify by engaging in various uses of social media, and how obtained (and un-obtained) gratifications, in return, shape the uses. We argue that young people's self-presentations are dynamic and are shaped by their social interactions with peers as well as their goals in using social media. Specifically, our research question is:

How do the uses and gratifications impact the dynamics of self-presentation on social media among young people?

Shao (2009) argues that the three usages of user-generated media (consuming, participating and producing) are interdependent, through their impacts on the gratifications. We

take this view to examine the dynamics of young people's self-presentations on social media and propose a research model to analyze how self-presentation is initiated to fulfill young people's needs and evolves over time. Our model includes social media activities that are results of uses (producing, participating and consuming) and the gratifications fulfilled by the uses (Shao, 2009). Specifically, following Chua and Chang's (2016) argument, we model the interdependent relationships among young people's self-presentation, peer feedback and peer comparison and the gratifications they fulfill. Each social media activity is the result of a social media use, which gratifies specific needs of young people. An activity, on the other hand, impacts the obtained gratifications, which influence the uses. Young people's activities on social media are shaped constantly by these circular relationships between uses, gratifications and activities. In this research, we examine the evolving of one activity---self-presentation.

We will use both survey and case study design to investigate young people's self-presentation on social media. High school students who are active users of social media sites will be recruited as the participants of this study. Participants will be selected through convenience sampling. The second author will recruit her classmates and friends who are engaged in all three activities on at least one social media site. The contents on social media such as text, pictures, videos, comments and number of likes will be used as sources of secondary data when available.

Taking a theoretical approach, this study will contribute to research on self-presentation on social media. Specifically, this research attempts to answer why young people post selective personal information on social media and how their self-presentations evolve over time. The insight gained from this study may enhance our understanding on the dynamics of self-presentation on social media and their impacts on young people.

REFERENCES

[1] Chou, H.-T. G., & Edge, N. (2012). "They are happier and having better lives than I am": The impact of using Facebook on perceptions of others' lives. Cyberpsychology, Behavior, and Social Networking, 15(2).

[2] Chua, T., & Chang, L. (2016). Follow me and like my beautiful selfies: Singapore teenage girls' engagement in self-presentation and peer comparison on social media. Computers in Human Behavior, 55, 190-197.

[3] Katz, E., Blumler, J. G., & Gurevitch, M. (1974). Utilization of Mass Communication by the Individual. In J. G. Blumler & E. Katz (Eds.), The Uses of Mass Communications: Current Perspectives on Gratifications Research. Beverly Hills: Sage Publications.

[4] LaRose, R., Mastro, D., & Eastin, M. (2001). Understanding Internet usage: a social-cognitive approach to uses and gratifications. Social Science Computer Review, 19(4), 395-413.

[5] Michikyan, M., Dennis, J., & Subrahmanyam, K. (2015). Can you guess who I am? real, ideal, and false self-presentation on Facebook among emerging adults. Emerging Adulthood, 3(1), 55-64.

[6] Shao, G. (2009). Understanding the appeal of user-generated media: a uses and gratification perspective. Internet Research, 19(1).

[7] Vogel, E. A., Rose, J. P., R., R. L., & Eckles, K. (2014). Social comparison, social media, and self-esteem. Psychology of Popular Media Culture, 3(4), 205-222.

How Does Use of Fitness Applications Influence Physical Activity?*

Ya Zhou
Department of Information Systems
and Analytics, School of Computing,
National University of Singapore
zhouya@comp.nus.edu.sg

Atreyi Kankanhalli
Department of Information Systems
and Analytics, School of Computing,
National University of Singapore
atreyi@comp.nus.edu.sg

ABSTRACT

This paper investigates the effects of fitness applications on physical activity performance, knowledge of which can help in feature design to improve users' utilization of the apps.

ACM Reference format:
Ya Zhou, and Atreyi Kankanhalli 2018. How Does Use of Fitness Applications Influence Physical Activity? In Proceedings of ACM SIGMIS-CPR, June 18–20, 2018, Buffalo-Niagara Falls, NY, USA, ACM, NY, NY, USA, 1 page. https://doi.org/10.1145/3209626.3209733

KEYWORDS

Physical activity, fitness applications, SNS, self-regulation, social comparison, social support

1 INTRODUCTION

In this paper, we propose a research model to address the following research question: *How do the use of various features of fitness apps influence users' physical activity?*

2 CONCEPTUAL BACKGROUND

2.1 Literature Review

Prior research has begun to investigate the effectiveness of fitness apps [e.g., 1-2]. However, prior studies have limitations in terms of small sample sizes, largely not being theory based, and not examining the separate effects of different app features. Such limitations could lead to inconsistent findings. These gaps motivate us to develop and test a theoretical model that explains the effects of different features of fitness apps using larger samples and objective performance data.

2.2 Social Cognitive Theory of Self-Regulation

This theory is useful here because people need to regulate themselves to overcome various impediments for conducting physical activities [3]. The components of self-regulation that we derived from integrating the social cognitive theory literature are forethought, performance volitional control, social influence, and self-reflection. Specifically, *goal setting* and *self- tracking* are the focal activities of forethought and performance volitional control respectively. Social influence includes both *social comparison* and *social support*. In fitness apps, using leaderboards, people could easily check their relative performance positions in their social network and conduct social comparison. Besides, by sharing one's physical activity data, users could obtain social support, such as by receiving "likes" or positive comments. An important outcome during self-reflection is *self-efficacy*, which further influences self-regulatory performance, i.e., physical activity performance in our study context.

3 MODEL DEVELOPMENT

Our model relates the features of fitness apps, such as goal setting, self-tracking, and SNS (for social comparison and social support) to self-regulation of physical activity. Specifically, we hypothesize that self-tracking, performance position (in the leaderboard) and social support are positively related to self-efficacy, while goal setting and self-efficacy are positively related to physical activity performance. Additionally, the effect of performance position is hypothesized to be negatively moderated by the performance difference between the individual and other users.

4 PROPOSED METHODOLOGY

To test our model, we will collect both survey and app data from fitness app users. Particularly, we will use app logged data (e.g., calories burned through exercise) to measure physical activity performance, which avoids self-report bias. We will be further refining the model and collecting data for the study in future.

5 EXPECTED CONTRIBUTIONS

Our study is expected to contribute to the literature on fitness apps, IS use, social cognitive theory, and social comparison. Practical implications for fitness app design are also expected.

REFERENCES

[1] King, A.C., Hekler, E.B., Grieco, L.A., Winter, S.J., Sheats, J.L., Buman, M.P., Banerjee, B., Robinson, T.N., and Cirimele, J., 2013. Harnessing Different Motivational Frames Via Mobile Phones to Promote Daily Physical Activity and Reduce Sedentary Behavior in Aging Adults. *PLOS One* 8, 4 (Apr).
[2] Walsh, J.C., Corbett, T., Hogan, M., Duggan, J., and Mcnamara, A., 2016. An Mhealth Intervention Using a Smartphone App to Increase Walking Behavior in Young Adults: A Pilot Study. *JMIR Mhealth and Uhealth* 4, 3 (Jul-Sep). DOI= http://dx.doi.org/10.2196/mhealth.5227.
[3] Bandura, A., 1991. Social Cognitive Theory of Self-Regulation. *Organizational Behavior and Human Decision Processes* 50, 2 (Dec), 248-287. DOI= http://dx.doi.org/10.1016/0749-5978(91)90022-l.

Are Friendly and Competent the Same? – The Role of the Doctor-Patient Relationship in Physician Ratings

Maximilian Haug
University of Applied Sciences Neu-Ulm
Neu-Ulm, Germany
maximilian.haug@hs-neu-ulm.de

Heiko Gewald
University of Applied Sciences Neu-Ulm
Neu-Ulm, Germany
heiko.gewald@hs-neu-ulm.de

ABSTRACT

More and more people regularly use physician rating websites to inform their choice of physicians. As physician rating websites attract more users, the number of such websites is expanding as well. Research on several German and English physician rating platforms has shown that despite similarities among the factors constituting ratings across platforms, there is no standardized set of such factors. The lack of a framework explaining how physicians are rated makes it difficult to compare how patients perceive and evaluate their doctor, and how physician ratings are calculated. As a step toward developing such a framework, this study identifies the factors influencing how satisfied patients are with their physician, and therefore how they rate them, assuming positive ratings on rating websites correlate with patient satisfaction. Past medical and healthcare-related research indicates that overall patient satisfaction is influenced by factors directly attributable to the physician, such as the quality of the medical treatment and the doctor-patient relationship, as well as by factors attributable to the administrative aspect of medical treatment services, such as waiting times, accessibility and the physical environment of the physician's office. This research focuses solely on the factors directly associated with the physician. The literature identifies two main determinants of patient satisfaction with the physician: the perceived competence of the physician and the interpersonal relationship between the doctor and the patient. The influence of perceived competence of the physician is a controversial construct among practitioners, who argue that in general most patients are laymen in the field of medical treatment and are not able to accurately assess treatment quality. In other words, this knowledge gap between patient and physician skews perceived competence. The second important determinant of patient satisfaction are interpersonal aspects such as how much the patient likes the physician, which influences the patient's perception of the physician's technical skills. This kind of satisfaction focuses on the short-term evaluation of the physician and does not consider medical treatment outcomes, which is often only possible after much more time has passed and, even then, may not necessarily be directly or solely attributed to the treatment. In this study, patients (n=115) in waiting rooms of five physicians in southern Germany were part of the quantitative data collection how satisfied they are with their physician and, therefore, how they would rate them. The data was evaluated using the partial least square method, and convergent validity, construct reliability and discriminant validity were tested. According to our results, the doctor-patient relationship and perceived competence are major determinants of satisfaction. More importantly, our findings indicate a strong influence of the doctor-patient relationship on perceived competence, supported by high cross-loadings of the two constructs. This finding indicates that patients who like their physician are likely to rate the physician's competence highly. This has important implications for the value of ratings as an information source. Patients may perceive ratings as an indicator of quality medical treatment, but the reviews and ratings on physician rating websites are a stronger indication of empathy, sympathy, amiability and likeability. The data also indicates that patients generally view their physicians positively, which is in line with previous research on physician ratings showing that patients ratings of physician rating websites usually favor their physician. This study fails to collect sufficient data about factors influencing patient dissatisfaction, since the sample had a heavy positive bias. In addition, this study does not measure rating behavior directly, but rather assumes strong correlation between high patient satisfaction and positive physician ratings. Further research will focus directly on the rating behavior on physician rating websites and the influence of treatment outcomes. To challenge the positive bias of patients, specialists should be chosen for the study, who are only visited few times by patients.

KEYWORDS

Doctor-patient relationship; Physician Rating; Perceived Competence

ACM Reference format:
Maximilian Haug, and Heiko Gewald 2018. Are Friendly and Competent the Same? – The Role of the Doctor-Patient Relationship in Physician Ratings In Proceedings of ACM SIGMIS-CPR, June 18–20, 2018, Buffalo-Niagara Falls, NY, USA, ACM, NY, NY, USA, 1 page. https://doi.org/10.1145/3209626.3209734

The Impact of Personality on Users' Specific Privacy Concerns Regarding Personal Health Information

Renée Pratt, PhD
Assistant Professor
Operations and Information Management
University of Massachusetts Amherst
rpratt@isenberg.umass.edu

Donald Wynn, Jr., PhD
Associate Professor
MIS, Operations Management and Decision Sciences
University of Dayton
wynn@udayton.edu

Oscar Lopez
Operations and Information Management
University of Massachusetts Amherst
olopez@umass.edu

ABSTRACT

The increased use of health information technology has made a wide range of personal health information available for practitioners and researchers alike. Notably, as more personal health information becomes available, there is increasing concern for the data's privacy. Personal electronic health information, i.e., digital report(s) of real-time patient-centered information, are a relatively new phenomenon for many of us to confront these days. Prior studies have examined the construct of privacy in-depth including cross-cultural perspective [1], analysis at different levels – organizational, group, and individual [2], literature reviews [3, 2] and more.

Expounding on these areas, research is now beginning to investigate the influence personal characteristics has on privacy. Rather than viewing privacy concerns as a single multidimensional consequence, our study examines the link between personality traits and individual privacy concern dimensions. A widely established proxy for privacy [4], known as the concern for information privacy (CFIP), consists of four components: collection, errors, unauthorized secondary use and improper access.

Unlike previous studies, we treat each of the privacy concern dimensions separately to determine how personality affects each specific concern. For some personality traits, we expect there to be a significant effect across all four dimensions; in others, the effect on some dimensions is expected to be significantly higher than others. In healthcare, the appropriate control of the information is viewed as an obligation of health care professionals from an ethics perspective but also as a function of their expertise, power and professional status [5]. We expect that characteristics such as the dynamic nature of healthcare and the private and intimate essence of patient information will highlight explicable relationships between personality traits and dimensions of privacy.

We have developed a Likert-scale-based survey instrument corresponding to the model, gathered data, and are currently analyzing the dataset using structural equation modeling. We hope that the results of our study (once completed) will be beneficial for subsequent studies as well as for practitioners interfacing with concerned users of health data.

CCS CONCEPTS

• **Security and privacy** → **Human and societal aspects of security and privacy** → Social aspects of security and privacy; • **Social and professional topics** → User characteristics

KEYWORDS

information privacy concerns, big five personality traits, personal health information

ACM Reference format:

R. Pratt, D. Wynn, Jr., and O. Lopez. 2018. The Impact of Personality on Users' Specific Privacy Concerns Regarding Personal Health Information. In *Proceedings of 2018 Computers and People Research Conference, Buffalo-Niagara Falls, NY USA, June 2018 (SIGMIS-CPR'18)*, 1 page. https://doi.org/10.1145/3209626.3209735

REFERENCES

[1] Markos, E., Milne, G. R., & Peltier, J. W. (2017). Information Sensitivity and Willingness to Provide Continua: A Comparative Privacy Study of the United States and Brazil. Journal of Public Policy & Marketing, 36(1), 79-96.
[2] Smith, H. J., Dinev, T., & Xu, H. (2011). Information Privacy Research: An Interdisciplinary Review. MIS Quarterly, 35(4), 989-1016.
[3] Bélanger, F., & Crossler, R. E. (2011). Privacy In The Digital Age: A Review Of Information Privacy Research In Information Systems. MIS Quarterly, 35(4), 1017-1042.
[4] Smith, H. J., Milberg, S. J., & Burke, S. J. (1996). Information Privacy: Measuring Individuals' Concerns About Organizational Practices. MIS Quarterly, 167-196.
[5] Anthony, D. L., & Stablein, T. (2016). Privacy in practice: professional discourse about information control in health care. Journal of Health Organization and Management, 30(2), 207-226.

Usage-Driven Personalized Mobile Banking Application: A Research Prototype

Mohammad Nawaz
University of Massachusetts Lowell
Lowell, Massachusetts, USA
mohammad_nawaz@student.uml.edu

Luvai Motiwalla
University of Massachusetts Lowell
Lowell, Massachusetts, USA
luvai_motiwalla@uml.edu

Amit V. Deokar
University of Massachusetts Lowell
Lowell, Massachusetts, USA
amit_deokar@uml.edu

ABSTRACT

Mobile banking (MB) services offered today by a majority of financial institutions are moving from being a strategic advantage to survival strategy in a highly competitive environment. The ubiquity of smartphones among banking customers to access a wide array of banking services including account balance check, money transfer, and mobile deposit has fueled MB services adoption. Personalization involves customizing the user interface and graphics to each users' need. Research on mobile usage shows that apps with personalization increases customer satisfaction, loyalty, continued usage and provide a higher return on investment for the banks [4]. Similarly, personalization increases perceptions of interactivity, in turn influencing customer trust and continued usage intentions [3]. While personalization features in the form of recommender systems are commonplace in ecommerce applications, personalization in mobile banking is yet in early stages. Personalized MB applications require use of customer profiles, customer preferences, prior usage data of MB service and social media data. This can restrain its' usage as users feel invasion of their privacy [1] creating a conflict in users. This personalization-privacy paradox is prominent phenomenon in mobile usage studies [6].

In this study, we designed a personalized MB application that conducts real-time analysis of user's prior interactions with the system to improve user experience with a personalized user interface (UI) while maintaining user privacy. The study uses design science methodology as the methodological foundation in developing this novel mobile app artifact [2, 5]. The requirements of integrating personalization features and analytics derived from mobile app usage were implemented through an architecture and prototype system that demonstrate the feasibility of the idea. The architecture of PERsonalized user interface in Mobile App (PERMA) system is modeled in terms of client-server architecture where the mobile app in a smart phone connects to a backend server in private cloud over mobile network. A hybrid app working on both iOS and Android platforms was designed with software layering. Design science guidelines are adopted in the

development of PERMA system [2]. Our mobile app is innovative, purposeful artifact for MB domain that yields performance utility for bank users, novel in delivering personalize banking services in a more effective and efficient manner. It utilizes the usage log of the user from database to determine the placement of the functions and information on the screen, predicts the next step of user with data analytics to make the app both purposeful and easy to use.

PERMA utilizes data analytic algorithm to determine recent highest viewed page and association rules to personalize the UI. In our preliminary tests with the best-case scenario, the personalized UI (PUI) user hits the user-desired screen right after sign-in, getting a hit success rate of 100%. In other scenarios, the user hits the desired page (1 out of 5 pages) getting a hit success rate of 20%. On an average, the user directly lands on desired page $(100 + 20)/2 = 60\%$ of time right after sign-in where rest 40% of time user needs an extra click. The static UI (SUI) user has to click twice to land on desired page in all cases. On the other hand, the PUI user has to click once 60% and twice 40% of time. This is a performance improvement for PUI over SUI. To assess the performance of our PUI with more complex use cases, we are conducting empirical studies with a field experiment in different MB task scenarios to test the efficacy of this approach. In sum, this design-science research-in-progress study, shows that personalized UI in a mobile app can enhance user performance significantly.

ACM Reference Format:
Mohammad Nawaz, Luvai Motiwalla, and Amit V. Deokar 2018. Usage-Driven Personalized Mobile Banking Application: A Research Prototype. In Proceedings of ACM SIGMIS-CPR, June 18–20, 2018, Buffalo-Niagara Falls, NY, USA, ACM, NY, NY, USA, 1 page. https://doi.org/10.1145/3209626.3209736

KEYWORDS

Mobile banking; personalized user interface; app behavior analytic; design science

REFERENCES

[1] Dhar, S. and Varshney, U. 2011. Challenges and business models for mobile location-based services and advertising. *Communications of the ACM*. 54, 5 (May 2011), 121–128. DOI:https://doi.org/10.1145/1941487.1941515.

[2] Hevner, A.R. et al. 2004. Design science in information systems research. *MIS Quarterly*. 28, 1 (2004), 75–105.

[3] Lee, T. 2005. The impact of perceptions of interactivity on customer trust and transaction intentions in mobile commerce. *Journal of Electronic Commerce Research*. 6, 3 (2005), 165–180.

[4] Merdenyan, B. et al. 2014. Icon and user interface design for mobile banking applications. *Proceedings of the International Conference on Advances in Computing and Information Technology (ACIT '14)* (2014).

[5] Peffers, K. et al. 2008. A design science research methodology for information systems research. *Journal of Management Information Systems*. 24, 3 (2008), 45–77.

[6] Xu, H. et al. 2011. The personalization privacy paradox: An exploratory study of decision making process for location-aware marketing. *Decision Support Systems*.51,1,(Apr.2011), 42–52. DOI:https://doi.org/10.1016/j.dss.2010.11.017.

Lifecasting a Living: Why did I choose this Technological Career?

Ye Han
Computer Information Systems
Department, Louisiana Tech
University, Ruston, LA, 71272, USA,
yha006@latech.edu

Tom Stafford
Computer Information Systems
Department, Louisiana Tech
University, Ruston, LA, 71272, USA,
stafford@latech.edu

ABSTRACT

Lifecasting is a business model conducted in online social media contexts, wherein site owners produce content that is intended to be interesting and even financially compelling to an audience of like-minded individuals who participate as both viewers and collaborative content producers on the topic of focus. Largely a business model practiced by young Chinese techno-entrepreneurs, Lifecasting demonstrates how interesting topic knowledge combined with entrepreneurial spirt and marketing sensibilities related to the promotion of the online social media of the Internet can turn into promising careers for certain individuals. A similar phenomenon exists in the West, called "live streaming," but while many might be tempted to compare Lifecasting with Western-style streaming, there are key distinctions for Chinese Lifecasters, leveraging the online social medium as a nascent and productive business model.

Lifecasting audience members can send instant messages as well as payments and electronic "gifts" to their favorite Lifecasters, a factor which makes Lifecasting as a career quite compelling to some practitioners because of the revenue production potential.

Any online social media user can be a 'caster, if they are willing to expend the time and effort to conceptualize, create, share, promote and exchange targeted personal information and experiences to interested groups of the Internet public. In this sense, modern Lifecasting represents a form of peer-to-peer (P2P) customized mass communication. As studied here, Lifecasting is a distinctly Chinese phenomenon. It is prevalent enough in China that the government formally tracks and reports on its progress. To that end, researchers interested in the concept as an aspect of emerging models of technological work should consider how likely the model is to prosper and grow in Western countries, specifically in view of its distinctly Eastern character in current use.

CCS CONCEPTS

•**Human Centered Computing** → Field Studies; Social Content Sharing;

KEYWORDS

Social Media; Live Streaming; Lifecasting

ACM Reference format:

Ye Han, and Tom Stafford. 2018. Lifecasting a Living: Why did I Choose this Technological Career? In *Proceedings of 2018 Computers and People Research Conference (SIGMIS-CPR '18)*. ACM, New York, NY, USA, 1 page. https://doi.org/10.1145/3209626.3209737

The Placement Evolution of Information Systems Graduates

Michelle Kaarst-Brown
Syracuse University, NY, USA
Mlbrow03@syr.edu

Indira R. Guzman
Trident University, CA, USA
Indira.guzman@trident.edu

ABSTRACT

Arguments have been made that the Information Systems (IS) workforce is changing and that as old roles disappear, new roles emerge. The idea that IS workers are only found in IS roles has changed to one where it is accepted that IS work may occur both inside and outside IS, and with co-creation by external stakeholders. Our research describes an empirical study of eight years of undergraduate IS placement data. The primary research question presented here is in response to arguments made in the theoretical paper by Neiderman, Ferratt, and Trauth (2016) with a goal to test if IS employment trends are shifting in response to the need for "bridging" workers who understand both IS and the business. Early findings and implications are presented.

CCS CONCEPTS

• **IS Workforce** → Human Factors; • **IS Curriculum** → Placement

KEYWORDS

Information Systems Personnel Placement; Bridger; IS workforce; IS education, Co-evolution

ACM Reference format:

M. L. Kaarst-Brown, and I.R. Guzman. 2018. Understanding the Placement Evolution of IS Graduates. In *Proceedings of ACM Computers and People Research conference, SIGMIS-CPR'18,Buffalo-Niagara Falls, NY, USA, June 18-20, 2018*, 1 page. https://doi.org/10.1145/3209626.3209738

EXTENDED ABSTRACT

It is important for academic institutions, academic administrators, hiring organizations, and graduates to understand the placement trends of graduates from IS related majors. Our research brings data to Niederman et al.'s (2016) theoretical explanation of co-evolution of technology and IS roles. We turned to placement data from an Information School in the North East. While the methodologies for calculating job placement rates vary from agency to agency (Jackson, 2016), in this research we refer to placement as "full-time job" obtained.

The "bridging role" is one of four categories Neiderman et al. propose. Their categorization clusters different IS roles into a classification scheme that addresses key skills and knowledge areas (KSAs) and eras of IT. The four categories are "Technical specialists" who focus on support and operations "domain specialists" who focus on coding and building, "Bridgers" who liaise or bridge between IS and business, and "IS managers" at various levels.

Our findings suggest several implications for IS jobs and for IS curriculum. First, there is early support for the differentiating categories proposed by Neiderman et al (2016). Second, over the eight years, there was an increased trend in graduates from the "moderately technical" undergraduate program to end up in "bridging" roles, such as the "Business Technical Analyst". It is interesting that increased demand for "Bridgers" also seems to be driving earlier job offers (prior to graduation). Another early implication of this study is that it reinforces the need for a diversity of degree programs or specializations with the information systems discipline, rather than being just technical or just managerial. Many iSchools already do this, which may also be why smaller, generic MIS programs in many business schools have died out.

More than a static report of one school's placement data, we see opportunities to track trends, and interpret curricular needs in relation to this co-evaluation of technology and KSAs.

ACKNOWLEDGMENTS

Our thanks to the university graduates and administration who shared their anonymized data with us. We also wish to thank our research assistants Pradeep Raja and Shashank Nadig.

REFERENCES

[1] Jackson, D. (2016). Modelling graduate skill transfer from university to the workplace. *Journal of Education and Work, 29*(2), 199-231.

[2] Niederman, F., Ferratt, T. & Trauth, E. (2016). On the Co-Evolution of Information Technology and Information Systems Personnel, *ACM SIGMIS Database: the DATABASE for Advances in Information Systems, v.47* n.1, February.

Improving Student-Driven Feedback and Engagement in the Classroom: Evaluating the Effectiveness of the Speed Dating Model

Sara Moussawi
Carnegie Mellon University
Information Systems
Pittsburgh, PA USA
smoussaw@andrew.cmu.edu

Jeria Quesenberry
Carnegie Mellon University
Information Systems
Pittsburgh, PA USA
jeriaq@andrew.cmu.edu

Randy Weinberg
Carnegie Mellon University
Information Systems
Pittsburgh, PA USA
randy2@andrew.cmu.edu

Megan Sanders
Colorado School of Mines
Trefny Innovation Instruction Center
Golden, CO USA
sanders@mines.edu

Marsha Lovett
Carnegie Mellon University
Eberly Center for Teaching Excellence
and Educational Innovation
Pittsburgh, PA USA
lovett@andrew.cmu.edu

Larry Heimann
Carnegie Mellon University
Information Systems
Pittsburgh, PA USA
lheimann@andrew.cmu.edu

Raja Sooriamurthi
Carnegie Mellon University
Information Systems
Pittsburgh, PA USA
sraja@andrew.cmu.edu

Don Taylor
Carnegie Mellon University
Information Systems
Pittsburgh, PA USA
dontaylor@cmu.edu

ABSTRACT

Information Systems (IS) pedagogy research supports the use of collaborative learning strategies that are based on the belief that learning increases when students work together to solve problems and develop cooperative learning skills. The use of innovative active learning approaches instead of lecture-based approaches have helped to engage student learning and build a broader range of skills and experiences (e.g., [1, 2]).

In this project, we present an empirical comparison of two active learning classroom approaches – the speed dating method and a traditional presentation format. The speed dating method supports low-cost rapid comparison of project ideas, design, application and progress in a structured and bounded series of serial engagements. In contrast, traditional student presentations allow individuals to provide content but offer somewhat limited interactions. We analyzed data from 174 student surveys and in-class researcher observations of student engagement in an undergraduate senior capstone course entitled, *Innovation in Information Systems*. The course is centered on studio-based learning as assignments are primarily project-based, students' work is periodically evaluated through critiques, and students continuously engage in critiquing peers' work [3]. The course utilized an alternating series of speed dating and presentation session formats.

Our analysis resulted in three main findings. First, students reported receiving and giving much more helpful feedback during the speed dating sessions than in the presentation sessions. Second, students reported being significantly more engaged during the speed dating sessions than in the presentation sessions Finally, classroom observations of engagement showed that students were significantly more engaged in the speed dating session as compared to the presentation session [4]. We believe these findings demonstrate that the speed dating method is a more effective alternative to a presentation format and is a useful complement to other collaborative learning methodologies.

ACM Reference Format:
S. Moussawi, J. Quesenberry, R. Weinberg, M. Sanders, M. Lovett, L. Heimann, R. Sooriamurthi, and D. Taylor. 2018. Improving Student-Driven Feedback and Engagement in the Classroom: Evaluating the Effectiveness of the Speed Dating Model. In Proceedings of ACM SIGMIS-CPR, June 18–20, 2018, Buffalo-Niagara Falls, NY, USA, ACM, NY, NY, USA, 1 page. https://doi.org/10.1145/3209626.3209739

REFERENCES

[1] Gan., B. Joshi, K.D., Lending, D., Outlay, C., Quesenberry, J., and Weinberg, R. (2014). "Active Learning Approaches in IT Pedagogy." *Proceedings of the 2014 ACM SIGMIS Conference on Computers and People Research,* ACM Press: New York, NY USA, 113-117.

[2] Potter, L.E., Lending, D. and Kaarst-Brown, M.L. (2015). "Panel: Preparing the Next Generation of Computer Personnel." *Proceedings of the 2015 ACM SIGMIS Conference on Computers and People Research* ACM Press: New York, NY, USA, 133-134.

[3] Carter, A. S., and Hundhausen, C. D. (2011). "A Review of Studio-based Learning in Computer Science." *Journal of Computing Sciences in Colleges,* 27(1), 105-111.

[4] Smith, M.K., Jones, F. H. M., Gilbert, S. L., and Wieman, C. E. (2013). "The Classroom Observation Protocol for Undergraduate STEM (COPUS): A New Instrument to Characterize University STEM Classroom Practices." *CBE Life Sciences Education,* 12(4), 618-627.

Online Advertising Research through the Ad Delivery Process: A Literature Review

Lea Müller
University of Bamberg
An der Weberei 5,
96047 Bamberg
Germany
lea.mueller@uni-bamberg.de

Jens Mattke
University of Bamberg
An der Weberei 5,
96047 Bamberg
Germany
jens.mattke@uni-bamberg.de

Christian Maier
University of Bamberg
An der Weberei 5,
96047 Bamberg
Germany
christian.maier@uni-bamberg.de

Abstract

Online advertising and the whole industry enabling and delivering online advertisements through the ad delivery process become more and more economically important, as it enables several Internet-based services and provides firms with the possibility to globally reach a broad range of consumers. The ad delivery process is concerned with the trade of ad spaces in the Internet and the placement of the right ad at the right time. To this end, it involves three major actors or perspectives: the advertiser, who places the ad, the publisher, who sells ad spaces to display the ad and the consumer, who interacts with the ad in the form of clicks or downloads. This consumer interaction is exactly what advertisers are paying for [1]. Hence, without consumers' interaction, in other words the consumers' acceptance and usage of online advertising, the whole ad delivery process collapses. Right now, the online advertising industry is facing precisely this issue of leaking user acceptance, causing severe challenges arising from each of the three perspectives: The majority of Internet users is unwilling to receive online advertising, as it is perceived as irrelevant and intrusive [3, 5]. This leads to the ignorance of ads [2]. However, publishers generate their biggest revenues with the consumer's interaction with ads, i.e. clicks, and downloads. Due to less consumer interaction, click-through rates (CTR) are dropping steadily and persistently. Furthermore, the effectiveness of online advertising is debatable, since consumers are less interested in online advertising [1, 2]. Therefore, advertisers question the amounts of money invested in online advertising and think about

ACM Reference Format:

Lea Müller, Jens Mattke, and Christian Maier. 2018. Online Advertising Research through the Ad Delivery Process: A Literature Review. In Proceedings of ACM SIGMIS-CPR, June 18–20, 2018, Buffalo-Niagara Falls, NY, USA, 1 page.
https://doi.org/10.1145/3209626.3209740

a potential redirection of those resources [1]. If those challenges remain unresolved, it could risk existing ad-dependent Internet-based business models and service infrastructures [2]. Now that we understand that there are several challenges jeopardizing the online ad delivery process and its related industry, we need to understand why and how those challenges arise. Therefore, we need to ground on a holistic view on online advertising research, involving marketing and especially IS research, as consumers' behavior towards online and offline advertising divers massively [4]. We conduct an ad delivery process guided literature review on the base of 46 papers, gathered from the most important IS and Marketing journals and conferences, following the framework after vom Brocke [6]. Using this literature review, future research might give more attention to online advertising research and especially to the challenges, the online advertising industry is exposed to.

References

[1] Yakov Bart, Andrew T. Stephen, and Miklos Sarvary. 2014. Which products are best suited to mobile advertising? A field study of mobile display advertising effects on consumer attitudes and intentions. *Journal of Marketing Research* 51, 3,

[2] Hyunsook Kweon, Dongsong Zhang, and Lina Zhou. 2012. User Privacy in Mobile Advertising. *AMCIS 2012 Proceedings.*

[3] Lea Müller, Jens Mattke, Christian Maier, and Tim Weitzel. 2017. The Curse of Mobile Marketing: A Mixed Methods Study on Individuals' Switch to Mobile Ad Blockers. *ICIS 2017 Proceedings.*

[4] Venkatesh Shankar, Amy K. Smith, and Arvind Rangaswamy. 2003. Customer satisfaction and loyalty in online and offline environments. *International Journal of Research in Marketing* 20.2

[5] Juliana Sutanto, Elia Palme, Chuan-Hoo Tan, and Chee W. Phang. 2013. Addressing the Personaliza-tion - Privacy Paradox: An Empirical Assessment from a Field Experiment on Smartphone Users. *MIS Quarterly* 37, 4,

[6] Jan vom Brocke and others. 2009. Reconstructing the giant: On the importance of rigour in documenting the literature search process. *ECIS 2009 Proceedings.*

The Individual Narrative of IS Project Success

Saifur Rahman Bhuiyan
Walton College of Business
University of Arkansas
Fayetteville, AR 72701
SBhuiyan@walton.uark.edu

Pankaj Setia
Walton College of Business
University of Arkansas
Fayetteville, AR 72701
PSetia@walton.uark.edu

ABSTRACT

"A satisfied IT staff can be an indispensable asset for any corporation, but keeping IT folks happy isn't about lofty titles or hefty raises. Two-thirds of IT professionals stay in their jobs because they are actively engaged with their colleagues, supported fairly by their managers and rewarded by opportunities to learn and grow within their varied roles" [3]. Previous research has studied organizational attributes such as governance, knowledge, and individual attributes mainly focused on project leadership that can affect performance. This study makes an effort to shift the focus to IS professionals who are at the core of IS projects and explores how IS professional's individual narrative of IS project success develops.

Researchers have expressed objective and subjective views on how to assess IS project performance. The objective approach depends on the assumption that the success or the failure of IS projects are based on factors that are objective [4]. For instance, previous research suggests quality, time, cost, use, product performance, process performance, and user satisfaction to assess performance [4, 14, 17, 18]. The narrative approach, on the other hand, views the success and failure of IS projects as a sense-making process which is represented by "narratives, interpretations, and discourses by different stakeholders" who are part of the projects [4]. Narratives are individual stories. Psychologists argue that human prefers to remember events in life as a story [16]. Sarbin argues that "narratives are not just ways of seeing the world; we actively construct the world through narratives, and we also live through the stories told by others and by ourselves – they have ontological status" [12]. Narrative of IS professionals are important because IS professionals are at the front and center of delivering IS Success. It is important to focus on the IS project member's perspective of success because it brings to fore a very different set of factors that are important to the individual and not necessarily written on either the job description or the requirements document provided to a project

SIGMIS-CPR '18, June 18–20, 2018, Buffalo-Niagara Falls, NY, USA
© 2018 Copyright held by the owner/author(s).
ACM ISBN 978-1-4503-5768-5/18/06.
https://doi.org/10.1145/3209626.3209630

team. Hence, assessing the success of the project as a narrative of the IS professionals provides a much richer understanding of the success of the project.

Narratives are also important because engagement is part of the narrative. There is a widespread problem of disengagement among US workers. A recent study by the Gallup among millions of US workers revealed that even with the improvement in recent years only 31.5% workers are engaged in their work and workplace [1]. The same study also notes that employees who do not hold management positions or those who are younger were found to be less engaged; a fact that should prompt researchers to study engagement among individual employees who are not in leadership roles. There is no literature to show that the IS professionals who are not in leadership positions are any different.

Even though narrative research of IS project performance have been limited, the existing literature provides interesting findings. Narrative approach is based on the assumption that the success or failure is not universal across various stakeholders in an IS project. Research shows that there are indeed well-documented differences between perceived and real success of IS projects pointed out by CIOs [13]. Other studies taking the narrative approach [2, 6, 19] also show that narratives of success and failure continually change at various stages of the project due to the influence of various stakeholders. However, the literature is limited on how the individual narrative of IS project performance develops and on specifics about how organizations may benefit from the individual narratives. We address this gap in the literature. In addition to studying the development of individual narrative, we also look at how the narrative can potentially impact individual well-being of the IS professional.

To understand how the individual narrative of IS success develops among IS professionals, we use the theoretical lens of attribution. Attribution theory is the study of the process by which people associate causes to events or outcomes they experience in life [8, 10]. It is important to study the attribution of cause because that helps us understand why people in an organization may get involved in productive or unproductive behaviours [11]. Specifically, we use attribution lens to see how IS professional's justice perception propels (deters) IS professional's engagement and how the narrative of success (failure) develops in a process of causal attribution. We examine this process by assessing individual IS professional's perception of justice, his or her level of engagement in the project and the organization and the individual perception of the project performance. Attribution of causes to entities by an individual is not an objective process and usually biased by the perception and circumstances which is why the attribution is an appropriate lens to study IS professional's narrative. We look at two important biases that are crucial to our understanding of the individual narrative of success.

The review of the project management literature reveals that most indicators of project performance are often divided in two aspects: process and product performance [7, 14]. Hence, based on these two aspects of performance, we define IS professional's perception project performance of an IT project as perception of the individual about the ability of the project team to utilize its organizational and project resources to deliver the desired IT artifact that satisfies the need of the client while remaining within the cost and time constraints. We define IS professional's perception of justice as the degree of fairness perceived by an IS professional in the personal treatment, the information, and the outcome received and how the outcome is determined during the tenure of his or her project and is drawn from Colquitt [5] who demonstrated that justice or the notion of fairness has four dimensions – distributive, procedural, interpersonal, and informational justice. IS professional's engagement is referred to how much an IS professional devotes his or her abilities to the IT project and the organization where he or she belongs. IS professional's project engagement is drawn from the concept of job engagement which refers to the employee's engagement to his or her work role [15]. Organization engagement refers to an IS professional's engagement to his or her organization as a member of the organization [15]. We define IS professional's well-being as the increase in job satisfaction and a decrease in the feeling of work exhaustion.

To study the development of IS professional's performance narrative, we surveyed seventy-nine IS professionals from various industries and locations both inside and outside of the USA. The survey included established measures from the information systems, project management, attribution, engagement, and the organizational justice literature. Each IS professional was requested to refer to an IT project s/he recently completed. The findings of our study from surveying various types of IS professionals corroborates our theory that IS professional's perception of justice and engagement play important role in forming the individual IS project performance narrative. The findings also include that the IS professional's individual narrative has a significant potential downstream effect on the individual well-being of the IS professional. These findings highlight the importance individual narrative in the context of IS projects. The current study is expected to make contribution to IT project management, social exchange and engagement literature. The primary contribution of our study to the IS project management literature is the examination of the development of IS individual narrative of project success. The study shows that the individual IS project success narrative is a cumulative product of justice perception, engagement, and perception of project performance and the relationships among these three constructs develop in a process of causal attribution that is driven by the perception of

individual IS professional. By utilizing the attribution theory to explain the complex social exchange of reciprocative behaviour in the context of IT projects this study highlights the social nature of IS projects.

KEYWORDS

Project Management, Narrative, Project Performance, Engagement, Justice, Attribution, Well-being, Job Satisfaction, Work Exhaustion

ACM Reference Format:
Saifur Rahman Bhuiyan, and Pankaj Setia. 2018. The Individual Narrative of IS Project Success. In Proceedings of ACM SIGMIS-CPR, June 18–20, 2018, Buffalo-Niagara Falls, NY, USA, ACM, NY, NY, USA, 2 pages. https://doi.org/10.1145/3209626.3209630

REFERENCES

[1] Adkins, A. 2015. "Majority of U.S. Employees Not Engaged Despite Gains in 2014," *Gallup* (available online at http://www.eeandra.com/wp-content/uploads/2016/04/Gallup-Article.pdf).

[2] Bartis, E., and Mitev, N. 2008. "A Multiple Narrative Approach to Information System Failure: A Successful System that Failed," European Journal of Information Systems (17), pp. 112-124.

[3] Bigelow, S. J. 2012. "Employment survey says IT job satisfaction is all about the work," *TechTarget* (available online at http://searchdatacenter.techtarget.com/feature/Employment-survey-says-IT-job-satisfaction-is-all-about-the-work).

[4] Cecez-Kecmanovic, D., Kautz, K., and Abrahall, R. 2014. "Reframing Success and Failure of Information Systems: A Performative Perspective," *MIS Quarterly* (38:2), pp. 561-588.

[5] Colquitt, J. A. 2001. "On the Dimensionality of Organizational Justice: A Construct Validation of a Measure," *Journal of Applied Psychology* (86:3), pp. 386-400.

[6] Fincham, R. 2002. "Narratives of Success and Failure in Systems Development," *British Journal of Management* 13(1), pp. 1-14.

[7] Gopal, A., and Gosain, S. 2009. "The Role of Organizational Controls and Boundary Spanning in Software Development Outsourcing," *Information Systems Research* (21:4), pp. 1-23.

[8] Jones, E. E., and Davis, K. E. 1965. From acts to dispositions the attribution process In person perception1. In *Advances in experimental social psychology* (2), pp. 219-266. Academic Press.

[9] Jones, S., and Hughes, J. 2001. "Understanding IS Evaluation as a Complex Social Process: A Case Study of a UK Local Authority," European Journal of Information Systems (10), pp.189-203.

[10] Kelley, H. H. (1973). The processes of causal attribution. *American psychologist*, 28(2), pp. 107.

[11] Luthans, F. and Church, A. H. 2002. "Positive organizational behavior: Developing and managing psychological strengths," *The Academy of Management Executive* (16:1), pp. 57-75.

[12] Murray, M. (2003). "Narrative psychology," Qualitative psychology: A practical guide to research methods, 111-131.

[13] Neves, F. G., Borgman, H., and Heier, H. (2016, January). Success Lies in the Eye of the Beholder: The Mismatch Between Perceived and Real IT Project Management Performance. In *System Sciences (HICSS), 2016 49th Hawaii International Conference on IEEE*, (pp. 5878-5887).

[14] Nidumolu, S. 1995. "The effect of coordination and uncertainty on software project performance: Residual performance risk as an intervening variable," *Information Systems Research* (6:3), pp. 191-219.

[15] Saks, A. M. 2006. "Antecedents and consequences of employee engagement," *Journal of Managerial Psychology* (21:7), pp. 600-619.

[16] Sarbin, T. (ed.) (1986) Narrative Psychology: *The Storied Nature of Human Conduct.* New York: Praeger.

[17] Subiyakto, A., Ahlan, A. R., Kartiwi, M., and Sukmana, H. T. 2015. "Measurement of information system project success based on perceptions of the internal stakeholders," *International Journal of Electrical and Computer Engineering* (5:2), pp. 271-279.

[18] Tiwana, A. 2009. "Governance-Knowledge Fit in Systems Development Projects," *Information Systems Research* (20:2), pp. 180-197.

[19] Wilson, M., and Howcroft, D. 2005. "Power, Politics and Persuasion in IS Evaluation: A Focus on 'Relevant Social Groups'," The Journal of Strategic Information Systems (14:1), pp. 17-43.

IT Enabled Frugal Innovation

Extended Abstract

Prem Bhushan Khanal
Victoria University of Wellington
Wellington, New Zealand
prem.khanal@vuw.ac.nz

CCS CONCEPTS

• **Social and professional topics** → **Socio-technical systems**;

KEYWORDS

Frugal Innovation, Effectuation, Digital Effectuation, IT Affordances

ACM Reference Format:
Prem Bhushan Khanal. 2018. IT Enabled Frugal Innovation: Extended Abstract. In *SIGMIS-CPR '18: 2018 Computers and People Research Conference, June 18–20, 2018, Buffalo-Niagara Falls, NY, USA*. ACM, New York, NY, USA, 2 pages. https://doi.org/10.1145/3209626.3209631

1 MOTIVATION AND RESEARCH PROBLEM

People living under $10 a day (Purchasing Power Parity) in Africa, Asia and the South Pacific represent 71% of world population [3]. This section of population, referred as Base of the Pyramid (BoP) could be served profitably by good enough products and services that are affordable and socially responsible [8]. Prolonged economic recession has forced lower and middle income customers in the West to look for good enough products and services which provide high value for money [5]. The innovation focus is shifting to product, service, process, or system that is affordable, sustainable, good-enough, and rooted in locality. It is often referred as frugal innovation [9]. There is a worldwide need for frugal R&D approaches to create more value from less resources for more people.

The entrepreneurial journey of frugal innovators provides an insight into the innovation process itself. Effectuation sketches theoretical representation of entrepreneurial journey. Entrepreneurs using effectuation (effectuators) extend scarce resources with their identity, knowledge, and immediate contacts; are flexible to switch new goals to go around institutional voids; do experiments to innovate; and develop partnerships to minimize uncertainty and risks [10]. Hence, it seems logical to study frugal innovation through the lens of effectuation.

The practices and behaviors of entrepreneurs are influenced by ubiquitously present digital technologies. IT extends the intellectual capabilities of innovators, creating endless opportunities of innovation [4] . IT plays an enabling role in the entire value chain of frugal innovation. Entrepreneurs using effectuation under extreme resource constraints can leverage the potential of IT to conceptualize and bring to market frugal innovation products and services.

This research attempts to investigate the Research Question (RQ): 'How do IT affordances enable frugal innovation?' Effectuation helps answer this question because a) effectuation differentiates innovation in frugal context, from innovation in affluent ones and b) effectuation describes key characteristics enabling the identification of specific ways IT can influence the innovation process. The research question could be further divided into two sub-questions: (Sub) RQ 1: How do IT affordances affect each effectuation dimension in the frugal innovation endeavors? (Sub) RQ2: How does each effectuation dimension contribute to frugal innovation outcomes?

2 LITERATURE REVIEW

Increasing reach and range, very low marginal costs, and high customizability of information technology (IT) opens up innumerable opportunities for frugal innovation. Frugal innovation is related to IT in two ways. The first stream explores the frugal ways of development and deployment of information systems (be it the entire information infrastructure of an enterprise or be it just the software development process). This approach is seen in the works of Watson, Kunene, & Islam [11]. Information system that utilizes minimal resources to achieve transcendent goals and is driven by ubiquity, uniqueness, unison, and universality is a frugal information system [11]. The second stream acknowledges the catalytic role of IT in frugal innovation value chain. The second approach is seen in the works of Ahuja & Chan [1] in which they map principles of frugal innovation with IT capabilities and propose frugal IT capabilities for social, technical and business innovation. In another explorative research absorptive capacity theory has been used to examine IT enabled frugal innovation [2] . These papers primarily focus on the organizational IT capabilities that enable frugal innovation. But what if the enterprise is still in formation and the innovation is still in its ideation (or earlier) phase? This research examines how IT enables the entrepreneurial journey of a frugal innovator. This, in turn, will help understanding the enabling role of IT in frugal innovation endeavor from ideation to disposal.

The entrepreneurial journey of frugal innovator could be explained by the theory of effectuation. Effectuation is intuitive, driven by identity and relies on informal relationships [10]. The effectual actions can be influenced by IT which in turn influence frugal innovation outcome. Proposed theory of digital effectuation explains how IT affordances influence actions and decisions of entrepreneurs using effectuation (effectuators) in frugal innovation endeavors [6]. Effectuators use their identity, knowledge, and immediate contacts as means on hand. The identity is extended by digital persona systems, which create a digital identity of effectuators, which in turn may help acquiring support and investment. The knowledge is extended by digital knowledge repositories and

Table 1: Methodological fit in field research

Research item	Proposed research design - phase 1	Proposed research design - phase 2
Research Questions	How do IT affordances affect each effectuation dimension in the frugal innovation endeavors?	How does each effectuation dimension contribute to frugal innovation outcomes?
Unit of Analysis	Frugal innovation endeavor in an entrepreneurial venture	Frugal innovation endeavor in an entrepreneurial venture
Type of data collected	Qualitative (Case Study)	Quantitative (Survey)
Illustrative methods for collecting data	Interviews, observations, documents and text analysis (media sources)	Survey instruments (questionnaire)
Constructs and measures	Constructs of IT affordances, effectual dimensions	Constructs of IT affordances, effectual dimensions, and frugal innovation outcome
Goal of data analysis	Develop a process model, which highlights the mechanisms tying digital effectuation to frugal innovation outcomes	Validate the refined model of digital effectuation in frugal innovation endeavor
Data analysis method	Inductive theory building	Partial least square method
Theoretical contribution	Provisional theory of digital effectuation that integrates previously separate bodies of work on IT affordances, Effectuation and Frugal Innovation	Validation of theory of digital effectuation and digital effectuation as antecedent of frugal innovation outcome

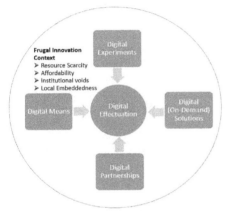

Figure 1: Digital Effectuation

learning opportunities. Digital connection with people (social media) and objects (IoT) extend the reach of effectuators. Usage of frugal information systems; on demand solutions on cloud; and free open source technologies help keeping tabs on losses. Virtual experiments using simulation and modelling not only provide frugal ways of evaluating the contingent effects but also provide flexibility to evaluate and choose among the contingent aspirations. Digital platforms and crowd funding help getting pre-commitments from partners. Also digital platforms, social media and crowd sourcing help creating strategic alliances with partners. The conceptual model of digital effectuation is shown in figure 1.

3 METHODOLOGY

Effectuation theory can be considered as a theory of intermediate maturity [7]. The reason is, a conceptual clarity has been established on the theoretical domain of effectuation and empirical research projects are sprouting. But the research on IT affordances and frugal innovation both are at the nascent stage as a conceptual clarity is yet to be developed in the domain and empirical research is scarce. Following the recommended 'hybrid' data collection for intermediate theories, I propose a two-phase research approach that progresses from a qualitative study to build/refine the theory of digital effectuation in frugal innovation endeavors to a quantitative survey that validates the theory. Methodological choices are shown in Table 1.

4 CONTRIBUTION

This research intends to make a number of contributions to both theory and practice. First, it extends the theory of effectuation to acknowledge the role of IT in frugal innovation endeavors and proposes a novel concept of digital effectuation. Second, it explains the antecedents of frugal innovation inherent in effectual actions. Third, it contributes to the frugal innovation literature by examining the influence of IT affordances on frugal innovation process and outcomes. For practice, entrepreneurs may refer to this research to formulate digital strategies while making business decisions. Lastly, frugal digital effectuation viewpoint helps understanding the actions and decisions of new generation tech-savvy entrepreneurs and prosumers who not only care about value for money but also care about value for many.

REFERENCES

[1] Suchit Ahuja and Yolande E. Chan. 2014. Beyond Traditional IT-enabled Innovation: Exploring Frugal IT Capabilities. In *Twentieth Americas Conference on Information Systems*.
[2] Suchit Ahuja and Yolande E. Chan. 2014. The Enabling Role of IT in Frugal Innovation. In *Thirty Fifth International Conference on Information Systems*. 1–20.
[3] Pew Research Center. 2015. World Population by Income: How Many Live on How Much, and Where. (2015). http://www.pewglobal.org/interactives/global-population-by-income/
[4] Manlio Del Giudice and Detmar Straub. 2011. IT and Entrepreneurism: An On-Again, Off-Again Love Affair or a Marriage? *MIS Quarterly* 35, 4 (2011), III–VII.
[5] Vijay Govindarajan and Chris Trimble. 2012. Reverse Innovation: a Global Growth Strategy That Could Pre-empt Disruption at Home. *Strategy & Leadership* 40, 5 (2012), 5–11.
[6] Prem Bhushan Khanal, Jean-Grégoire Bernard, and Benoit A. Aubert. 2017. IT Enabled Frugal Effectuation. In *ACM SIGMIS Computers and People Research Conference*. 71–78.
[7] John T. Perry, Gaylen N. Chandler, and Gergana Markova. 2012. Entrepreneurial Effectuation: A Review and Suggestions for Future Research. *Entrepreneurship: Theory and Practice* 36, 4 (2012), 837–861.
[8] C. K. Prahalad and Stuart L Hart. 2002. The Fortune at the Bottom of the Pyramid. *Strategy+Business Magazine* 26 (2002), 1–16.
[9] Navi Radjou and Jaideep Prabhu. 2015. *Frugal Innovation: How to do more with less.* The Economist.
[10] Saras D Sarasvathy. 2001. Causation and Effectuation: Toward a Theoretical Shift from Economic Inevitability to Entrepreneurial Contingency. *Academy of Management Review* 26, 2 (2001), 243–263.
[11] Richard T. Watson, K. Niki Kunene, and M. Sirajul Islam. 2012. Frugal information systems (IS). *Information Technology for Development* 19, 2 (2012), 1–12.

Social Media and Public Discourse: A Technology Affordance Perspective on Use of Social Media Features

Proposal for Doctoral Consortium

Sunil Reddy Kunduru
Indian Institute of Management Bangalore
Bangalore, India
sunil.kunduru14@iimb.ac.in

ABSTRACT

In this paper we present the proposal for a research study that aims at explaining the consequences of social media use on mass media content and public discourse. Social media is defined as a set of networked communication platforms that enable generation, distribution and consumption of user generated content. Technology features of the social media platforms are at the center of our analysis. The use of social media features is conceptualized using technology affordance theory. Borrowing from mass communication literature, we argue that media content is produced as a result of a dialectical relationship between media discourse and public opinion. The consequences of social media use on public discourse are conceptualized in terms of the changes in the dialectics between media discourse and public opinion resulting from the use of social media. Two types of public discourses are identified. We develop theory from extant literature to arrive at proposition on consequences of use of specific social media features on the media content and public discourse. Propositions are presented both for the general public discourse case and the context of particular type of discourses. We conclude this proposal by discussing the potential contributions of our study.

CCS CONCEPTS

• **Information systems** → Multimedia content creation;

KEYWORDS

Social media, affordances, mass media, user generated content, public discourse

ACM Reference Format:
Sunil Reddy Kunduru. 2018. Social Media and Public Discourse: A Technology Affordance Perspective on Use of Social Media Features: Proposal for Doctoral Consortium. In *SIGMIS-CPR '18: 2018 Computers and People Research Conference, June 18–20, 2018, Buffalo-Niagara Falls, NY, USA*. ACM, New York, NY, USA, 9 pages. https://doi.org/10.1145/3209626.3209627

1 INTRODUCTION

Mass media has been undergoing progressive digitization with penetration of the Internet and proliferation of software applications that support computer-mediated mass communication. As traditional media is moving to digital platforms, we also see the emergence of the new media, popularly referred to as social media. Social media is spearheading the emergence of new forms of public discourse [24] leading to new forms of organization of collective action [27, 28, 35]. It is of interest to both practitioners and academicians to study the effects of this digitization on technology mediated public discourse. We present a proposal to study how technology features of social media are shaping the content in mass media and the nature of public discourse.

Social media is an umbrella term used to refer to a broad range of Internet based networked communication platforms that are characterized by user generated content [7]. Social media is essentially an IT artifact and thus constitutes subject matter for Information Systems research. IS researchers have studied how social media is impacting the public discourse in different contexts. Various theories from IS and other disciplines were used to explain the impact of social media on collective efforts to shape public discourse and collective action.

Oh et al. used rumor theory to study how social media is used to share information during social crises [27]. Oh et al. used text mining concepts of milling and keynoting to show how individuals used social media strategically to communicate for mobilizing collective action during Egypt revolution of 2011 [28]. Vaast et al. used the concept of connective affordances to explain the role played by Twitter in emergent organization of public discourse around an issue of collective interest [35]. Miranda et al. used concepts such as frames and interpretive packages from mass communication theory to compare the effects of underlying technology on the nature and structure of content produced in public discourse [24]. We build on the work done by Miranda et al. and Vaast et al. by using concepts of mass communication theory and technology affordances theory to study how social media is changing the nature of media content and public discourse.

Public discourse is a way of making sense of public affairs [13]. Mass media is one of the many forums on which public discourse takes place. Media discourse is forged by professional journalists who draw opinions and facts from multiple forums. The task of the journalists is to organize media discourse in such a way that it helps normal citizens to make sense of the world around an issue. According to Gamson and Modigliani media discourse is organized as a set of interpretive packages [13]. Interpretive packages consist of catalogs of symbolic devices organized to constitute and enhance frames. Frames are used to organize the world around an issue by enabling causal analysis, consequences and moral evaluation.

Since public discourse takes place in multiple forums, there are multiple interpretive packages in the media discourse. Each interpretive package gives a unique meaning to world around the issue. For journalists to be relevant, their interpretive packages should be able to convey the meaning to a considerable size of audience. An interpretive package is said to have gained prominence if a very large segment of audience accepts its frames. Therefore, media content manifests as multiple interpretive packages competing to gain prominence in the media discourse.

The competition between interpretive packages leads to a dialectical relationship between media discourse and public opinion [13]. While the audience relies on the journalists account to make sense of the world around an issue, the journalists have to understand how an issue should be framed to gain and sustain prominence for their interpretive package in the discourse. The content produced in the media is the result of this dialectal relationship between media discourse public opinion.

Social media has the potential to change this dialectical relationship. Various features offered by social media sites enable generation, distribution and consumption of user generated content. User generated content can help journalists gauge public opinion better. At the same time journalists have to compete with user generated content in their efforts to gain and sustain prominence of their interpretive packages. User generated content gives consumers more alternatives to traditional media packages for understanding the world around an issue. Technology features that support building and maintenance of networks give individuals necessary resources for organizing public discourse on their own. For example, YouTube supports many independent websites that provide news coverage. As a result of these changes, the boundary between media discourse and public opinion becomes progressively narrow. This changes the nature of the dialectical process that produces media content. Thus social media has the potential to shape public discourse by changing the process through which media content is generated, distributed and consumed. In this research work we investigate into how use of social media technology features changes the nature of media content and public discourse. We aim to answer the following research question:

RQ: How does use of social media technology features for content generation, distribution and consumption change the nature of media content and public discourse?

The rest of the proposal is organized as follows. In section 2 we explain our approach to conceptualizing the social media artifact by clarifying on the paradigmatic assumptions and definition of social media. We also explain the reason for choice of technology affordance as the theoretical lens. In section 3 we explain how the dialectics between media discourse and public opinion unfold and develop propositions on how use of social media technology features for content generation and consumption, changes the nature of this dialectical relationship. In section 4 we present the design of our research study and in the final section we summarize the proposal and discuss implications of our work.

2 CONCEPTUALIZING THE ARTIFACT

We begin with delineating the definition and scope of the concept of social media and clarifying the paradigmatic assumptions underlying the conceptualization of the social media artifact. We present a brief review of the extant literature to support our choice of definition and research paradigm. We end this section with a discussion on the choice of technology affordances as the lens to operationalize the concepts of use and consequences of social media.

2.1 Definition and Scope of Social Media

Within the IS literature, there is an ongoing debate on which concept best represents the definition and scope of social media. In their seminal paper, Ellison et al. used the concept *social network sites* to describe websites such as MySpace, Facebook, etc [6]. These websites are presented as a segment of social media that allow users to articulate and make visible their social networks. Later, Ellison and Boyd revised the definition of social network sites to reflect the rapid changes that took place in the technology features of the sites [7]. Social network sites are now defined as networked communication platforms that allow generation, distribution and consumption of user generated content.

One of the primary alternative to the concept of social network site is put forth by Kane et al. [18]. The paper used the concept *social media networks* to emphasize the connectedness of the sites rather than the functionality of individual sites. Since we are interested in the patterns of use of individual sites and the consequences of use, the concept of social network sites as defined by Ellison and Boyd is more appropriate for our study. The user interacts directly with a specific site. The nature of use is dictated more by the features of the individual site rather than the whole network. Further, the network has different properties when viewed from different social network sites. For example, social distance between a user and a family member can be different depending on whether we view the network form the LinkedIn profile of the user or the Facebook profile of the user.

Following Ellison and Boyd we conceptualize social media as an ensemble of social network sites, which have the following features: each site is a networked communication platform connected to other such platforms; users have uniquely identifiable profiles that are built jointly by the user along with other users; the network of the user is publicly visible and can be traversed; and, importantly, the user can use the site to generate, distribute and consume streams of user-generated content that flows through the network.

We conceptualize the technology use at the level of feature set to incorporate the possibility of variation in use in practice [5]. According to this conceptualization, users interpret the social media artifact as a bundle of features. The goals and capabilities of use determine which bundle of features the user takes into account in a given social media site [23].

Ellison and Boyd argued that use of social network sites is driven by the desire to generate and share content. Such use is fostered by communication-oriented features that lower the barriers to generation and distribution of content. We classify communication-oriented features into two categories: network-oriented features (NOFs) and content-oriented features (COFs). COFs provide capabilities for effective generation of content. NOFs provide capabilities for efficient flow of content across connected user in a given site and across connected sites. Social media is thus the set of networked communication platforms with technology features that users find helpful in generation, distribution and consumption of user generated content.

2.2 Social Media Use and Consequences

In this subsection we present a brief review of the a portion of current literature on use and consequences of social media. The reviewed articles are accessed through the EBSCO SocIndex database by running a search using 'social media' in the 'subject terms' criteria for search. We present the analysis for articles published in MIS Quarterly and Information Systems Research journals only. These two journals accounted for close to half the papers published in IS Senior Scholars' Basket of Eight journals. The papers are reviewed to identify the technology features under study and the level of analysis of their use and consequences.

Table 1 gives the features analyzed in the research articles and the level of analysis of use and consequences in those articles. Out of a total of 40 papers, 18 papers conceptualized the social media artifact in terms of specific features. We separated the features studied into network-oriented features and content-oriented features. Adopting from Leonardi [21], we classified the studies into three levels of analysis of use: individual, group and organization. The original IS success model theorized impact of IS use at two levels: individual and organizational [4]. We chose community and society levels to represent aggregate level consequences in the non-organizational contexts. We used these levels of analysis for classification of consequences.

We can see from Table 1 that significant portion of this set of articles study the consequences of use at the society/community level of analysis. We position our study in this body of literature. When studying use and aggregate level consequences in the non-organizational context, the goals and capabilities of the users are heterogeneous and vary with time. Further, Table 1 also shows that social media has been conceptualized in terms of a wide range of technology features. Given the variety in the bundle of technology features and heterogeneity in goals and capabilities of the user, there is a lot of scope for unanticipated use and consequences [23]. To incorporate the possibility of unanticipated use and consequences, we need a non-essentialist research paradigm to study social media use in public discourse and its consequences. In the next subsection, we clarify our ontological and epistemological assumption about social media use and consequences.

2.3 Research Paradigm

IS researchers have been articulating the need for non-essentialist conceptualization of technology for over two decades [29]. Different research paradigms were used to conceptualize technology as not having essential properties. The proponents of sociomateriality have presented a critique of the humanist and the social constructivist approaches to non-essentialist conceptualization of technology. The humanist approach to technology has been criticized for its neglect of the material aspects of the phenomena [29]. Since our primary focus is on the material aspects of social media, the humanist approach is not suitable for our study. The social

constructivist view, has been criticized for its inability to account for performativity of the technology or the material agency in the human-technology interaction [17]. Sociomateriality overcomes the problems by the considering the social and material aspects as being inextricably related. We will briefly present the paradigmatic assumptions underlying sociomateriality and explain how we intend to adopt them in our study.

Wanda Orlikowski is often credited for adoption of sociomateriality in Organization research and Information Systems research [3, 10, 16]. The central arguments of and for sociomateriality are made in three research papers: Orlikowski [29], Orlikowski and Scott [31] and Orlikowski [30]. These papers point to the limitations in the insights acquired from Organization studies because of the neglect of the role material objects and spaces in organizing. The central premise in sociomateriality is that the material aspects of the organization are inextricably related to the social aspects of organization. The social aspects of the organization, such as identity, culture, etc. are the main subject matter of Organization studies. By ignoring the material aspects that are inextricably related with the social aspects, Organization researchers have developed a handicap in explaining technology driven processes, practices and structural changes. Studies that consider the role of technology conceptualize it as being independent of social aspects of organizing, irrespective of whether they assume one directional relation between the material and social aspects or a mutual dependence between them. Through various examples, the proponents of sociomateriality argue that neither of these studies reflect the empirical reality (e.g. [29], [31]. They argue that the social and material aspects exist in a state of constitutive entanglement. They call for the ontological assumption of constitutive entanglement to be adopted for making the concepts represent empirical reality more closely.

Critics argued that sociomateriality does not offer anything new [16]. Jones disagrees with the criticism, arguing that although there is nothing new about almost any principle of sociomateriality, it is the sum of all the principles that makes sociomateriality a useful research tool. Clarifying further, Jones identified five notions that are common in sociomateriality studies. The five notions and the problems with their definitions as pointed out by Jones are as follows:

Materiality. The notion of materiality calls of attention to the material aspects of organizing while not giving to primacy to either the social or material aspects. Jones finds that, within sociomateriality literature, the scope of materiality has been too wide, ranging from the tangible objects and objects to intangible entities such as algorithms.

Inseparability. The notion of inseparability states that materiality constitutes everyday life and that the social and material are inextricably related. This is an ontological assumption that stands in contrast to both unidirectional causality and mutual interaction between the material and social. However, Jones points out that there has been variation in sociomateriality literature with regards to adoption of inseparability. While some position them are inextricably related, others tend towards conceptualizing social and material as mutually interacting.

Table 1: Social media features conceptualized in IS research articles and the level of analysis in those articles

Paper	Content Oriented Feature	Network Oriented Feature	Level of analysis - Use	Level of analysis - Consequence
Oestreicher-Singer and Sundararajan, 2012	None	Networked recommendations on books e-retail	Individual/Group	Organizational
Zeng and Wei, 2013	Upload of photos on Flickr	None	Individual	Organizational
Oestreicher-Singer and Zalmanson, 2013	Community features	Social features	Organizational	Individual
Wu, 2013	None	Social networking tool	Organizational	Individual
Goh et al, 2013	UGC versus MGC	None	Individual	Individual
Dou et al, 2013	Community management	None	Organizational	Organizational
Oh et al, 2013	None	Collective reporting on Twitter	Individual	Society
Clausen et al, 2013	Limits on notifications to users of Facebook apps	None	Organization	Organizational
Dewan and Ramprasad, 2014	Content creation on blogs	None	Individual	Organizational
Beck et al, 2014	None	Interaction transparency	Individual	Organizational
Butler et al, 2014	Message tracking	Member tracking	Individual	Community
Levina and Ariagga, 2014	Reputation mechanism	None	Individual	Community
Du et al, 2014	Multi-tiered content management	None	Organization	Organizational
Kallinikos and Tempini, 2014	Computational abilities	Networking abilities	Individual	Community
Leonardi, 2014	None	Communication visibility	Group	Organizational
Oh et al, 2015	Hashtag as protest grammar	Hashtags as attention anchor	Individual	Society
Lowry et al, 2016	None	Anonymity	Individual	Society
Miranda et al, 2016	Information richness of content	Source and citation network	Individual	Society

Relationality. The notion of relationality points out at the explicit adoption of relational ontology in sociomateriality studies. According to relational ontology, the inherent properties of humans and technology are not important [20]. Only those properties that appear when humans interact with the technology are relevant. Jones points out that sociomateriality literature varies in its identification of what kind properties emerge out of the relationship. Another debate that is common in studies adopting relational ontology is with regard to the symmetry in the relationship and the question of giving primacy to humans or technology. Sociomateriality literature differs in this as well.

Performativity. The notion of performativity refers to the ontological position that relations and boundaries between technologies and humans are enacted in practice [31]. Some others defined performativity as the ability of the non-human entities to exert their agency by putting controls on what humans can and cannot do [20]. Jones points out that this notion is not unique to sociomateriality and it has been adopted in actor network theory and gender studies.

Practice. The notion of practice refers to the need to look at everyday practices to understand organization rather than looking at discourses and cognition. Jones points out that this notion is also not unique to sociomateriality but it can be used to understand how performativity is enacted.

We argue that notions of inseparability, relationality and performativity form the ontological positions of sociomateriality and the notions of materiality and practice form its epistemological position. Thus according to sociomateriality, social and material aspects are inextricably related and they exist in a state of constitutive entanglement. There are no inherent properties of either the material technology or the social beings that use it. All the properties arise only when the human and technology interact. Finally, the relations between the technology and the user are neither given a priori nor fixed. They are rather enacted in practice. Therefore, to study any aspect of organization, one needs to look into the practices associated with the phenomenon with focus on the material aspects of organizing.

Jones pointed out at the inconsistencies in the articulation of these ontological and epistemological assumptions in the IS literature that claims to use sociomateriality. He classified extant literature into two categories with each using a different level of sociomateriality. Research studies are said to use strong sociomateriality if they used all the five notions of sociomateriality in their conceptual development. Other studies that used a subset of the notions are said to use weak sociomateriality. Since we intend to adopt sociomateriality, it is important that we clarify how we are using the notions of sociomateriality. We adopt technology affordances theory as our theoretical lens for the study. In the next subsection we present our arguments for our choice of theoretical lens and discuss the five notions of sociomateriality for the case of use afforded by social media.

2.4 Theoretical Lens

Based on the discussion in this section, we see that IS researchers have identified three characteristics of social media. Firstly, social media constitutes a wide range of web sites that provide network organization and content organization capabilities to varying degree. Secondly, the technology features vary from site to site and different features have different consequence of use. Finally, the use of social media and its consequences happen at different levels of analysis. In this subsection, we will argue that given these characteristics, technology affordance theory provides a suitable theoretical lens for our study and clarify our ontological and epistemological positions.

Faraj and Azad defined technology affordances as action potentials that arise from an actor's interaction with a technology [10]. The concept affordance originated in ecological psychology in the works of J J Gibson. Gibson argued that perceptions and not cognition plays a crucial role in an individual interaction with its environment [14]. The properties of the environment are perceived by the individual through the sensory processing. Norman adapted this concept to the context of interaction between a technology and its user [26]. According to Norman, technology is designed in such a way that certain possibilities of action are easily perceivable by the user when the user interacts with it. These possibilities of action are called technology affordances. When the perceived action is enacted, it is said that the affordance is actualized. Affordances need not be anticipated by the designer nor the affordances as expressed by the designer may ever be actualized.

Technology affordances by definition subscribe to relational ontology because they arise as a result of the interaction between the technology and the user but are not inherent properties of either. Studies by Leonardi, Volkoff and Strong and Vaast et al. have explicitly mentioned taking relational ontology in their studies for conceptualizing technology affordances [20, 35, 37].

Relational ontology reflects the empirical reality of social media because it is a technological artifact with wide range of bundles of technology features. Many IS studies have used affordances to study use and consequence of social media (e.g. [22], [35]). Vaast et al. explicitly stated their adoption of relational ontology and used it to explain how connective affordance are actualized in practice.

IS research that uses technology affordances lens has tended towards considering mutuality of the social and material thus positioning itself away from the notion of inseparability. For example, Leonardi considered flexible technologies and flexible routines as two separate entities that can potentially have mutual interaction [20]. Similarly, Volkoff and Strong separated the real and actual domains clarifying that affordances can be conceptualized only if we do not assume inseparability [37]. In the real domain a material artifact can have any number of affordances. The actual domain differs from one actor to the other depending on other factors that lead to actualization of affordances. In this study also we consider the social and material as mutually interacting and not in constitutive entanglement.

According to the notion of performativity, the relations and boundaries between the social and material are enacted in practice [31]. Performativity reflects the empirical reality of the fluidity in the social and material aspects of social media. For example, the number of followers a social media handle has is a social concept: social capital [36]. At the same time, the number of followers a handle affords or constrains social influence of the posts made through the hand thus making it a material aspect in the discourse [15]. Similarly, posting a political opinion on social media is a social act. However, once it is posted the content triggers response from others thus exerting the materiality of the posted content [35]. Technology affordance theory can enable deeper exploration of performativity of social media.

The notion of materiality is inherent in our conceptualization as the technology is the primary focus of our conceptualization. In order to adhere to the notion of practice, we look into use of social media features in generating, distribution and consumption of user generated content. Recent literature using affordances to study social media use have studied patterns of feature use observable from the content [24, 35].

Thus, barring the notion of inseparability, we adhere to all the other four notions of sociomateriality while using technology affordances theory to study use and consequences of social media in the context of public discourse.

3 MASS MEDIA EFFECTS

It is now accepted that social media is being used to generate, distribute and consume large amounts of user generated content that shapes public discourse. In this section, we will present concepts that have been used to study the relationships between media discourse and public opinion. Using these concepts we develop propositions that will help answer our research questions on use and consequences of social media in the context of public discourse.

Discourse is defined as "a way of signifying experience from a particular perspective" [9, p. 138]. There are various forms of signifying such as oral or written texts, photographs and movies. Public discourse is a way of making sense of public affairs and takes place on many forums [13]. The various forums for discourse includes the *specialist forum*: discourse aimed at professionals with expertise in the issue, *official forum*: discourse that provides the perspective of the decision makers and the lobbyist interested in the issue and the *challenger forum*: discourse that challenges the status quo and seeks to mobilize collective action on the issue. On the issue of adopting nuclear energy, there is a specialist discourse on the viability of and risk involved in using nuclear energy. At the same time, there is an official discourse that emphasizes on the risk or the benefits depending on the priorities of the power elite. Finally, there is a challenger discourse that attempts to counter the official discourse.

Mass media is one of the forums for public discourse where professional journalists draw opinions and facts from any/all of the above discourse forums and forge the discourse as print or electronic content [13]. Media discourse dominates the culture around any issue of public interest. Culture can be understood as the ensemble of symbols, stories, rituals and world views that help make sense of public affairs [33]. The public opinion on any issue is shaped by the issue culture.

The role of journalists is to produce content that helps shape issue cultures and to make the content readily accessible for the audience. The audience actively uses media content to construct meaning of the world around the issue. Therefore, media discourse shapes issue cultures through professionally crafted content that is easily accessible to the audience. At the same time, media content is also shaped by the issue culture because its content is drawn from various forums hosting discourse on the issue. Media discourse can thus be viewed as having a dialectical relationship with public opinion. The content of media discourse is thus a product of a dialectical process.

3.1 Interpretive Packages and Structure of Media Content

The content of media discourse is structured as a set of interpretive packages, each of which represents a discourse on the issue. An interpretive package has an internal structure with a frame at its core. A frame organizes the world around the issue by use of various reasoning and frame enhancing devices. Reasoning devices present the claims for causal analysis, consequences and moral evaluation of an issue. Frame enhancing devices help present the ideas in shorthand using symbolic devices such as metaphors, exemplars, catchphrases, depictions and visual images [12].

According to Gamson and Modigliani, within a media discourse, multiple interpretive packages compete for prominence [13]. Each interpretive package must not only able to give meaning to an issue, it also should be able to incorporate new events into its frames to be viable in the long term. Three determinants combine to determine the viability of an interpretive package. They are cultural resonance, sponsor activity and media practices.

Cultural resonance occurs when the underlying cultural themes of a society match with the symbols, stories, narratives and world views depicted in the interpretive package. Frames with cultural resonance are familiar and easily accessible to the audience. Interpretive packages gain prominence through resonance between their frames and the issue cultures. Media content tends to reflect the cultural themes dominant in the society.

Sponsor activity involves generating ready-to-use content to promote an interpretive package. Organizations that sponsor a package maintain a symbiotic relationship with media organizations. Sponsor organizations provide content in the form of interviews with

journalists, open articles, advertisements etc. In return, media organizations give primacy to the content that promotes the sponsors' packages. The packages with stronger sponsorship tend to gain prominence.

Media practices refer to the ways in which the journalists assert their agency in content production process. According to Gamson and Modigliani empirical studies show that journalists give primacy to interpretive packages that support official discourse. Also, media content is shaped by the balance norm. The balance norm makes it preferable to use the frames of competing packages while reporting. In practice, balanced reporting is reduced presenting the package sponsored by the primary political opposition along with the official discourse package. The packages that are presented by sponsors outside the political establishment are not given enough legitimacy in the traditional media.

3.2 Social Media and Public Discourse

In this subsection, we theorize how social media changes the nature of dialectics between media discourse and public opinion. We focus attention of the three determinants of prominence of interpretive packages. For each of the determinants, we start with the set of users, their goals and capabilities with respect to the determinant. Based on the goal and capabilities, we formulate propositions with regards to the technology features that are necessary to make social media afford the users the realization of their goals.

3.2.1 Cultural Resonance. Journalists need cultural resonance in their frames. For creating frames which resonate with the culture of the audience, the journalists should understand the cultural themes related to the issue and also know symbols and narratives that make the frame familiar to the audience. Social media provides journalists access to abundance amount of user generated content that gives first hand knowledge of the symbols and narratives that the audience are familiar with. However, the abundance of content can make it difficult to build a coherent understanding of the issue culture. Journalists need tools to organize the content in a manageable way. Efficient search and filter features, such as hashtags, may help the journalists realize their goal.

Proposition 1: Social media sites with efficient search and filter features afford knowledge of issue cultures to journalists.

Content may assert its performativity when journalists are looking for issue cultures on the social media. If the issue cultures expressed on the social media vary significantly from the issue cultures expressed through an interpretive package, journalists may have to build the package again to ensure cultural resonance. Thus social media content may constrain journalistsâĂŹ agency in choosing and developing the interpretive packages.

Proposition 2: Social media content has the potential to constrain journalists' agency in developing the interpretive package of their choice.

3.2.2 Sponsor Activities. Sponsors can use social media as an alternative channel to promote their interpretive packages. In the traditional media setup, sponsors maintain a direct symbiotic relationship with the journalists. In the case of social media, they can use indirect methods that aim at creating issue cultures that support their interpretive package. Issues cultures are created in the social media through generation of messages that have potential to be distributed widely within a short period of time. The term used for such instantaneous ubiquity of the message is *virality*.

Marketing literature on new product diffusion through word-of-mouth marketing has examined how designing viral features can speed up the diffusion through peer influence and social contagion [2]. We argue that sponsors will use social media features to create messages with content that can make them go viral. For this to happen, the social media site should have features that enable creative crafting of messages using frame enhancing tools such as images, memes and videos.

Proposition 3: Social media sites with image and video posting features afford creation of message with viral content.

The ability to frame messages with viral features in a message can be developed with relatively less resources. Therefore, even individual actors can develop capabilities to be sponsors. This is in contrast to the traditional mass media where it is usually the organizations that take up sponsor activities. If the technology does allow individuals to act as sponsors, then social media can help ameliorate the lack of balance in reporting because of media practices. However, the performativity of the network constrains individuals from taking up sponsor activities on social media.

Literature on new product diffusion has found that opinion leaders aid in creating rapid diffusion of information in social networks [15]. Opinion leaders are those who have high centrality in their social networks. Thus to be able to influence issue cultures, one has to have high centrality in the network or have access to individuals with high centrality in the network. The #metoo movement owes its popularity significantly to the offline status of its proponents as movie stars. This offline star status translates into more number of online followers/friends thus giving their handles greater centrality in the online social networks.

Proposition 4a: Higher status of an individual in the offline world translates into higher centrality of the individual in the online social networks.

Proposition 4b: Social media sites with efficient message diffusion features afford sponsor activities to individuals with high centrality in the online social networks.

3.2.3 Media Practices. Social media and traditional media differ significantly in terms of the practices which lead to content generation, distribution and consumption. Traditional media practices give primacy to interpretive packages supporting the official discourse [13]. Interpretive packages on social media gain primacy because of the support they receive from the online community. Secondly, while the balance norm actively influences choice of frames in the traditional media content, balance happens in a more organic way in the social media. Miranda et al. has shown that when we take individual messages, then the balance of frames is greater in the traditional media than in the social media [24]. We argue that in social media, balance of frames happens at an aggregate level. Individual users post or share content that is in congruence with their attitude. Such messages are not crafted to have ideas from multiple frames. However, since posting and sharing is open to all users, at an aggregated level, consumers are exposed to multiple frames, thus ensuring balance. Even in the traditional media, balance norm is

observed at an aggregate level for syndicated columns and cartoons [13].

Proposition 5: Social media sites with open content posting and sharing features afford aggregate level balance in interpretive packages for consumers.

Content on social media undergoes multiple types of curation before it reaches the consumer [34]. One type of curation is algorithmic curation done by recommendation systems. These systems organize the content in such a way that the content that is more likely to be viewed by the viewer is pushed up in the recommended lists. The likelihood of views is determined by the consumption patterns of the individual and the history of consumption of other users who have similar pattern of consumption. Therefore, the recommendation system asserts its performativity by constraining the consumer from being exposed to balance of frames. If a consumer does not manage her online social network in such a way as to connect with people with different political beliefs, then she is more likely to consume content that does not have balance in frames.

Proposition 6: Social media with recommendation features constrains balance in interpretive packages to those consumers whose social networks are homogeneous in terms of political affiliations.

3.3 Types of Discourse and Social Media Content

In the previous subsection we used the concept of interpretive packages to understand how social media changes discourse practices in general. But discourses themselves are varied. We delineate two types of discourses: contested discourse and corrective discourse. In this subsection we will theorize on how social media affords participation in public discourse for normal citizens in the context of these two types of discourse.

We define normal citizens as the social media users who do not enjoy any enhanced offline status. We thus rule our political elite, artists/sportsmen who have attained stardom and any other person who has received widespread recognition for their work. Vaast et al. identified three emergent roles in a public discourse of social media: advocates, supporters and amplifiers. Normal citizens can potentially take up the roles of supporters or amplifiers.

3.3.1 Expression of Dissent: A Case of Contested Discourse. In a contested public discourse, there are at least two prominent frames that are mature. That is they have cultural resonance, sponsors and media support. A section of media is actively debating on these issues and frames from different perspectives are being actively promoted. Examples of contested discourses are debates on legislative bills, governance issues, demands of social movement organizations, etc.

In democratic political systems, mass media is given the responsibility to lead in open, free and balanced public discourse on government activities. Mass communication research has shown that the political elite have control over the discourse on the mass media [11]. Thus there are restriction on expression of dissent in traditional media. Social media is expected to overcome restrictions. Miranda et al. compared the ability of social media to emancipate public discourse from elite control. We build on this work by looking at the specific ways in which certain social media features afford normal citizens expression of dissent. As discussed above, normal citizens can take up the emergent roles of supporters or amplifiers. In their role as amplifiers, they can enhance the frames promoted by the opposition parties by using the metavoicing features. In their role as supporters, they may make innovative use of editing features to create signatures that enhance the messages. They may come up with innovative catchphrases, visual depictions to enhance the frames. In addition, they may also find ways to overcome performativity of recommendation systems in promoting attitude. This can be done through using searching and filtering tools in innovative ways to expose individuals to messages with multiple frames. The following propositions give a formal statement of our arguments.

Proposition 7a: Metavoicing features in social media sites afford enhancement of opposition frames for dissenting citizens.

Proposition 7b: Content editing features on social media sites afford innovative use of signatures to contest official frames for dissenting citizens.

Proposition 7c: Search and filter features on social media sites afford strategic use of attention anchors to counter attitude congruence of government sympathizers.

3.3.2 Fighting Media-promoted Prejudice: A Case of Corrective Discourse.
Corrective discourses are the discourses on issues that have not fully emerged yet but can potentially have adverse consequences. The corrective discourses usually take place in one forum and there is not more than one mature interpretive package. The objective of such discourse is to start a media discourse on the topic. The discourse on global warming prior to the 1972 Stockholm Conference is an example of corrective discourse. The discourse primarily took place in specialist forum, with occasional articles in the media discourse. The central theme of the Conference was to bring the discourse into the mainstream media by promoting official discourse on global warming. Note that today global warming discourse is a contested discourse [25]. A corrective discourse may eventually turn into a contested discourse.

One of the major categories of corrective discourses is the discourse against media promoted prejudices. In an attempt to frame an issue for the audience, journalists tend to simply the world by giving salience to certain aspects of reality [8]. In the process of to giving salience to certain aspects, they promote certain prejudices and stereotypes. Frame enhancing tools such as metaphors, catchphrases and visual depictions are especially prone to misinterpretations and thus promoting prejudice and stereotypes. Ana has shown how the metaphors used in anti-immigration discourse dehumanized immigrant workers in California. Klin and Lemish analyzed two decades of research on role of mass media in reducing stigma attached to mental illness. They found that mass media perpetuated misconceptions and stigma attached to mental illness.

Social media has the potential to counter the role of traditional media in creating and promoting prejudices. For example, #stigmawatch is being promoted by an Australia based organization with Twitter handle SANEAustralia. The handle urges the users to report, using the hashtag, media messages that stigmatize mental illness.

We argue that social media enables organization of discourse on the prejudices promoted by media. Vaast et al. showed how social media enabled organization of discourse around Gulf of Mexico oil leak in 2010. These organizations can mature into sponsors

to the interpretive packages that frame the media reporting as an issue. Features of virality in social media sites can help get widespread attention to the issue of prejudice and the need to counter the prejudices promoted by the mainstream media. Social media also helps overcome the fear of stigmatization as a result of participation in collective action against prejudices. Research has found that when an individual participates in a march or protest against prejudices, they become the targets of stigmatization [32]. Individuals avoid participating in these collective action efforts because of the fear of being stigmatized. Anonymity features on social media sites can help individuals overcome the fear of stigma and participate in the discourse on such social media sites. The following propositions give our arguments in a formal way.

Proposition 8a: Content editing and sharing features of social media sites afford organization of discourse against prejudices promoted by traditional media.

Proposition 8b: Social media sites with efficient information flow features afford attracting attention of large number of people to the prejudices promoted by media.

Proposition 8c: Anonymity features of social media sites afford safety from stigma attached to participating in discourse against prejudices.

4 RESEARCH DESIGN

As stated in Section 2, notions of materiality and practice describe our epistemological position. Social media site features and the pattern of their use in generation, distribution and consumption of user generated content are the are of particular interest in our study. We propose to take a multiple case study approach to this research study. Following the work done by Miranda et al. and Vaast et al. we will pick issue of interest public discourse as cases for our study of Propositions 1 through 6. Since we are looking at two types of discourses, we need two cases for studying Propositions 7 and 8.

For analysis, we will consider content from both traditional media and social media. Interpretive methods will necessary to understand the frames that are used to report on the focal issue. This will be followed by quantitative content analysis for establishing relationships between pattern of social media feature use and difference in the nature of the content traditional and social media.

5 SUMMARY AND CONTRIBUTION

Our study is motivated by the changing nature of media discourse because of emergence of social media, an IT artifact. We started our proposal by delineating the definition of social media for this study. Using extant literature on social media use and consequence we presented arguments in favor of choosing sociomateriality as the research paradigm and technology affordances as the theoretical lens for our study.

The arguments presented till here are applicable to social media use and consequence in general and not in particular for the case of public discourse. Therefore our arguments contribute to IS theory in many ways. First, we extended the definition of social media given by Ellison and Boyd to account for the presence of two types of features social media sites: network-oriented features and content-oriented features. Secondly, combined the debate on notions of sociomateriality and the conceptualization of social media affordances to clarify how affordance fits into the sociomateriality literature. This builds on the works of Jones and Faraj and Azad. Finally, in our propositions we deliberately included technology features, user goals and user capabilities to be true to the definition of affords as action potentials when these three aspects come together. We expect that such theorizing will help operationalization of affordances in a unique way. After building a general framework for studying social media, we moved on to the specific use of social media, in public discourse. Borrowing concepts from mass communication literature, we presented media discourse as having a dialectical relationship with public opinion. We then developed propositions on how social media features afford changes in the nature of the dialectics and hence public discourse. Further, we identified two types of public discourses based on the presence or absence of competing interpretive packages in the discourse. For each type of discourse, we presented propositions on how social media technology features will effect the public discourse on the issue.

Our propositions adds to the emerging literature on role social media in political participation in general and public discourse in particular. Since we have drawn significantly from Miranda et al. and Vaast et al., we are hopeful that we will contribute to conversations presented in these papers. Specifically, our propositions on balance of frames (Propositions 5 and 6) contradict the findings in Miranda et al.. Our disagreement with Miranda et al. stems from our conceptualization of balance at aggregate level in contrast to looking for balance of frames in individual messages. Secondly, our theory on role of social media in corrective discourse scenario builds on the concepts of emergent roles as theorized by Vaast et al. by applying it to the context of specific type of discourse. Thus our study has potential to make contribution to IS theory on social media in general and to theory on social media and public discourse in particular.

REFERENCES

[1] Otto Santa Ana. 1999. Like an animal I was treated': Anti-immigrant metaphor in US public discourse. *Discourse & society* 10, 2 (1999), 191–224.
[2] Sinan Aral and Dylan Walker. 2011. Creating social contagion through viral product design: A randomized trial of peer influence in networks. *Management science* 57, 9 (2011), 1623–1639.
[3] Dubravka Cecez-Kecmanovic, Robert D Galliers, Ola Henfridsson, Sue Newell, and Richard Vidgen. 2014. The sociomateriality of information systems: current status, future directions. *Mis Quarterly* 38, 3 (2014), 809–830.
[4] William H DeLone and Ephraim R McLean. 1992. Information systems success: The quest for the dependent variable. *Information systems research* 3, 1 (1992), 60–95.
[5] Gerardine DeSanctis and Marshall Scott Poole. 1994. Capturing the complexity in advanced technology use: Adaptive structuration theory. *Organization science* 5, 2 (1994), 121–147.
[6] Nicole B Ellison et al. 2007. Social network sites: Definition, history, and scholarship. *Journal of computer-mediated Communication* 13, 1 (2007), 210–230.
[7] Nicole B Ellison and Danah M Boyd. 2013. Sociality through social network sites. In *The Oxford handbook of internet studies*.
[8] Robert M Entman. 1993. Framing: Toward clarification of a fractured paradigm. *Journal of communication* 43, 4 (1993), 51–58.
[9] Norman Fairclough. 1993. Critical discourse analysis and the marketization of public discourse: The universities. *Discourse & Society* 4, 2 (1993), 133–168.
[10] Samer Faraj and Bijan Azad. 2012. The materiality of technology: An affordance perspective. *Materiality and organizing: Social interaction in a technological world* (2012), 237–258.
[11] William A Gamson, David Croteau, William Hoynes, and Theodore Sasson. 1992. Media images and the social construction of reality. *Annual review of sociology* 18, 1 (1992), 373–393.
[12] William A Gamson and Kathryn E Lasch. 1981. The political culture of social welfare policy. (1981).
[13] William A Gamson and Andre Modigliani. 1989. Media discourse and public opinion on nuclear power: A constructionist approach. *American journal of sociology* 95, 1 (1989), 1–37.
[14] JJ Gibson. 1979. The theory of affordances The Ecological Approach to Visual Perception (pp. 127-143). (1979).
[15] Raghuram Iyengar, Christophe Van den Bulte, and Thomas W Valente. 2011. Opinion leadership and social contagion in new product diffusion. *Marketing Science* 30, 2 (2011), 195–212.
[16] Matthew Jones. 2014. A Matter of Life and Death: Exploring Conceptualizations of Sociomateriality in the Context of Critical Care. *Mis Quarterly* 38, 3 (2014).
[17] Matthew R Jones and Helena Karsten. 2008. Giddens's structuration theory and information systems research. *MIS quarterly* 32, 1 (2008), 127–157.
[18] Gerald Kane, Maryam Alavi, Giuseppe Labianca, and Steve Borgatti. 2014. WhatâĂŹs different about social media networks? A framework and research agenda. *MIS quarterly* (2014), 275–304.
[19] Anat Klin and Dafna Lemish. 2008. Mental disorders stigma in the media: Review of studies on production, content, and influences. *Journal of health communication* 13, 5 (2008), 434–449.
[20] Paul M Leonardi. 2011. When flexible routines meet flexible technologies: Affordance, constraint, and the imbrication of human and material agencies. *MIS quarterly* (2011), 147–167.
[21] Paul M Leonardi. 2013. When does technology use enable network change in organizations? A comparative study of feature use and shared affordances. *MIS quarterly* (2013), 749–775.
[22] Ann Majchrzak, Samer Faraj, Gerald C Kane, and Bijan Azad. 2013. The contradictory influence of social media affordances on online communal knowledge sharing. *Journal of Computer-Mediated Communication* 19, 1 (2013), 38–55.
[23] M Lynne Markus and Mark S Silver. 2008. A foundation for the study of IT effects: A new look at DeSanctis and Poole's concepts of structural features and spirit. *Journal of the Association for Information systems* 9, 10/11 (2008), 609.
[24] Shaila M Miranda, Amber Young, and Emre Yetgin. 2016. Are social media emancipatory or hegemonic? Societal effects of mass media digitization. *MIS Quarterly* 40, 2 (2016), 303–329.
[25] Matthew C Nisbet. 2009. Communicating climate change: Why frames matter for public engagement. *Environment: Science and policy for sustainable development* 51, 2 (2009), 12–23.
[26] Donald A Norman. 1999. Affordance, conventions, and design. *interactions* 6, 3 (1999), 38–43.
[27] Onook Oh, Manish Agrawal, and H Raghav Rao. 2013. Community intelligence and social media services: A rumor theoretic analysis of tweets during social crises. *Mis Quarterly* 37, 2 (2013).
[28] Onook Oh, Chanyoung Eom, and H Raghav Rao. 2015. Research noteâĂŤRole of social Media in Social Change: An analysis of collective sense making during the 2011 Egypt revolution. *Information Systems Research* 26, 1 (2015), 210–223.
[29] Wanda J Orlikowski. 2007. Sociomaterial practices: Exploring technology at work. *Organization studies* 28, 9 (2007), 1435–1448.
[30] Wanda J Orlikowski. 2010. The sociomateriality of organisational life: considering technology in management research. *Cambridge journal of economics* 34, 1 (2010), 125–141.
[31] Wanda J Orlikowski and Susan V Scott. 2008. 10 sociomateriality: challenging the separation of technology, work and organization. *Academy of Management Annals* 2, 1 (2008), 433–474.
[32] Fay Cobb Payton and Lynette Kvasny. 2016. Online HIV awareness and technology affordance benefits for black female collegiansâĂŤmaybe not: the case of stigma. *Journal of the American Medical Informatics Association* 23, 6 (2016), 1121–1126.
[33] Ann Swidler. 1986. Culture in action: Symbols and strategies. *American sociological review* (1986), 273–286.
[34] Kjerstin Thorson and Chris Wells. 2016. Curated flows: A framework for mapping media exposure in the digital age. *Communication Theory* 26, 3 (2016), 309–328.
[35] Emmanuelle Vaast, Hani Safadi, Liette Lapointe, and Bogdan Negoita. 2017. Social media affordances for conective action: An examination of microblogging use during the Gulf of Mexico oil spill. *MIS Quarterly* 41, 4 (2017).
[36] Sebastián Valenzuela, Namsu Park, and Kerk F Kee. 2009. Is there social capital in a social network site?: Facebook use and college students' life satisfaction, trust, and participation. *Journal of computer-mediated communication* 14, 4 (2009), 875–901.
[37] Olga Volkoff and Diane M Strong. 2013. Critical Realism and Affordances: Theorizing IT-associated Organizational Change Processes. *Mis Quarterly* 37, 3 (2013).

Attention-based View of Online Information Dissemination

Ruochen Liao
State University of New York at Buffalo
rliao2@buffalo.edu

ACM Reference format:

Ruochen Liao. Attention-based View of Online Information Dissemination. In the Proceedings of *SIGMIS-CPR'18: 2018 Computers and People Research Conference, Buffalo-Niagara Falls, NY, USA,* 4 pages. https://doi.org/10.1145/3209626.3209703

1 INTRODUCTION

This is an early stage proposal for my dissertation essays. I have recently completed the course requirements of the Ph.D. program and preparing to embark on my dissertation research projects. I have recently submitted my first year paper and second year paper to journals for review. The first paper is on the topic of credibility of online consumer reviews, and the second paper is on the topic of user satisfaction on knowledge sharing communities. And I have collaborated with several other coauthors on one paper currently under the second round of review at JAIS, and another submission to the special issue on immersive systems at JMIS. Among these various topics, one particular salient factor emerges – the attention of the individual users. On e-commerce websites, online communities and forums, and collaborative or competitive networks (e.g. ERP systems and open-source software development platforms), users often face enormous amount of information that far exceed the information processing capacity of human beings. Although most literature acknowledge that users selectively process certain information, and the information they choose to process ultimately influence their decision (e.g. make a purchase online, read a post on the forum, and get involved in a discussion or a task), the actual effect of directed attention in this process has remain largely implicit. In this proposal, I lay out some of my early ideas about integrating the attention structure literature [e.g. 1] into the decision-making process of individual users in these contextual backgrounds. We propose that psychological states, cognitive feedbacks and personality traits together influence how individuals allocate their time and attention. In the following sections, I will briefly introduce the themes of the studies.

2 PAYING ATTENTION TO THE OPPOSITE? NEGATIVITY BIAS IN ONLINE CONSUMER REVIEW

With the advent in e-commerce, online consumers face enormous information asymmetry problem, as they cannot physically assess the product prior to purchase and often transact with a large group of unfamiliar e-commerce sellers [2-4]. Online consumer reviews (OCRs) have become an increasingly important source of information in the decision-making process of online buyers, as they are supposedly to be provided by other buyers as unbiased third parties. There has been a substantial body of literature in IS on the effect of product reviews [e.g., 5, 6-17]. Surveys indicate that almost 90% of online buyers consider opinions provided through feedback systems before making purchase decisions [18]. One of the most intriguing phenomena is the negativity bias: that is, online consumer reviews of a negative nature seem to have a greater effect on the psychological state and decision-making process of potential buyers than those of positive ones [19, 20]. There have been contradictory findings in the literature, for example, Li and Hitt [21] found that negative bias in early product reviews could affect long term sales. Sen and Lerman [22] found that product type (utilitarian vs. hedonic) affects how consumers perceive negative reviews. While Wu [19] argued that negativity bias is not present when controlling for review quality and base valance.

I posit to address these contradictory finding through the lens of attention-based view to explain how consumers choose to focus their attention on certain reviews and weigh them accordingly in the decision-making process. Consumers' attentional capabilities are limited compared to the huge volume of online OCRs, even some simple products on Amazon.com could have thousands of reviews. The consumers' behavior is both a structured decision, with some fixed expectations and established notions at the beginning, and an evolving cognitive process, with each new piece of information molding and shaping decision-making process of the consumer towards this product/purchase. The aim of this study is to explicitly model the interaction of these structured and evolving factors with consumers' attention, to find out how positive and negative reviews influence the decision. We based the analysis on three interrelated sub-dimensions:

1. The effect of the reviews on consumers' decision depends on what the consumers focus on.

2. The type of reviews that consumers focus their attention on depends on the particular cognitive feedback they receive in the decision making process.

3. How do consumers respond to the consonance or dissonance in the cognitive feedback depends on what they focus on, and the interaction with their personality traits in addressing problems.

The first sub-dimension refers to the structured part of the consumers' decision. Consumers reach the stage of purchase decisions with various expectation and individual evaluations. We identify three major factors that could influence the mindset of the consumers before they enter the decision-review process: Prior knowledge, visual appeal, and purchase involvement. Prior knowledge refers to consumer's pre-existing evaluation of the product, it could be the result of a prior purchase, word of mouth from friends and relatives, or brand image. Visual appeal refers to the first impression of the product, including the layout of the webpage, product pictures, verbal description of the product, and aesthetic elements such as font, color and design language. Purchase involvement refers to how important the purchase is to the consumer. Consumers assign importance to products based on price, utility, and relevance. For example, a consumer looking at a laptop priced at 1,000 dollars will likely have different expectations from another consumer who is looking at exactly the same laptop but at a discounted price of 500 dollars. And consumers purchasing medical supplies are more involved than those purchasing office supplies. These factors together decide whether the consumer views the purchase in a positive light or in a critical manner at the start of the evaluation process.

The second sub-dimension is the information input during the decision-making process. Consumers will direct their attention into two directions, confirmation and falsification. Confirmation is the attempt to seek out information to support the pre-existing expectations in the first dimension. Using the above example, if the laptop has 1,000 reviews with an average rating of 4.5 out of 5 stars. For consumers who had positive expectations, they can easily find confirmation in the large number of positive reviews. However, if the consumers had formed a negative expectation in the first dimension beforehand, they will not easily give up their predisposition and would question the authenticity and credibility of the reviews. They are more likely to focus their attention on negative reviews to confirm their risk evaluation. On the other hand, falsification refers to the effort to seek evidence that explains the cognitive dissonance. In this example, consumers who have formed a positive disposition towards the product will attempt to falsify the negative reviews they see, and try to find out if they are just isolated cases, or if the reviewers are just being overly finicky. Therefore, negative reviews may be the focus of information processing at this dimension, but as we can see, they are for completely different reasons.

The third sub-dimension focuses on the interaction between the previous two dimensions. Consumers with different personality traits are likely to solve the cognitive consonance and dissonance in the information in different ways. Assertive individuals are more likely to focus their attention on reviews that support their original expectations, and be more persistent in their confirmation or falsification process. On the other hand, individuals with high uncertainty-avoidance are likely to focus their attention on the reviews that is opposite to their original expectations, since the best way to avoid any uncertainty is to not make the purchase, positive reviews that contradicts negative expectations will also result in non-purchase, similar to that of negative reviews. Low involvement is likely to attenuate the effect of negative reviews, while high involvement is likely to amplify that.

From these three sub-dimensions, I posit that the negativity bias observed in the online consumers' decision-making process can be better explained by the redirection of attention at each sub-dimension. The introduction of attention structure of consumers can potentially provide insight into how different types of individuals direct their attention to attest their expectations, and close the gap between their established ideas and the new cognitive information they receive.

3 SOCIOEMOTIONAL SELECTIVITY IN PATIENT SUPPORT VIRTUAL COMMUNITIES

Socioemotional selectivity theory (SST) has been adopted by studies on the behavioral changes of older adults. Older adults display a tendency to reduce social interaction and separate themselves from making new social contacts because they selectively narrow down their social interactions to those that could provide optimal outcomes only, such as spending time with friends and families. For older adults who perceive future to be expansive, they tend to be future-oriented and pursue knowledge-related goals that could maximize their future prospective, whereas for those who perceive future to be limited, they tend to be present-oriented and focus on emotion-related goals that could bring immediate emotional gratification [23-25]. Apart from the general application of SST on senior and geriatric population, there is also the potential to apply this theoretical lens to examine the behavior pattern of patients in the healthcare arena.

The core concept of SST is that as people's perception of future time becomes limited, they are no longer willing to engage in social activities that involves uncertainty and cognitive effort [26, 27]. Instead, they prefer activities that could bring them immediate emotional confirmation and satisfaction. Therefore, older adults selectively narrow down their social interactions to close friends and relatives only so that the probability for positive emotional experience is maximized [28, 29]. This kind of selectivity in behavior is not only limited to older adults, younger people who are terminally ill, or migrating to another country also display similar behavioral patterns [24, 30]. On patient support communities for diseases such as cancer and HIV, the change in the psychological state of the patients are likely to go through a similar process to those of older adults. Patients that are future-oriented are more likely to appreciate the informational support of the community, while patients that are present-oriented are more likely to pursue emotional-related satisfactions.

As a result, I posit using the date of diagnosis as a reference point; individuals will direct their attention to different types of threads at different stages of the disease. Also, receiving responses in kind, e.g. receiving informational support for future-oriented individuals, and emotional support for present-oriented individuals will serve as the cognitive feedback, and are more likely to continue as a back-and-forth discussion. At the early stage, individuals are more likely to direct their attention to opinion leaders, and active members of the community. They also would prefer posting in threads that has received high level of attention within the community, as this maximizes their chance of obtaining useful information. As they progress into the focusing on emotion-related goals, they are likely to limit their interactions with a small but closely-knit group of users, and prefer to post in threads that receive fewer responses. This way they maximize the positive emotional satisfaction and make sure that their effort and time will not go wasted.

4 COMPETING FOR ATTENTION: COMPETITIVENESS AMONG PEERS

In the third study, I intend to study how observing other people's performance on a task or a challenge can affect people's own motivation and performance on task. In an organizational context where there are multiple tasks and multiple individuals engaged in different tasks, we propose that by adding a performance metric (e.g. scores, points) on a certain task will draw the attention of individual users to compare their performance with those of their peers. Seeking social status is a powerful motivator for individuals, and the attention drawn by the comparison is likely to further enhance the attraction. We intend to carry out our study in an informal learning environment in which there are several tasks that users can choose to take after their learning experience. We intend to track the number of users who are attracted to the task, their time spent on the task, their number of attempts and the performance they achieved on each attempt. We expect that attention will have an inverted U effect on the overall performance of users. As attention could positively drive the performance until a certain level, then the amount of attention creates pressure on the users to stop attempting when their performance is not considered to be competitive enough.

REFERENCES

[1] Ocasio, W. Towards an attention-based view of the firm. *Strategic Management Journal* (1997), 187-206.
[2] McKnight, D.H., Cummings, L.L., and Chervany, N.L. Initial trust formation in new organizational relationships. *Academy of management review*, 23, 3 (1998), 473-490.
[3] Rousseau, D.M., Sitkin, S.B., Burt, R.S., and Camerer, C. Not so different after all: A cross-discipline view of trust. *Academy of management review*, 23, 3 (1998), 393-404.
[4] Fan, M., Tan, Y., and Whinston, A.B. Evaluation and design of online cooperative feedback mechanisms for reputation management. *IEEE Transactions on Knowledge and Data Engineering*, 17, 2 (2005), 244-254.
[5] Chen, P.-Y., Dhanasobhon, S., and Smith, M.D. All reviews are not created equal: The disaggregate impact of reviews and reviewers at amazon. com. (2008).
[6] Chevalier, J.A., and Mayzlin, D. The effect of word of mouth on sales: Online book reviews. *Journal of marketing research*, 43, 3 (2006), 345-354.
[7] Gefen, D., and Straub, D.W. Consumer trust in B2C e-Commerce and the importance of social presence: experiments in e-Products and e-Services. *Omega*, 32, 6 (2004), 407-424.
[8] Ghose, A., and Ipeirotis, P.G. Estimating the helpfulness and economic impact of product reviews: Mining text and reviewer characteristics. *IEEE Transactions on Knowledge and Data Engineering*, 23, 10 (2011), 1498-1512.
[9] Grazioli, S., and Jarvenpaa, S.L. Perils of Internet fraud: An empirical investigation of deception and trust with experienced Internet consumers. *IEEE Transactions on Systems, Man, and Cybernetics-Part A: Systems and Humans*, 30, 4 (2000), 395-410.
[10] Hu, N., Bose, I., Koh, N.S., and Liu, L. Manipulation of online reviews: An analysis of ratings, readability, and sentiments. *Decision support systems*, 52, 3 (2012), 674-684.
[11] Hu, N., Liu, L., and Sambamurthy, V. Fraud detection in online consumer reviews. *Decision support systems*, 50, 3 (2011), 614-626.
[12] Jensen, M.L., Averbeck, J.M., Zhang, Z., and Wright, K.B. Credibility of anonymous online product reviews: A language expectancy perspective. *Journal of Management Information Systems*, 30, 1 (2013), 293-324.
[13] Miranda, S.M., Young, A., and Yetgin, E. Are social media emancipatory or hegemonic? Societal effects of mass media digitization. *Mis Quarterly*, 40, 2 (2016), 303-329.
[14] Mudambi, S.M., and Schuff, D. What makes a helpful review? A study of customer reviews on Amazon. com. *Mis Quarterly*, 34, 1 (2010), 185-200.
[15] Xiao, B., and Benbasat, I. Product-related deception in e-commerce: a theoretical perspective. *Mis Quarterly*, 35, 1 (2011), 169-196.
[16] Xu, Q. Should I trust him? The effects of reviewer profile characteristics on eWOM credibility. *Computers in Human Behavior*, 33 (2014), 136-144.
[17] Yin, D., Bond, S.D., and Zhang, H. Anxious or Angry? Effects of Discrete Emotions on the Perceived Helpfulness of Online Reviews. *Mis Quarterly*, 38, 2 (2014), 539-560.
[18] BrightLocal. Local Consumer Review Survey. 2016.
[19] Wu, P.F. In search of negativity bias: An empirical study of perceived helpfulness of online reviews. *Psychology & Marketing*, 30, 11 (2013), 971-984.
[20] Ito, T.A., Larsen, J.T., Smith, N.K., and Cacioppo, J.T. Negative information weighs more heavily on the brain: the negativity bias in evaluative categorizations. *Journal of Personality and Social Psychology*, 75, 4 (1998), 887.
[21] Li, X., and Hitt, L.M. Self-selection and information role of online product reviews. *Information Systems Research*, 19, 4 (2008), 456-474.
[22] Sen, S., and Lerman, D. Why are you telling me this? An examination into negative consumer reviews on the web. *Journal of interactive marketing*, 21, 4 (2007), 76-94.

[23] Carstensen, L.L. Evidence for a life-span theory of socioemotional selectivity. *Current directions in Psychological science*, 4, 5 (1995), 151-156 %\ 2015-2001-2016 2007:2047:2000.

[24] Charles, S.T., and Carstensen, L.L. Social and emotional aging. *Annual review of psychology*, 61 (2010), 383-409.

[25] Carstensen, L.L., Isaacowitz, D.M., and Charles, S.T. Taking time seriously: A theory of socioemotional selectivity. *American psychologist*, 54, 3 (1999), 165.

[26] Melenhorst, A.-S., Rogers, W.A., and Bouwhuis, D.G. Older adults' motivated choice for technological innovation: evidence for benefit-driven selectivity. *Psychology and aging*, 21, 1 (2006), 190.

[27] Fung, H.H., Carstensen, L.L., and Lutz, A.M. Influence of time on social preferences: implications for life-span development. *Psychology and aging*, 14, 4 (1999), 595.

[28] Baltes, P.B. On the incomplete architecture of human ontogeny: Selection, optimization, and compensation as foundation of developmental theory. *American psychologist*, 52, 4 (1997), 366.

[29] Baltes, P.B., and Baltes, M.M. Psychological perspectives on successful aging: The model of selective optimization with compensation. *Successful aging: Perspectives from the behavioral sciences*, 1, 1 (1990), 1-34.

[30] Carstensen, L.L., Fung, H.H., and Charles, S.T. Socioemotional selectivity theory and the regulation of emotion in the second half of life. *Motivation and Emotion*, 27, 2 (2003), 103-123.

Transforming Online Advertising:
A User Centric Approach to Bridge the Gap

Lea Müller

University of Bamberg
An der Weberei 5,
96047 Bamberg
Germany
lea.mueller@uni-bamberg.de

Abstract

Online advertising becomes more and more economically important, as it enables several Internet-based services and provides firms with the possibility to globally reach a broad range of consumers. Despite its huge significance, the whole industry is currently exposed to severe challenges concerning the ad delivery process, as click-through rates are declining rapidly, risking the effectiveness of online advertising and thus also the ad dependent business models, which contributed decisively to latest innovations in IS. To bridge the gap between the advertising industry and the consumer, we conducted a literature review on the most important IS and Marketing journals and conferences, to summarize the current evolution of online advertising research and, in a second step, to identify research gaps that need to be filled in the course of this dissertation. Therefore, we mainly base on mixed methods approaches involving QCA to identify the actual effects online advertising has on the consumers and on organizations.

Keywords

Online advertising, advertising avoidance, multi-channel advertising, ad delivery process, QCA, interviews, mixed methods

ACM Reference Format:
Lea Müller. 2018. Transforming Online Advertising: A User Centric Approach to Bridge the Gap. In Proceedings of ACM *SIGMIS-CPR, June 18–20, 2018, Buffalo-Niagara Falls, NY, USA* ACM, NY, NY, USA, 2 pages.
https://doi.org/10.1145/3209626.3209632

Introduction

Online advertising has become a key pillar of many Internet-based business models, as it enables free services and access to search engines, websites and social media platforms [10]. Revenues related to online advertising in the United States totaled 59.6 billion US dollars for 2015 and the amount of money firms spend on online advertising rises steadily [5]. Hence, online advertising and the whole industry enabling and delivering online advertisements through the ad delivery

process become more and more economically important. The ad delivery process is concerned with the trade of ad spaces in the Internet and the placement of the right ad at the right time [3]. To this end, it involves three major perspectives: the advertiser, who places the ad, the publisher, who sells ad spaces to display the ad and the consumer, who interacts with the ad in the form of clicks or downloads. This consumer interaction is exactly what advertisers are paying for [2]. Hence, without consumers' interaction, in other words the consumers' acceptance and usage of online advertising, the whole ad delivery process collapses. Right now, the online advertising industry is facing precisely this issue of leaking user acceptance, causing severe challenges arising from each of the three perspectives: The majority of Internet users is unwilling to receive online advertising [9], as it is perceived as irrelevant and intrusive. However, publishers generate their biggest revenues with the consumer's interaction with ads, i.e. clicks, and downloads. Due to less consumer interaction, click-through rates (CTR) are dropping steadily [1]. Furthermore, the effectiveness of online advertising is debatable, since consumers are less interested in online [2, 6]. Therefore, advertisers question the money invested in online advertising and think about a potential redirection of those resources [2]. If those challenges remain unresolved, it could risk existing ad-dependent Internet-based business models and service infrastructures [6]. Thus, we need to understand why and how those challenges arise.

Theoretical Background

Consumers' Perspective. Research has shown, that the overall perception of advertising is rather negative and that consumers have privacy concerns in the context of online advertising [6]. This emerges inter alia from inappropriate targeting mechanisms, involving a high level of personalization [11]. However, we need to understand why consumers are unwilling to receive online ads and of how we can influence their perceptions positively. This includes also individual differences in user perception [8], as acceptance can vary from person to person. We need to further investigate factors increasing consumers' acceptance, such as familiarity of the browsing environment, the influence of task orientation and an increased relevance of the ads, including the right amount of personalization or the involvement of social network data into targeting. Furthermore, we should think about the reallocation of control back to consumers. This means a higher involvement of consumers into the ad delivery process, including the choice of being advertised in general, by whom, using which of the personal data. Further, we need to investigate advertising resistance or workarounds [7] including ad blindness and the usage of ad-blockers [9].

Advertisers' Perspective. Despite the design and format of advertisements, advertisers should rather focus on the question what consumers see and why. This involves a better-structured usage of personal consumer data and the integration of consumers' preferences into ad design [4]. Furthermore, research should pay attention to the actual value of an audience to reduce ineffective spending. Therefore, it would be useful to exactly calculate a consumers advertising value and to involve this knowledge into pricing strategies. To increase the advertising effectiveness, further investigation on native ad formats would be necessary, which, embedded in the website, adapting its design, could reduce irritation and intrusiveness.

Publishers' Perspective. Especially publishers should have an interest in addressing the arisen challenges, as their business model might depend on the display of advertisements. A first approach for research to clarify the online advertising scope is to further investigate the automated real-time bidding process to assure transparency and effectiveness. Furthermore, the online advertising scope could be enlarged by the acquisition of the Internet of things as a possible online advertising channel to enrich publishers' possible income sources. This would require an even closer consumer targeting and the further investigation of cross-channel effects between online and offline advertising and conversions.

Methodology

We use a methodical pluralism mainly based on the conducted literature analysis, involving mixed methods approaches, using interviews, surveys, structural equitation modelling (SEM) and qualitative comparative analysis (QCA).

Prospects

The gained results will help to better assess the perceptions and behaviors of consumers with respect to online advertising (e.g., ad blocker usage, acceptance), which results in an increase of individuals being exposed to online ads and rises the profitability for publishers and advertisers. Therefore, the group of users actively perceiving online advertising would be enlarged, which raises the effectiveness of online advertising due to more receivers of online ads. Further, the results will help to better picture the users and their advertising value from an organizational perspective. Consequently, we can identify incongruences in the user-organization-relation and identify the major causes for the effectiveness gap. Furthermore, the measurement of advertising profitability and the placement of different ads could be improved and optimized. The specific placement of a targeted ad could furthermore reduce the information overload resulting from too many ads the user is exposed to and thus reduce ad blindness. Additionally, the field of ad choices is largely unrevealed in online advertising research, but opens the door to a completely new online advertising approach, including better ad design and targeting mechanisms. Giving users the choice of which ads they watch

and providing them with the possibility to give feedback on why they dissociate from certain ads could revolutionize the user-online advertising-relationship and improve the overall attitude towards online advertising. Capturing the reallocation of choice back to users, in a next step, we can address the reallocation of data control back to users. This requires the involvement of users into the ad delivery process. By controlling who is collecting which data, and who can deliver advertisements to a specific user, users would be an active part of the online advertising process and environment. This could possibly impose new problems to online publishers, if consumers prefer to pay for the provided context with money instead of data or it could simplify their business, as they can precisely target the users and therefor, deliver the right ad to the right person to the right time. However, the involvement of users could transform online advertising in accordance to users' needs.

References

[1] Kursad Asdemir, Nanda Kumar, and Varghese S. Jacob. 2012. Pricing Models for Online Advertising: CPM vs. CPC. *Information Systems Research* 23, 3-part-1, 804–822.

[2] Yakov Bart, Andrew T. Stephen, and Miklos Sarvary. 2014. Which products are best suited to mobile advertising? A field study of mobile display advertising effects on consumer attitudes and intentions. *Journal of Marketing Research* 51, 3, 270–285.

[3] Richard E. Chatwin, Ed. 2013. *An overview of computational challenges in online advertising.* IEEE.

[4] Shuk Y. Ho, David Bodoff, and Kar Y. Tam. 2011. Timing of Adaptive Web Personalization and Its Effects on Online Consumer Behavior. *Information Systems Research* 22, 3, 660–679.

[5] IAB. 2017. *IAB internet advertising revenue report. 2016 full year results* (2017). Retrieved May 2, 2017 from https://www.iab.com/wp-content/uploads/2016/04/IAB_Internet_Advertising_Revenue_Report_FY_2016.pdf.

[6] Hyunsook Kweon, Dongsong Zhang, and Lina Zhou. 2012. User Privacy in Mobile Advertising. *AMCIS 2012 Proceedings.*

[7] Sven Laumer, Chrisitan Maier, and Tim Weitzel. 2017. Information quality, user satisfaction, and the manifestation of workarounds: a qualitative and quantitative study of enterprise content management system users. *European Journal of Information Systems* 26, 4, 333–360.

[8] Chrisitan Maier. 2012. Personality Within Information Systems Research: A Literature Review. *ECIS 2012 Proceedings.*

[9] Lea Müller, Jens Mattke, Christian Maier, and Tim Weitzel. 2017. The Curse of Mobile Marketing: A Mixed Methods Study on Individuals' Switch to Mobile Ad Blockers. *ICIS 2017 Proceedings.*

[10] Jan H. Schumann, Florian von Wangenheim, and Nicole Groene. 2014. Targeted Online Advertising: Using Reciprocity Appeals to Increase Acceptance Among Users of Free Web Services. *Journal of Marketing* 78, 1, 59–75.

[11] Catherine E. Tucker. 2014. Social Networks, Personalized Advertising, and Privacy Controls. *Journal of Marketing Research* 51, 5, 546–562.

Toward a Grounded Theory of Game Development Work in the Philippines

Elcid A. Serrano
De La Salle University
Taft, Manila, Philippines
elcid_serrano@dlsu.edu.ph

Raymund C. Sison
De La Salle University
Taft, Manila Philippine
raymund.sison@delasalle.ph

ABSTRACT

The video games sector, an information technology-enabled services (ITES) industry, has rapidly expanded over the last four decades growing at 13.3% annually. In the Philippines, which is now one of the top destinations for ITES in the world, the number of game developers is predicted to grow to 9,100 in 2022 from 4,300 in 2016. This study will explore the experiences and concerns of game developers in the context of information technology-enabled services in the country, and the process by which they address these concerns, using the classic or Glaserian grounded theory method. The results of the study can help game development organizations improve work processes or working conditions, which in turn could lead to greater productivity and quality, and schools in the design and development of game-related programs and curricula.

KEYWORDS

Game development work; classic grounded theory; Glaserian approach; grounded theory

ACM Reference Format:

Elcid A. Serrano, and Raymund C. Sison. 2018. Toward a Grounded Theory of Game Development Work in the Philippines. In Proceedings of ACM *SIGMIS-CPR, June 18–20, 2018, Buffalo-Niagara Falls, NY, USA* ACM, NY, NY, USA, 2 pages. https://doi.org/10.1145/3209626.3209633

1 MOTIVATION AND PROBLEM STATEMENT

The video games sector is one of the fastest growing sectors of the entertainment industry [1], having almost tripled in size due to innovations [2]. In 2017 the global games market breached the $116 billion mark 10.7% higher than 2016 [3]. In the same report from Newzoo [3], the global games revenue was forecast to reach $143.5 billion in 2020. Asia Pacific, based on the Newzoo 2017 update, had a total revenue of $ 51.2 billion in 2017 [4]. The Philippines, which ranks among the top information technology-enabled services (ITES) destinations in the world in the Tholon and Kearney rankings [5], has continuous growth in the game development industry as Mitra [6] reports. The industry is growing by 13.3% annually. In 2017, the Philippines had games market revenues of $355 million [7]. Furthermore, the number of game developers was at 4,300 in 2016 and it is predicted to reach

9,100 in 2022 as per industry experts [8].

In this study we would like to investigate what the main psychosocial concerns of game developers are, and how they address these. At this stage, we do not yet know what these concerns and mechanisms are; therefore, we may not conjure a research question that is more specific than what has been stated in the previous sentence.

2 BACKGROUND LITERATURE

While the local game development industry continues to expand, there are few studies (none in the Philippines) conducted on the concerns of game developers. In a quantitative study of McGill [9] content analysis was performed on posted job advertisements for game developer positions that would determine the qualities what the industry desires when hiring game developers [9]. A categorization of qualities in the study of McGill was performed and five qualifications emerged that include: experience, education, interpersonal and personal abilities, technical skills, and supporting knowledge. Findings show that are education and experience levels, skills, abilities and knowledge are clearly sought by the industry. Yet certain qualities are sought with more frequency than others [10], in another quantitative study, it defines qualifications sought when hiring game developers for positions in industry. It used cross-sectional data, qualifications from job advertisements were coded, categorized and then subcategorized and weighted totals were calculated based on skills being either required or desired. Results show that required qualifications are more critical than the desired ones. Furthermore, according to the data, technical skills of languages and software development tools and environment are critical skills for those seeking game developer positions to possess.

Weststar examined the workers who make video games in a qualitative study [11]. The study used secondary analysis of online sources to demonstrate that video game developers can be understood as a unique social group or occupational community. In another qualitative study by O' Donnell, it argues that the daily activity of game development embodies the skills that are fundamental to creative collaborative practice and that these capabilities represent aspects of critical thought [12].

Another qualitative study by Wu investigates how programming education differs from other game-related disciplines, whether or not the current game education serves the purpose of producing employable game programmers and which types of curriculum are appropriate for students who wish to work as game programmers. Simply this study recommends education appropriate for game programmers [13]. Lastly, another study by Vanhala identified the peculiarity of computer game organizations and their human resources by presenting a stage model that includes four phases covering the growth from demo group to full business [14]. It presents its findings on what a computer game organizations go through when they evolve from demo group phase to full business. Thus, there is a lack of studies on game developers and their concerns.

3 METHODS

Grounded Theory is a systematic generation of theory from systematic approach that has a set of rigorous research procedures leading to the emergence of conceptual categories [15].

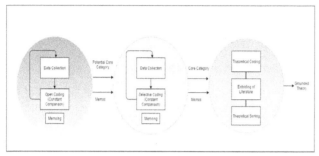

Figure 1: Research Framework

In gathering data, we will use multiple sources of data [15] like developers from Game Developers Association of the Philippines (GDAP). As we collect data, we will analyze them to look for interpretations thru the coding process while using constant comparative method. Data will be simultaneously collected, coded and analyzed [15]. Interview transcripts will be coded thru 'open coding' to identify and label common themes and categories. We will use memos in analysis to find similarities and differences within the data. We will break down data into units so we can analyze for inter-relationships. We will identify tentative categories and begin selective coding once we have discovered the core variable. We will write memos to be used in theory development [15]. After we have captured the emergent formation of ideas and concepts of substantive and theoretical categories and achieved theoretical saturation of the categories, we proceed to review, sort and integrate them related to the core category, its properties and related categories. They generate a theoretical outline or conceptual framework, for the full articulation of the GT through an integrated set of hypotheses [15].

Once themes, concepts and relationships have emerged, we will compare these with the literature [15] with the existing theories and integrate relevant literature into the study.

4 EXPECTED RESULTS

The study will provide understanding of game development work and game developers. Further, with the study addressing how game developers resolve their main concern, this will help game development organizations improve their work processes, procedures and collaborations. It could lead to greater productivity or quality of their artifacts. It can help organizations design interventions for the game developers in the conduct of their work. It can help schools in the design and development of curriculum. Finally, this study can contribute to a meaningful understanding of game development work in the Philippines by developing a theory or framework.

5 IMPLICATIONS

The study can contribute to providing understanding of game development work and game developers, and addressing how

game developers resolve their main concern. How game developers address their main concerns might turn out to be a set of skills; if so, then this study will not only identify and describe these skills at a more detailed level than what was done in previous studies, but will also provide a theory or framework that could be used to explain or understand why those skills are needed in the first place.

REFERENCES

[1] Dunklee, C. (2015). Video, computer, and virtual reality games. Salem Press Encyclopedia, January, 2015. 5p

[2] Superdata (2015). Playable media is the next big thing in $74B global games market. shttps://www.superdataresearch.com/blog/global-games-market-2015/

[3] Newzoo (2017). New Gaming Boom: Newzoo Ups Its 2017 Global Games Market Estimate to $116.0Bn Growing to $143.5Bn in 2020.

[4] Newzoo (2017). Q2 2017 Update. Global Games Market Report. www.newzoo.com/globalgamesnewsreport.

[5] Gott, J. & Sethi, A. (2016). 2016 A.T. Kearney Global Services Location Index™ Top 20. 2016 Global Services Location Index™. https://www.atkearney.com/strategic-it/global-services-location-index

[6] MDeC (2015).South East Asia Game Industry Initiative.

[7] Newzoo (2017). TOP 100 COUNTRIES BY GAME REVENUES. https://newzoo.com/insights/rankings/top-100-countries-by-game-revenues/

[8] TESDA (2017). Dimming or Brightening. Labor Market Intelligence Report. 2017.

[9] McGill, M. (2008). Critical skills for game developers: an analysis of skills sought by industry. Proceedings of the 2008 conference on future play: research, play, share. pp. 89-96.

[10] McGill, M. (2009). Weighted game developer qualifications for consideration in curriculum development. SIGSE '09Galarneau, Lisa (2014). Global Gaming Stats: Who's Playing What, and Why?.Big Fish Games.

[11] Weststar, J. (2015). Understanding video game developers as an occupational community. Information, communication & society. vol. 18. Issue 10. pp. 1238-1252.

[12] O' Donnell, C. (2009). The everyday lives of video game developers: Experimentally understanding underlying systems/structures. Transformative works and cultures.

[13] Wu, P. (2013). Education appropriate for game programmers. Consortium for computing sciences in colleges.

[14] Vanhala, E., et. al. (2015). Evolution of computer game developer organizations. Journal of advances in management research, vol. 12, issue 3, pp 268-291.

[15] Grounded Theory Institute (2008). What is Grounded Theory. 2008. http://www.groundedtheory.com/what-is-gt.aspx

Modeling and Evaluating Mobile-Based Interventions for Food Intake Behavior Change

Jieun Shin
Department of Information Systems and Analytics,
School of Computing, National University of Singapore,
15 Computing Drive, Singapore, 117418
jieun@u.nus.edu

ABSTRACT
Food intake is an important form of health information to observe the current status of personal health, which enables setting healthy eating goals and choosing a better diet. Based on monitoring food intake information, customized mobile interventions can help in advising users to consume a diverse and desirable quantity of healthy foods. However, previous research has not assessed whether mobile interventions enhance healthy eating behavior as an intermediary when determining whether the interventions impact health outcomes. To design mechanisms for behavior change, we need a better understanding of how mobile-based interventions affect users' motivation to change food intake behaviors and lead to healthier behavior. In this proposal, we categorize the prior interventions and behavior change techniques mainly based on three behavioral theories, i.e., control theory, theory of planned behavior, and theory of operant conditioning. Subsequently, the purpose of this thesis is: (1) to model theory-based mobile interventions for managing food intake, and (2) to investigate the impact of these mobile interventions on healthy eating behavior as an intermediary to better health outcomes. To this end, we propose three field experiment designs for future study.

Keywords
Food intake, Mobile Interventions, Healthy Eating, Control Theory, Theory of Planned Behavior, Theory of Operant Conditioning, Behavior Change

ACM Reference Format:
Jieun Shin. 2018. Modeling and Evaluating Mobile-Based Interventions for Food Intake Behavior Change. In Proceedings of ACM SIGMIS-CPR, June 18–20, 2018, Buffalo-Niagara Falls, NY, USA, ACM, NY, NY, USA, 2 pages. https://doi.org/10.1145/3209626.3209634

1. MOTIVATION AND BACKGROUND
Smartphone-based applications are a particularly important channel for delivering health interventions because of their widespread adoption - with powerful technical capabilities, ubiquitous access, people's attachment to their phones, and contextual awareness features such as for sensing GPS location, physical activity and others (Munos et al., 2016).

Previous research suggests that mobile-based interventions regarding users' food intake and provision of dietary recommendations can lead to better health promotion (Rollo et al., 2011; Rusin et al., 2013; Stumbo, 2013). However, prior studies have not examined the underlying mechanisms of mobile intervention effects on users' food intake, and their food consumption behavior changes for several reasons (Kato-Lin et al., 2016; West et al., 2017). First, they have not investigated mobile interventions for healthy eating behavior change as an intermediary when determining the relationship with health outcomes. Second, they did not theorize and test how mobile-based interventions affect users' motivation to change their diet and lead to healthier food intake behavior.

2. THEORY
Our proposal identifies several distinctive mobile-based interventions, which are used as behavior change techniques (BCTs) (Abraham and Michie, 2008), and aims to assess their effectiveness. Then, we categorize the interventions based on three behavioral theories, i.e., social cognitive theory, theory of planned behavior (TPB), and operant conditioning. By investigating theory-based interventions and their influence on healthy eating behavior, BCTs can be designed for achieving healthy eating behaviors and improving health outcomes.

3. METHOD
We conducted a systematic literature search from relevant publication databases according to PRISMA guidelines (Moher et al., 2010). Papers determined to be potentially relevant to the review were downloaded and analyzed by abstract followed by full text. At each stage, they were reviewed for eligibility to be further mapped into different BCTs. The search first identified 4,063 papers, from which 21 studies eventually met the inclusion criteria.

4. RESULTS AND FUTURE WORK
We identified which behavioral theories corresponded most closely to the mobile-based interventions in the studies selected through our literature review. As a result, control theory, theory of planned behavior, and operant conditioning were found to be the most prevalent theories. Based on the three focal theories identified in our literature review, we plan to develop three behavioral change models and design randomized field experiments to test each of them. This proposal expects to contribute to information systems research by providing a systematic review and proposing future research by identifying three key theories that can be used to understand the effects of mobile-based interventions for food intake on achieving healthy

food intake behavior and better health outcomes. This thesis is expected to offer important implications for mobile health application designers and policymakers.

5. REFERENCE

[1] Abraham, C., & Michie, S. (2008). A taxonomy of behavior change techniques used in interventions. Health Psychology, 27(3), 379.

[2] Kato-Lin, Y.-C., Abhishek, V., Downs, J. S., & Padman, R. (2016). Food for thought: The impact of m-health enabled interventions on eating behavior.

[3] Moher, D., Liberati, A., Tetzlaff, J., Altman, D. G., & Group, P. (2010). Preferred reporting items for systematic reviews and meta-analyses: The PRISMA statement. International Journal of Surgery, 8(5), 336-341.

[4] Munos B, Baker PC, Bot BM, Crouthamel M, Vries G, Ferguson I, et al. Mobile health: the power of wearables, sensors, and apps to transform clinical trials. Annals of the New York Academy of Sciences. 2016; 1375(1):3-18.

[5] Rollo ME, Ash S, Lyons-Wall P, Russell AW. Evaluation of a mobile phone image-based dietary assessment method in adults with type 2 diabetes. Nutrients. 2015; 7(6):4897-910.

[6] Rusin, M., Årsand, E., & Hartvigsen, G. (2013). Functionalities and input methods for recording food intake: A systematic review. International Journal of Medical Informatics, 82(8), 653-664.

[7] Stumbo, P. J. (2013). New technology in dietary assessment: A review of digital methods in improving food record accuracy. Proceedings of the Nutrition Society, 72(1), 70-76.

[8] West, J. H., Belvedere, L. M., Andreasen, R., Frandsen, C., Hall, P. C., & Crookston, B. T. (2017). Controlling your "App" etite: How diet and nutrition-related mobile apps lead to behavior change. JMIR mHealth and uHealth, 5(7).

Role of Absorptive Capacity, Knowledge Networks and Intellectual Property Rights in OSS Adoption of IT Firms*

Senthilkumar Thangavelu
Amrita School of Business
Amrita Vishwa Vidyapeetham
Bangalore, India
senmalkisasb@gmail.com

CCS Concepts

•Information systems~Open source software • Software and its engineering~Open source model

Keywords

Open Source Software; OSS Adoption; Absorptive Capacity; Networks; Intellectual Property Rights

ACM Reference Format:

Senthilkumar Thangavelu. 2018. Role of Absorptive Capacity, Knowledge Networks and Intellectual Property Rights in OSS Adoption of IT Firms. In Proceedings of ACM SIGMIS-CPR, June 18–20, 2018, Buffalo-Niagara Falls, NY, USA, ACM, NY, NY, USA, 1 page. https://doi.org/10.1145/3209626.3209629

1. Motivation

In recent times there is a disruptive change in the source of software and its development methodology. Most of the Information Technology (IT) product or service firms across the globe started adopting the Open Source Software (OSS) in different forms. As per a survey conducted by Blackduck software [65], 65% of the firms contributing to OSS and 59% of respondents participate in open source projects to gain competitive advantage. Two groups, the Free Software Foundation (FSF) and the Open Source Initiative (OSI) are recognized as founders of the OSS stream. FSF coined the term "free software,". In 1998, the OSI proposed replacing the term with "open source software". Open source software development is becoming familiar with software development communities and organizations. The IT firms continue to look for sources to create sustained competitive advantages over their competitors through various innovative initiatives. IT firms apply different strategies, including make or buy new products or services; acquire or merge with specialized product or service firms, enhance their productivity through new technologies; develop a relationship with knowledge sources like research institutes and firms; or, adopting to OSS. The OSS has become a strategic asset in the software development of 95% of mainstream IT firms [18].

OSS is becoming part of their mission-critical portfolios. The adoption of OSS by firms increases its OSS human capital and help to diffuse new knowledge arising from latest technological advances within the firms [41]. The firms leverage the OSS communities to access the knowledge and innovation capacity and change them into business values [48]. The empirical study by Piva et al. [50] shows that the ventures collaborating with the OSS community exhibit superior innovation performance when compared with those not adopting OSS. Many firms now realize the potential of OSS communities and starting their own OSS communities by sponsoring projects in order to leverage the advantages. But it is interesting to understand how do firms manage the OSS community members when the firms have less control over the behavior [64] of the community. Managing OSS communities and leveraging the potential will be a challenging task for firms as they will not fall under the traditional hierarchy of operations. After the success of the Linux operating system, Apache Web Server [45], Mozilla Firefox, Perl, Python, Eclipse and several other OSS, more firms are adopting OSS and is considered as a strategic need. The success of the collaborative development model of OSS projects is inspiring the software firms. The traditional IT firms want to leverage successes of OSS projects for their own distributed teams. There are various ways of adopting OSS adoption by IT firms. The firms benefit by deploying OSS products, using OSS in software development and in participating in the development of OSS. How IT firms adopt OSS and what are the categories of adoption? What are the factors influencing the OSS adoption? and what are the benefits and how they are realized? To get the answers to these questions, a deeper understanding of the OSS adoption with in-depth study at the firm level, including their knowledge absorption capacity, knowledge network, and governance mechanism is needed.

2. Literature Synopsis

OSS adoption is a matured research field and there are many research studies by scholars. But there are only a few papers that study the OSS adoption at firm level with empirical analysis, considering all forms of adoption. The existing OSS reviews deal with project characteristics, intercommunity process, and empirical studies related to how the IT firms adopt OSS, how OSS adoption benefits the firm that has been missing [7]. In a systematic literature review paper, Hauge et al. [29] reviewed OSS adoption research articles from 24 journals and 7 workshops and conference. From a population of 24,289 papers between 1998 and 2008 found that only 4.6% of them (112 papers) provided evidence for the empirical study on OSS adoption by firms. The author focuses his literature review on OSS adoption at the firm level, including the role of absorptive capacity, knowledge networks, and intellectual property rights. He focuses on OSS adoption frameworks and theories.

3. Research Gap

In the literature of OSS phenomenon, there are many studies related to OSS adoption. These papers study OSS adoption of specific products, communities or factors across selected IT firms or focus on OSS in general. OSS adoption happens at different levels, individual developer, group, project or program, firm, and country levels.

At the individual level like IT specialists [46] perception on the OSS concept, attitude towards individual OSS adoption using Linux operating system users [19] using Technology Acceptance Model (TAM) [13], the role of social identification in adopting OSS by end users [23]. The traditional models of innovation diffusion [13], [53] focus on when employees of a firm adopt innovation as a result of individual choice or mandated by authority.

There are research studies related to adopting OSS by firms on the individual product like web servers [59], OSS components reuse in the software development [2], adopting OSS in public administrations [43], adoption of OSS by an hospital using innovation adoption theory [20], successful and unsuccessful implementation of OSS study in an hospital [16], how human capital plays a role in organizational level OSS adoption [41], how the open strategy on adoption changes over the lifecycle of the organization [5]. There are studies on multi-level (country-level, firm-level, cross-level-IT based networks) adoption of OSS [52]. In the previous OSS adoption studies, very little information is available in the frameworks, theories, and models on the OSS adoption related to IT firms software adoption [39].

4. Problem Statement

An important unsolved question is whether a firm should take the closed approach to innovation or should use open sources for its innovation. Almirall et al. [4] developed a model and explored the factors that enhance the firm's organizational innovativeness. Many firms started using open innovation model, using external sources and actors to help them in the innovation processes and achieve and sustain innovation. The ability to exploit external knowledge is a critical component of a firm's innovative performance. There are many factors which influence the OSS adoption and diffusion within a firm.

The author proposes the following research questions (RQ) related to OSS adoption.

RQ1: How does the absorptive capacity of an IT firm influence the OSS adoption?

RQ2: How the knowledge networks of an IT firm affect the OSS adoption?

RQ3: How the intellectual property rights of OSS affect OSS adoption of IT firm?

RQ4: What are the characteristics of an IT firm that enable or inhibit its OSS adoption?

RQ5: How does IT firm adopt OSS?

RQ6: What are the dominating categories of OSS adoption?

5. Theoretical Support

There are many OSS adoption theories used by IS researchers which are applied at the individual, group, firm, country levels. The main OSS adoption theories are Technology Acceptance Model (TAM), Theory of reasoned action (TRA), the Theory of Planned Behavior (TPB), Unified Theory of Acceptance and Use of Technology (UTAUT), Diffusion of Innovation (DOI), and Technology, Organization, and Environment (TOE). The theories TAM, TRA, TPB, and UTAUT focus on individual OSS adoption. The DOI and TOE theories apply to firms OSS adoption.

Diffusion of Innovation (DOI) theory [53] explains how an innovation is adopted by the firms. The diffusion follows a normally distributed curve which is divided into five categories namely innovators, early adopters, early majority, late majority, and laggards. This model includes three key factors namely compatibility, complexity and relative advantage which influence the diffusion. This is mainly applied to groups and firms.

Technology-Organization-Environment (TOE) framework, one of the IS theories which is applied at the firm level is developed by Rocco DePietro et al [15]. The three main elements which influence the adaptation of technological innovation are the technological context, the organizational context, and the environmental context of the firm.

In this research study, the author invokes the TOE framework as it is applied at the firm level study which is the unit of analysis. The three elements, technology, organization and environment of TOE framework would include the study constructs and variables. The author also invokes the Absorptive Capacity theory (ACAP) [10], Social Network Theory (SNT) [21] and Property Rights Theory (PRT) [27] [22] to provide theoretical support to some of his study constructs and variables.

6. The Conceptual Research Model

The author proposes the conceptual model provided in Figure 6.1 for this research study. The influencing factors namely the firm's absorptive capacity, knowledge networks, and intellectual property rights will be further studied in detail to develop sub-hypotheses with suitable variables. The study will include the IT firm's demographic characteristics and external factors like government initiative and policies as controlling variables.

Figure 6.1: Conceptual Research Model

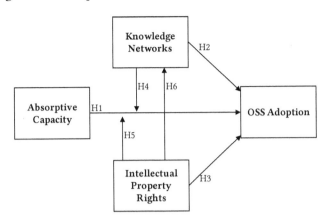

The author proposes to study, how absorptive capacity, knowledge networks, and intellectual property rights influence the IT firm's OSS adoption and their moderating effects on other study variables. This study adapts a framework developed by Hauge et al. [29] in their systematic review on OSS adoption. This framework is based on the review of publications from 24 journals, 7 conferences and workshop proceedings, between 1998 and 2008 that resulted in 112 empirical papers which provide evidence on OSS adoption [29]. This framework covers not just using the OSS products but includes all other possible ways of adopting OSS. This framework covers six different ways of adopting the OSS by a firm. These include

- Deploying OSS
- Using OSS CASE tools
- Integrating OSS components
- Participating in OSS communities
- Providing OSS products
- Using OSS practices

Hauge et al. [28] study the adoption of OSS in the Norwegian software industry using this framework which surveyed the usage of OSS components in the software development.

Author proposes to perform this research study in three tracks with an in-depth analysis of various important components of the influencing factors. This approach helps to perform a detailed study focusing on each influencing factor. The three tracks are:

Track1: Absorptive Capacity and OSS Adoption
Track2: Knowledge Networks and OSS Adoption
Track3: Intellectual Property Rights and OSS Adoption

7. Literature Review and the Hypotheses Development

Zaffar et al. [75] study the social and economic factors on the diffusion dynamics of OSS using Agent-based Computational Economics (ACE) approach. They find that network topology, network density, and interoperability costs are the key drivers of OSS diffusion. Li et al. [41] study the role

of human-capital (knowledge, skills, experience, abilities, and capacities possessed by employees) in the adoption of OSS among 215 firms and find that the adoption of OSS depends on the availability of OSS resources within a firm. Piva et al. [50] study of entrepreneurial ventures collaborating with the OSS community, exhibit superior innovation performance compared with their non-collaborating firms. Alexy et al. [3] study how OSS affects the administrative and technical dimensions of a large telecommunications firm using a mixed method of design that consist of interviews and survey. They find that the organizational innovation to commercially engage in OSS has different impacts on technical and administrative dimensions of different job roles. Sacks studies [55] the competition between a firm producing proprietary software (PS) and a community producing OSS and how they differentiate between each other. He finds the OSS caters to the most technologically savvy individuals, leading the firm to target even less savvy individuals than it would when acting as a monopolist.

Harison and Koski [26] study 170 Finnish software companies, how the characteristics of the firms like size, age, intellectual capital, absorptive capacity, and ownership structure affect their decision to adopt OSS. The intellectual capital which includes human capital and intellectual property determines its absorptive capacity with regards to the know-how of the business and technical knowledge. Their finding indicates adopting to OSS require relatively highly skilled employees, IT firms that have higher proportions of educated and skilled employees are more likely to be suppliers of OSS. Marsan et al. [47] study the OSS institutionalization in organizations by analyzing a total of 2840 articles on OSS from 251 professional journals published between 1988 and 2009 using the rhetorical theory of diffusion of innovations and the concept of organizing vision. Their study indicates that OSS institutionalization happens mainly in the back-end applications and gradually to front-end applications mainly in the SMEs. They also propose that future research on OSS institutionalization consider the multidimensional view of OSS adoption including firm members who actively participate in OSS development communities or use OSS development practices. Stam [61] studies how participation in open innovation communities influences the innovative and financial performance of OSS firms using a dataset of OSS commercializing firms in the Netherlands. His study reveals that higher technical participation in OSS projects is more strongly related to performance for larger size firms and firms with high R&D intensities. Marsan et al. [46] study the IT specialists perception of the discourse on OSS and how this plays a role in organization-OSS adoption by surveying 271 IT specialists. Their study indicates that a majority of IT specialists are neutral about the OSS concept and the detractors have more years of experience but have been less exposed to OSS than supporters. IT specialists' perceptions of the OSS concept are positively associated with their firm's openness to OSS adoption.

Lerner and Tirole [38] explore the open source software from the economics point of view to understand the nature of open source development through four case studies namely Apache, Linux, Perl, and Sendmail. They highlight the history of software development starting from operating systems and internet by academic institutions like MIT, Berkeley and industry R&D centers like Bell Labs during the 1960s and 1970s in a cooperative way. The paper consolidates the software development into three periods namely, the early 1960s to early 1980s, early 1980s to early 1990s, and early 1990s onwards. Many IT firms share the problems and projects with the development community outside their organizations to get solutions and encourage the open software development culture. OSS allows IT firms to incorporate the freely available source codes into their implementations. OSS provides many benefits to IT firms. Instead of a single firm, a community determines whether the contributions can be included in the source code or not. The OSS communities use collaborating tools to manage their work. The existence of freely available software allows faster adoption of technology, increased innovation, and reduced costs and time-to-market. OSS products have lower defect density than commercial software products. The OSS development communities rapidly respond to the user requests and problems.

Alexy et al. [3] study how OSS affects the administrative and technical dimensions of a firm. Sacks, [55] compares the Closed Source Software (CSS) and OSS and their competition. Harison and Koski [26] study the characteristics of the firms like size, age, intellectual capital, absorptive capacity, and ownership structure that affect their decision to adopt OSS in the context of 170 Finnish software companies. Their findings indicate adopting to OSS require relatively highly skilled people. Marsan et al. [47] study the OSS institutionalization in organizations. Their study indicates that OSS institutionalization happens mainly in the back-end applications and gradually to front-end applications mainly in the SMEs. But ignoring OSS-adoption would harm organizations. Stam [61] studies how the participation in OSS communities influence the innovative and financial performance of the firms which are commercializing OSS. Marsan et al.[46] study the IT specialists' perception of the discourse on OSS and how this plays a role in organization-OSS adoption.

7.1. Track1: Absorptive Capacity and OSS Adoption

The external and internal knowledge of a firm is very critical to its OSS adoption. A firm with diverse knowledge can quickly and easily acquire a new knowledge coming from various external sources. A simple static model was constructed by Cohen and Levinthal [10] on a firm's absorptive capacity using three determinants namely technological opportunity, appropriability, and competitor interdependence. This model was redesigned by Zahra and George to include the dynamic capabilities view of the firm [76]. The potential and realized absorptive capacities are used to explain how a firm can acquire a new knowledge from external sources and it is exploited internally within the firm. Todorova and Durisin [67] again re-conceptualized the absorptive capacity construct to remove ambiguities and introduced control and feedback mechanisms to bring dynamic nature to the model. The firm's absorptive capacity [10] depends on individual's absorptive capacity but the firm's absorptive capacity is not the cumulative sum of individual's absorptive capacities. Teigland et al. [64] analyze the relationship between firm's absorptive capacity, firm-sponsored OSS community's innovation capacity and its boundary management using the qualitative method. The absorptive capacity includes not only the acquisition or assimilation of knowledge but also exploiting it internally within the firm. There is always a trade-off between inward-looking and outward-looking absorptive capacities. Two key features of absorptive capacity are:

- Accumulating absorptive capacity in one period will permit its more efficient accumulation in the next.
- The possession of related expertise will permit the firm to better understand and therefore evaluate the import of intermediate technological advances.

March [44] in his study on organizational learning analyzes the two ways of acquiring knowledge namely the explorative learning and the exploitative learning and their cost-benefit analysis. There is always a trade-off between them to decide whether to build internally or to buy from external sources. He also analyzes the conditions which favor these two kinds of learning. A firm's Research and Development (R&D) expenses not only bring new innovations but also enhance a firm's absorptive capacity [11]. An empirical study on potential absorptive capacity, reveals that R&D cooperation, external knowledge acquisition, and experience with knowledge search are key antecedents of potential absorptive capacity [17]. Jansen [31] explores how the organizational antecedents, coordination capabilities, and socialization capabilities affect a firm's potential and realized absorptive capacity within units and why there is a difference in acquiring and assimilating new knowledge. Due to the uncertainty in the future technology trends, firms face an issue in developing required prior knowledge to understand a new knowledge. Vasudeva and Anand [73] further deconstruct absorptive capacity into longitudinal and latitudinal for distant and diverse knowledge through alliance portfolio-based capabilities. Lichtenthaler [42] explains the interfirm discrepancies in exploiting the external knowledge by considering marketing and technological knowledge as two components of absorptive capacity. Wales et al. [74] analyze the relationship between absorptive capacity and firm performance and argue they follow inverted-U shape. Rothaermel and Alexandre [54] hypothesize there is a curvilinear relationship that exists between a firm's technology sourcing mix and its performance, absorptive capacity acts a moderator which brings a positive effect on their relationship. Bosch et al. [9] added two more determinants of absorptive capacity namely organizational forms and combinative capabilities along with prior related knowledge suggested by [10] and illustrated the coevolving of firms along with their environment. The relationship between product innovation performance and various collaborating networks including supplier, customer, competitor, and research institution collaborations are studied by Tsai [68] using Taiwanese Technological Innovation Survey (TTIS) database. This paper highlights how the absorptive capacity influences relationships between collaborations. Tsai [70] [69] studies the interaction of absorptive capacity and firm's internal network positions. He argues that if a firm takes a central network position and its business units share their new knowledge, then it has a positive and significant effect on firm's innovation. Li et al. [40] argue the role of top management in identifying the new knowledge using search selection and search intensity using an empirical study. Tseng et al. [71] empirical study on knowledge input, knowledge spillover and absorptive capacity on innovation performance show a positive significance on the firm's innovation performance. Spithoven et al. [60] explore how firms with lack of enough absorptive capacity, manage the inbound open innovations using intermediaries collective research centers. Lane et al. [36] in their paper analyzed the usage of absorptive capacity among researchers using a model defined with the processes, antecedents, and outcomes. Szulanski [63] explores the internal stickiness to internal knowledge transfers and the related factors, lack of absorptive capacity of the recipients, casual ambiguity and the relationship between both parties. Teigland et al. qualitatively study [64] the relationship between firm's absorptive capacity, firm-sponsored OSS community's innovation capacity and its boundary management using the eZ Systems and its sponsored OSS community eZ Publish. Their results show that community's innovation capacity directly influences the firm's absorptive capacity. The firm can easily absorb and combine community knowledge with its internal knowledge to enhance and develop its products and services. Dahlander and Magnusson [12] study four in-depth case studies of OSS firms and their interaction and strategy with the development communities. They find that firms need to develop sufficient absorptive capacity to benefit from external developments, to identify, assimilate and apply the external knowledge.

H1: *Absorptive Capacity of the IT firm positively influences its OSS adoption.*

7.2. Track2: Knowledge Networks and OSS Adoption

In a network, diffusion can reach a larger number of people and greater distance in 'informal' ties than in 'formal' ties. The formal ties would limit the flow of information than the informal ties. Bridging the informal ties are important in the knowledge world to create influence or diffuse the knowledge. At the macro level, the informal ties play an effective role in social cohesion. The informal ties link members of different small groups than formal ties and help them integrate with the larger communities. The existence of related knowledge and a set of established linkage among business units are very important for interunit knowledge sharing. The corporate center plays a key role in developing required processes and policies to create a network to store and share knowledge gained from the projects across the firm. Uzzi [72] defines the term embeddedness in the networks context and explains how it creates the informal economic opportunities difficult to replicate in the formal structure. Embedded exchanges have different distinctive features like trust and personal ties, which reduce the monitoring cost and making expectations predictable. Two key ties are arm's-length ties (market relationships) and embedded ties (special relationships). Most of the interfirm relations are arm's-length relations but lesser significant than embedded ties. Three main components of embedded ties are trust, fine-grained information transfer, and

joint problem-solving arrangement. The information exchanged in embedded relations is more proprietary and tacit but price and quantity level information is shared in the arm's-length relations. Lane et al. [35] study the international joint ventures performance and learning by proposing three components of firm's absorptive capacity. The stronger intra-firm networks [34] help to acquire and assimilate new external knowledge within various business units of the firm. Mowery et al. [49] explore the knowledge transfer between alliance partners based on the citation patterns and conclude that alliance promotes the specialized knowledge of the firm. Firms in a network with diversely experienced firms would take better acquisition decisions [8] than in a network with homogeneously experienced firms. Ahuja [1] studies the impact of direct ties, indirect ties and structural holes in interfirm collaboration network on the innovation output. He predicts that direct and indirect ties support the innovation output but structural holes have a negative influence on it. Tiwana [66] explores the interaction of strong ties which provide integration capacity but lack innovation potential and bridging ties which has innovation potential but lack of integration in the innovation-seeking alliances. DeCarolis and Deeds [14] study the stocks and flows of organizational knowledge and firm performance. They use the Resource Based View (RBV) to test the relationship between the stocks and flows of knowledge. A firm's performance enhances when knowledge is shared more efficiently and effectively between various units of a firm. But the interrelationship between the units plays a key role in achieving this. Hansen [25] studies multiple networks by defining three stages of knowledge sharing, decision to seek knowledge, search cost, and transfer cost. Hansen [24] uses knowledge network to explain why some units perform better in acquiring knowledge from other units. Some business units and projects benefit from knowledge residing in other parts of the company. These project teams obtain more existing related knowledge from other teams and complete their projects with less effort and faster due to shorter network paths between the teams. The corporate center plays a key role in developing required processes and policies to create a network to store and share knowledge gained from the projects across the firm. There are direct and indirect (connection through intermediaries) interunit relations by which teams share or obtain related knowledge. The direct established relations give quick access to knowledge but some cost is involved to maintain them. Singh [58] also confirms that knowledge diffusion slows down when the path is longer in interpersonal networks. A firm to develop a new product or to find a solution for a problem gets input from its networks. It either searches internally or externally. Katila and Ahuja [33] explore how the firms find input or solution by defining search depth and search scope as two dimensions. Inkpen and Tsang [30] explore the interaction of social capital dimensions namely network ties, network configuration, network stability, shared goals, shared culture, and trust with three types of networks, namely intra-corporate networks, strategic alliances, and industry districts. Lee and Pennings [37] study the effect of external networks and internal capabilities on a firm's performance in start-up firms. Qi et al. [51] study the innovative performance of firms and their relationship with collaboration with central partners. They show that breakthrough innovations diminish beyond certain point. Sutanto et al. [62] investigate the factors which increase the popularity of OSS, from 176 OSS projects fromSourceforge.net and find that effective online user support is one of the antecedents along with the software quality. These studies show that OSS adoption by firms is impacted by the availability of both internal and external resources with OSS knowledge. The firms having OSS community's support perform well in their innovations.

H2: *Knowledge Networks of IT firm positively influence its OSS adoption.*

7.3. Track3: Intellectual Property Rights and OSS Adoption

The benefits of OSS to the user community are limited by the government policies and laws. These laws including the intellectual property rights (IPRs) reduce and limit the diffusion of new knowledge from the OSS community to others including IT firms, individuals who are interested to develop and contribute further. Sen et al. [57] study the relationship between the licenses and the effort involved in developing OSS among the developer community. They found that preference is given to less-restrictive licenses when more effort is needed and most-restrictive when less development effort. Many of the OSS firms like eZ follow dual-licensing models: General Public License and commercial license [64]. The strategy followed by some of the firms on IPR is "selective revealing" in order to encourage more participation in problem-solving [6]. While there has been the systematic study on IPR and licensing, there is a limited study in terms of exploring the characteristics of property rights. OSS while largely operates on a community or common property regime; firms largely operate in private property regime. The degree of 'rivalry' and 'excludability' give rise to different property regimes [32]. Private property regimes are also called as 'well-defined property rights regimes' whereas other property regimes are often known as 'ill-defined property rights regime'. In this context, the interaction of ill-defined and well-defined property regimes can have an influence on OSS adoption.

H3: *Intellectual Property Rights of OSS has a negative influence on OSS adoption of the IT firm.*

7.4 Moderating Effects

H4: *The Knowledge Networks of IT firm moderates the relationship between the Absorptive Capacity and its OSS adoption.*

H5: *Intellectual Property Rights of OSS moderate the relationship between the Absorptive Capacity of the IT firm and its OSS adoption.*

H6: *Intellectual Property Rights of OSS moderate the relationship between the Knowledge Networks of the IT firm and its OSS adoption.*

8. Methods

The author plans to use the following research process proposed by Saunders et al. [56]:

- Research philosophy: Positivism
- Research approach: Deductive
- Research strategy: Survey and interviews
- Research choices: Mixed method
- Time horizons: Cross-sectional
- Data collection techniques and analysis procedures: Mixed (Quantitative and Qualitative)

As a starting step, based on the research questions the study variables or constructs will be elicited from the literature. These will be validated with stakeholders using structured interview methods. The stakeholders would include the subject matter experts, the practitioners from the IT service and product firms, experts from the research institutes and academia, and the entrepreneurs from start-up firms. A conceptual model and hypotheses will be built with supporting theories and frameworks. A pilot questionnaire will be developed and validated with a small set of firms to get the feedback. The main survey questionnaire will be developed and administered online. The scope of the study is IT and IT-enabled services firms including Start-up firms. The firms would be identified from various sources including Centre for Monitoring Indian Economy Pvt. Ltd (CMIE) database, The National Association of Software and Services Companies (NASSCOM), the Technology Business Incubators (TBIs) initiated by academic institutions, Software Technology Parks of India (STPI), and Start-up India initiatives. The proposed hypotheses will be estimated using suitable statistical tools.

9. Expected Results and Implications

The findings of the three tracks of this study would help to advance the supporting theories and add to the literature by providing empirical support to the framework. This study would explicitly identify the role and characteristics of absorptive capacity, knowledge networks and help in devising suitable property regimes for the firms to optimize benefits from the OSS. This study would add to the paradigm shift in the traditional IS development methodology to OSS development methodology. The author hopes this study will highlight the influence of factors and help firms to develop strategies on OSS adoption, partnership with firms and institutions; reveal the processes to be followed in order to optimally exploit OSS; highlight the suitable approach to sponsor a new OSS project by IT firms; and help to understand how to balance between OSS communities and internal resources in order to maximize the firm benefits.

10. Future Work

In the near future, the immediate tasks to be performed by the author are:

- Identifying the dependent variables for each track, their related literature, operational definitions, and measurement.

- Developing sub-hypotheses with constructs and variables and validating them.
- Validating the consistency of the theories across all three tracks with a specific focus on organizational and institutional theories.

References

[1] Ahuja, G. 2000. Collaboration Networks, Structural Holes, and Innovation: A Longitudinal Study. *Administrative Science Quarterly.* 45, 3 (2000), 425–455.

[2] Ajila, S.A. and Wu, D. 2007. Empirical study of the effects of open source adoption on software development economics. *Journal of Systems and Software.* 80, 9 (2007), 1517–1529.

[3] Alexy, O. et al. 2013. From closed to open: Job role changes, individual predispositions, and the adoption of commercial open source software development. *Research Policy.* 42, 8 (2013), 1325–1340.

[4] Almirall, E. and Casadesus-Masanell, R. 2010. OPEN VERSUS CLOSED INNOVATION: A MODEL OF DISCOVERY AND DIVERGENCE. *Academy of Management Review.* 35, 1 (2010), 27–47.

[5] Appleyard, M.M. and Chesbrough, H.W. 2017. The Dynamics of Open Strategy: From Adoption to Reversion. *Long Range Planning.* 50, 3 (2017), 310–321.

[6] Arora, A. et al. 2016. The paradox of openness revisited: Collaborative innovation and patenting by UK innovators. *Research Policy.* 45, 7 (2016), 1352–1361.

[7] Ayala, C.P. et al. 2011. Five Facts on the Adoption of Open Source Software. *IEEE Software.* 28, 2 (2011), 95–99.

[8] Beckman, C.M. and Haunschild, P.R. 2002. Network Learning: The Effects of Partners' Heterogeneity of Experience on Corporate Acquisitions. *Administrative Science Quarterly.* 47, 1 (2002), 92–124.

[9] Van den Bosch, F. a. J. et al. 1999. Coevolution of Firm Absorptive Capacity and Knowledge Environment: Organizational Forms and Combinative Capabilities. *Organization Science.* 10, 5 (1999), 551–568.

[10] Cohen, W.M. and Levinthal, D.A. 1990. Absorptive Capacity: A New Perspective on Learning and Innovation. *Administrative science quarterly.* 35, 1 (1990), 128–152.

[11] Cohen, W.M. and Levinthal, D.A. 1989. Innovation and learning: The two faces of R&D. *The Economic Journal.*

[12] Dahlander, L. and Magnusson, M. 2008. How do Firms Make Use of Open Source Communities? *Long Range Planning.* 41, 6 (2008), 629–649.

[13] Davis, F.D. 1989. Perceived Usefulness , Perceived Ease Of Use , And User Acceptance of Information Technology. *MIS Quarterly.* 13, 3 (1989), 319–339.

[14] DeCarolis, D.M. and Deeds, D.L. 1999. The impact of stocks and flows of organizational knowledge on firm performance: an empirical investigation of the biotechnology industry. *Strategic Management Journal.* 20, 10 (1999), 953–968.

[15] DePietro, R. et al. 1990. The context for change: Organization, technology and environment. *The processes of technological innovation.* L.G. Tornatzky and M. Fleischer, eds. Lexington Books. 151–175.

[16] Fitzgerald, B. 2009. Anatomy of Success and Failure Open Source Software Adoption. *International Journal of Open Source Software Processes.* 1, March (2009), 1–23.

[17] Fosfuri, A. and Tribó, J.A. 2008. Exploring the antecedents of potential absorptive capacity and its impact on innovation performance. *Omega.* 36, 2 (2008), 173–187.

[18] Franco-Bedoya, O. et al. 2017. Open Source Software Ecosystems: A Systematic Mapping. *Information and Software Technology.* 0, Manuscript submitted for publication. (2017), 1–26.

[19] Gallego, M.D. et al. 2008. User acceptance model of open source software. *Computers in Human Behavior.* 24, 5 (2008), 2199–2216.

[20] Glynn, E. et al. 2005. Commercial adoption of open source software: An empirical study. *2005 International Symposium on Empirical Software Engineering, ISESE 2005* (2005), 225–234.

[21] Granovetter, M. 1973. The Strength of Weak Ties. *American Journal of Sociology.* 78, 6 (1973), 1360–1380.

[22] Grossman, S.J. and Hart, O.D. 1986. The Costs and Benefits of Ownership: A Theory of Vertical and Lateral Integration. *Journal of Political Economy.* 94, 4 (1986), 691.

[23] Gwebu, K.L. and Wang, J. 2011. Adoption of open source software: The role of social identification. *Decision Support Systems.* 51, 1 (2011), 220–229.

[24] Hansen, M.T. 2002. Knowledge Networks: Explaining Effective Knowledge Sharing in Multiunit Companies. *Organization Science.* 13, 3 (2002), 232–248.

[25] Hansen, M.T. et al. 2005. Knowledge sharing in organizations: Multiple networks, multiple phases. *Academy of Management Journal.* 48, 5 (2005), 776–793.

[26] Harison, E. and Koski, H. 2010. Applying open innovation in business strategies: Evidence from Finnish software firms. *Research Policy.* 39, 3 (2010), 351–359.

[27] Hart, O. and Moore, J. 1990. Property Rights and the Nature of the Firm. *The Journal of Political Economy.* 98, 6 (1990), 1119.

[28] Hauge, Ø. et al. 2008. Adoption of open source in the software industry. *IFIP International Federation for Information Processing, Open Source Development, Communities and Quality.* 275, (2008), 211–221.

[29] Hauge, Ø. et al. 2010. Adoption of open source software in software-intensive organizations - A systematic literature review. *Information and Software Technology.* 52, 11 (2010), 1133–1154.

[30] Inkpen, A.C. and Tsang, E.W.K. 2005. Social Capital, Networks and Knowledge Transfer. *Academy of Management Review.* 30, 1 (2005), 146–165.

[31] Jansen, J.J.P. et al. 2005. Managing Potential and Realised Absorptive Capacity: How do Organisational Antecedents Matter? *Academy of Management Journal.* 48, 6 (2005), 999–1015.

[32] Jyotishi, A. et al. 2017. Gold Mining Institutions in Nilgiri – Wayanad A Historical-Institutional Perspective. *Economic and Political Weekly.* LII, 28 (2017), 57–63.

[33] Katila, R. and Ahuja, G. 2002. Something old, something new: A longitudinal study of search behavior and new product introduction. *Academy of Management Journal.* 45, 6 (2002), 1183–1194.

[34] Khoja, F. and Maranville, S. 2009. The power of intrafirm networks. *Academy of Strategic Management Journal.* 8, (2009), 51–70.

[35] Lane, P.J. et al. 2001. Absorptive capacity, learning, and performance in international joint ventures. *Strategic Management Journal.* 22, 12 (2001), 1139–1161.

[36] Lane, P.J. et al. 2006. THE REIFICATION OF ABSORPTIVE CAPACITY: A CRITICAL REVIEW AND REJUVENATION OF THE CONSTRUCT. *Academy of Management Review.* 31, 4 (2006), 833–863.

[37] Lee, C. and Pennings, J. 2001. Internal Capabilities , External Networks , and Performance: A Study on Technology- Based Ventures. *Strategic Management Journal.* 22, (2001), 615–640.

[38] Lerner, J. and Tirole, J. 2002. SOME SIMPLE ECONOMICS OF OPEN SOURCE. *The Journal of Industrial Economics.* 50, 2 (2002), 197–234.

[39] Lewis, J.A. 2010. *Government Open Source Policies.*

[40] LI, Q. et al. 2010. Top Management Attention to Innovation: The Role of Search Selection and Intensity in New Product Introductions. *Academy of Management Journal.* (2010).

[41] Li, Y. et al. 2013. It is all about what we have: A discriminant analysis of organizations' decision to adopt open source software. *Decision Support Systems.* 56, 1 (2013), 56–62.

[42] Lichtenthaler, U. 2009. ABSORPTIVE CAPACITY, ENVIRONMENTAL TURBULENCE, AND THE COMPLEMENTARITY OF ORGANIZATIONAL LEARNING PROCESSES. *Academy of Management Journal.* 52, 4 (2009), 822–846.

[43] van Loon, A. and Toshkov, D. 2015. Adopting open source software in public administration: The importance of boundary spanners and political commitment. *Government Information Quarterly.* 32, 2 (2015), 207–215.

[44] March, J.G. 1991. Exploration and Exploitation in Organizational Learning. *Organization Science.*

[45] Margan, D. and Čandrlić, S. 2015. The success of open source software: A review. *MIPRO* (2015), 1463–1468.

[46] Marsan, J. et al. 2012. Adoption of open source software in organizations: A socio-cognitive perspective. *Journal of Strategic Information Systems.* 21, 4 (2012), 257–273.

[47] Marsan, J. et al. 2012. Has open source software been institutionalized in organizations or not? *Information and Software Technology.* 54, 12 (2012), 1308–1316.

[48] Morgan, L. and Finnegan, P. 2014. Beyond free software: An exploration of the business value of strategic open source. *Journal of Strategic Information Systems.* 23, 3 (2014), 226–238.

[49] Mowery, D.C. et al. 1996. Strategic Alliances and Interfirm Knowledge Transfer. *Strategic Management Journal.* 17, Winter Special Issue (1996), 77–91.

[50] Piva, E. et al. 2012. Is Open Source Software about Innovation? Collaborations with the Open Source Community and Innovation Performance of Software Entrepreneurial Ventures. *Journal of Small Business Management.* 50, 2 (2012), 340–364.

[51] Qi Dong, J. et al. 2017. How Central Is Too Central? Organizing Interorganizational Collaboration Networks for Breakthrough Innovation. *Journal of Product Innovation Management.* 34, 4 (2017), 526–542.

[52] Qu, W.G. et al. 2011. Multi-level framework of open source software adoption. *Journal of Business Research.* 64, 9 (2011), 997–1003.

[53] Rogers, E.M. 1995. *Diffusion of innovations 3rd Edition.*

[54] Rothaermel, F.T. and Alexandre, M.T. 2009. Ambidexterity in Technology Sourcing: The Moderating Role of Absorptive Capacity. *Organization Science.* 20, 4 (2009), 759–780.

[55]   Sacks, M. 2015. Competition between Open Source and Proprietary Software: Strategies for Survival. *Journal of Management Information Systems*. 32, 3 (2015), 268–295.

[56]   Saunders, M. et al. 2009. *Research Methods for Business Students*. Pearson Education Limited.

[57]   Sen, R. et al. 2011. Open source software licenses: Strong-copyleft, non-copyleft, or somewhere in between? *Decision Support Systems*. 52, 1 (2011), 199–206.

[58]   Singh, J. 2005. Collaborative Networks as Determinants of Knowledge Diffusion Patterns. *Management Science*. 51, 5 (2005), 756–770.

[59]   Spinellis, D. and Giannikas, V. 2012. Organizational adoption of open source software. *Journal of Systems and Software*. 85, 3 (2012), 666–682.

[60]   Spithoven, A. et al. 2011. Building absorptive capacity to organise inbound open innovation in traditional industries. *Technovation*. 31, 1 (2011), 10–21.

[61]   Stam, W. 2009. When does community participation enhance the performance of open source software companies? *Research Policy*. 38, 8 (2009), 1288–1299.

[62]   Sutanto, J. et al. 2014. Uncovering the relationship between OSS user support networks and OSS popularity. *Decision Support Systems*. 64, (2014), 142–151.

[63]   Szulanski, G. 1996. EXPLORING INTERNAL STICKINESS: IMPEDIMENTS TO THE TRANSFER OF BEST PRACTICE WITHIN THE FIRM. *Strategic Management Journal*. 17, 1 (1996), 27–43.

[64]   Teigland, R. et al. 2014. Balancing on a tightrope: Managing the boundaries of a firm-sponsored OSS community and its impact on innovation and absorptive capacity. *Information and Organization*. 24, 1 (2014), 25–47.

[65]   The Tenth Annual Future of Open Source Survey: 2016. *https://www.blackducksoftware.com/2016-future-of-open-source*.

[66]   Tiwana, A. 2008. DO BRIDGING TIES COMPLEMENT STRONG TIES? AN EMPIRICAL EXAMINATION OF ALLIANCE AMBIDEXTERITY. *Strategic Management Journal*. 29, (2008), 251–272.

[67]   Todorova, G. and Durisin, B. 2007. ABSORPTIVE CAPACITY: VALUING A RECONCEPTUALIZATION. *Academy of Management Review*. 32, 3 (2007), 774–786.

[68]   Tsai, K.H. 2009. Collaborative networks and product innovation performance: Toward a contingency perspective. *Research Policy*. 38, 5 (2009), 765–778.

[69]   Tsai, W. 2001. Knowledge Transfer in Intraorganizational Networks: Effects of Network Position and Absorptive Capacity on Business Unit Innovation and Performance Wenpin Tsai KNOWLEDGE TRANSFER IN INTRAORGANIZATIONAL NETWORKS: EFFECTS OF NETWORK POSITION AND ABSORPTIV. *Academy of Management Journal*. 44, 5 (2001), 996–1004.

[70]   TSAI, W. 2001. KNOWLEDGE TRANSFER IN INTRAORGANIZATIONAL NETWORKS: EFFECTS OF NETWORK POSITION AND ABSORPTIVE GAPAGITY ON BUSINESS UNIT INNOVATION AND PERFORMANCE. *Academy of Management Journal*. 44, 5 (2001), 996–1004.

[71]   Tseng, C.-Y. et al. 2011. Knowledge absorptive capacity and innovation performance in KIBS. *Journal of Knowledge Management*. 15, 6 (2011), 971–983.

[72]   Uzzi, B. 1997. Social Structure and Competition in Interfirm Networks: The Paradox of Embeddedness. *Administrative Science Quarterly*.

[73]   Vasudeva, G. and Anand, J. 2011. Unpacking absoprtive capacity: A study of knoweldge utilization from alliance portfolios. *Academy of Management Journal*. 54, 3 (2011), 611–623.

[74]   WALES, W.J. et al. 2012. TOOMUCH OF A GOOD THING? ABSORPTIVE CAPACITY, FIRM PERFORMANCE, AND THE MODERATING ROLE OF ENTREPRENEURIAL ORIENTATION. *Strategic Management Journal*. (2012).

[75]   Zaffar, M.A. et al. 2011. Diffusion dynamics of open source software: An agent-based computational economics (ACE) approach. *Decision Support Systems*. 51, 3 (2011), 597–608.

[76]   Zahra, S.A. and George, G. 2002. Absorptive capacity: A review, reconceptualization, and extension. *Academy of Management Review*. 27, 2 (2002), 185–203.

Author Index